Yale Historical Publications, Miscellany, 116

KRAAL AND CASTLE

Khoikhoi and the Founding of White South Africa

Richard Elphick

New Haven and London   Yale University Press

1977

Published under the direction of the Department of History of
Yale University with assistance from the income of the
Frederick John Kingsbury Memorial Fund

Designed by John O. C. McCrillis
and set in Baskerville type.
Printed in the United States of America by
The Alpine Press, South Braintree, Massachusetts.

Published in Great Britain, Europe, Africa, and Asia
(except Japan) by Yale University Press, Ltd., London.
Distributed in Latin America by Kaiman & Polon, Inc.,
New York City; in Australia and New Zealand by Book & Film
Services, Artarmon, N.S.W., Australia; in Japan by Harper &
Row, Publishers, Tokyo Office.

Library of Congress Cataloging in Publication Data

Elphick, Richard.
    Kraal and castle.

    (Yale historical publications: Miscellany; 116)
    A revision of the author's thesis, Yale University, 1972.
    Bibliography: p.
    Includes index.
    1. Khoikhoi (African people)   2. South Africa—
Native races.   3. South Africa—History—To 1836.
4. Cape of Good Hope—History.   I. Title.   II. Series.
DT764.K45E4   1977   968'.004'961   76–49723
ISBN 0-300-02012-0

To Ester

Contents

PART I
The Cape Khoikhoi before the Arrival of Whites

Europeans and the Western Cape Khoikhoi, 1488–1701

4   Peninsular Khoikhoi on the Sea Route to the Indies,
    1488–1652   71

    From Armed Conflict to a Trading Bonanza, 1488–1610   71
    Coree the Saldanian and the Decline in Trade, 1610–1626   76
    Harry, the Strandlopers, and the Post Office, 1627–1652   82
    Europeans and Khoikhoi on the Eve of Colonization   86

5   Peninsular Khoikhoi at the Gateway to Southern Africa,
    1652–1662   90

    The Peoples of the Cape Peninsula   91
    The Years of Tense Cordiality   95
    The Three Interpreters: Harry, Eva, and Doman   103
    The First Khoikhoi-Dutch War and Its Aftermath   110

6   The Cochoqua and the North: The Failure of
    Noncooperation   117

    The Cochoqua and Their Neighbors before 1658   117
    The Cochoqua and Their Neighbors, 1658–1672   121
    Gonnema Falls out with the Dutch   126
    The Second Khoikhoi-Dutch War (1673–77) and the Decline of
       the Cochoqua   130
    The Northern Borderlands   134

7   The Chainouqua and Hessequa: The Perils of
    Cooperation   138

    The Chainouqua and Hessequa before 1673   138
    Klaas, Koopman, and the Company's Trade, 1673–1692   141
    The Downfall of Klaas, 1693–1701   144

PART 3
Processes of Decline among the Western Cape Khoikhoi, 1652–1701

8   The Trade in Cattle and Sheep   151

    The Dimensions of Demand   151
    The Conditions of Supply   154
    The Company and Khoikhoi: Profit and Loss   162
    How the Khoikhoi Lost Their Livestock   170

PART 4
Denouement and Retrospect

Maps

Abbreviations

AS	*African Studies*
BS	*Bantu Studies*
BVR	R. Raven-Hart, *Before Van Riebeeck*
CGH	R. Raven-Hart, *Cape Good Hope*
DR	Dagregister
JAH	*Journal of African History*
KA	Koloniaal Archief (in the Algemeen Rijksarchief, The Hague)
KP	*Kaaps Plakkaatboek*, ed. M. K. Jeffreys
KZ	Kamer Zeeland (in the Algemeen Rijksarchief, The Hague)
RZA	*Reizen in Zuid-Afrika in de Hollandse Tijd*, ed. E. C. Godée Molsbergen
SAAB	*South African Archaeological Bulletin*
SAJS	*South African Journal of Science*
Staf	Staffordshire County Record Office, Stafford, England
VRJ	*Journal of Jan Van Riebeeck*, ed. H. B. Thom
VRS	Van Riebeeck Society
XVII	The Lords Seventeen

Acknowledgments

This book is a revised version of a doctoral dissertation submitted to Yale University in 1972. While preparing the dissertation I received financial help from many sources: first, from the Yale Council on Comparative and European Studies for a preliminary study-visit to South Africa; later, from the Canada Council and the Yale African Studies Council for the main period of research in the Netherlands; and finally, from the Netherlands government and Wesleyan University for a final year of study and writing. I am deeply grateful to all these institutions. I am also grateful to the staffs of the libraries and archives where most of my research was done: the Cape Archives; the South African Public Library (and particularly Mrs. Sue Sturman and Miss Margaret Saunders); the Algemeen Rijksarchief in the Hague (where Miss Miriam van den Berg and Mr. A. J. H. Rozemond were particularly kind); the Suid-Afrikaanse Instituut in Amsterdam (and especially Miss J. Bakker and Mrs. Rachel Conradie); the Koninklijke Bibliotheek at the Hague; the Staffordshire County Record Office; and, in London, the libraries of the School of Oriental and African Studies and the Royal Commonwealth Society.

I have received generous help, on both academic and practical matters, from Mr. James Armstrong, Dr. René Baesjou, Dr. Anna Böeseken, Dr. Christopher Ehret, Dr. H. B. Giliomee, Dr. Shula Marks, and Professor Robin Winks. The last four also read the manuscript and made many helpful suggestions. Warm thanks are due to Mrs. Edna Haran, Mrs. Dorothy Hay, and Mrs. Melody Martin for typing the manuscript; to Mr. L. M. J. de Bie for preparing the original version of the maps; to Mr. William Martello for checking the footnotes and bibliography; and to my mother, Mrs. A. G. Elphick, for her generous and efficient work on the index. The Countess of Sutherland has kindly made available the valuable papers of Colonel R. J. Gordon, and the Nasionale Opvoedkundige Uitgewery has allowed me to use a map from one of their publications as the basis of one of my own (see map 4, p. 93).

I am particularly indebted to four people. Professor Leonard Thompson first interested me in South African history, supervised this work in its thesis stage, and provided much guidance thereafter; throughout he has proven, not only a great scholar and teacher, but a wise counselor and loyal friend. Dr. David Robinson mastered the argument of the early chapters in first draft and later prepared detailed and powerful commentaries on their many revisions. My colleague, Professor Jeffrey Butler, reassured me when I was despondent, goaded me when I was complacent, and hunted through the manuscript for jargon, inconsistency, illogicity, and cant. Finally, my wife, Ester Timbancaya Elphick, has helped me in so many ways that it is quite impossible to list them. To her this book is most affectionately dedicated.

Introduction

The word *Hottentot* is occasionally heard even in the 1970s, but few outside South Africa know its precise meaning. Perhaps for most it is merely a nonsense word: school children in the Netherlands maintain that the longest Dutch word is *Hottentottententententoonstellingsterrein* (an exhibition ground for Hottentot tents). And for a whimsical example in English, consider Dame Edith Sitwell's lines:

> "For the minx,"
> Said she
> "And the drinks
> You can see
> Are as hot as any Hottentot and not the goods for me!"

Unfortunately, there is a rather more sinister side to this word. *The Oxford English Dictionary* defines *Hottentot* as, figuratively, a "person of inferior intellect or culture," while a standard Dutch dictionary has "a rough, unmannerly person." In Portuguese a *Hottentotismo* is a "*pronúncia viciosa.*" These connotations are faint vestiges of the intellectual climate of eighteenth-century Europe, where "Hottentot" was a widely accepted symbol for irredeemable savagery and the very depths of human degradation. In one of that era's most celebrated insults, Lord Chesterfield declared Dr. Samuel Johnson to be no more than a "respectable Hottentot." And even in the nineteenth century a British prime minister, Lord Salisbury, created an uproar among Irishmen and sensitive Englishmen when he publicly equated Irish and Hottentot capacities for Home Rule.

This book is a study of the "Hottentots," or rather of the South African people whom Europeans have long called by that name. The people themselves did not use this word (which appears to have derived from one of their dance chants) but called themselves Khoikhoi in the Namaqua dialect, and Kwena and perhaps Kwekwena in the Cape dialect. Kwena means "men," while Khoikhoi and Kwekwena mean "men of men."[1]

---

1. G. S. Nienaber, *Hottentots* (Pretoria: J.L. van Schaik, 1963), pp. 310–11. For a discussion of the terms used by Khoikhoi to refer to themselves, see A. J. Böeseken, "The meaning, origin

The Khoikhoi became a symbol for all that was raw and base in mankind, not only because many aspects of their culture were repellent to Europeans, but because their territory, the hinterland of the Cape of Good Hope, lay along the sea route which Europeans traveled on the way to the Orient. Thus, of all the preliterate peoples in the eastern hemisphere, they were the most frequently observed and intensively discussed, and for a while their supposed savagery was a focal point in learned speculation about the nature of the human race. This early, and somewhat naïve, obsession with Khoikhoi was followed in the nineteenth and twentieth centuries by more scholarly investigation of this atypical African people. The Khoikhoi language with its unusual "clicks" (implosive consonants) intrigued first amateur, and later professional, linguists. The brown skin of the Khoikhoi and their material and intellectual culture set them apart from all their negro neighbors and thus attracted the interest of anthropologists. Furthermore, because the Khoikhoi had once occupied vast territories, they figured in historians' descriptions of the expansion of white settlement in many regions of southern Africa.

Despite the abundant attention which has been bestowed on Khoikhoi over the centuries, there is still no comprehensive account of their history. Nor will there be one for some time to come, for the materials which must be examined are dauntingly extensive. Khoikhoi can be divided into several large tribal[2] clusters, the Cape Khoikhoi, the Einiqua, the Korana, and the Namaqua.[3] All the tribes of each cluster were related genealogically to each other, and they all spoke the same dialect and practiced roughly the same culture. This study deals only with the Cape Khoikhoi, that is, the Khoikhoi dwelling in the modern

---

and use of the terms Khoikhoi, San and Khoisan," *Cabo* 1 no. 1 (Aug. 1972):5–10; *Cabo* 2, no. 2 (Jan. 1974):8–10; and *Cabo* 2, no. 3 (Nov. 1975):16–18; and replies with the same title by R. H. Elphick in *Cabo* 2, no. 2 (Jan. 1974):3–7 and *Cabo* 2, no. 3 (Nov. 1975):12–15.

2. The term *tribe* is defined on pp. 45–46.

3. In Khoikhoi speech, tribal names normally ended in -*qua* or -*n(a)*, respectively the masculine and common plural terminations of Khoikhoi nouns. Names in this form were taken over into European documents, where they were even used incorrectly as singular nouns and adjectives (e.g. "a Chainouqua" or "three Chainouqua captains"). I have followed the documents in this practice and have parted company with modern Africanists, who usually prefer to use only the roots of tribal names. I have done this for two reasons. Firstly, almost all the tribes discussed in this work are extinct, and we can no longer determine with certainty the original root of their names. Secondly, Khoikhoi suffixes, unlike Bantu prefixes, do not impede English speakers in their reading. For consistency's sake I also use Korana, Namaqua, San (=Sana), rather than Kora, Nama, or Sa; but I have shrunk from abandoning the well entrenched term Khoikhoi in favor of Khoikhoin.

Cape Province south of the Orange River Valley and west of the area already occupied by Bantu-speaking negroes in the seventeenth century. The Cape Khoikhoi can in turn be arbitrarily divided into three subgroups of tribes: the Eastern Cape Khoikhoi (consisting of Gonaqua, Damasqua, and several other peoples); the Central Cape Khoikhoi (most notably the Inqua, Attaqua, and "Gouris"); and the Western Cape Khoikhoi, who resided within a hundred miles of the Cape of Good Hope. The tribes of this last group accounted for the majority of Cape Khoikhoi in the seventeenth century, and it is to them that almost all contemporary documents on Khoikhoi refer.

The Western Cape Khoikhoi figure prominently in African history because they were the first indigenous people to confront the Dutch refreshment station founded in 1652 at the Cape of Good Hope: this station soon became a colony of white settlement which in later centuries effected the deepest and most lasting European penetration of the African continent. Within sixty years of 1652 the traditional Khoikhoi economy, social structure, and political order had almost entirely collapsed. My main goal here is to understand this collapse. It cannot be explained purely in military terms, for the whites in this period were few in numbers, and yet had to resort to arms against Khoikhoi only infrequently and briefly. Neither can it be seen merely as a result of the smallpox epidemic of 1713, even though this swept away the bulk of the Western Cape Khoikhoi population. Khoikhoi decline was far advanced and probably irreversible well before this final catastrophe.

Each of the four parts of this work is an attempt to explain one aspect of this problem. Part 1 reconstructs the precolonial social history of Khoikhoi with an eye to locating traditional weaknesses later exacerbated by the European presence. A major challenge in this part is to unravel the complex relations between Khoikhoi and another category of people, also brown-skinned and speaking "click" languages, who were known to the Khoikhoi as "San" and to the whites (since the 1680s) as "Bushmen." For reasons explained below (pp. xxi–xxii) I have not myself used these traditional names but have replaced them with several descriptive terms, of which the most common is "hunter."

The next two parts investigate interaction between Khoikhoi and Europeans, part 2 focusing on military and diplomatic events, part 3 on the processes of political, social, and economic change which underlay them. The fourth part describes the final collapse of Khoikhoi society in the first two decades of the eighteenth century.

The sources for this work are entirely written: virtually no oral traditions are available, the Cape Khoikhoi being now extinct. Part 1 (precolonial history) consists largely of deductions made from data furnished by linguists, archaeologists, anthropologists, and other specialists. It is also based on the diaries of the first European visitors to regions of Khoikhoi occupation; these provide useful demographic and cultural information from which conditions in even earlier centuries can sometimes be inferred.

The sources for parts 2, 3, and 4 (the history of Khoikhoi-European interaction) are of two main types. The first consists of seventeenth- and eighteenth-century accounts of South Africa published in Europe for European readers. Many of these yield information which is trivial, false, or pirated from earlier authors. However, the major works (e.g. by Schreyer, Kolbe, and Grevenbroek) give useful general analyses of Khoikhoi life, though they are almost devoid of information on specific tribes and on the processes of change which are the focus of this book.

The second and more useful category consists of the official papers of the Dutch East India Company, now housed at the Hague and Cape Town. The Company founded and administered the Cape Colony, and most of the unpublished documentation on the early settlement was written by its employees. The most important Company documents are (1) accounts of the formation of Dutch policy toward Khoikhoi (instructions from higher to lower officials, resolutions of the ruling Council of Policy, and proclamations); (2) descriptions of Khoikhoi-Dutch relations (reports, diaries, and the indispensable journal or *Dagregister* of the colony); (3) judicial records, which have scattered information on the status of Khoikhoi in the colony; and (4) statistical sources (chiefly trading books and the annual censuses).

The East India Company's papers have several strengths as sources for Khoikhoi history. They are fairly extensive (when compared, for example, to records of Dutch activities in West Africa and Malaya); they are preserved almost in their entirety, and in several copies; they were written mainly by competent, businesslike observers; and they are remarkably candid about Dutch mistreatment of Khoikhoi, despite falsification to cover corruption among Company officials. Their cardinal weakness is the failure of Company employees to interest themselves in the subtleties of an alien society more simple than their own. In general, they were less perceptive than the nineteenth-century imperial agents whose observations have been used by many historians of African peoples, and they only rarely questioned how Khoikhoi perceived their own problems and determined their strategies.

It is striking that only two or three contemporaries offered even a casual analysis of the disintegration of Khoikhoi society in this period. Even more amazing is the failure of later scholars to recount in detail, much less explain,[4] these first events in the long story of settler-native relations in South Africa. In the hope of remedying this failure I have written this book.

4. However, for a stimulating introduction to the period, see Shula Marks, "Khoisan Resistance to the Dutch in the Seventeenth and Eighteenth Centuries," *JAH* 13, no. 1 (1972):55–80. Also useful is the old-fashioned but generally reliable work of H. J. le Roux, "Die Toestand, Verspreiding en Verbrokkeling van die Hottentotstamme in Suid-Afrika 1652–1713," (M. A. thesis, Stellenbosch University, 1945). This work has been unjustifiably ignored by scholars. It consists largely of painstaking reconstruction of the location, wealth, and political structure of each Khoikhoi tribe and clan. Le Roux's analysis of Khoikhoi decline is quite brief and conflicts with my own at crucial points.

Note on Terminology

In this work I consider a Khoikhoi to be *any person accepted as a full* (i.e. not a subordinate) *member of a Khoikhoi community*. A Khoikhoi community was *one where a dialect of the Khoikhoi language was spoken and where pastoralism was the preferred mode of economic life*. This definition corresponds fairly closely to that commonly used by scholars, except that it allows for the possibility that not all Khoikhoi groups or individuals actually possessed livestock at all times.

It is appropriate to use the ethnic name "Khoikhoi" because Khoikhoi were a relatively homogeneous group of peoples with common origins, common language (divided into dialects), common culture, and common economic aspirations. This, however, was not the case with the "San," who were extremely heterogeneous linguistically, culturally, and economically. Partly for this reason, I have avoided giving them a generic, ethnic name and have dispensed entirely with "San" and "Bushman" except when referring to the usage of others.

These old terms were used in a bewildering variety of ways, first by the Khoikhoi, whose concept "San" (pp. 23–28) was much too vague to be of use in a scientific work, and later by scholars. Some scholarly definitions have been suitable from the perspective of a single discipline—for example, if a linguist defined "San" solely in terms of the languages they spoke—but have been too narrow for the multifaceted concerns of the historian. On the other hand, historians' definitions have tended to be too broad, encompassing more than one distinct category and giving rise to faulty reconstructions of history. The most serious error is to regard "San" *both* (1) as those inhabitants of any region of southern Africa before the arrival there of Khoikhoi, and (2) as those brown-skinned people, described in seventeenth-century documents, who did not keep cattle but lived solely by hunting and gathering. I call the first group *aborigines*[1] and

---

1. This term does not mean that the designated people were the first humans in their region, only that they were there before Khoikhoi.

the second *hunter-gatherers*, or more simply *hunters*.[2] I thus avoid the assumption that the latter are necessarily direct descendants of the former. A major theme of part 1 is the complex development from the Khoikhoi-aborigine dichotomy of prehistoric times to the Khoikhoi-hunter dichotomy of the early colonial period.

The economic term "hunter" has a further advantage over the quasi-ethnic name "San" in that it allows for possible overlap with Khoikhoi, who, it must be remembered, were people who preferred pastoralism but could not always practice it. Thus the terminology allows for Khoikhoi-speaking hunters should the documents point to their existence. Heretofore most scholars have relied on mutually exclusive definitions of "San" and "Khoikhoi" and have hence failed to perceive the complex movements which took place between the two groups.

There are two further meanings of the words "San" and "Bushman" found in the literature. They are used (1) to denote people who lived chiefly by stealing and slaughtering the livestock of their Khoikhoi neighbors, and (2) to denote people in a servile position in Khoikhoi society whom Khoikhoi deemed to be both alien and inferior. Both groups of people were normally hunters or ex-hunters, and may be so designated. But this was not invariably the case. Thus I sometimes call them *robbers* and *alien-clients* respectively, especially when the documents give no hint of their origin.

2. It would be awkward and pedantic to repeat the hyphenated form *hunter-gatherer* throughout this work. The reader is asked to remember that *hunter* refers to all nonpastoral brown-skinned people, even though most of these people actually lived as much from gathering as from hunting. I even use it to refer to the scavenging Strandlopers who hunted little, if at all.

Part 1   The Cape Khoikhoi before the Arrival of Whites

1

The Early History of the Khoikhoi

KHOIKHOI AND HUNTERS: SURVIVING EVIDENCE OF PAST RELATIONSHIPS

The Opinions of Writers concerning the Origin of the *Hottentot* Nations are as various and dissonant as the Methods they have taken to account for the Name of 'em; and indeed, 'tis a difficult Matter to settle it. Nor am I myself, after all my Researches, able with any Certainty to point it out. All I can undertake in the Matter is to do it with more Probability than others have done; or, at least, to furnish out more Lights and better Materials for such an Enquiry.[1]

—Peter Kolbe (1719)

It is now more than two and a half centuries since Peter Kolbe wrote these sober words. Since that time information on Khoikhoi origins has increased a hundredfold, but no author who explores this problem today can be more ambitious than Kolbe of finding the final answer. At most he may hope only to write "with more Probability than others have done" and to provide "better Materials for [further] Enquiry."

The usual raw materials of historical research—written documents or inscriptions—are virtually nonexistent for this problem. Oral traditions are also lacking, at least for the southwestern Cape. This is partly because traditions were not collected by early European travelers, and partly because they later disappeared during the rapid decline of independent Khoikhoi societies in the region. Thus the historian must

1. Peter Kolben [Kolbe], *The Present State of the Cape of Good Hope*, trans. Guido Medley (London: W. Innys, 1731), 1:29. Peter Kolbe was a German astronomer who resided at the Cape from 1705 to 1712. His detailed account of the Khoikhoi, though in parts inaccurate, is generally of immense value. It first appeared, in German, under the title *Caput Bonae Spei Hodiernum* (Nürnberg: Pieter Conrad Monath, 1719). For this study I have used a later German edition of 1745 (see chap. 3, no. 1), and have normally had recourse to the highly unreliable English edition only when I wished to exploit the raciness of Guido Medley's translation.

3

turn to the evidence of linguistics, archaeology, and anthropology to find the clues he needs.

The problem of Khoikhoi origins is entangled in that Gordian knot of South African ethnography, the enigmatic relationship between Khoikhoi and those people whom I call "the hunters" (i.e. the San or Bushmen). The hunters resembled the Khoikhoi in many respects, but were conventionally distinguished from them by their sole reliance on hunting and gathering and by their lack of livestock, a conspicuous feature of Khoikhoi life. At the beginning of European contact the hunters were scattered throughout the entire region inhabited by Khoikhoi. For centuries the question has been raised: are the Khoikhoi and the hunters simply economically differentiated segments of the same people?

One can discern three phases in the answers offered to this question. In the seventeenth and eighteenth centuries, whites met Khoikhoi and hunters primarily in the southwestern part of the modern Cape Province. During this period it was almost universally assumed that the "Bushmen" were a subspecies of "Hottentot"—indeed, they were often called "Bossiesmans Hottentots." This identification was based chiefly on easily made observations: e.g. that both groups had brown skin, small stature, and peppercorn hair, and spoke a "click" language.

It was not until the beginning of the nineteenth century that a view was put forward based on the observations of a number of scholarly minded travelers. In 1812 Hinrich Lichtenstein asserted that:

> They [the hunters] are, and ever have been, a distinct people, having their own peculiar language, and their own peculiar customs. . . . No Hottentot understands a word of the Bosjesman language, and the nation was hated by all others on account of its habits of plunder, and disregard for the right of property long before the Europeans settled in Southern Africa.[2]

Lichtenstein's three propositions (namely, that Khoikhoi and hunters were distinct, that they *always* had been distinct, and that they were normally in conflict with one another) were shared by most of his successors throughout the nineteenth century. This new view was conditioned in part by the new locales in which whites now observed

---

2. Henry Lichtenstein, *Travels in Southern Africa, in the Years 1803, 1804, 1805, and 1806*, trans. Anne Plumtre, Van Riebeeck Society Publications, nos. 10, 11 (Cape Town: Van Riebeeck Society, 1928, 1930), no. 10, p. 143. The Van Riebeeck Society Publications are hereafter designated as VRS.

Khoikhoi and hunters. After 1750, colonial settlement had passed north of the central Cape mountain barrier into Bushmanland, and soon after crossed the Orange River into Transorangia. In both these regions the pastoral Khoikhoi and their Colored descendants were recent immigrants and were engaged in bitter warfare with hunter-gatherers who undoubtedly spoke languages quite unlike their own, lived by different norms, and seemed quite irreconcilable to the presence of the newcomers. While early Dutch observers often had difficulty distinguishing Khoikhoi from "Bushmen" by sight, W. H. I. Bleek spoke for most nineteenth-century scholars when he wrote in 1871:

> As regards the difference in appearance between [Korana] Hottentots and Bushmen ... it is so marked as, in rare instances only, to leave one in doubt regarding the nationality of an individual of either nation.[3]

This second position, which I loosely call the "nineteenth-century view," was systematized and supported by much new material in George W. Stow's *The Native Races of South Africa*. This massive work was finished in 1880, but was published only in 1905 at the instigation of George McCall Theal, the influential historian of South Africa. It expounded a historical corollary to the current view of Khoikhoi-hunter relations; namely that the hunters were the original inhabitants of southern Africa and that the Khoikhoi were the first aliens to invade the region from the north. Theal drew heavily upon Stow's work in his own reconstruction of precolonial history.[4] The prestige of Theal's works probably accounts for the persistence of the nineteenth-century view in much historical literature of our own times.

Since Theal, no professional historian has undertaken a thorough and fundamental review of the question of Khoikhoi origins. During this third phase initiative has shifted entirely to linguists, anthropologists, and other specialists who have investigated the similarities and differences between Khoikhoi and hunters in the "ethnographic present": i.e. at the various times, chiefly in the late nineteenth and twentieth centuries, when these peoples and their cultures have been

3. W. H. I. Bleek and L. C. Lloyd, *Specimens of Bushman Folklore* (London: George Allen & Co., 1911), p. 436.

4. George W. Stow, *The Native Races of South Africa*, ed. George McCall Theal (London: Swan Sonnenschein & Co., 1905), p. 178 and passim; George McCall Theal, *Ethnography and Condition of South Africa before A.D. 1505*, 2d ed. (London: George Allen and Unwin, 1919), pp. 80–90.

studied by trained observers. A mass of literature has accumulated on the subject, much of which is amateurish or limited to the perspectives of a single discipline, and almost all of which is fiercely controverted.[5]

Fortunately, there is now unanimity on one point of critical importance to the historian, namely, the close relationship between the Khoikhoi tongue and a specific group of hunter languages. Formerly such a connection was denied, most notably by Carl Meinhof, who argued early in this century that the inflections (noun terminations) of Khoikhoi were absent in hunter languages but closely paralleled in the languages of the North African "Hamites." This theory dovetailed neatly with the then current belief of physical anthropologists that Khoikhoi and hunters were somatically distinct, and with the historians' view that Khoikhoi had obtained their cattle in eastern Africa during their migrations from the far north. However, Meinhof's theory was severely damaged in 1934 when L. F. Maingard showed that inflections were neither absent in hunter languages nor present in all Khoikhoi dialects. Since then studies by Oswin Köhler (working in the field) and Joseph Greenberg (in his classification of all African languages) have led to these conclusions: (1) that there is no significant vocabulary common to Khoikhoi and "Hamitic" languages; and (2) that the few terminations which Khoikhoi shares with "Hamitic" languages are also shared by the Central group of hunter languages.[6]

As the belief in a Khoikhoi-Hamitic link receded, more attention was given to possible connections between Khoikhoi and hunters. In 1927 Dorothea Bleek classified all the known hunter tongues into three families, "Northern Bush," "Central Bush," and "Southern Bush." She noted that the language of the Naron, a "Central Bush"-speaking people, was very close to Khoikhoi. However, so entrenched was the Khoikhoi-hunter dichotomy in scholarly circles that neither Bleek nor her immediate successors were willing to consider the logical deduction from this fact. Indeed, it was comparatively recently (1963) that E. O. J. Westphal classified the entire "Central Bush" language family

5. For a much fuller discussion of this literature, see Richard Hall Elphick, "The Cape Khoi and the First Phase of South African Race Relations," (Ph. D. diss., Yale University, 1972), pp. 7–25.

6. Carl Meinhof, "Ergebnisse der afrikanischen Sprachforschung," *Archiv für Anthropologie,* n.s. 9, nos. 3–4 (1910):200; Carl Meinhof, *Die Sprachen der Hamiten* (Hamburg: L. Friederichsen & Co., 1912), p. 216; L. F. Maingard, "The Linguistic Approach to South African Prehistory and Ethnology," *SAJS* 31 (Nov. 1934):122–29; Oswin Köhler, "Sprachkritische Aspekte zur Hamitentheorie über die Herkunft der Hottentotten," *Sociologus,* n.s. 10, no. 1 (1960):69–77; Joseph H. Greenberg, "The Languages of Africa," *International Journal of American Linguistics* 29, no. 1, pt. 2 (Jan. 1963):66–84.

(which he rechristened Tshu-Khwe) as a subgroup of Khoikhoi. In the same year L. F. Maingard published a comparative study of two dialects of Tshu-Khwe and Korana (a dialect of Khoikhoi). Of a core vocabulary of 300 roots, fully 120 (i.e. 40 percent) were found in all these three languages. Striking resemblances were also found in their morphologies, all having similar pronouns, postpositions, and verb formations.[7]

Khoikhoi is thus clearly related to a particular family of languages spoken by hunters. This family is now found chiefly in northern Botswana. Since it is highly unlikely that a whole family of languages (particularly languages spoken by hunters) could move long distances *as a group*, it seems that Khoikhoi originated in or near Botswana, and not in distant parts of northern or eastern Africa. Their ancestors were southern African hunters, not intrusive pastoralists.

This conclusion is compatible with the tendency of twentieth-century anthropologists to stress similarities between Khoikhoi and hunter cultures. These correspondences are so numerous that they cannot be attributed to independent development. There are only two possibilities: either that Khoikhoi and hunter cultures had a common origin, or that the similarities are due to transfer between groups. Many researchers have chosen the latter explanation. For example, J. F. Schofield concluded that almost all pottery styles found among hunters had been borrowed either from Khoikhoi or Bantu-speakers, and Percival Kirby traced much of the hunters' musical tradition to their Khoikhoi neighbors. Similarly, L. F. Maingard opted for a diffusionist view in his study of the bow and arrow in southern Africa, though he saw the transfer going in the opposite direction, that is, from hunters to Khoikhoi. Together these studies suggest continuing and intimate interaction between Khoikhoi and hunters in recent centuries —a subject to which I shall return in chapter 2.[8]

7. D. F. Bleek, "The Distribution of Bushman Languages in South Africa," *Festschrift Meinhof: Sprachwissenschaftliche und andere Studien* (Hamburg: L. Friederichsen & Co., 1927), p. 63; E. O. J. Westphal, "The Linguistic Prehistory of Southern Africa; Bush, Kwadi, Hottentot, and Bantu Linguistic Relationships," *Africa* 33, no. 3 (July 1963): 249 ff; L. F. Maingard, "A Comparative Study of Naron, Hietshware and Korana," *AS* 22, no. 3 (1963): 97–108; Oswin Köhler, "Die Wortbeziehungen zwischen der Sprache der Kxoe-Buschmänner und dem Hottentottischen als geschichtliches Problem," *Neue Afrikanistische Studien*, ed. Johannes Lukas (Hamburg: Deutsches Institut für Afrika-Forschung, 1966), pp. 144–65; Greenberg, "Languages of Africa," pp. 66–84.

8. J. F. Schofield, *Primitive Pottery*, The South African Archaeological Society Handbook Series, no. 3 (Cape Town: By the Society, 1948), pp. 51–55, 69; Percival R. Kirby, *The Musical Instruments of the Native Races of South Africa* (London: Oxford University Press, 1934), pp. 135 ff, 166–67, 177–81, 249 ff; L. F. Maingard, "History and Distribution of the Bow and Arrow in South Africa," *SAJS* 29 (Oct. 1932): 711–23.

These conclusions do not, however, rule out the common origin demanded by the linguistic evidence. Common origin is indicated by aspects of culture more complex than pottery style and musical instruments, and hence less likely to be transferred without major alterations. For example, in 1930 Isaac Schapera concluded that Khoikhoi and hunter religions had a common heritage, one clearly distinct from that of the Bantu-speakers. Schapera's analysis was based, not so much on the names and attributes of individual gods or on specific myths (both of which could easily be borrowed), but on underlying cosmological and theological structures, where transfer was much less likely. He linked Khoikhoi particularly with the central and northern hunter groups, a view which supports the linguistic evidence. The validity of Schapera's general conclusions seems to be confirmed by recently published studies of hunter religions.[9]

Of perhaps greater value to the historian is the comparative study of social structures. Here we find that two hunter communities of the central group (Naron and G/wi) have a classificatory kinship system much like that of Khoikhoi but radically unlike that of a northern hunter people, the !Kung. Many specific parallels between G/wi and Namaqua Khoikhoi systems strike even the nonspecialist observer; if these were to be confirmed by a qualified anthropologist-linguist, they would strongly corroborate the view that Khoikhoi society had evolved from a simpler hunter society in Botswana.[10]

Among physical anthropologists there has also been a long debate

9. I. Schapera, *The Khoisan Peoples of South Africa: Bushmen and Hottentots* (London: Routledge & Kegan Paul, 1960), pp. 395–99; Lorna Marshall, "!Kung Bushman Religious Beliefs," *Africa* 32, no. 3 (July 1962):221–52; G. B. Silberbauer, *Report to the Government of Bechuanaland on the Bushman Survey* (Gaberones: Bechuanaland Government, 1965), pp. 95 ff.

10. Both systems classify kin primarily according to generation and further by means of sex-endings. Siblings are clearly divided between those older and younger than "ego"; in both systems ego calls his mother's brother "grandfather" and his brother's wife "wife"; his sister's offspring are called "grandchildren," while his brother's offspring are merely "children." In both cases the levirate is practiced, and very respectful behavior is enjoined toward siblings of the opposite sex, as well as to parents. There are only a few obvious cognates in kin terms between G/wi and Namaqua, but many between Naron and Namaqua. See Lorna Marshall, "The Kin Terminology System of the !Kung Bushmen," *Africa* 27, no. 1 (Jan. 1957):1–25; G. B. Silberbauer, "Aspects of the Kinship System of the G/wi Bushmen of the Central Kalahari," *SAJS* 57, no. 12 (Dec. 1961):353–59; D. F. Bleek, "Bushman Terms of Relationship," *BS* 2, no. 2 (Dec. 1924):57–70; A. Winifred Hoernlé, "The Social Organization of the Namaqua Hottentots of Southwest Africa," *American Anthropologist*, n.s. 27, no. 1 (Jan.–March, 1925):17–23. The classificatory system was noted among the Cape Khoikhoi as early as 1695: J. G. de Grevenbroek, "Elegans & Accurata Gentis Africanae ... Descriptio Epistolaris," *The Early Cape Hottentots*, ed. and trans. I. Schapera and B. Farrington, VRS 14 (Cape Town: Van Riebeeck Society, 1933), p. 287.

about the relationship between Khoikhoi and hunters. Little has emerged from this argument that can be of use to the historian. True, the study of blood types has confirmed what simple observation suggests: that Khoikhoi and hunters are sufficiently like each other, and unlike the Bantu-speakers, that one can justifiably bracket them as a biological group.[11] But the exact somatological relationship between Khoikhoi and hunters is not clear. Before 1923 the consensus among physical anthropologists coincided with the "nineteenth-century" view that the two groups were utterly distinct and had thus probably originated in different places. Between 1923 and 1937 it was generally thought that both groups had descended from the same prehistoric stocks long resident in southern Africa. Since 1937 various theories have been proposed which allow for both local development from earlier races and for admixture from outside.[12] None of these theories commands a consensus among experts. Moreover, the methods of classification which underlie these comparative studies do not inspire confidence. Since only a small number of complete skulls have been found in archaeological sites, and since almost none of these can be unambiguously identified by their cultural association as Khoikhoi, it is very difficult to establish statistically meaningful categories. In the case of living populations, rapid hybridization has made it doubtful that specimens of "pure" races—particularly pure Khoikhoi—can be found.

Complex hybridization now seems to be assumed by all investigators. L. H. Wells, for example, sees three components leading into his "Hottentot" type, while Phillip V. Tobias erects a more complex structure in which seven ancient races intermix with each other to produce six modern Khoikhoi and "Bushmen" physical types. Others who concentrate more on classification than evolutionary reconstruction arrive at similar conclusions.[13] Without committing himself to any

11. Ronald Singer and J. S. Weiner, "Biological Aspects of Some Indigenous African Populations," *Southwestern Journal of Anthropology*, 19, no. 2 (Summer 1963):168–76; Trefor Jenkins et al., "Red-Cell Enzyme Polymorphisms in the Khoisan Peoples of Southern Africa," *The American Journal of Human Genetics* 23 (Sept. 1971):529.

12. Phillip V. Tobias, "Physical Anthropology and Somatic Origins of the Hottentots," *AS* 14, no. 1 (1955):1–15.

13. L. H. Wells, "Bushman and Hottentot Statures: A Review of the Evidence," *SAJS* 56, no. 11 (Nov. 1960):279; Tobias, "Physical Anthropology," p. 13; J. A. Keen, "Craniometric Survey of the South African Museum Collection of Bushman, Hottentot and Bush-Hottentot Hybrid Skulls," *Annals of the South African Museum* 37, pt. 2 (Aug. 1952):217; C. S. Grobbelaar, "Report on Eight Bushman-Hottentot Skulls from the South East Coast, Cape Province," *SAJS* 59, no. 6 (June 1963):285.

one view, the historian can make use of one underlying conclusion. Clearly the somatic history of the modern Khoikhoi has been exceedingly confused, entailing much mixture between previously distinct groups. This is a conclusion which complements the evidence of complex cultural exchange already presented.

In summary, the evidence from the three fields most pertinent to this question—linguistics, cultural anthropology, and physical anthropology—can best be explained by assuming both that Khoikhoi originated as a hunter group in southern Africa[14] and that Khoikhoi and hunters subsequently interacted at many stages of their history. From these abstract but important conclusions the historian must begin his reconstruction of the Khoikhoi past.

The Pastoral Revolution: The Khoikhoi Diverge from the Hunter-Aborigines

In recent centuries brown-skinned pastoralists have occupied a vast swath of territory stretching from northern Namibia to the Cape Peninsula and then east to the region of the Fish River. The Khoikhoi language was spoken with only minor variations over this whole area and was hence one of the most widely diffused tongues in Africa. By contrast, the hunters' languages were purely local: those which survived have been grouped into five families, most of which comprise several distinct tongues. Early travelers noted that the hunters' languages varied even from band to band, although immediate neighbors could usually understand one another.[15] This extraordinary linguistic diversity indicates that hunters spread throughout southern Africa a very long time ago—certainly much earlier than the Khoikhoi, whose linguistic homogeneity points to a comparatively recent dispersal. For this reason I refer to "aborigines" or "hunter-aborigines," by which I simply mean those hunters who were in occupation of any region of

14. Several scholars still contend for a northern origin of Khoikhoi. For detailed and critical discussion of their views, see Elphick, "Cape Khoi," pp. 34–40.

15. Westphal, "Linguistic Prehistory," p. 249; Monica Wilson, "The Hunters and Herders," *The Oxford History of South Africa*, ed. Monica Wilson and Leonard Thompson (Oxford: Clarendon Press, 1969), 1:43–44. On the similarity of Namaqua and Einiqua languages, see Staffordshire County Record Office, D 593 /U/4/1/3, Gordon, Vierde Reyse, Sept. 28, 1779, n.p. (The Staffordshire County Record Office is hereafter designated as Staf.) On hunter languages, see J. W. Janssens, "Journaal en Verbaal eener Landreyse in den Jaare 1803 . . . gedaan," *Reizen in Zuid-Afrika in de Hollandse Tijd*, ed. E. C. Godée Molsbergen, 4 vols. (The Hague: Martinus Nijhoff, 1916, 1922, 1932), vol. 4: *Tochten in het Kafferland, 1776–1805*, pp. 191–92. (This work is hereafter cited as *RZA*.) See also Lichtenstein, VRS 11, p. 467.

southern Africa at the time when Khoikhoi first reached that region.[16]

Apart from a few exceptions explained in chapter 2 all brown-skinned stock-keepers in South Africa in historical times have spoken the Khoikhoi language; conversely, all but a very few speakers of Khoikhoi were associated with stock-keeping communities. Thus it is reasonable to assume that the spread of the Khoikhoi language has been related to the expansionist needs of a pastoral economy.[17] The hunters were usually loath to leave their ancestral hunting grounds; and their population, strictly controlled by the harsh realities of their economy and by infanticide, apparently did not force them into rapid movements. By contrast, the pastoralists, always seeking new pastures in the dry climate of South Africa, would be likely to expand rapidly into all contiguous areas that could support cattle. A regular supply of cows' milk would support a growing population, which in turn would foster territorial expansion. Moreover, movement over long distances was comparatively easy, since oxen were available to transport not only the portable Khoikhoi huts but also a supply of water; this convenience made Khoikhoi somewhat less dependent on reliable water holes than were their hunting brethren.

It seems, then, that one or several hunting bands—consisting of Central "Bush" speakers in or near northern Botswana[18]—acquired stock and became by that act the first Khoikhoi. They presumably obtained their livestock from a pastoral or mixed farming people who

16. The use of the term *aborigine* does not imply that such persons were necessarily the first human inhabitants of a given region. The long history of the various hunting cultures in southern Africa is a complex province of archaeology, and one that does not directly relate to this history of the Khoikhoi.

17. While the Khoikhoi language could not have expanded so far without pastoralism, it is possible that stock spread among some hunters in advance of the Khoikhoi language. If this in fact happened, the non-Khoikhoi-speaking pastoralists were later absorbed into Khoikhoi communities. Such a dispersal is more likely with sheep than with cattle. Bones of domesticated sheep have recently been found 100 miles east of Cape Town and dated to the fourth and fifth centuries A.D. See F. R. Schweitzer and Katharine J. Scott, "Early Occurrence of Domestic Sheep in Sub-Saharan Africa," *Nature* 241 (Feb. 1973):547. There is also evidence from rock paintings that sheep preceded cattle into the western Cape: see Jalmar and Ione Rudner, *The Hunter and his Art* (Cape Town: C. Struik, 1970), p. 239. However, since the number of sheep paintings in the area is extremely small (five), the corresponding absence of cattle paintings may be purely a matter of chance (ibid., p. 267).

18. T. M. O'C. Maggs has recently suggested the Vaal-Orange confluence as one of several areas where the pastoral revolution might have taken place ("Pastoral Settlements on the Riet River," *SAAB* 26, pts. 1 and 2, nos. 101 and 102 [Aug. 1971], p. 59). The homogeneity of Khoikhoi language and culture makes it unlikely that the acquisition of pastoral culture could have taken place in widely different areas, unless of course one newly pastoral people was later absorbed by the expanding Khoikhoi-speakers. However, such a complicating assumption is unnecessary

had moved into their midst, probably in rather small numbers. The linguistic affiliations of this donor group may eventually be determined through systematic study of all Khoikhoi vocabulary related to stock-keeping. Christopher Ehret has recently linked a number of Khoikhoi words (including those for cow, goat, ram, milk ewe) to Central Sudanic languages that he believes were spoken in central Africa before the arrival of Bantu-speakers. Central Sudanic speakers were presumably more oriented to pastoralism than the Bantu-speakers, a fact which strengthens their claim to donorship.[19]

It is implausible that the small hunting bands should have conquered and absorbed the pastoral intruders. More probably they attached themselves to the newcomers' society and subsequently seceded. Alternatively, they simply stole the livestock and learned how to tend it by intermittently working for the pastoralists or by observing them at a distance. The essence of the pastoral revolution was not the mere acquisition of stock but the development of the patience to let it breed before slaughtering. We need not doubt the ability of hunters to acquire these new values without prolonged tutelage. Stock-breeding techniques among pastoral Khoikhoi were very simple and required no knowledge that would not be possessed by a hunting people who had had long familiarity with animals (see p. 59). A similar process of transfer by robbery probably accounted for the spread of horses among Indian peoples on the North American plains.[20]

The Khoikhoi must have acquired livestock at least a century before 1488, by which date they had moved as far south as Mossel Bay and were seen there by Bartolomeu Dias.[21] We cannot yet be more specific about the date. However, a number of factors suggest that the pastoral revolution did not take place at an extremely early period: these include the very low population density of Khoikhoi in the Cape Province in the seventeenth century, their apparent absence in the

in this case, because the demographic pattern to which Maggs draws attention (i.e. a climate-dictated frontier between farming Bantu-speakers and pastoral Khoikhoi) is fully explained if Khoikhoi expanded westward along the Orange River system followed by the cultivators—as is argued in this chapter. In my view, the linguistic evidence virtually forces us to regard the Central Bush region as the Khoikhoi cradleland.

19. Christopher Ehret, "Patterns of Bantu and Central Sudanic Settlement in Central and Southern Africa," *Transafrican Journal of History* 3, nos. 1, 2 (1973): 13, 64.

20. Frank Gilbert Roe, *The Indian and the Horse* (Norman: University of Oklahoma Press, 1955), pp. 72–92; and Evon Z. Vogt, "Navaho," in *Perspectives in American Indian Culture Change*, ed. Edward H. Spicer (Chicago: University of Chicago Press, 1961), pp. 295–96.

21. R. Raven-Hart, *Before Van Riebeeck: Callers at South Africa from 1488 to 1652* (Cape Town: C. Struik, 1967), p. 1 (Dias, 1488). This work is hereafter referred to as *BVR*.

good pastures abutting the mountain ranges of the central Cape Province, and the continuing uniformity of the Khoikhoi language over a wide area. It is also notable that few rock paintings of sheep, and none of cattle, have been found in the western Cape or Namibia, and that remains of cattle have not so far been discovered in Late Stone Age sites in South Africa.[22]

It is unlikely that even an approximate date for the Khoikhoi genesis can be obtained through linguistic research, even in the improbable event of a reliable glottochronological date being obtained for the divergence of proto-Khoikhoi from Central "Bush." Divergence could easily have taken place many centuries before the arrival of cattle. The only hope would seem to be that archaeological sites be found with nonnegroid skeletal remains and domestic animal deposits, and then reliably dated by the carbon-14 process.

The pastoral revolution explains a number of indices in which Khoikhoi differ from all known hunter societies. Certainly the taller stature of Khoikhoi, noted by many early travelers,[23] can, in part at least, be attributed to the effect of a comparatively regular milk diet. (There is modern evidence that the average height of hunters increases as a result of the better food they receive on white farms.)[24] Much of Khoikhoi culture can be similarly explained in terms of economic change; after the pastoral revolution, Khoikhoi largely replaced their traditional garb of wild-animal furs with clothing of calf- and sheep-skins, and greasing of the body with animal fat became more common. Livestock moved to the very center of the Khoikhoi value system. Private property became more extensive, and as a result cleavages between rich and poor developed, wars became more common, and political authorities emerged whose prestige was based on livestock wealth.

Of course, the largest units of Khoikhoi political organization, the "tribes," were considerably more extensive and complex than the hunter bands which anthropologists have studied in recent years. In the Khoikhoi tribe a number of clans had coalesced and chieftainship had emerged, hereditary in a senior clan. But these agglomerations

22. Rudner and Rudner, *The Hunter and His Art*, p. 267; R. R. Inskeep, "The Archaeological Background," in Wilson and Thompson, *Oxford History*, 1:22.

23. This impression seems to be confirmed by modern physical anthropology: see L. H. Wells, "Bushman and Hottentot Statures," p. 281.

24. Phillip V. Tobias, "On the Increasing Stature of the Bushmen," *Anthropos* 57 (1962): 801–10.

of clans were often far less stable than the clans of which they were composed. The chief was almost always a weak figure; and indeed, some Khoikhoi had only clan headmen and no chiefs at all. We must also remember that hereditary chiefs were by no means absent among hunters; chieftainship of a sort exists in modern !Kung society and was noted formerly among the Naron and among hunting bands on the Orange River.[25] The evolution from this office to the weak chieftainship of the Khoikhoi involved only a minimal adaptation induced by the leadership requirements of a society with large herds and flocks to defend. In respect to political structure—and in other respects as well—we can agree with George Peter Murdock's confident assertion that "Hottentot culture is still recognizably Bushman in all its basic patterns, and its deviations are about the minimum to be expected in a hunting people adapting to a more stable pastoral economy."[26]

The Khoikhoi Move into the Cape Region

Earlier writers on African history were fond of speculating about "migration routes." When we turn to the problem of Khoikhoi movement into the western Cape we are not dealing with a migration, and only in the broadest sense with a route. It is not likely that Khoikhoi set out on a rapid, long-distance trek: such movements, when they have occurred in African history, have usually involved militaristic societies that could support themselves during their long march by raiding the wealth of local peoples. With the Khoikhoi we have no evidence of their having once been a formidable military machine, and no stock-owning societies existed ahead of them to supply their needs. Their movement was probably stimulated mainly by the need to find and exploit new pastures, and is best described by the term "migratory drift."[27]

In regions occupied by Khoikhoi in recent centuries, the pasture

25. Lorna Marshall, "!Kung Bushman Bands," *Africa* 30, no. 4 (Oct. 1960):349; Dorothea F. Bleek, *The Naron, a Bushman Tribe of the Central Kalahari* (Cambridge: Cambridge University Press, 1928), p. 36; Stow, *Native Races*, p. 183 and passim.

26. George Peter Murdock, *Africa: Its Peoples and Their Culture History* (New York, London, and Toronto: McGraw-Hill Book Company, 1959), p. 57.

27. Derrick Stenning distinguishes three types of movement among pastoralists: transhumance (seasonal migrations in search of water and pasture but in long-occupied territories); migration proper (rapid movement under abnormal circumstances); and migratory drift (gradual deviance from traditional transhumance patterns because of competition with other peoples). We are probably dealing with this last phenomenon, though we posit natural growth as a stimulus to movement, along with possible competition. See Derrick J. Stenning, *Savannah Nomads* (London: Oxford University Press, 1964), pp. 206–07.

is generally inferior, requiring from five to over thirty acres to support one stock unit (i.e. one head of cattle or seven sheep or goats).[28] Furthermore, much of this veld is not suitable for premodern pastoralism, since water supplies are often inadequate or unreliable, and since good pastureland is rendered inaccessible by mountains. These difficult circumstances doubtless accelerated Khoikhoi expansion into contiguous pastures, as did the loosely organized nature of Khoikhoi society, which readily permitted fission among disputing clans.

No doubt the Khoikhoi initially dispersed in different directions, but because of the presence of more populous farming peoples to their north and east, the ultimate tendency of movement was southward into regions inhabited only by hunters. Complex interaction with hunters probably took place at many stages of the Khoikhoi dispersal, the Khoikhoi facing fierce resistance from hunters but also gaining numerous recruits from their ranks: such recruits would adopt the Khoikhoi language and pastoral culture. The widespread interbreeding of Khoikhoi with different hunters in many parts of southern Africa explains why physical anthropologists have such difficulty in satisfactorily distinguishing the physical remains of the "Hottentot" and "Bushman" races.

For our present purposes we can regard the termination of Khoikhoi wanderings as their settlement pattern at the time they were first seen by whites. This pattern is shown in map 2 (p. 51).[29] The heaviest population densities were along the western sector of the Orange River and in the southwestern Cape; these two regions were linked by sparsely populated Little Namaqualand near the Atlantic coast, and conceivably by trade routes (but so far as we know, no settlement areas) up the center of the continent.

This distribution has often been explained by positing a movement of Khoikhoi down the west coast to the Cape Peninsula, and thence eastward along the south coast toward the Fish River.[30] This theory seems to be supported by one Korana tradition,[31] but was probably inspired largely by the fact that for the last 150 years the core of

28. Monica Mary Cole, *South Africa* (London: Methuen & Co., 1961), p. 226.

29. It should, however, be noted that very little is known about Khoikhoi north of the Orange River prior to 1800.

30. Stow, *Native Races*, pp. 234 ff; Theal, *Ethnography*, pp. 80–90; C. K. Cooke, "Evidence of Human Migrations from the Rock Art of Southern Rhodesia," *Africa* 35, no. 3 (July 1965): 263–85.

31. Stow, *Native Races*, p. 267.

Map 1 : Suggested Khoikhoi Expansion Patterns

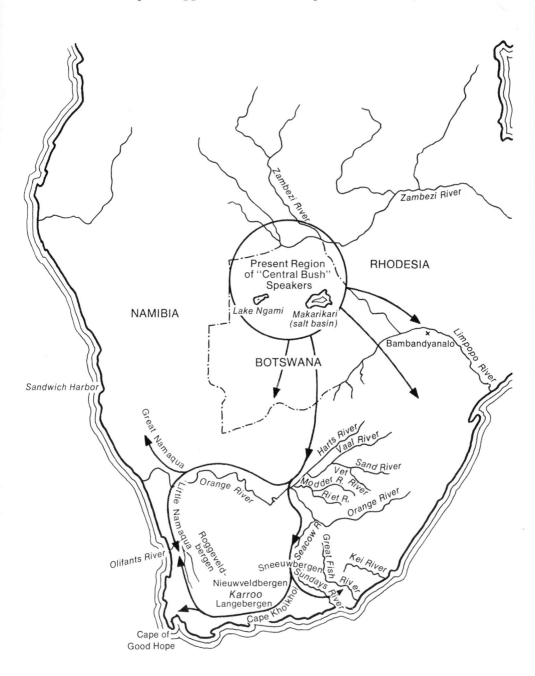

Key: — · — · — Boundaries of Botswana

0   Miles   400

Khoikhoi settlement has been in Namibia. Indeed, C. K. Cooke, in a recent defense of this view, relied entirely on modern distribution maps and ignored historical evidence of earlier patterns of settlement.

The cardinal difficulty with the west-coast view is the nature of the terrain. Most of the Khoikhoi dispersal area now consists of thorn veld savannah receiving only 10 to 20 inches of rain a year. It is presently suitable only for "ultra-extensive" (i.e. nomadic) pastoralism, and the carrying capacity of the veld is very unfavorable, being about 40 acres per cattle unit.[32] Even if the veld had not then deteriorated to its present level, one would expect a growing pastoral society to expand out of this region quickly, given the opportunity. However, one would expect such expansion to be toward the east (i.e. into Matabeleland and the Transvaal) rather than into the western coastal region; for the stock-carrying capacity of the latter region is far lower than that of the former. Rainfall in this eastern corridor is presently 20 to 30 inches a year, while in the western corridor it is only 5 to 20 inches in the wetter sections, and below 5 inches in some of its southern zones.[33] In particular, the area south of the Orange (Little Nama-qualand) is extremely difficult to cross with livestock. The Dutch tried to do this several times in the seventeenth century, but always in vain: they learned from local Khoikhoi that it could be so traversed only in the wet season, and then only if the rains were unusually plentiful.[34]

Moreover, there is linguistic, and perhaps archaeological, evidence of contact between Khoikhoi pastoralists and Bantu-speaking cultivators on the high veld east of the Khoikhoi dispersal area. This contact undoubtedly occurred at a time when both groups were few in numbers, but the order of their arrival in each area cannot yet be determined. Over the decades and centuries each would slowly expand, the farmers growing more rapidly in numbers, and the pastoralists more rapidly in terms of territory occupied. As a result of this internal

32. John H. Wellington, *Southern Africa: A Geographical Study* (Cambridge: Cambridge University Press, 1955), 2:112.

33. Ibid., 1, maps 3 (Mean Annual Rainfall) and 4 (Vegetation); and 2, map 1 (Land Classification).

34. Evidence could be cited from virtually every expedition sent north in the seventeenth century. See, for example, Journal of Cornelis de Cretser, in *Journal of Jan Van Riebeeck*, ed. H. B. Thom, 3 vols. (Cape Town and Amsterdam: A. A. Balkema, 1952), 3:468–69; and Second Diary of Olof Bergh, in *Journals of the Expedition of the Honourable Ensign Olof Bergh (1682 and 1683) and the Ensign Isaq Schrijver (1689)*, ed. and trans. E. E. Mossop, VRS 12 (Cape Town: Van Riebeeck Society, 1931), p. 165. The former work will hereafter be cited as *VRJ*.

growth, each would expand into lands to the south but would also expand into each other's proximity. Some of the Khoikhoi would borrow from the cultivators, then ally with them, and finally intermarry with them—just as they did later, on the Khoikhoi-Xhosa and the Khoikhoi-Tswana frontiers. Other Khoikhoi, retaining their pastoral culture, their language, and their original racial stock, would slowly be forced out of their pastures and pushed ahead of the cultivators in search of new lands. These processes can be likened to the events of the seventeenth century, when the Dutch farming frontier in the southwestern Cape absorbed some Khoikhoi and pushed others ahead into the interior.

As a result of these processes, one would expect that all purely pastoral Khoikhoi communities would disappear from areas occupied by the cultivators—as in fact has happened. One would also expect to find indications of Khoikhoi occupation in the Bantu languages of the region's present inhabitants and in the archaeological record. Indeed, some linguistic data show that Khoikhoi words were borrowed both by the ancestral language of the Southeast Bantu and later by individual languages which developed from it. The large number of cattle-related words among these borrowings suggest that the Southeast Bantu derived much of their modern pastoral culture from this contact with Khoikhoi.[35] Moreover, the archaeological sites of Bambandyanalo and Mapungubwe (in the Limpopo Valley) contain human remains that one physical anthropologist described as Khoisan and mixed negro-Khoisan, repectively.[36] Though these identifications are viewed skeptically by many modern scholars, they fit neatly into the pattern of interaction suggested by the linguistic evidence.

From the high veld the Khoikhoi probably penetrated the drier western regions by moving along the tributaries of the Orange River (the Riet, Modder, Vet, Vaal, and Harts) and later the Orange itself. This supposition is based in part on an analogy to later Korana movements in the eighteenth and nineteenth centuries, which almost invariably followed these rivers,[37] and in part on the fact that, when they were first visited by whites, Khoikhoi dwelt in tightly packed

35. Christopher Ehret et al., "Outlining Southern African History: A Re-evaluation, A.D. 100–1500," *Ufahamu* 3, no. 1 (Spring 1972) : 18.

36. Raymond A. Dart, foreword in Alexander Galloway, *The Skeletal Remains of Bambandyanalo* (Johannesburg: Witwatersrand University Press, 1959), pp. xiv, xvii.

37. See the map, "Migrations of the Korana," in *BS* 6, no. 2 (June 1932), opposite p. 205.

communities along the Orange River. They had apparently been there
for some time, as their language was then spoken by many nearby
groups of hunters (see p. 29). This Khoikhoi concentration along
the river contrasted with the situation between the river and the southwestern Cape, where there were almost no pastoralists to be found.
For cattle-keepers good pastures are useless in the absence of adequate
water for man and beast; and in much of south-central and southwestern Africa the rainfall is so low, and the evaporation of summer
rain so rapid, that the inhabitants are forced to cluster along river
banks.[38]

As some Khoikhoi began to move westward down the river system,
others continued to press south and east through the grasslands of the
Orange Free State. A very old and very specific Korana tradition may
refer to this split. In 1858, C. F. Wuras informed Sir George Grey that
a Korana, then almost a hundred years old, had told him that

> a tradition exists, that in ancient times the whole nation of
> Hottentots lived close together along the banks of [the] Vaal and
> Orange River. Their chief settlement ... was not far from the
> junction of the Orange and Vaal River. But in consequence of a
> great quarrel which arose amongst them, they divided, one part of
> their nation went in the direction of Cape Town and settled
> there; another part went down the Orange River and the Korana,
> the greatest and richest tribe, remained.[39]

The Khoikhoi in the western prong slowly differentiated themselves
into three great clusters of riverain tribes: (from east to west) the
Korana, the Einiqua (River People), and the Namaqua. Even today
the languages of Korana and Namaqua are closer to each other than
to that of the Cape Khoikhoi, who descended from the southward-
moving prong.[40] The Namaqua, as the advance guard of the westward
expansion, finally reached a point, not far from the Atlantic Ocean,
where increasing aridity forced them to discover pastures away from
the river if they were to sustain further population growth. By the
time they were first contacted by whites, they had begun their two-
pronged movement south over the dry stretches of Little Namaqualand
toward the southwestern Cape and north into modern Namibia. This

38. I. Schapera, *The Tswana* (London: International African Institute, 1953), pp. 19 and 47.
39. C. F. Wuras, "An Account of the Korana," *BS* 3, no. 3 (July 1929):290.
40. Christopher Ehret, personal communication.

latter movement, which is confirmed by Heinrich Vedder's analysis of Great Namaqua traditions,[41] was clearly under way well before 1677, when the crew of the *Boode* met cattle-keeping Khoikhoi as far north along the Atlantic coast as Sandwich Harbor.[42] Northward migrations continued over a long period, for in 1760 Jacobus Coetsé met some Great Namaqua who said that they had left the river and moved into Namibia just twenty years previously.[43]

Meanwhile, far to the east, the ancestors of the Cape Khoikhoi made their way south to the coast. It is difficult to determine their exact route until more is learned about Khoikhoi settlement patterns in the eastern Cape—either from the Graaff-Reinet records or from Xhosa traditions about Khoikhoi. Still, one can point out that the most obvious route would have been by the Seacow River, over the good pastures of the Sneeuwbergen, into the valleys of the Sundays or the Great Fish Rivers—or via some parallel route farther east. P. J. van der Merwe has shown that the Dutch *trekboers*, who in the eighteenth century expanded with sheep and cattle in exactly the opposite direction of the Khoikhoi we are discussing, found all routes to the north of the Roggeveld-Nieuwveld blocked by inadequate pasture and water: it was only when they had pushed east to the Sneeuwbergen that they found a well-watered corridor north into the Free State and the Transvaal.[44]

In the coastal areas of the southeast Cape Province, further Khoikhoi expansion may have been stimulated by Bantu (Nguni) pressure as well as by shortage of pasture, and it proceeded westward through the narrow defiles of suitable pasture to the southwestern Cape. The

41. Heinrich Vedder, *South West Africa in Early Times*, trans. and ed. Cyril G. Hall (London: Oxford University Press, 1938), pp. 125–26. Vedder advanced this view in spite of his belief that Khoikhoi had originated as "Hamites" in northern Africa.

42. Algemeen Rijksarchief, The Hague, Koloniaal Archief, vol. 3990, Journal of the *Boode*, March 5–6, 1677, pp. 949–50v. The crew had already had contact with Namaqua—"real Hottentots, but [whose] language did not correspond with [that of] our Hottentots"—at a coastal point north of the Orange River mouth and south of Lüderitzbucht (entry of Feb. 17, 1677, p. 944). In identifying these locations I have followed Vedder (*South West Africa*, pp. 10–15). The Koloniaal Archief is henceforth cited as KA.

43. "A Narrative ... by the Burger Jacobus Coetsé ... ," *The Journal of Hendrik Jacob Wikar (1779) and the Journals of Jacobus Coetsé Jansz (1760) and Willem van Reenen (1791)*, ed. E. E. Mossop and A. W. van der Horst, VRS 15 (Cape Town: Van Riebeeck Society, 1935), p. 281. This movement occurred early enough that it was probably independent of white activity in southern Africa. White expansion was subsequently responsible for still further northward migrations.

44. Petrus Johannes van der Merwe, *Die Noordwaartse Beweging van die Boere voor die Groot Trek (1770–1842)* (The Hague: W. P. Van Stockum & Zoon, 1937), pp. 4–7.

Khoikhoi expansion route at this stage probably corresponded almost exactly to the narrow chain of Khoikhoi habitation which was noted near the coast by seventeenth- and eighteenth-century travelers. When they reached the southwestern Cape, the Khoikhoi discovered an almost ideal region: there they found no Bantu-speaking cultivators competing with them for land, and there was sufficient water and abundant pasture. Under these conditions Khoikhoi expanded rapidly to form the cluster of wealthy and culturally uniform Western Cape Khoikhoi who were met by the Dutch after 1652. It was the northwestern edge of this dilating cluster of tribes which encountered the southern flank of the Namaqua near the Olifants River (see pp. 135–36).

In the seventeenth century, the Western Cape Khoikhoi had their most important economic links with the Namaqua to their north, but they were far better informed about peoples to the east, even those living at distances of several hundred miles. Moreover, they explicitly recognized the political suzerainty (in the sense of lineage seniority) of eastern peoples, whom they tended to rank hierarchically with people farthest east at the top. This curious phenomenon, which is discussed in chapter 3, strongly suggests that the Cape tribes were descendants of clans which had split from more senior clans in the east.

The Cape Khoikhoi attitude to the Namaqua, who were geographically closer to them, was quite different: they never linked them genealogically with the Cape tribes, and they dwelt on the fact that Namaqua had strange weapons, clothing, crafts, and speech. European observers also noted that Cape Khoikhoi and Namaqua sheep, though of the same basic breed, had developed in different directions.[45] So important were these differences, that some Cape Khoikhoi even denied that Namaqua were Khoikhoi at all.[46] This striking cultural discontinuity between Cape Khoikhoi and Namaqua is what one would expect if the two peoples had met again after splitting previously in a distant region of South Africa. It must be remembered in discussing the origins of the Western Cape Khoikhoi that the presence of the Karroo and the evidence of demographic patterns leave us with only two choices: the Cape Khoikhoi came either from the north or from the east. Of these alternatives the latter is clearly the more likely.

45. H. Epstein, *The Origin of the Domestic Animals of Africa* (New York, London, Munich: Africana Publishing Company, 1971), 2: 155–57. Epstein believes that Namaqua sheep changed through interbreeding with stock of the Bantu-speakers.
46. The evidence is presented in Elphick, "Cape Khoi," pp. 193–94.

CONCLUSION

The foregoing reconstruction is of course speculative, and some parts of it are more probable than others. We may be quite confident that the Khoikhoi were descendants of hunters who acquired stock in or near northern Botswana, but the precise circumstances I have suggested for this pastoral revolution are less certain. It is highly probable that the Khoikhoi expanded because of the needs of their pastoral economy, but the routes I have suggested for this dispersal must be regarded merely as informed guesses.

The least certain facets of this reconstruction are those concerning interaction with Bantu-speakers. On this subject only one statement can now be made with virtual certainty: that some Khoikhoi arrived in the southwestern Cape with their pastoral values intact and without any striking evidence of having been deeply involved with Bantu-speakers. As a result they continued to practice a livestock economy in a region abundantly blessed with good pastures and rainfall, a region which was, in fact, eminently suitable for cultivation. Thus they were singularly fortunate among African pastoralists, most of whom find themselves excluded from the most attractive lands by their cultivating neighbors. The anomalous position of the Cape Khoikhoi can best be explained by assuming that the Bantu-speaking, mixed farming communities, which supported a much larger population on much less land, had expanded more slowly but also more decisively than the Khoikhoi; and that the Khoikhoi had been pushed ahead of them into seemingly more arid regions. By a happy stroke of fortune these regions issued, not into desert, but into the rich grasslands of the southwestern Cape.

2

Hunters and Khoikhoi:
The Ecological Cycle of Hunting and Herding

WHO WERE THE "SAN"?

When Khoikhoi wandered into the southwestern Cape, or into any pastures previously unknown to them, their discovery was usually marred by the realization that the region was already inhabited by aboriginal hunters. The ensuing relations between the newcomers and the hunters entailed war, trade, clientage, and intermarriage, and resulted in the widespread transfer of cultural traits from one society to the other. Nowhere did Khoikhoi societies attain a high population —in 1660 there could have been no more than 100,000 Khoikhoi in the southwestern Cape[1]—and nowhere, so far as we know, did they succeed in eliminating the hunters, either by war or by absorption. Whenever whites visited Khoikhoi societies in the seventeenth and eighteenth centuries, they found people without livestock residing in Khoikhoi camps or else dwelling nearby, sometimes on good pastures but more typically in hilly regions or on the seashore.

It must be remembered that for decades after 1652 these white observers applied the word *Hottentot* (or *Hottentoo*) indiscriminately to

1. Several estimates have been made of Khoikhoi population at the time of the first Dutch settlement. About 1811, M. H. C. Lichtenstein suggested a mere 10,000 (*Foundation of the Cape/ About the Bechuanas*, trans. and ed. O. H. Spohr, [Cape Town: A. A. Balkema, 1973], p. 37, n. 3). In 1837, the *Report of the Parliamentary Select Committee on Aboriginal Tribes*, pub. for the Aborigines Protection Society (London: William Ball, Aldine Chambers, 1837), p. 30, opted for the much higher figure of 200,000. The most frequently quoted estimate is that of 45–50,000, first made by George McCall Theal (*History of South Africa under the Administration of the Dutch East India Company, 1652–1795* [London: Swan Sonnenschein & Co., 1897], 1:126). In my view, Theal is a fairly reliable guide on this issue. The highest possible figures for the total Peninsular population are 8,000 and, for the Cochoqua, 16,000. It is conceivable that the Chainouqua and the Hessequa were more numerous—say, 25,000 each. But the Guriqua and Little Namaqua populations were both smaller. Thus a total of 100,000 is almost certainly on the far side of the truth. For discussions of tribal population figures, see pp. 91–92, 117–18, 134, 136–37, 139.

all brown-skinned, noncultivating natives of South Africa, both those who kept stock and those who did not. Cattleless people were conceived as a subspecies of Hottentot[2] and were initially described by three names: (1) "Strandloper" (i.e. Beachranger), which referred to the fisher-scavenger folk of Table Bay and later, by extension, to many other coastal peoples; (2) "Sonqua" or "Soaqua" (which were the Cape Khoikhoi equivalents of Namaqua "San"); and (3) "Ubiqua" and its variant "Obiqua."[3] The terms "Sonqua" and "Ubiqua" were the words the Khoikhoi used themselves; they were virtually synonymous,[4] referring not to specific bands but to a category of people scattered all over southern Africa. By 1685 the term "Bosjesman" was first used in a colonial document,[5] and within a few years it had, along with "Bosjesman Hottentot," become the standard Dutch equivalent of the older Khoikhoi terms.

As we noted in chapter 1 the seventeenth-century view on Khoikhoi-hunter relationships was replaced in the nineteenth century by a conviction that "Hottentots" and "Bushmen" were two distinct peoples, each with its own language(s), culture, economy, and racial type. When investigators imbued with this new conception searched the archives of the old Dutch colony, they read contemporary conceptions back into the events of previous centuries and confidently

2. See, for example, the following lists in which Sonqua or Ubiqua are listed among Khoikhoi tribes: Kolbe, *Cape of Good Hope* (English ed.), 1:63; Olfert Dapper, "Kaffrarie of Lant der Kaffers ...," in Schapera and Farrington, *The Early Cape Hottentots*, VRS 14, pp. 31–33; and Wilhelm ten Rhyne, "Schediasma de Promontorio Bonae Spei," in ibid., p. 111.

3. *Sonqua* was a Khoikhoi word formed by adding the masculine plural termination *-qua* to a root which Theophilus Hahn (*Tsuni-//Goam, The Supreme Being of the Khoi-Khoi* [London: Trübner & Co., 1881], p. 3) identified with the Namaqua *saa*, with the vowel nasalized, meaning "to settle." Heinrich Vedder (*South West Africa*, p. 124) preferred the Namaqua *saa* without the nasal, which means "to gather or collect." The word might thus mean either "aborigine" or "gatherer." As for *Ubiqua*, Theal argued that it meant "murderer," a plausible explanation which has, however, been rejected on linguistic grounds by L. F. Maingard. See Theal, *History of South Africa*, 1:173; and L. F. Maingard, "The First Contacts of the Dutch with the Bushmen until the Time of Simon van der Stel (1686)," *SAJS* 32 [Nov. 1935]:486.) Maingard is possibly correct in identifying the Ubiqua with the "Fishermen," but is wrong in supposing them to be a single group.

4. Examples of the use of *Ubiqua* and *Sonqua* as synonyms are found in KA 3989, Dagregister March 26, 1676, p. 207; and KA 3992, Dagregister Sept. 30, 1679, p. 285. The Dagregister is henceforth cited as DR.

5. D. Moodie, *The Record* ... (Cape Town: A. S. Robertson, 1838–42), pt. 1, p. 399, n. 1. Moodie wrongly gives the date as Oct. 3, 1685; it should be Oct. 31 (KA 3999, DR Oct. 31, 1685, p. 306). For an interesting discussion of the evolution of this word in the mouths of non-whites, see Marius F. Valkhoff, *Studies in Portuguese and Creole, With Special Reference to South Africa* (Johannesburg: Witwatersrand University Press, 1966), p. 8.

classified all native peoples as "Bushmen" or "Hottentots," even if the documents gave them no warrant for doing so. This Bushman-Hottentot (or Khoikhoi-San) dichotomy has become one of those time-honored pairing mechanisms by which scholars automatically organize, but also distort, the complexities of historical reality.

Underlying this practice is the assumption that there were two distinct and nonoverlapping economies among brown-skinned South African natives—hunting-gathering and pastoralism—and that the pastoralists recognized this division by calling themselves Khoikhoi and consistently reserving the term *San* for the hunters. There is much evidence against this assumption, but before presenting it we must admit that in a few cases where the Dutch or the Khoikhoi gave a brief explanation of the status of "San" they made reference to absence of livestock. Simon van der Stel's view was typical:

> [The Ubiqua] maintain themselves by robbing and stealing from other Hottentots, having no cattle at all nor anything else on which to live.[6]

In reality, however, the seventeenth-century Dutch had very little opportunity to confirm these statements, and even in this period of limited contact there is considerable evidence that many so-called San had some acquaintance with sheep and cattle.

On January 16, 1669, a Dutch party under Corporal Jeronimus Cruse was attacked by a group of "Ubiqua" (i.e. San), a robber people who dwelt to the east of the Chainouqua. The robbers showered the Europeans with poisoned arrows (a weapon more characteristic of hunters than of Khoikhoi), but were repelled by musket fire. Cruse retaliated by marching to the Ubiqua's empty camp, where he destroyed a large cache of weapons and seized 139 cattle and 31 sheep which the Ubiqua had been keeping in kraals. The Ubiqua themselves dwelt in a single community of more than four hundred people—a significant number even by pastoral Khoikhoi standards.[7]

6. Gilbert Waterhouse, *Simon van der Stel's Journal of his Expedition to Namaqualand, 1685–6* (London: Longmans, Green, and Co., 1932), p. 115.

7. KA 3981, Journael ... gehouden by den Corpal Jeronimus Croes, Jan. 16, 1669, pp. 766–67v. Their strength was about 100 arms-bearing men; therefore their total population must have been well over 400. This group of "Ubiqua" has long been known to historians, and because it combined a typically "Bushman" culture with cattle keeping, it has often been identified as a community of mixed Khoikhoi-hunter descent. Such physical intermixture is, of course, perfectly possible but is in no way suggested by the evidence. As the next few pages will show, it was common for communities of non-Khoikhoi culture to own small numbers of livestock.

Subsequent contacts between Dutchmen and "San" east of Cape Town were normally hostile and occasionally gave the Europeans an opportunity to seize cattle or sheep. But even peaceful encounters could involve livestock: for example, in March 1674 five "Ubiqua" emissaries brought six sheep to the Cape governor as a gesture of good will.[8] So-called Sonqua with considerable cattle holdings were also found in the region just north of Cape Town. A significant example was one Kees, whom both Europeans and Khoikhoi identified as a "Sonqua" captain, yet who possessed modest amounts of stock over a period of at least twenty-four years.[9]

It is, of course, possible that some of the tribes designated "San" were robber groups who had recently acquired their stock from other Khoikhoi, especially as Khoikhoi often used the words *Sonqua* and *Ubiqua* in the same breath with "robber." The crucial point, however, is not the means by which stock was obtained—for most Khoikhoi possessed cattle seized in war from other Khoikhoi—but whether or not the stock was immediately consumed by the robbers in the classic hunter pattern. The keeping of herds in kraals, the use of sheep as diplomatic gifts, and the long history of Kees's livestock holdings suggest that, in several cases at least, this was not the case.

In the eighteenth century, scholarly whites penetrated far into the interior and wrote more perceptive and detailed accounts of people called "San." In the 1770s Andreas Sparrman met, at the Klein Zondag River, three old "boshis" who called themselves "good Bushmen," as they did not rob but raised (*élevoient*) a few cattle. That such activity was not limited to those in direct contact with whites is shown by Sparrman's statement that some of the "Chinese Bushmen" raised cattle well beyond the colony.[10] Furthermore, Robert Gordon, while wandering in the remote region known as Bushmanland, was given milk by four "Bosjesmans," a fact which strongly indicates that these people had not stolen cattle simply for immediate slaughter.[11]

8. KA 3991, DR March 24, 1678, p. 390v.

9. Moodie, *The Record*, p. 388, n. 2; Suid-Afrikaanse Argiefstukke, *Resolusies van die Politieke Raad*, 6 vols. (Cape Town and Johannesburg: Publikasie-Afdeling van die Kantoor van die Direkteur van Argiewe, 1961), vol. 3, entry of Nov. 28, 1689, p. 213; KA 3989, Daghregister gehouden op de Expeditie na de rebellerende Gonnemase Africanen, Nov. 11, 1676, p. 337v; KA 3989, Bax to XVII, March 14, 1677, p. 16v; KA 4024, DR Nov. 29, 1701, p. 177.

10. André Sparrman, *Voyage au Cap de Bonne-Espérance et autour du Monde*, 2 vols. (Paris: Buisson, 1787), 2:23, 156.

11. Staf D 583/U/4/1/3, Gordon, Vierde Reyse, Sept. 26, 1779, n.p.

Most conclusive of all was the evidence of Hendrik Jacob Wikar, a Swedish deserter from the Dutch East India Company's service; Wikar lived several years among the Khoikhoi far beyond the colony and spoke their language well. On one of his trips along the Orange River he encountered a group called Samgomomkoa (a word which probably means Cattle San), who had "cattle, but only a few"; they did not steal, but lived primarily by gathering and hunting, and were called Chaboup (lit. "wanderers") or Bushmen by the Namaqua. Near the Samgomomkoa the party met another "Bushman" group, the Nanningai or Mountain Climbers, who likewise had sheep and cattle which they were willing to trade.[12]

All these testimonies clearly prove that at various points inside and outside the colony there were groups who were called (or in two cases, who called themselves) "San" or "Bushmen," yet who held small numbers of livestock on a permanent basis.

Further indication of the broad and imprecise meaning of the concept "San" can be found in an unexpected place. Khoikhoi designated certain small local groups with compound names in which the word *San* was apparently a part. Peoples called by these compound names were found over the whole of southern Africa. The Hori*sans*,[13] the Coche*sons*,[14] and the Dama*sonquas*[15] were found near the "Eastern Frontier"; the Kame*son* (Cumis*soquas*)[16] and *Sam*gomomkoa[17] on the Orange River; the *Son*damrocqua (also Damras*sen*)[18] in Namibia; and

12. Hendrik Jacob Wikar, "Report to His Excellency Joachim van Plettenbergh . . . ," Mossop and Van der Horst, *Journal of Wikar* . . . , VRS 15, pp. 29–33, 35.

13. Probably Hori-sa-na: an unidentified adjective + San + the common plural ending. KA 4027, Interrogatorien . . . Willem van Sijburg, Oct. 23, 1702, pp. 444–44v; and KA 4027, Interrogatorien . . . Lambert Symonsz, Oct. 24, 1702, p. 448v. This information must be correlated with the evidence in KA 4027, Vraagpoincten . . . Soetekoek et al., Nov. 7, 1702, pp. 469v–70: Soetekoek's "Bushman" kraal Kannou was the same as the Dutchmen's Horisons.

14. KA 4027, Vraagpoincten . . . Soetekoek et al., Nov. 7, 1702, p. 469v.

15. Journal gehouden door den Adsistend Carel Albregt Haupt," *RZA*, 3: 282–83.

16. Probably //*Gami-son-qua* or Water People, although E. E. Mossop (Wikar, VRS 15, p. 27, n. 16) identified them as the !Gami-≠nun, a Namaqua group. See Waterhouse, *Van der Stel*, p. 148; *VRJ*, 3:477 (Feb. 22 and 23, 1662); KA 3999, S. van der Stel to XVII, April 4, 1686, pp. 643–44.

17. These people kept livestock, and their name was probably *San-goma-qua* or Cattle San. Wikar, VRS 15, pp. 30–31.

18. These are the Bergdama(ra) of Namibia. See "Dag Register gehouden op den Landtogt . . . onder het Commando van . . . Hendrik Hop . . . ," *The Journals of Brink and Rhenius*, ed. E. E. Mossop, VRS 28 (Cape Town: Van Riebeeck Society, 1947), p. 50; Willem van Reenen, "Journal Kept on the Inland Journey . . . to the Rhenius Berg," Mossop and Van der Horst, *Journal of Wikar* . . . , VRS 15, p. 315.

the Hou*swaana* in the Sneeuwberg.[19] The word *San* could thus be exceedingly flexible in reference. It was applied not only to hunter-gatherers but to .small-scale stock breeders like the Horisans and Samgomomkoa. It included both brown- and black-skinned persons, for the Sondamrocquas were the black people generally known as Bergdamara. And finally, it encompassed both Khoikhoi speakers (e.g. the Sondamrocquas) and non-Khoikhoi speakers (e.g. the Houswaana).

On the other hand, the name San was never applied to a group that was large or prosperous, and never to groups that we are able to relate genealogically to one of the great clusters of Khoikhoi clans. In other words, it connoted low status in regard to wealth or lineage; this was the case whether the reference was to aboriginal hunter bands, to impoverished fragments which were formerly pastoral, or to cattleless people within Khoikhoi society. Thus Theophilus Hahn noted that nineteenth-century Namaqua could even call fellow Namaqua "Bushmen" if they were poor (i.e. had no cattle or sheep) or if they worked as servants. The words *Sab* (singular) and *San* (plural) were regularly used as insults:

> One . . . often hears, "*Khoikhoi tamab*, Sab ke," he is no Khoikhoi; he is Sā, which means to say, "he is no gentleman, he is of low *extraction, or he is a rascal*." [Italics in original]

Namaqua even referred to indigent Europeans as "!Uri San" (white Bushmen).[20] It is clear, then, that "San" were not perceived as an ethnic group but as an undesirable social class, however vaguely demarcated; they were, as Simon van der Stel remarked in 1685, "the same as the poor in Europe."[21]

Thus "San" or "Bosjesmans" of the old colonial documents are not necessarily to be identified with the *hunter* "Bushmen" of modern writers. But is it still possible that the Khoikhoi-San dichotomy is valid? Could there have been two distinct peoples even though

---

19. These people lived in the Sneeuwberg and were known by Khoikhoi as d'Gauas and by whites as "Chinese Bushmen." The form *Houswaana* derives from Le Vaillant and is probably *d'gau* (presumably a click plus *au*) +sa +na. This supposition is supported by the fact that ≠*ou* means "tame" in Namaqua; these people had an early reputation for timidity, later completely reversed. See Beutler (Haupt), *RZA*, 3:324, 327; François le Vaillant, *Voyage de Monsieur le Vaillant dans l'intérieur de l'Afrique*, 2 vols. (Paris: Chez Leroy, 1790), 2:341; Sparrman, *Voyage*, 2:155.

20. Hahn, *Tsuni-//Goam*, pp. 3, 101. The quotation is on p. 3.

21. Waterhouse, *Van der Stel*, p. 121.

contemporary whites and Khoikhoi were fuzzy in perceiving the difference between them? At least partial answers can be sought in a survey of the languages spoken by hunters. If some cattleless people spoke Khoikhoi rather than aboriginal languages, then a fundamental assumption of the Khoikhoi-San dichotomy will be demolished—the belief that hunters of recent times are *necessarily* practitioners of an aboriginal culture and hence direct cultural descendants of peoples who lived in particular regions of southern Africa before the Khoikhoi.

It seems that at least some cattleless groups spoke Khoikhoi as their first language. For example, early Dutch officials stated that the Strandlopers (or Goringhaicona), a scavenging people on the Cape Peninsula, spoke the same language as the neighboring Goringhaiqua, a cattle-keeping Khoikhoi group.[22] This assertion might be questioned on the grounds that early settlers thought all "click" languages to be alike: but this view is made unlikely by the extremely close lineage ties between Strandlopers and Goringhaiqua, by the relatedness of their tribal names, and by the absence of communication problems between them (see p. 94). More valuable, perhaps, is the expert testimony of Wikar and Gordon that many hunter groups in the Orange River Valley spoke Khoikhoi fluently. The Khoikhoi language had probably displaced aboriginal tongues in this region, for "Bushmans' language" was still used in magical rituals—a facet of culture where linguistic relics are often found.[23]

A rather different pattern of bilingualism was exhibited by the cattleless people living in the mountain ranges parallel to the Atlantic coast north of Cape Town. These peoples had, like most aboriginal hunters, a variety of their own languages; but among them, as Jan Danckaert noted in 1660, "there [was] also one language which all their great ones understand but which the common people do not."[24] This lingua franca was doubtless Khoikhoi, for this was the only native language which Khoikhoi guides from Table Bay could understand, and they had no difficulty communicating with these hunters.

We also have evidence of hunters who did not speak Khoikhoi at all. These were found chiefly in the mountains of the central Cape Province, like the Roggeveld and Sneeuwberg. In the Sneeuwberg they were

---

22. *VRJ*, 1:71 (Oct. 9, 1652).

23. Staf D 593 /U/4/1/3, Gordon, Vierde Reyse, Aug. 20, 1779, n.p.; Wikar, VRS 15, p. 164, n. 138; and p. 55; Staf D 593 /U/4/2, R. J. Gordon, Journaal der Derde Reis door een Deel van zuidelyk Africa gedaan, . . . , Jan. 4, 1779, n.p.; and Dec. 8, 1778, n.p.

24. *VRJ*, 3:300 (Dec. 14, 1660); see also Waterhouse, *Van der Stel*, p. 164.

called "Chinese" and their language was probably a member of Bleek's Southern "Bush" category.[25] This was the only hunter group associated with rock paintings in the writings of travelers before the nineteenth-century,[26] a fact which strengthens its claim to having a relatively pure aboriginal culture.

Clearly the Khoikhoi language had greater influence in regions, like the Cape Peninsula and the Orange Valley, where Khoikhoi had long been settled, and in large numbers. The fact that hunters of these regions spoke Khoikhoi as their first language (and as a second language elsewhere) suggests that other aspects of their culture could be at least partly Khoikhoi, and hence not purely aboriginal in nature. This conclusion threatens a crucial facet of the Khoikhoi-San dichotomy— the assumption of uninterrupted continuity between aboriginal and seventeenth-century hunter communities. The evidence based on language can be accounted for in two ways: by allowing that some immigrant Khoikhoi communities lost their livestock and reverted to hunting, or by assuming that some aboriginals acquired Khoikhoi culture through prolonged contact with Khoikhoi. In fact there is considerable evidence for both processes, and to accommodate this we must replace the static Khoikhoi-San classification with a dynamic model of interaction between Khoikhoi and their neighbors.

THE ECOLOGICAL CYCLE: UPWARD PHASE

In the documentation at our disposal we can distinguish many different modes of contact between Khoikhoi immigrants and the aboriginal hunters of different regions. The foremost of these were: (1) contact solely through armed conflict, (2) contact through trade and other forms of economic cooperation, (3) incorporation of hunters as subordinate clients in Khoikhoi communities, and (4) the final absorption of these clients into Khoikhoi society through intermarriage. These modes of contact could have followed each other as phases in a gradual accommodation and amalgamation of Khoikhoi and hunters in specific regions.

---

25. Beutler (Haupt), *RZA*, 3:324; Lichtenstein, VRS 10, p. 146; Sparrman, *Voyage*, 1:245; 2:435–38; Staf D 593 /U/4/2, Gordon, Derde Reis, Nov. 12, 1778. The provisional identification of this language with the Southern Bush family has been made by comparing Sparrman's vocabulary items (and scattered items from Gordon) with Dorothea F. Bleek, *A Bushman Dictionary* (New Haven, Conn.: American Oriental Society, 1956).

26. See, for example, Joachim Baron van Plettenberg, "Dagverhaal van de Landryse...," *RZA*, 4:40–41.

We may assume that the cycle of cultural assimilation began at the point when a Khoikhoi group arrived in a Cape region previously inhabited only by aboriginal hunter-gatherers. At this point the two communities were clearly differentiated by the languages they spoke and by the economies they practiced. However, they had at least one institution in common that would ultimately facilitate both conflict and cooperation between them. The Khoikhoi, it must be recalled, practiced a culture which itself had originally been based on hunting and gathering. The acquisition of sheep and cattle had barely diminished the importance of the old activities in their economic and cultural life. The Khoikhoi diet still consisted largely of *veldkos* (berries, roots, etc.) which was collected daily by the women.[27] Furthermore, the hunt, which was prosecuted with techniques similar to those of "Bushmen,"[28] retained great prestige. Khoikhoi leaders preferred to dress in wild animal skins rather than cowhide or sheepskin,[29] and at least one chief insisted on payments from his people each time they killed an animal in the hunt.[30]

These traditional hunting customs were retained in "pastoral" society in part because livestock provided inadequate nourishment for the Khoikhoi, who slaughtered only on special occasions. Even milk was not usually available all year round, because its supply was dependent on the state of the pasture and the presence of newborn calves.[31] Khoikhoi were probably more reliant on the hunt than were their Bantu-speaking neighbors in southern Africa, for not only did they lack the basic foodstuffs available to the cultivators, but the mobile nature of their society made hunting comparatively easy.[32]

27. Grevenbroek, VRS 14, p. 197; Schapera, *Khoisan Peoples*, p. 316.

28. Schapera, *Khoisan Peoples*, p. 301.

29. Soeswa, the Chainouqua chief, was clad in "splendid leopard skins" (*VRJ*, 3:302 [Dec. 16, 1660]). Among the Gonaqua, chiefs wore tiger skins, while commoners had only calf skins: C. P. Thunberg, *Voyages de C. P. Thunberg, au Japon, par le Cap de Bonne-Espérance* ..., 2 vols. (Paris: Benoît Dandré, Garnery, Obré, 1796), 1:229, 293. The Great Namaqua wore jackal skins (Coetsé, VRS 15, p. 285). In *VRJ*, 3:352 (Journal of Pieter van Meerhoff, Feb. 20, 1661), we hear of a magnificent skin used by Little Namaqua as a seat for visitors.

30. Schrijver, VRS 12, pp. 234–45. Schapera (*Khoisan Peoples*, p. 291) quotes Wandres on the Namaqua, who regarded game as the herds of the chief. Hunters were obliged to give the chief the head and lower legs of any animal killed; in the case of small game they donated part of the meat.

31. Schapera, *Khoisan Peoples*, pp. 294–95.

32. This conclusion is suggested by the columns of George Peter Murdock, *Ethnographic Atlas* (Pittsburgh: University of Pittsburgh Press, 1967), p. 62, col. 7. Murdock has attempted, on the basis of published ethnographic material, to quantify the relative importance of different forms of economic endeavor in a large number of societies. His figures are of course only approx-

Moreover, Khoikhoi males, unlike their Bantu-speaking counterparts, were permitted by custom to leave their livestock in the care of the women while they ventured far afield after game.

The fact that Khoikhoi economy was merely an extension of aboriginal economy meant that coalescence of the two societies was fairly easy. At the outset, however—when Khoikhoi first arrived in an aboriginal area—this feature probably intensified conflict. Not only did the two groups find themselves competing for the same game, but they also had to fight over waterholes and rivers which were gathering places for game as well as for cattle. It probably took somewhat longer for hunter-aborigines to realize that Khoikhoi stock was destroying the pastures on which the game herds depended. Sooner or later they would feel justified in attacking Khoikhoi cattle and sheep which, in the view of the hunters, were merely animals that had wandered into their ancestral hunting zones. A bitter struggle of raid and counter-raid would ensue. This form of conflict has been described so often, and is so widely regarded as the typical form of Khoikhoi-hunter interaction,[33] that only the briefest discussion of it is necessary here.

Confrontation probably led to a tightening of the social structure of both communities. Among the Khoikhoi, competent military leaders emerged who could unite several clans into the moderately large tribes common in the western Cape in the seventeenth century. Such leadership counteracted the centrifugal pull which the open veld otherwise exerted on Khoikhoi political institutions. Among the aborigines, some fled the strife and established themselves in mountain and desert areas where the pastoralists would not follow; others united into large robber communities such as those we often meet in the seventeenth-century documents. These latter groups normally had a form of chieftainship, an institution unknown in some of the isolated Bushman communities which have been studied by modern anthropologists.[34] The techniques of the robbers can be seen in several

---

imate, and even impressionistic. It is nonetheless striking that among the Namaqua (the only Khoikhoi group on which adequate data are available) hunting is assessed at 30 percent of total economic activity. This is as great or greater than the figures given for so-called hunter groups (the Naron and !Kung Bushmen are given 30 percent and 20 percent, respectively), and is much greater than the figures for the numerous Bantu-speaking cultivating societies south of the Zambezi (which are variously assessed at 0–10 percent). It is equally noteworthy that the Herero, the only other pastoral and noncultivating society in southern Africa, are also given a hunting figure of 30 percent even though they are culturally and racially unrelated to the Khoikhoi.

33. E.g. by Theal in *History of South Africa*, 1:227–28.
34. E.g. KA 3991, DR March 24, 1678, p. 390v.

Dutch accounts. Schrijver described how in 1689 the "Hongliqua Hottentots" (a robber group in Hessequa country) approached his camp at night and "chased one or maybe two oxen with much shouting and yelling and other uproar into our kraal, in order by such a stratagem to throw our men and cattle into disorder."[35]

Such conflict, however painful, was still a form of culture-contact. It taught the robbers much about handling livestock, and probably awakened in them a desire for the benefits of pastoralism. Most importantly, war led to negotiations, and negotiations often resulted in a peaceful modus vivendi between the two groups. Many South African historians still assume that hunters and herders will always be engaged in bitter and irreconcilable conflict with each other.[36] This belief is derived largely from the observations of whites in the central Cape mountains and Transorgania after 1750. By contrast, in the Orange River Valley and the western Cape, areas of relatively long pastoral occupation, cooperation was just as common as strife.

Probably the first stage of cooperation involved the periodic exchange of goods and services. The hunters brought animal skins, honey, items of *veldkos*, and their finely constructed weapons: bows, arrows, and quivers.[37] In exchange they probably received milk or an occasional piece of meat. In places where Khoikhoi had access to the trade lines from European and Bantu-speaking societies, they also gave the hunters beads, tobacco, and apparently small pieces of iron: eighteenth-century travelers often found hunters with iron arrow heads.[38] However, the most important service the hunters could render the Khoikhoi was to procure game for them. Along the Orange River, hunters were repaid for these services in an interesting way: they were permitted to eat any game they found in game traps owned by Khoikhoi, on condition that they immediately reset the traps.[39]

The hunters, too, were anxious to guarantee a regular food supply and would naturally prefer to bring game to Khoikhoi in return for

35. Schrijver, VRS 12, p. 240.

36. See e.g. Arthur Keppel-Jones, *South Africa: A Short History* (London: Hutchinson & Co., 1961), p. 35.

37. KA 4037, Dagverhaal gehouden op de vee Ruyling ... onder 't Gezag van den Baas Thuijnier Jan Hartogh, Nov. 11, 1707, p. 906v; *VRJ*, 3:315 (Dec. 7, 1661). In 1661 some hunters promised to bring the Dutch ivory, honey, and wax (*VRJ*, 3:373 [April 20–23, 1661]): this may reflect a traditional barter in these products.

38. E.g. Sparrman, *Voyage*, 1:214.

39. Wikar, VRS 15, pp. 119–21. This reference does not specifically state that these privileges were given in return for hunting, but this seems very likely.

permanent and regular payment. Such desires led to the transition from the symbiotic relationships described above, to an incorporation of aborigines as an occupational (i.e. hunting) class in Khoikhoi society.[40] At first these hunters probably lived under their own chiefs in an encampment close to that of their employers. Arrangements like this were noted by Slotsboo in the country of the Guriqua and Little Namaqua, and by Wikar along the Orange River.[41] With the passage of time, some hunters came to live in Khoikhoi kraals, but in huts that were clearly set aside from those of Khoikhoi: in 1661 Van Meerhoff described a Little Namaqua kraal as follows:

> There is a circle of 73 huts, and outside this kraal there are three huts whose occupants have no cattle but are like messengers, who run from one kraal to another at the king's command.[42]

These alien clients were often used as messengers, probably because of their expert knowledge of local terrain. From being a messenger it was a short step to becoming an ambassador: in 1687 the king of the Inqua tribe sent as his envoy to the Cape government a captain of the *struijkrovers* (i.e. highwaymen or San).[43]

Starrenburgh noted that the hunters also served as soldiers for the Khoikhoi, and the two functions easily overlapped, as both demanded tracking skills, dexterity, and accurate aim. We have many examples of hunters who acted as frontier guards to spot approaching intruders, as spies and informers between Khoikhoi groups, as watchmen protecting Khoikhoi kraals at night, and as soldiers in full-scale combat.[44] These warriors were paid during peacetime in meat or other foods; in war they shared in the booty. Often they employed the robbing techniques they had previously learned, always—so our sources allege—stealing from neighboring Khoikhoi and never from their own employers.[45] In such cases Khoikhoi regarded patrons as

40. KA 4031, Dag Verhaal van den Land-drost Johannes Starrenburgh, Oct. 30, 1705, p. 746.

41. Algemeen Rijksarchief, The Hague, Kamer Zeeland 3193, Dagh Verhaal van den Luytenant Kaij Jessen Slotsbo, Nov. 16, 1712, n.p.; Wikar, VRS 15, pp. 117–23 and passim. The Kamer Zeeland is hereafter denoted by KZ.

42. *VRJ*, 3:353 (Journal of Pieter van Meerhoff, Feb. 20, 1661).

43. KA 4002, DR Feb. 4, 1687, p. 168.

44. J. C. Rhenius, "Dagh Register gehouden op de Togt naar de Amaquas Hottentots...," Mossop, *Journals of Brink and Rhenius*, VRS 28, p. 136; Waterhouse, *Van der Stel*, p. 121; Moodie, *The Record*, p. 263.

45. Wikar, VRS 15, p. 205; Waterhouse, *Van der Stel*, p. 121.

responsible for the actions of their hunter-clients, and disputes over the clients' actions often led to wars among Khoikhoi.[46]

Khoikhoi also hired ex-hunters to tend their all-valuable herds, even though this could mean letting the herdsmen take the cattle hundreds of miles from the owner's kraal.[47] Such arrangements were striking proof of the good relations that could exist between Khoikhoi and hunters, and also of the effect which contact could have in breaking down the Khoikhoi-San dichotomy. This practice of lending out cattle was widespread throughout southern Africa. Among the Namaqua the herdsmen were usually given one-half of the increase of the stock in their charge, as well as all the milk.[48] If former aborigines received treatment similar to that of Khoikhoi herdsmen, it is likely that many acquired their own fledgling herds and flocks in this manner.

So common were these various systems of incorporation that Simon van der Stel could assert that all Khoikhoi communities in Little Guriqualand had "Sonquas" under their protection, and Wikar testified the same for the Orange River Valley. Similar conclusions can be deduced from documents for every Cape Khoikhoi tribe from Table Bay as far east as the Inqua.[49] Former hunters who were partially absorbed into Khoikhoi society were easily distinguishable from those who remained alienated, as they suffered less from the effects of malnutrition and chronic insecurity.[50] Lichtenstein and other travelers commented that the "Bushmen" of the Orange River were more "gentle and sociable" than other Bushmen, and this doubtless derived from their long involvement with Khoikhoi.[51]

The foregoing process of incorporation was an important facet of the periodic upward phase in local Khoikhoi economies. Under ideal conditions the upward swing was a self-perpetuating spiral. The transformation of the hunters' hostility into cooperation permitted the peaceful growth of Khoikhoi herds and flocks, as did the acquisition of reliable herdsmen. Increased herds meant a secure food supply, and human population consequently grew. As wealth was a very important

46. Wikar, VRS 15, p. 171.

47. KZ 3193, Dagh Verhaal . . . Kaij Jessen Slotsbo, Oct. 23, 1712, n.p. The case of the Sonqua-Guriqua Kees is probably another good example; Kees apparently pastured many of the Cochoqua's cattle: see above p. 26.

48. Schapera, *Khoisan Peoples*, p. 294.

49. Waterhouse, *Van der Stel*, p. 121; Wikar, VRS 15, p. 161; Guy Tachard, *Voyage de Siam* . . . (Paris: Arnold Seneuze et Daniel Horthemels, 1686), p. 96; Schrijver, VRS 12, p. 228.

50. Wikar, VRS 15, p. 205.

51. Lichtenstein, VRS 11, p. 290.

basis of political power in Khoikhoi society, prosperity favored the emergence of more prestigious rulers and the formation of larger political units. Under these conditions the lot of unabsorbed hunters became increasingly difficult: those who did not wish to flee to inhospitable mountains were induced to capitulate and enter Khoikhoi society. Their absorption was facilitated by the demand for herdsmen to tend the expanding Khoikhoi herds and for warriors to fight in their defense. Thus the independent hunter population of a given area decreased at the same time as the Khoikhoi population was on the rise.

At some point in this process the hunter-clients began to intermarry into Khoikhoi society. This development could not have come easily, as Khoikhoi had considerable disdain for those they called "San"; and when it did come, the pattern could well have been hypergamous, Khoikhoi men marrying hunter-client women and not vice versa.[52] (There is evidence of such a one-sided pattern when Khoikhoi and former hunters were living on white farms.)[53] Women were made available for marriage to Khoikhoi by the well-known hunter custom of giving away or "selling" their children to avoid starvation in difficult times.[54] In the expanding Khoikhoi society a few individuals were becoming rich enough to become polygamous and there was doubtless a demand for wives. It is perhaps an index of the effects of intermarriage that, in areas of long contact, the Dutch noted no differences in stature between Khoikhoi and hunters, while in other areas, for example in the region north of Cape Town, they described the Khoikhoi as being very tall and the hunters as very short.[55]

From the evidence cited on pages 29–30, it would seem obvious that intermixture (both economic and through marriage) led to former hunters speaking Khoikhoi, first as a second language and later as their own. It is striking that Khoikhoi speech remained so uniform from Namibia to the Eastern Frontier in view of the wide variety of aboriginal tongues with which it had come into intimate contact. This was only in part due to far-reaching transhumance, which discouraged the development of local Khoikhoi dialects. More important was the fact that children of Khoikhoi-hunter marriages

52. Stow, *Native Races*, p. 308 (quoting J. Campbell); Staf D 593 /U/4/1/3, Gordon, Vierde Reyse, Sept. 28, 1779, n.p.

53. E.g. Lichtenstein, VRS 10, p. 69.

54. Staf D 593 /U/4/1/3, Gordon, Vierde Reyse, Oct. 10, 1779; Janssens, *RZA*, 4:183; Lichtenstein, VRS 11, 74–75.

55. *VRJ*, 3:351 (Journal of Pieter van Meerhoff, Feb. 19, 1661); *VRJ*, 1:305 (April 3, 1655).

naturally learned Khoikhoi, since it was the prestigious language of cattle-keeping, of tribal affairs, and of intertribal relations. On the other hand, in the small, generally nonpolygamous Khoikhoi families, these children were not influenced by their mothers' aboriginal languages as much as children often are in bilingual marriages in Bantu Africa. Even those aboriginal languages which did not entirely disappear bore the imprint of their contact with Khoikhoi. For example, Maingard was able to discover eight words in /Xam "Bushman" which had been derived from Cape Khoikhoi; two of these (the words for "to ride an ox," and "metal") almost certainly corresponded to items of culture borrowed from Khoikhoi.[56]

No doubt Khoikhoi also learned much from hunters, particularly lore about the flora and fauna of their region. They also took over the use of the bow and arrow, probably from different hunter groups at different times. In general, however, Khoikhoi culture displaced aboriginal cultures rather than the reverse. The association of aborigines with pastoral societies resulted linguistically in the spread of the Khoikhoi language, somatically in the emergence of a mixed people of higher stature, and economically in the diffusion of skills related to cattle and sheep raising.

THE ECOLOGICAL CYCLE: DOWNWARD PHASE

People did not move only from hunting to herding communities. Quite the contrary, we have much evidence of individual Khoikhoi temporarily or permanently going to dwell among the hunters. In many cases we do not know the reason; but in one documented case the exile was a woman who had recently been widowed, and in another, a man who had been banished from his own tribe for the particularly heinous crime of incest.[57] In fact, at least one cattleless group, the Strandlopers near Table Bay, consisted largely of outcasts from neighboring Khoikhoi tribes (see pp. 94–95).

However, the important point is not that surviving hunter bands offered a refuge for the rejects of Khoikhoi society, but that the whole hunting way of life always remained a viable option for Khoikhoi who—in whatever numbers—had fallen on hard times. The upward movement of the cycle was dependent on the maintenance of prosperity, and prosperity is extremely fragile in purely pastoral societies. The

56. Maingard, "First Contacts," p. 486.
57. Moodie, *The Record*, p. 395, n. 2; *Resolusies*, 3: 213 (Nov. 28, 1689); Dapper, VRS 14, p. 69.

whole delicate structure could topple if herds were diminished by one
of many common cattle diseases, by the failure of waterholes because
of drought, by the destruction of pasture through overstocking, or by a
massive attack of robber-hunters. In addition, the depredations of
robbers were often exacerbated by epidemics that rendered the
Khoikhoi defenseless.[58]

Even apart from these externally stimulated disasters, prosperity
could be swept away by the almost automatic operation of the balance
of power. Whenever a Khoikhoi clan or tribe became wealthy, there
was a tendency for a hostile coalition to form against it, led not, says
Wikar, by the wealthy, but by the poorer members of neighboring
groups.[59] Cattleless hunters eagerly joined the coalition, hoping for
booty. The first robbery led to retaliation and the development of a
feud. In each attack and counterattack cattle were slaughtered, not so
much because of the war itself, but because Khoikhoi, who rarely
killed their own cattle, slaughtered large numbers of captured beasts to
celebrate their victories.[60] Since relatively few Khoikhoi were killed in
war, the overall effect of such conflict was for the total population of
stock per capita to drop over a whole region. Even more significant
was the sudden impoverishment of the losers in a particular battle.
Both sorts of decline in the cattle population encouraged new wars, as
individuals and groups sought to recoup their losses. The erosion of
wealth meant the collapse of political authority and stimulated the
movement of individuals to new, more secure groups.

In Khoikhoi society cattle was owned, not by the clan or tribe, but
by families and individuals.[61] Hence an individual Khoikhoi could
easily be rendered destitute by one disastrous attack. He could then
try to obtain a position as another man's herdsman, but in a deteriorating situation such positions were few; and often individuals, then
families, and finally whole clans, were forced back into hunting and
gathering in order to avoid starvation. As the requisite skills had
never been forgotten, this transition was made smoothly but not
without much regret and hardship.

Here the Khoikhoi experience contrasted sharply with that of most

58. E.g. Rhenius, VRS 28, p. 142.

59. Wikar, VRS 15, p. 208.

60. Simon van der Stel, "Instructie bij ons . . . aan den Ed[le] Heer Wilhelm Adriaan van der
Stel . . . nagelaten," *Collectanea*, VRS 5 (Cape Town: Van Riebeeck Society, 1924), p. 20.

61. Schapera, *Khoisan Peoples*, p. 293.

eastern and southern African peoples, who combined a ritual and emotional attachment to pastoralism with an economic reliance on cultivation. In Southern Bantu society, for example, all persons have the right to use a section of tribal land, even though the actual distribution of the land rests in the hands of the chief. Thus, though individuals and lineages may be poor in stoçk, they rarely starve unless the whole community is starving with them. The Khoikhoi approach to wealth was by contrast individualistic; fortune was unstable, and the gap between rich and poor could be very pronounced.

The Khoikhoi failed to develop a form of hereditary chieftainship that could hold society together even during relatively short periods of hardship, and furthermore they lacked the segmentary lineage system and age-grade institutions which gave some measure of cohesion to pastoral societies in eastern Africa. Consequently, the disintegrative effects of the economic downswing probably were more severe among Khoikhoi than among most African peoples, and it was common for Khoikhoi to be forced into reliance solely on hunting and gathering. Therefore, when we see allusions to "Bushmen" in the documents we must not uncritically assume that these are aborigines with no previous experience of pastoralism.

During 1701–02 the northwest frontier of the Cape Colony was in great turmoil; both whites and Khoikhoi lost stock to marauding groups which struck in widely separate areas. The attackers were normally identified as "Sonquas" or "Bosjesmans."[62] Three years later a government expedition under Johannes Starrenburgh visited the area and found evidence that some, at least, of the robbers were in fact dispossessed Khoikhoi. One group described what had happened to them after losing all their cattle to a white freebooter:

> [They were forced] to go to the remotest Dutch farms to rob cattle and to steal from their own countrymen if they could get anything. With this they roamed in the mountains until it was all gone; then they took some more cattle ... of which they still possess only a few.[63]

Starrenburgh went on to summarize the plight of Khoikhoi in the region:

62. KA 4024, DR June 16, 1701, p. 145.
63. KA 4031, Dag Verhaal van ... Starrenburgh, Oct. 26, 1705, p. 743v–44.

those who used to live contentedly under chiefs, peacefully sup-
porting themselves by breeding cattle, have mostly *all become
Bushmen, hunters and robbers*, and are scattered everywhere among
the mountains. [Italics mine][64]

It is true that in this case the tragedy was partly set in motion by a
white man. But there are many examples where whites were not
involved.

In 1752 Ensign August Frederik Beutler journeyed to the region
later known as the Eastern Frontier. En route he found some
"Gamtoos" in a very impoverished condition; they reported "that the
Bushmen had robbed all their cattle and that they now had to live only
by hunting and what they could find in the veld." Yet this group had
once possessed cattle and had not been regarded as San by the
Khoikhoi.[65] Beutler went on to describe the situation of several groups
even further east, near the Gonaqua.

All these Hottentots who formerly were rich in cattle are now,
through the thefts of the Bushmen, entirely destitute of them.
Some have been killed and some are scattered through wars with
each other and with the Caffers. Those who are still found here
and there consist of various groups which have united together.
They live like Bushmen from stealing, hunting and eating anything
eatable which they find in the field or along the shore. [Italics
mine][66]

Similar cases of retrogression to hunting and gathering can be found
in the recorded history of other major Khoikhoi groupings in southern
Africa; for example, among the Namaqua and the Korana.[67]

One of the long-term effects of the downward cycle was the extension
of Khoikhoi culture beyond the bounds of the pastoral economy.
This transmission was obvious in cases like those documented above,
where the new "San" groups consisted of Khoikhoi speakers with
pastoral tastes and skills. However, the downward phase of the
ecological cycle did not always result in the impoverishment of entire
tribes. In other and less catastrophic cases, only the poorest members
of Khoikhoi society returned to the hunt. Individual refugees of this

64. Ibid., Nov. 4, 1705, p. 749v.
65. Beutler (Haupt), *RZA*, 3:280; KA 4027, Vraagpoincten . . . Soetekoek et al., Nov. 7,
1702, p. 469v.
66. Beutler (Haupt), *RZA*, 3:292.
67. W. van Reenen, VRS 15, p. 315; Stow, *Native Races*, pp. 276, 336.

sort would normally gravitate to hunting groups already in existence—a process well documented in the case of the Strandlopers of the Cape Peninsula—and some uniquely talented Khoikhoi, like the eighteenth-century Ruyter, might possibly use their skills to organize hunter bands, lead them in battle, and even teach them the virtues of husbanding and breeding stolen cattle.[68]

The downward phase of the ecological cycle could be halted by circumstances roughly opposite to those which had first precipitated it. Benevolent trends in nature, such as abundant rainfall or a reduction of cattle disease, could create the preconditions for a new prosperity; but the decisive turning point would be passed when strong political units emerged among the remaining pastoralists—units which could attract a large human following and provide security for the accumulation of large herds and flocks. Such expanding tribes would soon come into contact with the hunter groups that had been created or enlarged by the recent misfortunes; and then, either at the stage of conflict or at the stage of symbiosis, the cycle of Khoikhoi-hunter relations would begin again.

Conclusion

I began this chapter by rejecting the belief that two completely distinct and nonoverlapping peoples inhabited southern Africa—the hunting "San" of aboriginal descent and the stock-keeping Khoikhoi descended from rather recent immigrants. While such a dichotomy must clearly have existed when Khoikhoi first penetrated any new region of southern Africa, it had been greatly blurred by the time whites first came upon the scene. Khoikhoi themselves made no such clear and systematic distinction between peoples, their term "San" having wide reference to both hunter and small-scale pastoral groups; moreover, many cattleless peoples spoke the Khoikhoi language and thus could not be direct *cultural* descendants of aborigines.

These facts can be explained by positing a cycle of Khoikhoi-hunter interaction—a cycle that likely occurred many times, in varying forms, in regions of long Khoikhoi occupation. This interaction illuminates the patterns of physical and cultural hybridization which had obscured the original differences between Khoikhoi and aborigines. Because people moved in both directions between hunting and herding groups, there was miscegenation in both sorts of host societies. By contrast, the

68. Sparrman, *Voyage*, 2:168–69.

transmission of languages and culture traits went mainly in one direction; namely, from the prestigious and widespread Khoikhoi culture into the despised and localized cultures of the hunters. These patterns are repeatedly suggested by the evidence of seventeenth- and eighteenth century travelers.

Not only does the cyclical theory account for physical and cultural hybridization, it also explains why in the western segment of southern Africa these processes were slower than elsewhere on the continent, and why in this region alone significant numbers of hunters survived late enough to be observed by Europeans. By contrast, in those regions of Africa where the immigrants were Bantu-speaking hoe-cultivators, only small pockets of hunters were still to be found at the beginning of the present century. The less drastic fate of the hunters of southern Africa can be explained by the fact that Khoikhoi culture differed from most immigrant cultures in that (1) it did not demand that the hunter drop his own culture, only that he add to it; and that (2) it was subject to the severe and sudden "downswing" which I have described. These factors, along with the comparative military weakness of the Khoikhoi, tended to preserve the hunting-gathering economy in this region.

3

Power and Wealth in Traditional
Cape Khoikhoi Society

THE TRIBE AND ITS RULERS

Seventeenth-century observers often described Khoikhoi social structure in terms appropriate to societies based on permanent occupation of land, like those they knew in Europe and southern Asia. Thus, for Kolbe the main units of Khoikhoi society were the "village" and the "nation."[1] In reality the Khoikhoi "village" (in South African terminology, the kraal) was both mobile and exceedingly unstable in its composition. Among Cape Khoikhoi, as among Korana and Namaqua, kin groups, not geographical units, were the component parts of society. Cape Khoikhoi displayed an eager interest in kinship matters—so much so that when an official Dutch party first visited the camps of the Cochoqua they were persistently asked "whether the Dutch chief was also of high descent . . . and who the ensign's ancestors were, etc."[2] Nonetheless, the Europeans were oblivious to this facet of Khoikhoi culture and collected virtually no data on kinship (apart from chiefly succession), and no genealogies.

We do, however, obtain a few glimpses of Cape Khoikhoi social structure in the writings of Peter Kolbe and other seventeenth- and eighteenth-century observers. Since this information is usually vague and fragmentary, it can be coordinated by referring to Agnes Hoernlé's description of Namaqua in the early twentieth century: her data provide a plausible model which can then be tested against the evidence we have on the earlier Cape Khoikhoi. Among the Namaqua Hoernlé perceived three levels of organization: the (extended) family, the "sib" (i.e. clan), and the "tribe." She provided little information on the family, the smallest of her three units, except to indicate that clans

1. Peter Kolbe[n], *Beschreibung des Vorgebürges der Guten Hoffnung* (Frankfurt and Leipzig: Pieter Conrad Monath, 1745), pp. 76, 153.
2. *VRJ*, 2:366 (Oct. 31, 1658).

usually comprised only a few families, and often only one.[3] Seventeenth-century sources cast even less light on the family among the Cape Khoikhoi.

On the clan we are somewhat better informed. Namaqua clans consisted of people who claimed to be related to each other patrilineally: similar relations between clans were also asserted but could not be traced genealogically. Hoernlé observed that "through the whole course of Nama history the sib [i.e. the clan] was the strongest social unit the Nama ever attained." Individuals were usually more loyal to their clan than to their tribe, and clans occasionally broke off from the tribe to form a new tribe.[4] Our seventeenth-century observers did not perceive this clan structure among Cape Khoikhoi, but it is likely that the "kraal" which they described as the unit of local government consisted roughly of a clan (with the addition of affines, hunter-clients, and other hangers-on). The Dutch felt that the kraals were the chief living units when the tribe was dispersed, and when it camped together they could still recognize the preexisting kraals which comprised it. Namaqua tribes were composed of several exogamous clans united in allegiance to a hereditary chief. Each tribe claimed prior right to use certain springs, and these served to demarcate its territory.[5] Among the Cape Khoikhoi, who inhabited much wetter terrain than the Great Namaqua, springs were apparently not of vital significance, although rivers (along with mountains) were sometimes indicated as the boundaries between tribal territory, and some groups named themselves after the rivers along whose banks they dwelt.[6]

Unfortunately, Hoernlé's definition of a tribe, which was based on the structure of the twentieth-century Namaqua, does not neatly accommodate all of the so-called nations into which the seventeenth-century Cape Khoikhoi were conventionally divided. The tribe lists which Khoikhoi furnished to early white officials usually included (apart from "San" and some eastern tribes that were not well known) most of the following names: Goringhaicona, Goringhaiqua, Gorachouqua, Cochoqua, Chainouqua, Hessequa, Hamcumqua, Guriqua (usually given as Chariguriqua), and Namaqua. Of these,

3. Hoernlé, "Social Organization," pp. 9, 11.

4. Ibid., pp. 9, 15. On p. 11, Hoernlé also says that the genealogical relationships between families could not then (1925) be traced, but she hints that formerly this might have been possible.

5. Ibid., p. 6.

6. Beutler (Haupt), *RZA*, 3:292.

the Goringhaicona were a tiny cluster of cattleless people of diverse tribal origins; the Namaqua were a group of many tribes (in Hoernlé's sense) which the Cape Khoikhoi grouped together because they perceived their culture as alien to their own; Cochoqua were, in fact, two tribes with a common name but each with its own able leader; and the Guriqua had no chiefs at all other than at the kraal (i.e. clan) level. The Goringhaiqua and Gorachouqua, though clearly distinct political entities, were united in allegiance to a common chief, and acted so much in common that the Dutch invented a term (Capemen) to refer to them together.[7] Thus, of the nine "nations" recognized by Western Cape Khoikhoi in the 1660s, only three can be called "tribes" in Hoernlé's sense.

As we discovered in chapter 2, static categories often fail accurately to describe the reality of Khoikhoi societies, which are typically in a state of constant flux. Hoernlé has described the constant process of fission in Namaqua society, and this process is amply confirmed by the documents relating to the Cape Khoikhoi. When a clan prospered in numbers or wealth, or when it was blessed with dynamic leadership, it might flake off from its parent tribe, occupy new pastures, and establish itself as a new tribe. Such fission also occurred commonly as part of tribal disintegration after the death of a great chief. In all these cases it was customary for the new tribe to continue to recognize the lineage superiority of the old.

In the flux of frequent fission and consolidation the existence of supraclan political units was unstable. It seems that Khoikhoi terminology did not keep abreast of changing reality; thus, names like Cochoqua and Chariguriqua remained in current use even after the tribes to which they referred had split into two or more parts. Nonetheless, the lag between terminology and reality was not unduly great, as can be seen from the bewildering alteration of tribal names which occurred in the seventeenth century: the name of one important tribe, the Chainouqua, changed twice between 1660 and 1700.

In view of this endemic flux, and also of our ignorance of most kin relationships among Cape Khoikhoi, it would be futile to try to employ Hoernlé's concepts "tribe" and "clan" with an anthropologist's precision. So when I use the term "tribe" I mean a group of Khoikhoi who habitually called themselves, or were called by others, by a specific name: I do not necessarily imply that such a tribe was an effective

7. All of these tribes are discussed in detail in chapters 5, 6, and 7 of this work.

political unit, but in cases where it was, I assume it to have been the largest political unit to which its members belonged.[8] When tribes divided into two segments, I call the new units "sub-tribes." Smaller but relatively cohesive units I call "clans," even though the documents do not usually give us proof of those lineage ties by which anthropologists identify a clan.

The Dutch called each Khoikhoi ruler a "king," "chief," or "captain," thus haphazardly recognizing a certain hierarchy of leadership among them. The Cape Khoikhoi also ranked their own leaders in ways of which we are only partially informed. We hear once of the term *khoebaha*, which Jan van Riebeeck believed to mean "supreme ruler of the whole Hottentot race," and "overlord of all the kings and chiefs of the country": this title was held only by the chief of the Hamcumqua. In other tribes the most commonly used title was *khoeque* (Namaqua !*khu-khoi-b*, rich man) which could refer to eminent rulers and, at least in the eighteenth century, to very petty chieftains. A less prestigious term was *humque* (Namaqua $\neq$ *am-khoi-b*, headman) which, according to the biased testimony of the Chainouqua, was the lowly title of the chiefs of the Chariguriqua and Cochoqua. The subordinate chief in a divided tribe like the Cochoqua was called *chamhuma* (apparently the Namaqua word /*gam* "second," plus *humque*).[9] Since it is rarely known what title Khoikhoi gave to individual leaders, I use the European terms "chief" and "captain," the former in reference to tribal leaders and the latter to denote heads of clans.

Among the Cape Khoikhoi, as among the Namaqua, chieftainship passed from father to eldest son and remained in the tribe's dominant clan until that clan died out or was displaced by another.[10] Very often, if the chief lived to an old age, his son took over effective leadership during the life of his father, though the latter retained his ritualistic

8. These statements must be modified in regard to the Namaqua and the Korana, the sub-sections of which are properly called tribes. The supratribal designations *Namaqua* and *Korana* drew attention to the common history, culture, and location of a group of tribes, but had no political significance. The analagous supratribal term for the Khoikhoi studied in this book is *Cape Khoikhoi*, a designation of purely scholarly origin. If the Cape Khoikhoi themselves had an equivalent term, it is not known; however, they sometimes used the word *Kwena* (i.e. "people," the equivalent of Namaqua *Khoi-na*) to refer to themselves and to exclude the Namaqua.

9. Most of the evidence on the political titles of Cape Khoikhoi is found in *VRJ*, 3:258–60 (Sept. 21, 1660). For linguistic analysis of the titles, see Nienaber, *Hottentots*, p. 309 (*hoofman*), pp. 330–31 (*kaptein*), pp. 349–51 (*koning*), pp. 384–85 (*meneer*), p. 406 (*onderkaptein*), p. 435 (*ryk*), p. 483 (*troonopvolger*), and passim.

10. Tachard, *Voyage de Siam*, p. 95; Hoernlé, "Social Organization," p. 10.

prerogatives.[11] On the other hand, when a chief died young and left a child heir, the dead chief's brother could be installed as regent.[12] If there were no direct male heirs, a brother or brother's son of the dead chief could be chosen as his successor, probably by the council of clan heads, as was definitely the case among the Korana.[13] Despite the somewhat flexible nature of Khoikhoi succession, wars between disputing contenders do not seem to have been common among Cape Khoikhoi.

In the western Cape it was very common for a chief to have a second-in-command (often his "brother" or a "brother-in-law")[14] who was always present at parleys with the Dutch. For example, in 1707 a traveler among the Chainouqua and Hessequa listed two leaders for almost every kraal he encountered.[15] This pervasive pattern of dual leadership may well have been a precondition for the splitting of tribes into two parts, as among the Cochoqua, or into the "Big" and "Little" segments found so often in Khoikhoi history.

The chief was assisted by a council consisting of the clan captains under his jurisdiction. The council met at the chief's kraal and under his chairmanship; one of its main functions was the adjudication of interclan disputes. In most matters affecting only one clan, the captain, and not the chief, had effective authority. Individual justice was normally meted out at a gathering of all the males of a clan, though apparently some chiefs could exert influence on the outcome of the proceedings. Even in matters of tribal significance the chief was no autocrat; he could often be overruled by his council, though he was theoretically sovereign in decisions relating to war and transhumant movements.[16]

The honors and prerogatives associated with chieftainship varied

11. See, for example, Waterhouse, *Van der Stel*, p. 130; KA 4037, Dagverhaal . . . Hartogh, Nov. 8, 1707, pp. 905–05v. See also p. 91 of this study, on Gogosoa's son, and p. 140, on Soeswa's son.

12. KA 3986, Accordt by den E. Heer Albert van Breugel . . . en den Hottentosen Overste Dackkgy . . . aangegaan, May 3, 1672, p. 270; KA 4030, DR Sept. 1, 1705, pp. 205v–06.

13. KA 4050, DR Feb. 15, 1714, p. 277v; J. A. Engelbrecht, *The Korana: An Account of Their Customs and Their History* (Cape Town: Maskew Miller, 1936), pp. 89–90.

14. Here, and often throughout this work, kinship terms will be placed in quotation marks to remind the reader that under the Khoikhoi classificatory kinship system, terms often had far wider reference than their English equivalents.

15. *VRJ*, 3:205 (April 27, 1660); *VRJ*, 3:276 (Nov. 3, 1660); KA 4011, DR Jan. 8, 1694, p. 114v; KA 4037, Dagverhaal . . . Hartogh, pp. 905–09.

16. Engelbrecht, *Korana*, p. 89; Kolbe, *Beschreibung*, pp. 76–83; Schrijver, VRS 12, p. 248.

from tribe to tribe, and were doubtless partly a function of the wealth
and prestige of the individual chief. Chiefs often practiced polygamy,
which was otherwise rare among Khoikhoi and a sign of unusual
wealth. They smeared their bodies with extra grease and could afford
to feast themselves to the point of corpulence. Their position was
usually made evident by subtle externals—a larger hut than their
subjects, a more magnificent animal skin, or a copper-studded wooden
throne.[17] We have little evidence of chiefs receiving tribute or services
from their subjects: however, among the Inqua, subjects who had
killed wild game were obligated to pay their chief a fat sheep.[18]

The Khoikhoi were vigilant that their chiefs did not overstep the
circumscribed scope of their authority. Hahn recounts that Namaqua
chiefs whose actions savored of despotism could be openly and viciously
ridiculed by the women of the tribe:

> Once I saw a chief sitting by, when the young girls sang into
> his face, telling him "that he was a hungry hyena and a roguish
> jackal; that he was the brown vulture who is not only satisfied
> with tearing the flesh from the bones, but also feasted on the
> intestines."[19]

We also know of one case where the majority of a tribe, led by the
younger people, rose in rebellion against their chief.[20]

All this was very distressing to the Dutch, who were always hoping
to find Khoikhoi monarchs surrounded by the splendor of the semi-
divine rulers of the Orient. In their bitter disillusion with the Khoikhoi
chieftains, they may often have left us with an unduly negative
impression: one of the most thoughtful of European observers insisted
that the honor which Khoikhoi gave their chiefs was "much greater
than one would be able to believe from outward appearance."[21]
In any event, the effective power of chiefs varied as much as the trap-
pings of their office: the spectrum stretched from the Inqua chief
whose orders were obeyed "with running and jumping," to Gogosoa
of the Goringhaiqua, who was allegedly treated as a beggar by his
own children.[22]

17. *VRJ*, 2:367 (Oct. 31, 1658); *VRJ*, 3:352 (Journal of Pieter van Meerhoff, Feb. 20,
1661); Kolbe, *Beschreibung*, p. 77.

18. Schrijver, VRS 12, pp. 234-35.

19. Hahn, *Tsuni-//Goam*, p. 28.

20. *Resolusies*, 3:55 (Dec. 8, 1682).

21. A. Hulshof, "H. A. van Reede tot Drakestein, Journaal van zijn verblijf aan de Kaap,"
Bijdragen en mededeelingen van het Historisch Genootschap (gevestigd te Utrecht) 62 (1941): 203.

22. Schrijver, VRS 12, p. 233; *VRJ*, 3:444 (Dec. 1, 1661).

Bonds between Tribes

Virtually all tribes were ex-clans which had established their independence from their parent tribe and had perhaps since gained new followers and new wealth. Thus, in a sense, intertribal relations were an extension of kin relations at a higher level. For example, all of the seven Namaqua tribes that were "indigenous" to Namibia (i.e. those that did not trek north in response to the growth of the white colony) claimed to be related to one another by ties of kinship. Five of the seven were allegedly descended from five brothers, the eldest of whom was the founder of the Gei / /Khauan, whose seniority was recognized by the other tribes.[23]

A roughly similar situation existed among the Cape Khoikhoi, where some tribes recognized the suzerainty of others by paying tribute in the form of cattle or, in one case, in the form of bundles of assegais (spears).[24] Though we have only the vaguest information on these transactions, we can still conclude that the ranking of the Cape tribes was based, like that of the Namaqua, on kinship rather than conquest. Most of our information on this subject derives from tribes who conceded their inferiority to others on the hierarchy of lineage precedence. Such information is naturally more reliable than aggressively asserted claims of dominance. Our major sources are tribes in the extreme southwest corner of the Cape Province: in general, they recognized the lineage superiority of peoples to their east, whom they ranked with those farthest east at the top. Because of these various levels of prestige, patterns seem more complex among the Cape Khoikhoi than among the Namaqua; the reader may find these easier to understand by referring to the chart on page 53.

In the 1650s Goringhaiqua, Gorachouqua, and other groups near Table Bay (whom I collectively call Peninsulars) were all united in allegiance to Gogosoa, chief of the Goringhaiqua. All of Gogosoa's followers, along with the "Chariguriquas," were subject in some sense to the nearby Cochoqua, the most numerous and powerful tribe close to Table Bay. In turn, the Cochoqua explicitly acknowledged their own subordination to the Chainouqua to their east. Thus, the Chainouqua were the leading tribe among all the Western Cape Khoikhoi, barring perhaps the Hessequa.[25]

---

23. Hoernlé, "Social Organization," pp. 4–5; Vedder, *South West Africa*, p. 126. The Taaibosches held a similar position among the Great Korana (see Stow, *Native Races*, p. 277).

24. *VRJ*, 3:259 (Sept. 21, 1660); 3:448 (Dec. 7, 1661).

25. *VRJ*, 3:259–60 (Sept. 21, 1660); 3:265 (Sept. 28, 1660).

However, there were at least two peoples who lived beyond the western Cape and yet were regarded by Western Cape Khoikhoi as their superiors. First were the Hamcumqua (Inqua),[26] who in the late seventeenth century were a large and wealthy society under an unusually powerful king. According to Western Cape Khoikhoi informants, the Hamcumqua enjoyed the allegiance, not only of the Chainouqua, but of many Central Cape Khoikhoi peoples as well—the Chamaqua, Omaqua, Atiqua (=Attaqua), Houtunqua, and Cauqua. The leaders of these subordinate tribes seem somehow to have been related to the Hamcumqua monarch: the Chainouqua chief was, for example, said to be the "representative of the next-of-kin of the Paramount King;" and Gaukou, the chief of the wealthy Hessequa, was his "brother."[27]

The most striking feature of Khoikhoi lineage patterns was the recognition by some Western Cape Khoikhoi that their supreme rulers were a negro people located hundreds of miles away—the so-called Chobona (or Coboqua). The name Chobona may derive from the Nguni salutation *sakubona*.[28] It was used by all Khoikhoi and had a racial connotation that allowed it to refer to blacks, including slaves of Europeans, in a variety of situations.

In the 1650s the Western Cape Khoikhoi had spasmodic contact with Bantu-speakers. The wife of a leading Chainouqua captain had been brought up in a Bantu royal kraal; and black visitors, perhaps traders, were seen at the Chainouqua camps.[29] As a consequence, Western Cape Khoikhoi knew a fair amount about Bantu-speakers— for example, that they cultivated the soil, were rich in metals, spoke languages radically unlike Khoikhoi, and dwelt in stone buildings. This last point probably refers to highveld Sotho-Tswana. Nevertheless, the Chobona whom Western Cape Khoikhoi regarded as their dominants were probably Nguni-speaking Xhosa, since these Chobona were always mentioned in connection with other peoples east of the Cape.[30]

---

26. On the identification of Inqua with Hamcumqua, see Gerrit Harinck, "Interaction between Xhosa and Khoi: Emphasis on the Period 1620–1750," in *African Societies in Southern Africa*, ed. Leonard Thompson (London, Ibadan, and Nairobi: Heinemann, 1969), pp. 162–63. For other views, see Le Roux, "Hottentotstamme," pp. 16, 141–42.

27. *VRJ*, 2:171 (Oct. 31, 1657); 3:259 (Sept. 21, 1660); 3:303 (Dec. 16, 1660); KA 4002, DR Feb. 4, 1687, p. 168.

28. M. D. W. Jeffreys, "The Cabonas," *AS* 27, no. 1 (1968):41–43.

29. *VRJ*, 2:170–72 (Oct. 31, 1657); 2:406 (Dec. 31, 1658); 3:268 (Sept. 29–30, 1660); 3:303 (Dec. 16, 1660).

30. See e.g. KA 4027, Vraagpoincten . . . Soetekoek et al., Nov. 7, 1702, p. 469v.

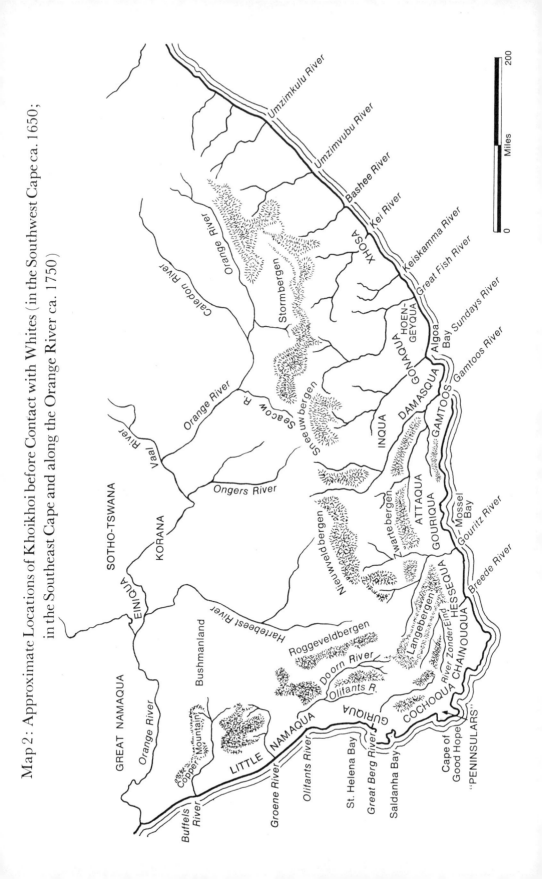

Map 2: Approximate Locations of Khoikhoi before Contact with Whites (in the Southwest Cape ca. 1650; in the Southeast Cape and along the Orange River ca. 1750)

The rule of the Chobona was, of course, purely honorary, and seems not to have been recognized by all Cape Khoikhoi.[31] Yet it seems strange that any Khoikhoi would give any honor at all to a non-Khoikhoi people who could not have been their ancestors. Of course, it is possible that there had been real or imputed marital links between some Xhosa royal line and the ancestors of the chiefly Khoikhoi lineages. An alternative solution to this puzzle may be found in the vague racial connotation of the word *Chobona*. Evidence given by the Attaqua strongly suggests that the Khoikhoi also denoted as "Chobona" other Khoikhoi—specifically the Gonaqua—who as a result of intermixture with negroes were darker than normal.[32]

It is thus possible that the Western Cape Khoikhoi, who were very far from the tribes in question, confused traditions about two "Chobona" groups—the Xhosa proper and the Gonaqua (or some other Xhosa-Khoikhoi group). These latter Chobona might have been the ancestors of the Khoikhoi who had long ago begun the dispersal westward along the south coast toward Table Bay, and their exalted position would then derive from their lineage superiority. The fact that they later came deeply under the influence of the Xhosa would only increase their prestige, as Khoikhoi throughout South Africa regarded Nguni with fear or awe. The beginning of profound Xhosa influence on the Chobona, and of subsequent miscegenation between them, must have taken place after the beginning of the westward movement of Khoikhoi, since no results of it were blatantly obvious in Western Cape Khoikhoi culture. Gerrit Harinck has shown that the first oral traditions of such interaction refer to the reign of the Xhosa paramount, Togu (c. 1590–1620, according to Harinck's altered dating of his life), a date which fits this argument admirably.[33]

However it is explained, the Chobona "paramountcy" is fully consistent with the broader patterns of tribal seniority among Cape Khoikhoi: namely, a multitiered hierarchy with eastern peoples usually taking precedence over peoples to their west. This pattern is summarized in figure 1, in which the solid lines link subordinates with their dominants higher on the page. It must be remembered that the actual lineage patterns were probably even more complex than our meager evidence would suggest.

31. *VRJ*, 2:184 (Nov. 15, 1657).
32. KA 3981, Journal of the *Voerman*, Oct. 4, 1668, p. 657v; and Oct. 5, 1668, p. 658v.
33. Harinck, "Xhosa and Khoi," pp. 154–55 and n. 30.

Figure 1 : Lineage Patterns among the Cape Khoikhoi

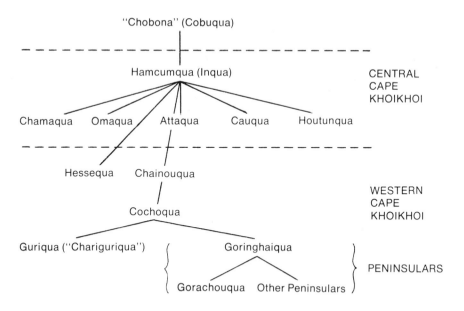

WAR: ITS PURPOSES AND PROSECUTION

Khoikhoi were not a martial people: they had no standing armies, no professional soldiers, and no military leaders apart from their chiefs. Apparently they did not admire valor nearly as much as wealth or success in the hunt. Nor were they, on the whole, bloodthirsty. In their wars with the Dutch they killed only if it was necessary; and when they were allies of the Europeans they disappointed their mentors by zealously pursuing the enemy's cattle and neglecting to slay the enemy himself.[34]

Nonetheless, Khoikhoi fought many wars among themselves, and these were fought vigorously and not without incidents of brutality. Khoikhoi were very keen on mock combats: some of these were witnessed by European visitors, who were extremely impressed by the skill of the participants in hurling and ducking projectiles, and by the order and precision of their manoeuvres. This last observation was

34. *VRJ*, 1:196 (Dec. 18, 1653); 3:63 (June 3, 1659); KA 3988, DR April 7, 1674, p. 108.

inconsistent with the Europeans' conviction that actual Khoikhoi battles were very disorderly.[35]

The causes of war were varied but were all related to two conspicuous characteristics of Khoikhoi society: the great fluidity of wealth and prestige, and a deeply ingrained zeal for vendettas. As in other parts of southern Africa, cattle robberies were a common prelude to war; but on this score Kolbe makes a significant statement:

> 'tis very rare that one *Hottentot* Nation steals . . . cattle of another but with a pure Design to irritate and mad that other and bring her into a War.[36]

Engelbrecht also notes that the traditional Korana usually stole cattle only when deliberately provoking a conflict.[37] Cattle theft was such a grievous matter to Khoikhoi that they did not normally undertake it except with premeditation and in company with so many people that it became virtually a crime of the whole tribe, and hence a casus belli. Other disputes over livestock arose from the common Khoikhoi practice of hiring out cattle to members of a neighboring tribe.[38] Quarrels over pastures were likewise common. Even though each tribe had a recognized grazing terrain, conflict could arise as a result of tribal fission, or because one tribe granted pasture to another and then claimed it back. Kolbe also asserted that the common Khoikhoi practice of burning the veld (to improve it for next year's grazing) led to fires that spread rapidly to neighboring pastures and precipitated strife.[39] I have found no confirmation of this in the Company records.

Most white observers were shocked or amused that Khoikhoi so often went to war over incidents of woman-stealing. In fact, several of the leading disputes of seventeenth-century Khoikhoi history were fired by such abductions. Normally the victim of abduction was the wife of a chief or an important personage, and it is likely that prestige was as great a motive as passion in many of these incidents.[40]

---

35. *VRJ*, 3:70 (June 20, 1659); Hulshof, "H. A. van Reede . . . Journaal," p. 35; François Valentyn, *Oud en Nieuw Oost-Indiën* (Dordrecht and Amsterdam: Joannes van Braam & Gerard Onder de Linden, 1726), 5 (2): 105.

36. Kolbe, *Cape of Good Hope*, 1:285.

37. Engelbrecht, *Korana*, p. 193.

38. *VRJ*, 3:373 (April 23, 1661).

39. Kolbe, *Beschreibung*, p. 84.

40. *VRJ*, 3:266 (Sept. 28, 1660); Kolbe, *Beschreibung*, pp. 84–85.

Wars were also caused by individual acts of provocation, like murder. In one case the brother of the Cochoqua chief Oedasoa killed a Goringhaiqua in what was alleged to be a hunting accident. The Goringhaiqua retaliated by trying to murder the guilty Cochoqua, again during a hunt, and again trying to make it look like an accident. Grievances of this sort led to feuds that were passed down from one generation to the next.[41] In fact, vendettas often gave a certain stability to intertribal politics which counteracted the fluidity of alliances: Khoikhoi changed their allies freely but tended to keep the same enemies for decades.

Several seventeenth-century writers described Khoikhoi methods of warfare at some length, but they presumably obtained their information second hand from farmers who had witnessed battles in the interior. These descriptions are markedly at variance with those found in diaries of officials who actually fought against Khoikhoi. It is likely that Khoikhoi had two distinct forms of warfare, and that the Dutch themselves experienced the brunt of the second type only.

The first, more formal type probably occurred in disputes over pasture or lineage subordination, or when fighting broke out after the breakdown of prolonged negotiations between the assembled tribes. A confrontation of this sort took place near the walls of the Dutch fort in late 1661. For roughly two weeks the numerous Cochoqua, along with their cattle and sheep, pressed down on the Peninsular tribes, and by sheer force of numbers pushed them out of their pastures and induced them to signify publicly their submission to their oppressors.[42]

In other cases such confrontations led to full-scale battles. These were fought on open fields, near which the kraals were placed, women and children being left in the huts, safe from the fray. Combat commenced when one side attacked en masse with wild shouts and war-calls. According to Kolbe, there was a certain precision to these attacks:

> When a soldier has thrown his assegai or fired his arrow, he steps back a few paces and leaves space for another who stands ready. While this man uses his weapon, the first man prepares himself, and returns to his place when it is again empty. . . .[43]

---

41. *VRJ*, 3:444 (Dec. 1, 1661). The vendetta was also characteristic of the Namaqua in the nineteenth century (Hoernlé, "Social Organization," p. 16).

42. *VRJ*, 3:436–48 (Nov. 21–Dec. 7, 1661).

43. Kolbe, *Beschreibung*, p. 87.

Offensive weapons were throwing assegais (spears), bows, stones, and short sticks (*rackums*)[44] used as darts. It is clear from the Company records that Khoikhoi preferred the assegai to the bow and rarely used the latter with poisoned arrows, at least in war. The poisons, whose use some Cape Khoikhoi definitely understood, worked far too slowly in close combat: a wounded enemy might fight for several hours before he dropped. The only defensive weapon appears to have been the *kirri* or walking stick, which could be used to parry arrows, assegais, and *rackums*.[45] Large oxhide shields were used by Namaqua but not by the Cape Khoikhoi.[46] One curiosity of Khoikhoi warfare was the use of oxen in battle: since Khoikhoi cattle responded well to verbal orders, they could be used as ramparts for defense against a charging army, or could be driven forward as a flying wedge to gore and trample the enemy.[47]

The battle, which normally constituted the whole war,[48] was over in a day. The victors plundered their enemy's huts, drove off their livestock, and sometimes slaughtered those warriors who failed to escape. Kolbe argued that Khoikhoi did not steal from, or otherwise misuse, dead enemy soldiers, though he did concede (and this is amply confirmed by the Company records) that they customarily executed all prisoners of war.[49] Nonetheless, the Khoikhoi sometimes tried to ransom prisoners taken by the Dutch, and this suggests that ransom and prisoner-of-war exchanges were known to them.

The second type of Khoikhoi combat can loosely be called guerilla warfare. It was par excellence the tactic used by robber groups, but was also appropriate in intertribal vendettas over cattle- or wife-stealing and in cases where one side had been defeated in formal battle and was trying to regroup. The Khoikhoi also invariably employed guerilla warfare against the Dutch, since they could not stand

44. A creole word apparently coined from the Dutch verb *raken*, "to hit a target."

45. Kolbe, *Beschreibung*, pp. 86–87; R. Raven-Hart, *Cape Good Hope, 1652–1702*, 2 vols. (Cape Town: A. A. Balkema, 1969), 2:505–10 (index entries "bows and arrows," "assegais," "darts," "kirri," and "rakum"); Nienaber, *Hottentots*, pp. 336–37. *Cape Good Hope* is henceforth cited as *CGH*.

46. *VRJ*, 3:353 (Journal of Pieter van Meerhoff, Feb. 20, 1661).

47. *BVR*, p. 10 (d'Almeida, 1510); *CGH*, 1:124 (Schreyer, 1668); Kolbe, *Beschreibung*, pp. 87–88; Johan Daniel Buttner, Waare Relation und Beschrybung von Cabo de Goede Hoop (Unpubl. MS, South African Public Library, Cape Town), n.p.; Grevenbroek, VRS 14, p. 189.

48. Kolbe, *Beschreibung*, p. 85.

49. Ibid., pp. 89–90; KA 3989, Dagelyckse Aanteyckening op de Expeditie na de rebellerende Gonnemase Africanen, April 12–13, 1676, p. 224; KA 3987, DR Aug. 20, 1673, pp. 227v–28.

in open combat against gunfire. In these cases their main offense was a series of sudden and massive attacks on the herds of the enemy. Faced by a strong opposing force, they would melt away into the bush, even if this meant abandoning their homes, their sick cattle, and the elderly members of the tribe. Khoikhoi were exceedingly clever at deceiving Dutch punitive expeditions by artfully laying false trails and by setting fires or placing stray cattle in such a way as to give the enemy false ideas of their location.[50] In this form of hit-and-run warfare the Khoikhoi relied on their hunter-clients, whose knowledge of the terrain made them ideal spies and pickets.

We know rather little about the manner in which peace was concluded. Envoys, often close relatives of the chief, were sent from one tribe to another to conduct negotiations, and sometimes the same individuals seem to have been used regularly for this purpose.[51] Many disputes probably "wound down" without any formal declaration of peace. However, Grevenbroek describes a peace ceremony in which the ex-combatants slaughtered a heifer on their common frontier and pronounced ritual curses against anyone who might in the future break the treaty.[52] Such curses were not very effective, for all available evidence suggests that animosity between two tribes could flare into violence repeatedly over the years, and even over the decades.

CATTLE, SHEEP, AND THE KHOIKHOI

Cattle and sheep played an extremely important role in Khoikhoi society and, by extension, in Khoikhoi history. Possession of livestock was the main criterion by which Khoikhoi were distinguished from hunters, and rich Khoikhoi tribes from poor. Within each tribe, livestock was important in almost every realm of life: the economic, aesthetic, political, and social. Unlike most other pastoral Africans, Khoikhoi did not divide their time between livestock and tilling the soil; and unlike pastoral peoples in some other parts of the world, they had neither the camel nor the horse to share the glamor with cattle and sheep. The Namaqua, however, did have goats: they had presumably acquired these from the Tswana (whom they called Birina or "goat people") and were herding them in small numbers close to the Cape as early as 1661. By the twentieth century, goats had replaced

50. See description of the Second Khoikhoi-Dutch War on pp. 130–32.
51. *VRJ*, 3:374 (April 20–23, 1661).
52. Grevenbroek, VRS 14, p. 191.

sheep as the main subsistence of poor Namaqua, but in the seventeenth century they were of little importance and were virtually unknown among Cape Khoikhoi.[53]

Since livestock needed vast pastures in the dry climate of South Africa, and since oxen provided a useful means of transporting people and their possessions, the acquisition of cattle intensified the mobile character which Khoikhoi society had already possessed when it was dependent on hunting. Khoikhoi transhumance patterns were never regular enough to enable the Dutch to forecast the location of a particular tribe without hesitation, but each tribe seems to have followed a generally consistent itinerary. The patterns were sometimes repeated annually, and sometimes over a period of two years. In some particularly well-watered regions, Khoikhoi remained in the same general region for the entire year; one such region lay behind the Tigerberg close to Cape Town. In the western Cape there was a marked tendency for Khoikhoi to push into the Cape Peninsula in the dry midsummer, while tribes further north were gathering along the rivers. The Little Namaqua, like the Boers after them, preferred the mountains in the hot season and the valleys in the cold.[54]

Another characteristic of Khoikhoi movement was a periodic pattern of dispersal and reunification: dispersal was necessitated by the search for pasture at times when it was scarce; reunification, which could entail one or several tribes, was caused either by the need to gather at a river for water or by social and ritual reasons at which we can only guess.[55] Khoikhoi did not move their kraals only to find pasture: they also moved on the death of one of their number, for the camp where he died was henceforth deemed accursed.[56]

At night Khoikhoi cattle were kept within the circular enclosure of the huts, or just outside, the legs of the animals being tied to prevent their escape.[57] Kolbe states that the whole herd and the whole flock

---

53. *VRJ*, 3:343, (March 10–11, 1661). It is possible that goats were still rare even among the Little Namaqua at this date, since when someone had offered a Dutch party a gift of one goat, "there had been a great deal of mumbling among them over this goat before they handed it over." On goats among the Great Namaqua, see Leonhard Schultze, *Aus Namaland und Kalahari* (Jena: Verlag von Gustav Fischer, 1907), pp. 263–64.

54. *VRJ*, 1:126 (Jan. 9, 1653); 2:174 (Nov. 5, 1657); KA 3969, Van Riebeeck to XVII, March 5, 1657, p. 1v; Waterhouse, *Van der Stel*, pp. 113–14, 161.

55. See, for example, KA 3992, DR March 22, 1679, p. 244v.

56. KA 4008, DR Aug. 21, 1692, pp. 292v–93; Sparrman, *Voyage*, 1:331.

57. Kolbe, *Beschreibung*, p. 161; Engelbrecht, *Korana*, p. 91; *VRJ*, 1:227 (April 7, 1654) and 320 (June 23, 1655).

pastured together, and were driven out by two or three men at 7:00 A.M. and brought in at 5:00 or 6:00 P.M. Among the Namaqua, however, cows and calves pastured separately under different herders; oxen and old cows were allowed to wander to new pastures alone and were not brought in at night. Khoikhoi made no attempt to control contact between cows and bulls or between ewes and rams, and they ridiculed the Dutch ranchers who did. This does not mean that they had no notion at all of controlled breeding, for they did castrate male animals—not only the steers, which they needed as pack oxen, but the rams as well. Castrations were an occasion for great feasting.[58]

Livestock in the southwestern Cape were threatened by drought and failing pasture, but not to the extent that they were in the drier interior of South Africa. In normal years the more immediate danger came from stock disease and from attacks by wild animals. Lions and leopards trailed Khoikhoi tribes around the countryside and often attacked the stock enclosures at night, creating havoc and killing both animals and Khoikhoi watchmen. Once they had victimized a kraal, the predators would attack it again and again.

Though Khoikhoi often acted with incredible bravery against lions, it seems that they had only partially successful means of coping with this pervasive danger. On many occasions Dutch observers would arrive at a kraal and find that Khoikhoi had surrounded a lion in a thicket or in the midst of their cattle: though they had the beast at bay, and though they terrified it by wearing reeds and branches around their heads, they could not kill it. It is particularly interesting that they often arranged their cattle as a defensive breastwork over which they hurled their assegais at the attacking animal: the Dutch noted that cattle which they had bought from Khoikhoi, when threatened by a wild animal, "all collected in a body with their horns towards the door and formed a crescent, so that the animal had all he could do to keep clear of their horns and escape."[59]

Livestock was by far the most valued form of private property in a society where land was never divided among individuals. The animals were, of course, chiefly of value as a mobile source of food that was more reliable than game and more nourishing than veldkos. We should not, however, exaggerate this factor, for neither sheep nor cattle were

<hr />

58. Kolbe, *Beschreibung*, pp. 158–59; Schultze, *Namaland*, pp. 258–62; KA 4037, Dagverhaal ...Jan Hartogh, Nov. 9, 1707, p. 906.

59. KA 4031, Dag Verhaal ... Johannes Starrenburgh, Nov. 2, 1705, p. 748v; *VRJ*, 1:317 (June 10–12, 1655); 2:41 (June 16, 1656). The quotation is from *VRJ*, 1:315 (June 1, 1655).

regularly slaughtered. Slaughter was undertaken chiefly to celebrate special occasions like weddings or farewells to visitors, or as a sacrifice to combat illnesses among humans or stock.[60] In general, Khoikhoi slaughtered sheep more readily than cattle, and according to some of our sources, women ate only mutton, and not beef.[61] There is not much evidence that Khoikhoi consumed cattle blood in the manner of some East African peoples, except in the sense that they did not wash or drain their meat after slaughter: Simon van der Stel, however, claimed that Guriqua collected and drank the blood of animals they had slaughtered.[62]

Milk was on the whole a more important product of stock-keeping than meat, but it was by no means in constant supply. Though cows and ewes were milked morning and evening, their supply of milk was closely dependent on the presence of a suckling calf or lamb. If a cow's calf died, the Khoikhoi stimulated her milk supply by presenting her with another calf covered with the skin of her dead offspring; if that failed, they blew air into the cow's genitals, a practice also encountered in parts of Europe. Unlike their Bantu-speaking counterparts, Khoikhoi women did most of the milking. We have no way of determining the daily yield of Cape Khoikhoi cows, but during the dry season the milk was sufficient only for the calves, or did not come at all.[63]

Khoikhoi did not strain their milk but stored it, often for very long periods, in cowhide sacks with the hair side inward. Men were allowed to drink only cows' milk, but women and children were apparently able to drink ewes' milk as well. The milk that was not consumed was made into butter by the simple process of shaking the sack.[64] This butter was used solely as body grease, a function which it shared with the fat both of wild game and domestic animals. In 1688 an ambassador from the Inqua boasted to Simon van der Stel that his people were so rich in cattle that "they often slaughtered an ox or a cow in order to smear themselves with fat, and leave the meat lying about."[65] This was probably a flamboyant exaggeration, but it well illustrates the importance that animal fat had on the Khoikhoi value scale. The

60. *CGH*, 1:119 (Schreyer, 1668); Hulshof, "H. A. van Reede ... Journaal," p. 203; Waterhouse, *Van der Stel*, p. 124; Dapper, VRS 14, p. 55; Kolbe, *Beschreibung*, p. 167.

61. Ten Rhyne, VRS 14, p. 125; *CGH*, 1:130 (Schreyer, 1668).

62. Waterhouse; *Van der Stel*, p. 124.

63. Kolbe, *Beschreibung*, p. 159; Schultze, *Namaland*, pp. 257–58; Hendrik Swellengrebel, "Journaal van eenen Landtogt ...," *RZA*, 4:68.

64. Kolbe, *Beschreibung*, pp. 159–60; *CGH*, 2:506 (index entry "butter").

65. KA 7571/KZ 3179, DR Dec. 22, 1688, n.p.

mythological and aesthetic reasons behind these usages are not known in detail, but the essential association of ideas is clear: grease connoted wealth, security, and tranquility. Theophilus Hahn, who intimately knew the nineteenth-century Namaqua, wrote:

> A rich man (*gou-aob*) was a fat man; he could afford to be fat (*gousa*) he could anoint himself with fat (*goub*). Therefore the word *gou-aob*, *fat-man*, is identical with *!khu-aob*, *rich-man*, and both have become the words by which rulers, kings, chiefs, masters and lords are addressed.[66]

Given the central position of livestock in the Khoikhoi economy, it is not surprising that exchanges of stock were an important phase of social relationships. Stock was transferred in connection with marriages, but apparently not in the vast quantities customary among some southern Bantu-speaking communities. For example, among the Orange River Khoikhoi, the groom gave cattle to his parents-in-law, but while Gordon stated that he regained most of these within three or four years, Wikar seemed to imply that he received other animals immediately in exchange.[67]

All Namaqua children were assigned a cow for their own use, and as soon as they were old enough, they were supposed to milk it. Among the Namaqua and the Cape Khoikhoi, newly married couples often received a few cows from their parents to begin their herds: this was the origin of the family's holdings, which would grow or dwindle with the vicissitudes of climate, disease, and war.[68] These holdings could be dramatically increased when parents died. Inheritance patterns were complex: among the Korana the eldest son inherited *most* of his father's cattle and sheep, while the youngest son received all of the mother's (in other words, what she had brought to the marriage, plus its issue). The middle sons received the remainder of the father's holdings, which were distributed among them by the eldest son. Daughters inherited large numbers of stock only if there were no living sons.[69]

Livestock were also commonly used as fines which, at least in the case of the Korana, were paid not to the injured party in a dispute,

---

66. Hahn, *Tsuni-//Goam*, p. 16.

67. Staf D 593 /U/4/1/3, Gordon, Vierde Reyse, Sept. 23, 1779, n.p.; Wikar, VRS 15, pp. 89–91. See also Schultze, *Namaland*, p. 298.

68. Schultze, *Namaland*, p. 299; Kolbe, *Beschreibung*, p. 123.

69. Engelbrecht, *Korana*, pp. 191–92; see also Kolbe, *Beschreibung*, p. 123.

but to the old men of the tribe.[70] Cattle were also important links
between rich and poor, for the former often lent out their cattle to
poor clients who herded them in return for a percentage of their yield.
Such relations were common not only within tribes but between them,
for wealthy tribes wished to disperse their possessions widely in order
to forestall the growth of covetousness among their neighbors.[71]

NARCOTICS, METALS, AND LONG-DISTANCE TRADE

Despite the extraordinary value that Khoikhoi placed on their
livestock, they also were anxious to consume products which the
pastoral economy alone could not provide. As a result, there was much
local trade between Khoikhoi and hunters, of a nature described in
chapter 2. In addition, there were extensive long-distance trade networks which kept distant Khoikhoi societies in contact with each other
and with Bantu-speaking Africans. The main goods exchanged in this
barter were cattle, dagga, iron, and copper.

Dagga, a form of hemp, was a highly valued intoxicant among Khoikhoi. Earliest observers of its use say that it was chewed or mixed with
water and drunk; it appears, as Raven-Hart suggests, that Khoikhoi
began to smoke dagga (sometimes mixed with imported tobacco) only
when taught the use of pipes by Europeans.[72] Dagga is apparently not
mentioned in the numerous accounts of the Cape Khoikhoi before
1652. Furthermore, the first Dutch commander, Jan van Riebeeck
(1652–62), usually referred to it, not in connection with Western Cape
Khoikhoi, but with inland tribes who were alleged by Western
Cape Khoikhoi to cultivate it. Throughout the seventeenth century, it
was usually mentioned only by close students of Khoikhoi culture and
not by the myriad of casual visitors to the Cape.[73] In view of all these
facts, it is likely that Western Cape Khoikhoi knew and esteemed
dagga, but that their supply of it was too small to make it a conspicuous part of their everyday life. Such a situation would explain

70. Dapper, VRS 14, p. 69; Engelbrecht, *Korana*, p. 193.

71. For example, see the evidence that Harry herded for Khoikhoi not in his own tribe, in
VRJ, 2:302 (July 6, 1658); see also ibid., 3:373 (April 20–23, 1661).

72. *VRJ*, 2:286 (June 21, 1658); *CGH*, 1:126 (Schreyer, 1668); ibid., 2:507 (index entry
"dagga"); KA 3976, Journael ... van de heen ende wederom Reyse gedaen ... by den Sergiant
Jonas de la Guerre, Dec., 1, 1663, n.p. Brian M. du Toit has suggested that some early references
to dagga at the Cape point to *Leonotus leonurus*, not to hemp (*Cannabis sativa*): see Brian M. du
Toit, "*Cannabis sativa* in sub-Saharan Africa," *SAJS* 70 (Sept. 1974):268.

73. Nienaber, *Hottentots*, pp. 241–43 (*dagga*); *VRJ*, 3:264 (Sept. 27, 1660) and 303 (Dec. 16,
1660).

the enthusiasm with which they greeted European tobacco, which rapidly became a mild dagga-substitute.

Western Cape Khoikhoi must have obtained their dagga by trade, since they apparently did not grow it themselves. They consistently stated that Khoikhoi to the east were growers of dagga, and named, first the Hamcumqua, then the Hessequa, and later a host of other Central Cape Khoikhoi tribes.[74] Though this testimony has been doubted,[75] later travel accounts clearly show that some Khoikhoi practiced the extremely rudimentary form of cultivation which dagga required. Most of this evidence refers to the Central Cape Khoikhoi, beginning with Cruse's visit to the Attaqua in 1668—when he was told that "it was still one month too early [to buy dagga] and it was not yet ripe"[76]—and including two direct observations of dagga fields by the eighteenth-century travelers, Sparrman and Thunberg. In these latter cases it is remotely possible that Khoikhoi had learned the technique from whites, but this explanation will not do for the Namnykoa, whom Wikar discovered planting dagga on the islands of the Orange River in 1779.[77]

Greater difficulties surround the question of Khoikhoi knowledge of metals prior to white settlement in South Africa. In 1956 the archaeologist A. J. H. Goodwin concluded that "the Cape Peninsula Hottentots had no metals and no knowledge of metal-working in 1650."[78] This statement is contradicted by abundant evidence. In the very first year of the European settlement the Dutch became aware that the copper they were trading was being made by Khoikhoi into bracelets and chains,[79] and evidence of similar activities can be found in travelers' accounts long before 1652. The more interesting question is whether these skills could have been learned from the many whites

74. *VRJ*, 3:303 (Dec. 16, 1660).

75. L. F. Maingard, "The Lost Tribes of the Cape, "*SAJS* 28 (Nov. 1931):492–93.

76. KA 3981, Journal of the *Voerman*, Oct. 5, 1668, p. 659.

77. Thunberg, *Voyages*, 1:140; Sparrman, 1:286; Wikar, VRS 15, p. 123. For an Australian example of possible cultivation among a people conventionally regarded as noncultivating, see F. R. Irvine, "Evidence of Change in the Vegetable Diet of Australian Aborigines," *Diprotodon to Detribalization*, ed. Arnold R. Pilling and Richard A. Waterman (East Lansing: Michigan State University Press, 1970), pp. 278–79.

78. A. J. H. Goodwin, "Metal Working among the Early Hottentots," *SAAB* 11, no. 42 (June 1956):50. In 1969, R. R. Inskeep advanced a similar but less radical view when he stated that historical sources "leave us in little doubt that these peoples [the Cape Khoikhoi, but not necessarily the Namaqua] were still ignorant of the processes of metallurgy at the time of the arrival of the first Europeans" ("The Archaeological Background," p. 21).

79. *VRJ*, 1:116 (Dec. 18, 1652), 128 (Jan. 14, 1653).

who called at the bay in the century and a half before Van Riebeeck's landing.

This possibility is made unlikely by the following fact: when Vasco da Gama, the discoverer of the sea route to India, visited St. Helena Bay in 1497, he found Khoikhoi (or hunters?) wearing copper beads in their ears and desiring to buy more copper from the Portuguese. Da Gama did not mention copper in connection with the Khoikhoi inhabitants of Mossel Bay whom he subsequently visited: our first reference to these Khoikhoi wearing copper ornaments dates from 1595—that is, just before the institution of regular visits by Dutch and English ships.[80] These later ornaments could, of course, have derived from Portuguese visits, which were mainly of a century earlier, but a source from inland trade is much more likely.

The Cape Khoikhoi seem to have had little iron before contact with whites, as the earliest description of their assegais speak merely of fire-hardened tips (i.e. tips without metal).[81] However, in 1506 a Portuguese vessel put into Mossel Bay to look for the ship of Pedro de Mendoça, which had been wrecked there the previous year: they reported finding the burnt timber of the lost ship and concluded "that the fire had been made by the Cafres [i.e. Khoikhoi] to get the nails of her, iron being so much esteemed among them."[82] Even if the Portuguese were wrong in their suspicion (which was confirmed by many incidents in later centuries), it is significant that Khoikhoi already had a reputation for desiring iron a mere nine years after da Gama's visit. It is very unlikely that the extremely small numbers of Portuguese who had visited them in the interim could have instructed them in the use of iron and the techniques of melting and fashioning it: contacts were too brief for this, and were usually hostile; besides, the Portuguese would have no reason to give Khoikhoi information on the making of weapons which the Khoikhoi might well use against them.

By the beginning of the seventeenth century, when regular visits of European ships had assured Khoikhoi of a steady supply of junk iron, we have ample evidence that they were fashioning this iron into assegai heads.[83] In 1595 a Dutch observer noted that the Table Bay Khoikhoi called iron cori. The same word was also attested at Saldanha Bay in 1655 and in the eastern part of the Cape province in the late eighteenth century. It is the same as the modern Namaqua /urib, which in similar

80. BVR, pp. 4 (da Gama, 1497) and 18 (de Houtman, 1595).
81. Ibid., pp. 3 (da Gama, 1497) and 11 (d'Almeida, 1510).
82. Ibid., p. 9 (Quaresma and Barbudo, 1506).
83. Ibid., pp. 47 (de Laval, 1610) and 48 (Downton, 1610).

forms is also found in modern Korana.[84] The wide diffusion of this root in space and time suggests that it was an original Khoikhoi root, and hence that Khoikhoi had possessed iron before the divergence of Namaqua from Cape Khoikhoi.[85] It is also likely that Khoikhoi knew iron before other metals, for both Namaqua and Cape Khoikhoi used the word /urib to mean both iron and metal in general, calling copper "red iron," gold "yellow iron," and so on.

Since significant quantities of dagga, iron, and copper were not available in the southwestern Cape, they had to reach the hinterland of Table Bay by means of trade routes from the interior. The metals required by the Cape Khoikhoi originated among the Damara of Namibia and among the Tswana (Bricqua, Bri) of the Bechuanaland region of the Cape Province. They then flowed south to the Orange River, west toward the coast, and thence south toward the Cape Peninsula. They were taken moderate distances by each carrier, perhaps only to the next tribe—where they were then sold for various goods, but chiefly for livestock. Having thus passed through the hands of several middlemen, they reached the Little Namaqua, who then carried them south to the Cape Khoikhoi, adding copper which they themselves had mined in their own region.[86]

A second trade route in metals began among the Tswana and proceeded south to the Hamcumqua (Inqua), a tribe which dwelt farther inland than other Central Cape Khoikhoi. From the Hamcumqua the metals were passed westward to the Attaqua and eastward to a number of Eastern Cape Khoikhoi communities like the Gonaqua, and then on to the Xhosa. At the earlier stages of this chain, metals were traded against livestock, but at the later stages chiefly against dagga.[87]

Gerrit Harinck has tried to link this Inqua-Xhosa system with the Western Cape in what he called the "Xhosa-Khoi trade diffusion network," a transcontinental system in which Dutch products (chiefly copper and beads) flowed east from Table Bay and dagga flowed west from the Xhosa.[88] The evidence for such a neat pattern is not very good. Harinck is forced to rely on two sorts of evidence: the data on east-west *political* relations among the Khoikhoi (which I have interpreted in

84. Nienaber, *Hottentots*, p. 537 (*yster*).
85. Alternative interpretations of this evidence are discussed in Elphick, "Cape Khoi," pp. 113–14.
86. For a full discussion of the evidence, see ibid., pp. 115–18.
87. Ibid., pp. 118–19.
88. Harinck, "Xhosa and Khoi," pp. 164–65.

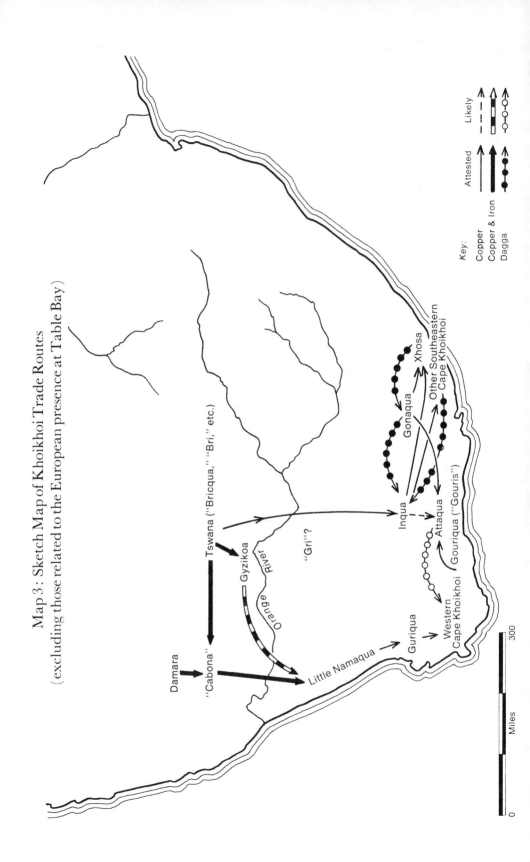

Map 3: Sketch Map of Khoikhoi Trade Routes
(excluding those related to the European presence at Table Bay)

Key:

	Attested	Likely
Copper		
Copper & Iron		
Dagga		

Damara

"Cabona"

Tswana ("Bricqua," "Bri," etc.)

Gyzikoa

Orange River

"Gri"?

Little Namaqua

Guriqua

Western Cape Khoikhoi

Inqua

Attaqua

Gouriqua ("Gouris")

Gonaqua

Xhosa

Other Southeastern Cape Khoikhoi

Miles

0   300

terms of lineage recognition), and the claims of Western Cape Khoikhoi that the inland Khoikhoi chieftains planted dagga. However, one cannot deduce from lineage patterns the nature of trade; and, as to the second point: it is very likely that the Western Cape Khoikhoi obtained dagga from people to the east; but, as I have explained, it probably originated with the Central Cape Khoikhoi, not with the Xhosa.

It is on the metals, and not dagga, that we should focus our attention. Copper and iron had to be obtained from great distances and were very highly valued by Khoikhoi. Indeed, the main purpose of long-distance Khoikhoi trade was to obtain these products, and a measure of their importance is seen in the commodity that was normally traded for them, namely, the highly valued livestock of the Khoikhoi. By contrast to the metal trade, exchanges involving dagga were probably more localized. Dagga can be grown in most areas, and with almost no effort; thus it was not a commodity that one would expect to be traded in large quantities over long distances. In fact, the evidence does not allow us to go further than to state that (1) in certain cases dagga replaced livestock as the article exchanged against incoming metals, and (2) that it was also traded into the western Cape where it was apparently not grown. In this latter case it was probably exchanged against cattle before 1652 but later, as Harinck suggests, against European trade goods.

Though our evidence on Khoikhoi trade networks is rather fragmentary, it recurs persistently enough in the travel accounts to indicate that long-distance trade was an important, and regular, facet of Khoikhoi life. However, the trade was not of sufficient scale to alter fundamentally the Khoikhoi economy or political structure. It gave rise to no regular markets; it created no merchant class; and it did not facilitate such large accumulations of nonpastoral wealth that previously existing differences between rich and poor, or between ruler and ruled, were markedly intensified.

KHOIKHOI AND THE IMPENDING CHALLENGE FROM EUROPE

The traditional society I have described was destined to be swept away rapidly when European adventurers, administrators, and settlers arrived in South Africa. Confronted by this challenge to their ancestral pastures, Khoikhoi were to prove comparatively passive; against the threat of rapid social and cultural innovation, they were to offer remarkably little resistance.

Their compliancy and flexibility are partially explained by the fact that they enjoyed neither the isolation of a small-scale society nor the strong traditions and institutions of a large-scale society—both of which can be sources of conservatism. The pastoral Khoikhoi were in no way parochial, being well informed of tribes hundreds of miles away, to which they were bound by trade, and in many cases by kinship and common culture. Their perspective was much broader than that of the local hunting bands which later put up fierce and protracted resistance to European penetration. Khoikhoi had come to appreciate goods and services which economies other than their own could provide, and consequently they later showed little hesitation in trading with Europeans. They were familiar with a "labor" system whereby clients from one tribe worked for employers in another, and hence they were to have no objections on principle to taking employment in the European colony.

On the other hand, unlike large, long-established African kingdoms, the Khoikhoi lacked institutions that could have been a bulwark against outside challenges. Though the spread of Khoikhoi culture was extensive, Khoikhoi polities were small, exceedingly unstable, and apparently incapable of uniting for a prolonged period against a common enemy. Much of this instability was rooted in the nature of the pastoral economy. Unending and rapid transhumant movement discouraged the accumulation of personal goods which in other contexts might have formed the basis of a strong political center; furthermore, this mobility, and the wide dispersal of the tribe at certain seasons of the year, necessitated a decentralization of decision making, and hence of political control. Pastoralism favored an individualistic society, one in which authority derived less from birth than from skill and wealth. Since skill was not always heritable, and since livestock wealth was highly volatile, political power remained unstable. The mobile nature of pastoral wealth also facilitated intertribal theft and fuelled the virtually unresolvable vendettas that were endemic in Khoikhoi, as in many other pastoral societies.

Many of these problems were intensified by the fact that pastoralism had not entirely supplanted the hunter-gatherer economy in southern Africa. Hostile hunters contributed greatly to the uncertainty of pastoral prosperity; friendly hunters eagerly participated as soldiers and allies in inter-Khoikhoi wars. Together the Khoikhoi-hunter cycle and the political weaknesses of pastoralism led to a fluid situation in which people and livestock flowed rapidly from tribe to tribe, and from herding to hunting communities and back again. The ways in which this fluidity shaped the Khoikhoi response to European pressure will be a major theme in the chapters that follow.

Part 2   Europeans and the Western
Cape Khoikhoi, 1488–1701

4

Peninsular Khoikhoi on the Sea Route
to the Indies, 1488–1652

FROM ARMED CONFLICT TO A TRADING BONANZA, 1488–1610

From the perspective of previous chapters, the western Cape has been seen as a cul-de-sac, a distant corner remote from the movements of people and ideas which accompanied the Bantu-speakers' occupation of southern Africa. In this favored and isolated region the ancient pastoral culture of the Khoikhoi was able to survive and flourish, cut off from most of Africa by mountains and deserts, and from the rest of the world by oceans which no African peoples could cross. In the late fifteenth century this isolation was broken suddenly, dramatically, and forever. By a trick of geographic fortune the Khoikhoi found that their peninsula lay athwart one of the most important trade routes in the history of mankind, the sea link between the vigorous Europe of the late Renaissance and the enticing wealth of the Orient.

To the mariners who sailed this route, the Cape was only in theory a part of Africa. The majority of them sighted no other part of the continent on their long voyage, and the Cape might well have been merely another convenient island like Mauritius or St. Helena. For 164 years contact between Europeans and Khoikhoi was intermittent, brief, almost purely commercial, and limited to the small Khoikhoi groups on the peninsula.[1] Yet the Cape was in fact to become Europe's gateway to Africa; and the forms of exchange, the fears and prejudices which developed in these early spasmodic encounters were to be important when Europeans later began their penetration of the continent.

---

1. The scattered sources for this period have recently (1967) been brought together in Major Raven-Hart's superb compendium, *Before Van Riebeeck* (cited in this work as *BVR*). Raven-Hart is more complete on English than Dutch sources, and for the latter I have had recourse to a number of items in the Algemeen Rijksarchief at The Hague. I am indebted to Jan Lucassen, a student at Leiden University, for directing me to those accounts which are most valuable on Khoikhoi.

In 1488 the Portuguese navigator Bartholomeu Dias was cruising down the west coast of Africa. At one point in his voyage he turned his ship toward the east and was surprised to find no land. Rightly suspecting that he had rounded the tip of the continent, he struck north and put into Mossel Bay on Africa's southern shore. The Portuguese named this bay Angra dos Vaqueiros "because of the many cows seen there watched by their herdsmen." The herdsmen—who were in fact Khoikhoi—were terrified by these pale apparitions from another world, and hastily drove their cattle inland.[2]

Dias was followed in 1497 by Vasco da Gama, the pioneer of the sea route to India. Before rounding the Cape, da Gama visited St. Helena Bay, where he encountered a people who may have been Khoikhoi but were probably hunters: they apparently had no cattle, and lived on "sea-wolves," whales, roots, and honey. They wore copper ornaments, and fought with assegais and possibly arrows.[3] After several days of friendly relations, the Portuguese and the hunters came to blows, and da Gama and three or four Europeans were wounded. Later, the Portuguese explorer put in at Mossel Bay, where he met a native people who rode on cattle, played flutes, danced in the manner of later Khoikhoi, and wore ivory armlets.[4] These two descriptions by da Gama's expedition are the earliest accounts we have of South African hunters and Khoikhoi, and they say nothing in regard to the culture or location of peoples which is inconsistent with our knowledge of later centuries.

The Table Bay Khoikhoi were probably first met by Europeans in 1503, when Antonio de Saldanha accidentally put into the bay, his pilot having erroneously concluded that the Cape had already been rounded. On his second visit ashore Saldanha was ambushed by some two hundred Khoikhoi, and he escaped with a wound in one arm. By now the Khoikhoi had earned a reputation for ferocity and military prowess, a reputation which was to be enhanced in 1510. In that year

2. *BVR*, p. 1 (Dias, 1488). Barros's description of Dias's visit does not mention a violent encounter, but Velho's account of da Gama's voyage says that Dias had killed one Khoikhoi with a crossbow (*BVR*, p. 5).

3. Raven-Hart argues that the words *frechas* and *pijlen* (respectively, Portuguese and Dutch for arrows *or* darts) always mean "darts" prior to 1610, when the first clear reference to a bow is found (*BVR*, p. 192, index entry "darts"). His view is probable in most cases; but in the da Gama incident, where hunters were apparently involved, it is reasonable to assume the use of arrows, and there is no reason in the text for not doing so.

4. *BVR*, pp. 3–7 (da Gama, 1497).

Francisco d'Almeida, the first Portuguese viceroy in India, was on his way home after a distinguished career of colonial conquest in Asia and along the East African coast. After he had dropped anchor in Table Bay, d'Almeida sent his men ashore, where they soon found themselves in disputes with local Khoikhoi. The viceroy was induced to mount an expedition to teach the Khoikhoi a lesson. The Portuguese party marched to an inland kraal and there decided to seize children as hostages; this act so enraged the Khoikhoi that they counterattacked, using their oxen as a defensive rampart from behind which they hurled stones and assegais. The Portuguese retreated to the beach only to find that their boats had been taken out to sea for protection against the breakers. Floundering in the deep sand, the heavily armored Europeans were at the mercy of the fleet-footed Khoikhoi, who moved "so lightly that they seemed birds." Before the expedition could set out to sea, fifty Portuguese, including the viceroy, lay dead, and almost all the rest were seriously wounded.[5]

If the chronicler Barros is reliable in his description of this clash, more Europeans perished here than in any engagement between Khoikhoi and Europeans in the following three centuries. This was due in part to the fact that Europeans were not yet carrying efficient firearms.[6] Nevertheless, the Khoikhoi seem to have been far more capable of mounting concerted resistance to Europeans then than they were a century later. Khoikhoi pugnacity was probably one reason why the Portuguese rarely called at the Cape in the following century, although they were sole masters of the route around Africa. Many of their ships victualled at Mozambique on their outward voyage and at St. Helena on the way home; a surprising number undertook the six- to eight-month voyage from Lisbon to Goa with no stopover at all.[7]

In the 1590s the Portuguese commercial empire was penetrated by mariners from the emerging Protestant states of England and the

5. Ibid., p. 8 (de Saldanha, 1503); pp. 9–10 (d'Almeida, 1510).

6. The main weapon used on the Iberian peninsula in the early sixteenth century was the arquebus, a weapon that was "very heavy, most unwieldy, tiresome to load, and continually missing fire" (W. W. Greener, *The Gun and Its Development*, 9th ed. [New York: Bonanza Books, n.d.], p. 58). I am indebted for this reference to Prof. Willard Wallace of Wesleyan University. In the d'Almeida incident, the Portuguese soldiers were carrying only lances and swords. *BVR*, p. 10 (d'Almeida, 1510).

7. *The Tragic History of the Sea, 1589–1622*, ed. C. R. Boxer, The Hakluyt Society, 2d ser., 112 (Cambridge: Cambridge University Press, 1959), p. 6.

United Netherlands. Many ships of both nations stopped in Table Bay (or Saldanha Bay, as the English called it)[8] on the outward and homeward voyages. The Cape was convenient for the Dutch and English, not only because they had no African bases like the Portuguese, but also because they avoided the east coast of Africa and cut directly across the Indian Ocean, via the "roaring forties" passage from the Cape to the Sunda Straits.[9] At Table Bay their crews could recover their strength, refreshed by an abundant supply of fresh water and by the benign Mediterranean climate of the region. The Khoikhoi were often induced to trade a few cattle or sheep, for fresh beef and mutton were eagerly sought by the sailors who had been living for several months on salty or rancid pork.

After 1590 most outward-bound ships visited the Cape in June or July, and most homeward-bound ships, between February and May. No clear correlation can be found in any period between the month of arrival and the availability of Khoikhoi stock. In early years almost any month was good, in later years any month could be bad. Of fifteen English and Dutch accounts examined for the period 1591–1610, almost all attest that Khoikhoi brought sheep and cattle regularly, often in amounts larger than the ships needed for immediate or future use. The figures cited by these early voyages would be considered wildly improbable (in view of later experience), were it not that the sources of information are so numerous and varied. The four highest recorded figures were:[10]

		Sheep	Cattle
Lancaster	(1601)	1000	42
Middleton	(1604)	214	12
Keeling	(1607)	450	66
Matelief	(1608)	175	29

The willingness of Khoikhoi and Europeans to trade was no index of the trust they placed in each other. Both sides desperately feared

8. The Portuguese named Table Bay "Aguada de Saldanha" after the navigator Antonio de Saldanha, who had visited it in 1503. English visitors followed this Portuguese usage from the time of Sir James Lancaster (1591) until well into the seventeenth century. However, in 1601 the Dutch navigator Joris van Spilbergen transferred the name "Saldanha" to the modern bay of that name, and christened the bay near the Cape "Table Bay." This became standard Dutch usage and became universally recognized after the founding of the Dutch colony in 1652 (*BVR*, pp. 8, 15, 25, 27, and passim.)

9. C. R. Boxer, *The Dutch Seaborne Empire, 1600–1800* (London: Hutchinson & Co., 1965), p. 197.

10. *BVR*, pp. 23, 30, 34, 40.

trickery, the Khoikhoi being especially terrified that the Europeans would turn their firearms on them. An account of Matelief's visit of 1608 shows the tense manner in which trade proceeded:

> [The Khoikhoi] brought a sheep along, which they held fast by the forelegs. At this the Admiral showed them a copper bracelet, and they agreed to the bargain, so he grasped the sheep by one leg and reached out the ring to them, and when they let loose the sheep he also let the ring loose.[11]

Also, the Khoikhoi were apparently suspicious that Europeans would settle permanently at the Cape. Thus they were willing to barter with Sir James Lancaster in 1601 until his herds grew larger than the needs of his ships, at which time they withdrew; on another occasion they told Cornelis Matelief that if he wanted to barter, he and his men should not venture inland.[12]

Despite such mutual suspicion, incidents of violence were fewer in the period 1591–1610 then they had been in the past, and fewer than they would be in the future. This was due in part to the Khoikhoi thirst for European iron, and in part to the growing realization among whites that it was folly to risk the cattle supply, and indeed their own lives, by responding violently to petty thefts by Khoikhoi. It was better, said a member of Matelief's expedition, "to endure the thievery rather than lose the trade."[13]

Considerable wisdom was often shown by expeditions under the command of an admiral or other person of strong authority. Sir James Lancaster, for example, insisted on going ashore himself and winning Khoikhoi good will with gifts of knives and pieces of iron. As the chronicler stated, "he spoke to them in Cattels Language (which was never changed at the confusion of Babell) which was *Moath* for Oxen and Kine, and *Baa* for Sheepe." Only when he had gained the confidence of the Khoikhoi did he allow his men to come ashore and pitch tents. When Khoikhoi came to trade, only five or six Europeans were permitted to approach them directly: thus Khoikhoi were not alarmed, but security was guaranteed by keeping at least thirty musketeers and pikemen ready nearby.[14]

The aspect of the trade which most delighted Europeans was the

11. Ibid., p. 38 (Matelief, 1608).
12. Ibid., p. 23 (Lancaster, 1601); p. 38 (Matelief, 1608).
13. Ibid., p. 40.
14. Ibid., p. 23 (Lancaster, 1601).

extraordinarily small payment the Khoikhoi demanded. In 1591 an ox could be purchased for two knives, a sheep or a calf, for one or less. In 1595 the English paid for stock in "old Iron and spike Nailes"; the best cattle cost no more than a pennyworth of iron per head. Until 1609 almost all stock was purchased with iron, nails soon giving way to iron barrel hoops. The high prices Khoikhoi were willing to pay, and the acrimony with which they quarreled among themselves over bartered iron, showed that to them iron was just as valuable as livestock was to the Europeans.

Apart from knives, which they probably used intact, Khoikhoi desired iron primarily for use in the manufacture of assegai heads.[15] The earliest descriptions of Khoikhoi assegais (1497 and 1510) mention that they were fire-hardened at the points or else were tipped with fire-hardened horns. Effective as these weapons were, they could be greatly improved by the addition of metallic heads, and the Khoikhoi seem to have retained the requisite metal-working skills acquired earlier in their history (see p. 64). By 1595 Cornelis de Houtman reported that some of the assegais of the Peninsular Khoikhoi were iron-tipped and some were not. In 1610, after two decades of flourishing trade, two observers (Laval and Downton) mentioned only spears with iron points, as did the majority of visitors who commented on Khoikhoi weapons for the rest of the seventeenth century.[16]

Coree the Saldanian and the Decline in Trade, 1610–1626

This incredible boom—which allowed whole fleets to be fed in return for miscellaneous junk readily available on any ship—came to a sudden end. In 1609 Khoikhoi were selling cattle for both iron and copper; in 1610 they abruptly refused to take iron at all and would accept only copper. The disinterest in iron lasted for a decade, and indeed for the ensuing half-century we find only scattered references to the once valuable metal. Nicholas Downton incorrectly supposed that the declining demand for iron meant an end to wars in the hinterland of the Cape.[17] More probably the market for iron had become saturated. Only a small amount of iron was needed to outfit all able-bodied male Khoikhoi near the peninsula with several iron-tipped assegais. Soldiers probably did not exceed 1,200 in number, and they

15. Ibid., p. 15 (Lancaster, 1591); p. 20 (Davys, 1598); p. 48 (Downton, 1610).
16. Ibid., p. 19 (de Houtman, 1595); p. 47 (de Laval, 1610); p. 48 (Downton, 1610); see also index entry "assegais," p. 186, and the corresponding entry in *CGH*, 2:505.
17. *BVR*, p. 46 (Claesz. van Purmerendt, 1609); p. 48 (Downton, 1610).

had been virtually inundated with the metal: William Keeling in
1607 had left no fewer than two hundred iron hoops.[18] The market
could become glutted because Peninsular Khoikhoi would naturally
not trade iron inland to improve the spears of their enemies: no great
inland market could develop, as later was the case with copper. One
effect of the glut in iron was that after 1610 this metal was even used
in the making of ornaments.[19]

Copper, in contrast to iron, was purely an item of luxury for Khoikhoi. As I have shown in chapter 3, copper ornaments were first noted
by Europeans in 1497 at St. Helena Bay and in 1595 at Mossel Bay,
but most early descriptions emphasize the use of ivory in making arm
bands. The Europeans brought a new and more abundant source of
copper which soon replaced ivory as the conventional Khoikhoi orna-
ment: observers of Khoikhoi between Sir Thomas Herbert's visit (1627)
and the founding of the colony (1652) mention only metal armlets.[20]

The shift to copper raised the price of livestock for Europeans, for
copper ranked higher than iron on their own value scale and was less
readily available aboard ship. Moreover, the copper had to be of the
right sort: Khoikhoi particularly desired small thin squares that were
easily formed into various sorts of jewelry. The sailors often cut these
from kettles and other pots or pans.[21] However, no sooner had the
Europeans accustomed themselves to the demand for copper, than the
market shifted again and only brass was acceptable.

Khoikhoi perceived brass as a species of copper and probably
favored it because of its hardness, shininess—observers agree that
Khoikhoi jewelry was highly polished—and resistance to corrosion.
Furthermore, it is very probable that the native copper they had long
obtained from Little Namaqualand was yellowish in color: a merchant
on Matelief's voyage of 1608 found a Khoikhoi with a bracelet which
he insisted had been made by Khoikhoi of metals found in South
Africa. This claim was probably true, as European trade in copper
had been slight before this date. It is significant that the metal looked
to the European like "something between copper and gold," i.e.
something more yellow than copper.[22]

The European sailors were outraged by the rising Khoikhoi de-

18. Ibid., p. 34 (Keeling, 1607). On the Peninsulars' population figures, see p. 92.
19. Ibid., p. 122 (Herbert, 1627).
20. Ibid., index entry "Hottentots: armlets," p. 198.
21. Ibid., p. 48 (Downton, 1610); p. 51 (Diecksz., 1610).
22. Ibid., p. 39 (Matelief, 1608).

mands. They put the blame on the shoulders of Coree, a Khoikhoi who had visited England; they suspected that he had given the Khoikhoi knowledge of brass and had told them of the low esteem in which all these metals were held by Europeans. When Coree was present at the barter, Khoikhoi would accept only "brasse Kettels which must be verie bright," and they had to be paid lavishly in "Skillets, Basons and Scummers," all of which meant that one could no longer buy even a sheep with the merchandise which formerly would have bought two or three oxen.[23]

Coree's adventures had begun in May 1613, when the crew of the *Hector* had seized him and another Khoikhoi and taken them on board their Europe-bound vessel.[24] As long as their compatriots were gone, the Khoikhoi retaliated as best they could against English shipping which happened into the bay.[25] Though his companion died at sea, Coree reached England and there received considerate treatment from Sir Thomas Smythe, the governor of the English East India Company. It will not surprise a modern reader that a pastoralist from South Africa reacted with little enthusiasm to an English winter and to the filth and boisterous activity of Stuart London, but contemporaries professed to be appalled by his attitude and labeled him "an ungrateful dogge":

> now one would think that this wretch might have conceived his present, compared with his former condition, as Heaven upon Earth; but did not so. . . . for never any seemed to be more weary of ill usage than he was of courtesies; none ever more desirous to return home to his country than he; for when he had learned a little of our language he would daily lie upon the ground, and cry very often this in broken English, "Coree home go, Souldania go, home go."[26]

Coree's wish was soon granted, as the English, who were imitating a kidnapping technique long used on the West African coast,[27] intended that he should return home and manage the barter on their

23. Ibid., pp. 64–67 (Downton, 1614); pp. 70–71 (Milward, 1614).

24. Ibid., p. 87 (Jourdain, 1617). For previous accounts of the life of Coree, see D. H. V.[arley], "A Note on Coree the Saldanian," *Quarterly Bulletin of the South African Library* 1, no. 3, (March 1947):78–81, and John Cope, *King of the Hottentots* (Cape Town:Howard Timmins, 1967). This latter work must be used with caution.

25. *BVR*, p. 54 (Saris, 1614).

26. Edward Terry, *A Voyage to East India* (London:J. Wilkie, 1777; orig. ed. 1655), p. 20.

27. Winthrop D. Jordan, *White over Black* (Baltimore:Penguin Books, 1968), p. 6.

behalf. He was taken aboard the *Hector* the following spring and deposited on the shores of the bay in June 1614. Wasting no time, he departed inland with his "tinckerlie treasure" (a suit of copper armor made for him by the East India Company) and did not appear again as long as the fleet was in the bay. Rightly or wrongly, the English thought that he was responsible for the failure of his people to trade; and when another tribe, over which he had no apparent influence, arrived and traded abundantly at low rates, a consensus formed among the English sailors that it "would haue bynn much better for vs and such as shall come hereafter yf [Coree] had neuer seene England."[28]

Though prices remained high for some time, it soon became apparent that Coree had formed a certain cautious affection for the English. The following year an English fleet arrived with Sir Thomas Rowe, special envoy from King James I to the Great Moghul in India. Coree hastened down to welcome the fleet, his people traded freely, and a party of Englishmen was taken upcountry to see Coree's kraal. The members of this party reported that Coree's people greeted them with joyous cries of "*Sir Tho: Smithe English Shipps*, which they often repeat & that with great glorye." Several Khoikhoi even expressed a desire to visit England.

This same fleet also dropped ashore a number of condemned criminals whose sentences had been commuted to transportation in the hope that they might found an English "plantation" (i.e. colony) in South Africa. Coree's Khoikhoi were at first hostile to these Newgate men, and in fact killed some and wounded others. However, when it was explained that they had been sent by Sir Thomas Smythe, Coree's attitude changed. He urged that the convicts be armed with muskets and suggested that he, his family, and his cattle come down to the shore to live under the protection of their guns.[29]

At this juncture it became obvious that Coree's surprising warmth toward his ex-captors was dictated in large part by his desire for aid in a struggle against an indigenous enemy. Attempts to form mutually beneficial alliances with Europeans were to be made by resourceful Khoikhoi on many later occasions, often with considerable success. In Coree's case, however, the tactic almost certainly failed. The Newgate men remained at the Cape for only two or three years, and though

28. As in n. 23. The quotation is on p. 67.

29. *BVR*, pp. 67–69 (Dodsworth, 1615); pp. 71–75 (Peyton, 1615, 1617). The quotation is on p. 72.

their final fate is obscure, it seems unlikely that they ever aided Coree in any decisive way. In 1617 Coree was still at war, and he took an English party inland to see his enemies assembled. His foe numbered about 5,000 and their cattle about 10,000, while his own following were estimated at about 1,000 armed men and 5,000 cattle. In the face of such unfavorable odds, the English refused all Coree's pleas that they intervene on his behalf. Later in the same year, however, Coree persuaded a Dutch party to march inland to attack his indigenous antagonists. This action was successful: 120 cattle and 160 sheep were seized and three enemies taken prisoner.[30]

Coree himself lived at least until 1624, appearing occasionally to English (and in one case to French) ships in the bay. Nothing further is known about his inland war. He himself probably perished in 1626, for the following year an anonymous Welsh sailor reported that one "Cary who was in England" had been killed by Dutch mariners for refusing to give them food.[31] No direct confirmation of this statement has yet been found in Dutch records, but the story is not improbable. In 1626 a very large number of Dutch ships had visited Table Bay, and during that year the Khoikhoi traded generously with the English but not with the Dutch, because of "their ill euill useadge of the blackes." This tension might well have been either the prelude to or the aftermath of the killing of Coree.[32]

It now remains to locate Coree, his people, and his mysterious inland enemies in the structure of Khoikhoi society as we know it from later sources. When the Dutch formed their settlement at mid-century, they found a group in the immediate vicinity of Table Bay called the *Gora*chouqua, under a chief Choro or Chora. (As *ch* and *g* had equal value in Dutch spelling, the name of the chief was clearly eponymous.) There can be little doubt that Coree had been a previous leader of this tribe, or at least a member of the same family after which it was named.[33] Apart from the clear correspondence in his name, Coree's

30. Ibid., pp. 87–88 (Jourdain, 1617); KA 977, Letter of Hans Bartholomensz van Rosendal et al., July 18, 1617, p. 69v. It is very likely that Coree was the Khoikhoi who took them inland, even though the Dutch source does not specifically say so.

31. Great Britain, Historical Manuscripts Commission, *Report on Manuscripts in the Welsh Language* (London: Eyre & Spottiswoode, 1905), vol. 1, pt. 3, p. 1012.

32. *BVR*, p. 115 (Minors, 1626).

33. His name appears as Coree, Corre, Quore, Cary, etc. The consistent use of the ending *e* is curious, as this is much more typical of Namaqua proper names than of Cape Khokhoi. It is possible that the English assimilated the Khoikhoi name *Chora* to their own surname *Cory*, in which form it became widely used. The word *tribe* is here used in the sense explained on pp. 45–46.

kraal (one hundred huts about eight English miles inland) fits in very well with later data on the Gorachouqua.[34]

In 1652 the Gorachouqua were one of several groups under the largely nominal authority of one chief, Gogosoa. All these peoples (whom I call Peninsular Khoikhoi) were periodically at loggerheads with the Cochoqua, a much larger inland tribe which asserted some sort of lineage suzerainty over them. Our scattered fragments of evidence suggest that the situation was roughly similar in Coree's day. Information on Khoikhoi political structure is rare in these years, but we do get occasional references to a "commander" or "Great Capitaine" who had authority over the course of the trade. Though some of these references may be to different people, at least two (Milward in 1614 and Minors in 1624) mention Coree and make it clear that he, though influential, was less important than this chief. It is possible that this personage, to whom the English gave a brass breastlet with the royal coat of arms, was Gogosoa or his predecessor, and thus the overchief of the Peninsular Khoikhoi.[35]

There is no unambiguous evidence that either the Europeans or the Khoikhoi regarded Coree as a chief. Nevertheless, after his visit to England he displayed considerable influence over barter and the conduct of war; he was also polygynous[36] and rich in metals and cattle. All this makes it conceivable that his authority among Khoikhoi derived, like that of several later Khoikhoi, from his influence with Europeans, and that we are witnessing in this period the consolidation of the Gorachouqua under Coree's leadership as a subgroup of the Peninsular Khoikhoi.

We are on surer ground when we speculate about the identity of Coree's enemies. In 1615 Coree informed Edward Dodsworth of "cyvill discorde amongst themselves, that many times he and his friends were robbed by the mountainers." Subsequent encounters between the Europeans and the "mountainers" showed that the latter were not cattleless robbers, as might be suspected from their name, but were a numerous stock-keeping group whose population, wealth, and location make it probable that they were the Cochoqua. The Dutch always referred to them as "the people of Saldanha Bay." Since the Dutch, unlike the English, used the name Saldanha to refer to the modern bay of that name, and since they doubtless derived this location from

34. *BVR*, p. 72 (Peyton, 1615).
35. Ibid., p. 52 (Saris, 1611); p. 70 (Milward, 1614); p. 114 (Minors, 1624).
36. Ibid., p. 68 (Dodsworth, 1615).

Peninsular Khoikhoi informants, the identification with Cochoqua (who often occupied Saldanha Bay) is very strong.[37]

HARRY, THE STRANDLOPERS, AND THE POST OFFICE, 1627–1652

The death of Coree in the mid-1620s deprived the Europeans of their last chance of reviving the livestock trade, which had by then been in decline for a decade. Our last reports of abundant trading come from 1617. Between 1617 and 1652 we have forty-two accounts of visits to Table Bay in which some reference is made to Khoikhoi or to livestock. Of these, only two mention trade in more than ten cattle and only two mention more than ten sheep. Two others state that the trade was adequate; a few speak of one or two cattle; eleven state clearly that no meat at all could be obtained; and an even larger number, though mentioning Khoikhoi, say nothing at all about trade —which suggests that there was none. In no case was there a repetition of the astounding figures of the period 1590–1610. The Cape, though it was now a much frequented stopover, was no longer regarded as a paradise for meat-eating seamen.[38]

It is likely that the decline in trade was intimately linked to a decline in trust between Europeans and Khoikhoi. Transient sailors were not the best people to try to build up a happy relationship with a suspicious native population. When they arrived in the bay they were usually starved, exhausted, and frustrated by the close confinement of the voyage: many of their members were miserably ill, many had died en route. Suddenly they found themselves in a verdant paradise, far from the laws and inhibitions of their own society and confronted by a native population which commanded seemingly endless supplies of fresh nourishment in the form of cattle and sheep. The sailors were usually a rough lot, swept together from the squalid quarters of North European ports; and their leaders often could not, or would not, restrain their bellicose instincts. Egged on by incidents of petty thievery and undeterred by the comparatively ineffective weapons of the Khoi-

37. Ibid.; KA 977, Letter of Hans Bartholomensz van Rosendal et al., July 18, 1617, p. 69v; KA 974, Journal of Franco van der Meer, 1616, p. 8v. The mystery of the "mountainers" can be partially solved if it is remembered that the source for the name was Coree, who had obtained a basic English vocabulary. He would use the word *mountain* only if it were a translation of all or part of the ethnic name of a Khoikhoi group. Nienaber (*Hottentots*, p. 217) lists the following forms of the Khoikhoi word for mountain attested for the western Cape: *cou* (1655), *khoe* (1660), *k'koe* (1691). This is possibly the first syllable in *Co*choqua.

38. *BVR*, passim.

khoi, the sailors had every motive to attack and plunder. The only
consideration which sometimes restrained them was the fear that the
Khoikhoi would retaliate on the next unsuspecting crew to set foot on
land. Sailors who had had armed clashes with Khoikhoi sometimes
buried letters on the beach to warn those who followed them of likely
Khoikhoi hostility.[39]

Many crews, however, resisted the temptation to resort to force, and
the Khoikhoi had no way of knowing beforehand whether or not they
would be misused if they approached the newcomers. As a consequence,
their own behavior soon became as unpredictable as that of the Europeans. They waxed alternatively meek and bold. Sometimes they
would flee inland with their cattle at the first glimpse of a ship; at
others they would attack small groups of Europeans who left their
main party in order to fish.[40]

In the period after the death of Coree our information on Khoikhoi
events in the interior drops to almost nothing. This is due largely to
the fact that channels of information were blocked by the decline of
peaceful barter between Khoikhoi and Europeans. However, while
our knowledge of cattle-keeping peoples decreases, we obtain our first
information about the cattleless community whom the Dutch called
Strandlopers (i.e. Beachrangers) or Watermen. These people were
almost certainly an impoverished offshoot of the Peninsular Khoikhoi
(see p. 94).

No unambiguous reference to Strandlopers has been found before
1632, but after that date references are numerous and unmistakable.[41]
It must be tentatively concluded that, although similar scavenging
groups may well have lived earlier on the shores of the bay, the fairly
cohesive community of Van Riebeeck's day probably first emerged in
the late 1620s or early 1630s. The clearest early definition of their
nonpastoral economy was provided in 1639 by Johan Albrecht von
Mandelslo:

> The inhabitants of this country are of two sorts: some which live
> very miserably by the waterside, but without ships or boats. They

39. E.g. *BVR*, p. 172 (Geleynsz., 1648).
40. E.g. *BVR*, p. 126 (Van den Broeck, 1630); p. 97 (Hore, 1620).
41. Algemeen Rijksarchief, Collectie Geleynssen de Jongh, no. 31, Briefboeck ..., Letter
from the ship *'s Gravenhage* in Table Bay, Dec. 2, 1632, n.p.; KA 1033, Journael van 't Schip
Banda, May 20, 1636, p. 1387. A possible earlier reference to people like the Strandlopers is
found in *BVR*, p. 41 (Jourdain, 1608).

live on herbs, roots and fishes, and especially on the dead whales
which are cast ashore by storms, which must serve as their best
food. They are called the *Watermen*. . . . The other sort which live
further inland are called Solthanimen . . . they have lovely cattle,
sheep and goats.[42]

The formation of the Strandloper community was doubtless caused
by disintegrative tendencies in Peninsular Khoikhoi society. It owed
its longevity in part to two factors: the periodic benefits it could derive
from the visits of Europeans and the extraordinary character of its
chief, Autshumato, who was known to the Europeans as Hadah, Adda,
or Haddot—and after 1652, as Harry. This was the Harry who was
later to become famous for his intrigues with and against the Dutch.
However, in this early period Harry's chief contacts were with the
English, and it was the English who took him to the Javanese port of
Bantam (probably in 1631–32) and taught him the essentials of their
language.[43]

In view of Harry's confident and cheerful demeanor with Europeans,
it is not likely that he was kidnapped in the way Coree had been. In
any event, the motive of the English was different in the two cases:
Harry was a cattleless person who could not be expected to bring stock
to passing ships. The English hoped, rather, that he would become
their agent in South Africa, keeping letters from one fleet to the next
and reporting on the movements of friendly and hostile shipping in
the bay. In 1632 they transported Harry and more than twenty of his
followers to Robben Island. Less than a year later, a Dutch vessel
acceded to the earnest request of thirty more Strandlopers and carried
them over to join the original party on the island.[44]

This location was very appealing to the Strandlopers, as it offered
complete security against their cattle-keeping enemies (the Cochoqua
and to some extent the Peninsular Khoikhoi), none of whom had any
knowledge of sailing. The island also supported an enormous supply of
penguins and seals, which had only to be clubbed to death and eaten.
(Both animals were rare on the mainland, probably because they had
been previously hunted out by Khoikhoi.) From their vantage point
on the island, the Strandlopers could spot all ships entering the bay

42. Ibid., p. 152 (Van Mandelslo, 1639). The reference to goats is an error.
43. Ibid., p. 127.
44. Collectie Geleynssen, no. 31, Briefboeck . . . , Letter from the ship *'s Gravenhage*, Dec. 2,
1632, n.p.

and could gain their attention by lighting a smoky fire. Many vessels stopped at the island on their way in or out of the harbor, or else sent their longboats from shore to pick up the mail. Quite often they would take several Strandlopers to the mainland to visit their relatives and then deposit them back on the island.

Harry considered himself to be an agent of both the Dutch and the English, even though his main contacts were English and the English language was always his means of expression. In 1632 a French ship stopped at the island, possibly with the intention of making train oil from whale blubber. Harry told the Frenchmen that he was "au service de messejieurs Holandois et de messjeurs les Anglois," and he used the persuasiveness for which he was afterward famous to induce the new-comers to remove themselves to Saldanha Bay. During the 1630s both the Dutch and the English left their letters with him, though the Dutch were normally less trusting and many buried a second copy on the mainland. On at least one occasion the Dutch employed him as a translator on a barter expedition inland, and it may be that his later aptitude for the trade dated from such early experience.[45]

The Strandlopers probably left Robben Island for good sometime in the early 1640s. In 1638 they were found on the mainland by Artus Gijsels, who later reported that the island was almost depleted of penguins and seals. Gijsels concluded that the Khoikhoi had virtually exterminated the animals on which they lived. Quite probably the Strandlopers had asked to be removed well before the animals were gone, for the next year (1639) fifteen returned to the island and found it considerably restocked. This small party probably remained there only a short time, for most of our records of the 1640s suggest that the island was uninhabited.[46]

The postal service continued to operate in whichever location the Strandlopers happened to be. It even underwent a brief period of expansion. In 1638 we find indications of *two* Khoikhoi who spoke English; the second of these may be the same person as "Isaac," a Khoikhoi whom the Dutch later took to Batavia and returned to the bay in January 1642. Doubtless the Dutch intended that Isaac should serve as their counterpart to Harry. There was a brief period when Isaac was regarded as the "Dutch Caffer" and Harry as the "English

45. *BVR*, p. 137 (French at Saldanha Bay, 1632); Collectie Geleynssen, no. 31, Briefboeck ..., Letter from the ship *Amsterdam*, April 14, 1635, n.p.

46. *BVR*, pp. 148–49 (Gijsels, 1638); p. 153 (Von Mandelslo, 1639).

Caffer," but after 1646 Isaac disappeared from the records, leaving Harry alone to reap the benefits of the founding of the colony in 1652.[47]

EUROPEANS AND KHOIKHOI ON THE EVE OF COLONIZATION

By 1652, when the Dutch East India Company established a permanent colony at the Cape, Europeans and Khoikhoi had had 164 years of contact with each other. To be sure, most of the contact had been in the last fifty years of this period, and all of it had involved very small groups of Khoikhoi in spasmodic relations with constantly changing groups of Europeans. Nonetheless, a great deal had been learned by both sides, and the shape of their relations in the new colony cannot be understood unless it is realized that Khoikhoi and whites already had much information—and misinformation—about one another.

The Peninsular Khoikhoi had acquired some elementary knowledge of European shipping: the usual date and duration of the fleets' visits, the needs of the ships, and the strengths and weaknesses of the newly arrived crews. Their early panic at the mere sound of gunfire had given way to a healthy and realistic fear of the damage firearms could inflict. Khoikhoi had learned to distinguish the different European nations, and were well aware of the advantages of playing one off against the other. Several of their leaders had mastered European tongues—a significant achievement, as no European could utter a sentence of Khoikhoi—and had visited Europe or Asia, bringing back tales about European society, values, and skills. Perhaps most importantly, the Khoikhoi had appraised the value of different forms of the Europeans' merchandise and had formed views as to the advantages to be gained in bartering with them. As we shall see shortly, the Peninsular Khoikhoi had developed a small inland barter system based on the intermittent supply of European copper; when the colony was founded in 1652, the Peninsulars were to exploit this preexisting system to the full, thus acquiring an importance in South African history out of all proportion to their numbers and wealth.

In one respect at least, the Khoikhoi had formed a conviction about Europeans which was later to prove disastrously false. Originally, as

47. Ibid., p. 148 (Gijsels, 1638); pp. 164–65 (Wurffbain, 1646); KA 1046, Cornelis Jansen Silvius and Andries Araenss to François Caron, Jan. 5, 1642, p. 298. The term *Kafir*, originally an Arabic word for "infidel," was possibly acquired by the Dutch during their contacts with the Portuguese throughout the Indian Ocean region. For an early Portuguese use of this term in reference to Khoikhoi, see *BVR*, p. 9 (de Saldanha, 1503).

I have noted, they reacted strongly to any hint that the Europeans intended to settle at the Cape. Throughout the seventeenth century various ships built minor redoubts and other fortifications while they were stationed in Table Bay. As time went by, the Khoikhoi became less alarmed by such activity and the conviction grew that Europeans, no matter how long they stayed, would eventually leave.

This idea was initially challenged but subsequently confirmed in 1647. In March of that year the ship *Haerlem* was wrecked in the bay. The crew began building a fort immediately; and although most of them soon returned to Holland in other vessels, Leendert Janssen and sixty men stayed on in the fort to salvage the ship's cargo. In June, Harry came by with five sheep—this is our first indication of a Strandloper reacquiring stock—and asked permission to inspect the fort. He was clearly trying to ascertain its permanence, for by September he had assured himself that the Dutch intended to stay and he begged to be allowed to live under their guns for protection from his enemies. This request was turned down. The Dutchmen remained in the bay an entire year, until in March 1648 they were repatriated to Europe on the home fleet of that year.[48]

The *Haerlem* episode had great impact on South African history. On the Khoikhoi side, it confirmed the false notion that Europeans were by nature birds of passage. Thus, when in 1652 a party of Europeans, only slightly larger than the *Haerlem's* rump crew, landed and began to build a fort, it took several years before the Peninsular Khoikhoi realized the significance of the move—namely, that the Dutch constituted a permanent threat as well as a passing opportunity. On the European side, the *Haerlem* experience crystallized a large amount of previously fragmentary information about the Cape and proved to be the impetus to the eventual decision to establish a Dutch post there.

Janssen himself was one of the two authors of the "Remonstrance"[49] of July 26, 1649, which urged the Lords Seventeen (of the Dutch East India Company) to consider such an action. Like many documents of its kind, the Remonstrance drew as much on optimism as on confirmed fact in setting forth the benefits it envisaged. Only passing reference was made to the Cape as a source of beef and mutton, the palmy days of abundant barter being now only a faint memory. Emphasis was placed, rather, on the Cape's potential as a self-sufficient vegetable- and

48. *BVR*, pp. 166–72 (Janssen, 1647).
49. Moodie, *The Record*, pp. 1–4.

fruit-growing colony, manned by a small garrison, three or four Dutch gardeners, and possibly a few Chinese assistants.

Alongside his cheerful economic prognosis, Janssen put in a favorable assessment of the Khoikhoi as potential neighbors. He denied the common view that they were savages and cannibals:

> that some of our soldiers and sailors have also been beaten to death by them, is indeed true; but the reasons why, are, for the exculpation of our people who give them cause, always concealed; for we firmly believe, that the farmers in this country [the Netherlands], were we to shoot their cattle or take them away without payment, if they had no justice to fear, would not be one hair better than these natives.[50]

Janssen reported that, in his experience, friendly treatment was all that was required to induce Khoikhoi to trade regularly and to refrain from hostilities. He was convinced that a Dutch fort, "being provided with a good commander, who would treat the natives kindly and pay them thankfully for all that was bought of them,"[51] would not only have little to fear from Khoikhoi, but could expect them to learn the Dutch language and be won over to the Christian faith.

The Lords Seventeen accepted Janssen's recommendation and during the course of 1650 and 1651 made plans for founding a station at the Cape of Good Hope. After their first commander-designate refused the post, they turned to Jan van Riebeeck, who accepted the challenge and in June 1651 drafted a commentary on Janssen's original Remonstrance. Van Riebeeck had been aboard the fleet which picked up the *Haerlem's* crew in 1648, and during his short stay at the Cape had formed some views of his own. He reacted somewhat negatively to Janssen's enthusiasm for Khoikhoi; in his view they were "by no means to be trusted but are a savage set, living without conscience, and therefore the Fort should be rendered totally defensible, for I have frequently heard . . . that our people have been beaten to death by them without having given the slightest cause."[52]

The unresolvable difference between Janssen's view, based on his own experience, and Van Riebeeck's, based mainly on the experiences of others, summarizes the ambiguous legacy of the first years of Khoi-

---

50. Ibid., p. 3.
51. Ibid., p. 4.
52. Ibid., pp. 5–7. The quotation is on p. 5.

khoi-white relations. Khoikhoi opinions about whites were doubtless
equally inconsistent, for in 1652 the record of relations between them
was almost equally balanced between peace and fighting, cooperation
and strife. South African racial attitudes, which one day were to attract
the attention of the whole world, were still only tentatively formed,
and their future shape was by no means predetermined.

5

Peninsular Khoikhoi at the Gateway
to Southern Africa, 1652–1662

The Lords Seventeen of the East India Company had the most
modest of motives when they founded the Cape settlement in 1652:
they wished to create, not an expanding colony, but merely a fort and
a garden to welcome Company ships, refresh their crews, and hasten
them on their way to Europe or to the Indies. Consequently, the Cape
outpost was at first confined to a tiny area and its population, white
and slave, was numerically small, reaching a mere 133 in 1656 and
394 in 1662. Initially most contacts were with Peninsular Khoikhoi,
themselves few in numbers.[1] Thus, for several years Khoikhoi-white
relations continued to be small in scope and were dominated by cattle
barter and petty thievery, much as they had been when Europeans
visited the bay on a purely seasonal basis.

Yet by the end of Van Riebeeck's ten-year command dramatic
transitions had taken place, usually in response to problems that were
fundamental to the nature of the Dutch settlement. By then the Company's insatiable demand for meat had forced it to establish trading
relations with distant Khoikhoi chieftains; its need for Khoikhoi labor
had created the beginnings of a multiracial society; and its agricultural
requirements had led to the foundation of a settler community and to
the outbreak of the first "native war" in South African history. In
these diverse ways the Cape was soon transformed from a mere way-
station into the gateway by which Europeans intruded themselves,
their commerce, and their culture into the African continent.[2]

---

1. On the colony, see population musters in KA 3968, p. 284v, and KA 3974, n.p. The
population of Peninsular Khoikhoi is discussed below, pp. 91–92.

2. This brief period of transformation is far better documented than the periods preceding
and following it. This is due almost entirely to the so-called Van Riebeeck Journal, the official
logbook of the settlement compiled under the eye of the commander. Though this is an exceedingly valuable source on Khoikhoi, it must be used with great caution: many early entries
must be reviewed in the light of later revelations made when the Dutch were more knowledgeable
about Khoikhoi, and no tribal identifications should be accepted without first being questioned.

THE PEOPLES OF THE CAPE PENINSULA

The "Peninsular Khoikhoi"[3] consisted of various groups of cattle-keepers and hunter-gatherers that were united by two bonds: their common claim to the pastures of the Cape Peninsula and its adjacent hinterland, and their nominal allegiance to chief Gogosoa. Gogosoa was known to the Dutch as the Fat Captain, and his corpulence, an unusual trait among Khoikhoi, was associated in Khoikhoi values with wealth, and hence with political power. He had once been a powerful chief, but by the 1650s he had grown old and his great weight had made him inactive and ineffectual. He no longer exerted noticeable influence over the Peninsular peoples apart from his own tribe, the Goringhaiqua. Even there, effective power had devolved upon his sons, Osinghkhimma (known to the Dutch as Schacher), Khuma, and Otegno, who were said to treat their father like a miserable beggar.[4]

Of the cattle-keeping tribes which comprised the Peninsular Khoikhoi, the most important were Gogosoa's own Goringhaiqua, and the Gorachouqua ("Tobacco Thieves"), who were ruled by chief Choro with the help of his brother Gakingh.[5] The two communities occasionally feuded, but most often during the 1650s and 1660s they were camped together in order to present a united front against the Cochoqua or the Dutch.[6] They were not the only cattle-keeping groups on the peninsula; other wealthy stockowners seem to have had small followings that were largely independent of the two main tribes. The best known of these was Ankaisoa, the owner of large flocks of sheep, who camped sometimes with Gogosoa, sometimes with Choro, and often alone.[7]

By Khoikhoi standards the Peninsular tribes were quite small and

3. I use this term instead of *Capemen*, which was used by the Dutch in Van Riebeeck's period but was rather ambiguous in its reference.

4. Fat Captain may be a direct translation of the name Gogosoa. Note that *gousa* is the Namaqua adjective for "fat." On Gogosoa see *VRJ*, 1: 208 (Jan. 28, 1654); 2: 270 (May 12, 1658); 3:444 (Dec. 1, 1661).

5. Wuras ("Account of the Korana," pp. 288–89) interprets Goringhaiqua as "those who dip water out of fountains," and Gorachouqua as referring to digging tools used by the Khoikhoi. Much more likely are Maingard's reconstructions !Kuriŋ//aikwa ("High-standers") and !Korakhwekwa ("Men of !Kora"): see his "Studies in Korana History, Customs and Language," *BS* 6, no. 2 (June 1932):111. The Dutch called the Gorachouqua "Associates of the Capemen" or "Tabackteckemans" (i.e. Tobacco Thieves). The latter word is a creole term invented by Khoikhoi to refer to the Gorachouqua involvement in a robbery of Dutch tobacco in 1657. It derives from the Dutch noun *tabak* and the English verb *to take*.

6. For quarrels between them, see *VRJ*, 2:271 (May 13, 1658); 3:133 (Sept. 21, 1659).

7. Ankaisoa was also known as Siginman, probably a derisive nickname (see Nienaber, *Hottentots*, p. 471). On Ankaisoa, see KA 3972, Van Riebeeck to Batavia, June 4, 1659, p. 38v; *VRJ*, 2: 295 (July 2, 1658).

only moderately wealthy. In his report to his successor (1662), Van Riebeeck estimated the population of the Goringhaiqua at 300 and that of the Gorachouqua at 600 to 700 able-bodied men. These figures are roughly consistent with observations he had made on two personal visits to their camps in 1661 and 1662, and are doubtless as close as we will ever come to an accurate estimate.[8] On this basis the total Peninsular population, including women and children, was probably between 4,000 and 8,000. In January 1658, Van Riebeeck reckoned the combined wealth of the Goringhaiqua and Gorachouqua at a mere 3,000 cattle and 2,000 sheep;[9] these figures are almost certainly too low, for Khoikhoi did not usually have all their animals in one place. The fact that sheep were outnumbered by cattle in spite of the faster breeding rate of sheep, suggests that the Peninsulars kept part of their flocks in hilly areas where the Dutch did not see them.

All the groups under Gogosoa laid consistent claim to the entire Cape Peninsula and its immediate hinterland. If this claim did not entail ownership in the modern sense, it certainly implied grazing rights in the area and authority to exclude neighboring tribes from using these pastures without permission. Among the Peninsulars' favorite camping areas were the mouth of the Salt River, the Hout and Berg valleys, the shores of False Bay, and the Bosheuvel. The inland limits of their territory are not clear: Harry maintained that all peoples south of the Great Berg River were Gogosoa's subjects, but this is doubtful, as the powerful Cochoqua were often south of the river in summertime.

As for their transhumance pattern, Harry stated that the Peninsular Khoikhoi trekked each year toward Mossel Bay and then northwest toward Saldanha Bay before turning back toward the Cape.[10] In normal times it is unlikely that they reached either of these bays,[11] since even when they were "inland" they could be reached quickly from the fort. They tended to be near Table Bay in the dry summer months (December to March), though, as their involvement with the Dutch increased, they also came often in winter.

8. KA 3974, Memorial Van Riebeeck to Successor, May 5, 1662, pp. 7–7v. In 1661 he said the combined Peninsulars had 90–100 huts with eight to ten able-bodied men in each (*VRJ*, 3:439 [Nov. 25, 1661]), and in 1662 that the Peninsulars had 104 huts with more than twenty men, women, and children in each (*VRJ*, 3:478 [Feb. 24, 1662]).

9. *VRJ*, 2:211 (Jan. 3, 1658).

10. Ibid., p. 184 (Nov. 15, 1657); 1:126 (Jan. 9, 1653).

11. Their presence at Saldanha Bay during the First Khoikhoi-Dutch War was apparently anomalous: they had first to ask the permission of the Cochoqua to use these pastures.

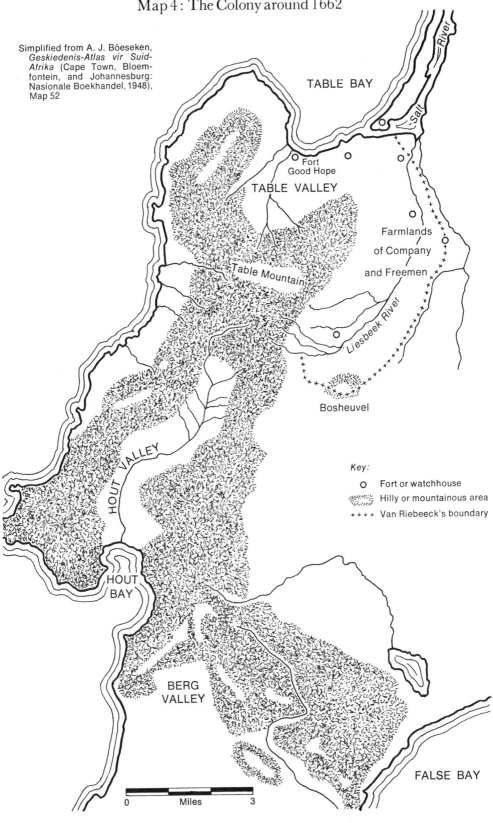

Map 4: The Colony around 1662

Simplified from A. J. Böeseken, *Geskiedenis-Atlas vir Suid-Afrika* (Cape Town, Bloemfontein, and Johannesburg: Nasionale Boekhandel, 1948), Map 52

TABLE BAY

Salt River

Fort Good Hope

TABLE VALLEY

Farmlands of Company and Freemen

Table Mountain

Liesbeek River

Bosheuvel

HOUT VALLEY

Key:

○ Fort or watchhouse

Hilly or mountainous area

+ + + + Van Riebeeck's boundary

HOUT BAY

BERG VALLEY

FALSE BAY

0   Miles   3

The Strandlopers, the cattleless scavengers who lived along the shores of the bay, numbered no more than forty or fifty persons in 1652.[12] Nonetheless, they were quite important since from their members came the first subordinate native group in colonial society. Though the Strandlopers probably called themselves by a "tribal" name (Goringhaicona), one must avoid the common mistake of considering them as a clearly defined tribe like the others, as well as Stow's misleading view that they were closer to "Bushmen" (i.e. aborigines) than "Hottentots."[13] They were, as suggested in the last chapter, an offshoot of the cattle-keeping societies of the Cape region. They spoke exactly the same language and wore exactly the same clothing as their pastoral neighbors. They were indistinguishable from the latter by sight, except for the fact that they were less well fed. Like the pastoralists they recognized Gogosoa as their overlord. And despite the occasional hostilities which arose between Strandlopers and cattle-keepers, there was easy movement of individuals back and forth between the two societies, and Strandlopers and pastoralists occasionally camped together. Most of the Strandlopers recognized Harry as their chief; but when he later became wealthy, Harry was influential among the Goringhaiqua and Gorachouqua as well.[14]

The Strandlopers consisted not only of the poor of Peninsular Khoikhoi society, but also of refugees, outcasts, orphans, and other persons without family. Olfert Dapper cited the case of one recruit to their ranks, a high-ranking Cochoqua, who had been exiled from his tribe for committing incest. The pastoralists, who regarded all Strandlopers with contempt, accused Harry of gathering followers from the robber "Sonqua," from those who were not "his own people," and from those

---

12. VRJ, 1: 80 (Nov. 13, 1652).

13. Goringhaicona is usually construed as "children of the Goringhaiqua," since |kona means "children." For Stow's view, see Native Races, p. 245. The Goringhaicona belong to that group of peoples (discussed on pp. 29–30) which are Khoikhoi rather than aboriginal in language and culture, yet cannot be classified as a Khoikhoi community because they owned no livestock and probably never did own any, as a group. They belong to the category "hunter-gatherers," which includes all African peoples with nonpastoral, noncultivating economies. The Goringhaicona are the best-known "Strandloper" group, though the latter term was later applied to cattleless people on the shores of other South African bays. The term Strandloper usefully denotes a subgroup of hunter-gatherers, namely, those with a predominately scavenging and gathering economy. However, one cannot assume that all Strandloper communities had the same language, culture, and background as the Goringhaicona.

14. VRJ, 1: 71 (Oct. 9, 1652); 2: 184 (Nov. 15, 1657). For information on kin ties between Strandlopers and cattle-keepers, see data on Eva below, and compare data on Boubo (Sijmon) in VRJ, 2:307 and 338 (July 8 and Sept. 15, 1658).

"whose parents and husbands were dead." Thus the Strandlopers, unlike the members of most Khoikhoi tribes, were not bound together by kinship so much as by their common misfortunes and their means of livelihood. Commander Wagenaar was substantially correct, if uncharitable in his choice of words, when he said that their numbers were recruited from "rabble out of the interior."[15]

THE YEARS OF TENSE CORDIALITY

In the last chapter we saw that, during 164 years of contact, Europeans and Peninsular Khoikhoi had both clashed and cooperated with each other. Memories of these experiences overshadowed the responses of Khoikhoi after 1652 and caused them to exhibit an uncertain mixture of boldness and timidity. Sometimes they would venture close to the fort, but usually they tried to keep most of their cattle inland. Whenever a Dutch party penetrated up-country, the Khoikhoi, who associated such expeditions with the cattle-raids of the past, often abandoned their stock without resistance and fled in disorder.[16]

Van Riebeeck had to take great pains to overcome these fears: in December 1653 he and a party of twenty men approached a group of Khoikhoi:

> Every now and then as we came gradually nearer ... some of them would get up and in great fear take to their heels, afterwards returning again. When this had happened 10 or 12 times we at last left another 4 of our men behind, and when the 3 of us alone advanced they waited for us, not daring, however, to trust us completely yet and trembling and shaking with fear.
>
> At long last 8 or 10 of them awaited us, the rest standing at a distance to see how matters would develop. When we reached them they immediately saw and recognized the Commander of the fort in person, and stepping towards him held out their hands in welcome and as a further sign of good feeling and friendship clasped us around the neck.[17]

The trust which the Khoikhoi began to place in the commander himself was doubtless very important in the improvement of Khoikhoi-white relations after 1652. There was now continuity of leadership among the Europeans who came into contact with Khoikhoi; and the com-

---

15. Dapper, VRS 14, p. 69; *VRJ*, 2: 50 (July 16, 1656); Moodie, *The Record*, p. 291.
16. *VRJ*, 1: 113 (Dec. 15, 1652); 126 (Jan. 9, 1653).
17. Ibid., p. 197 (Dec. 20, 1653).

mander, who disciplined the unruly elements that threatened the
Khoikhoi, became for them a symbol of good will.

Indeed, Van Riebeeck exercised considerable tact and wisdom in
dealing with Khoikhoi. It is true that he had formed a hostile view of
them even before the colony was formed, and that this prejudice had
not evaporated after a year at the Cape, when he wrote to the directors
that Khoikhoi were a "dull, rude, lazy, stinking nation." This harsh
comment has been quoted over and over again by historians in order
to prove that Van Riebeeck had a deep antipathy to Khoikhoi.[18] It
is well to remember that he wrote these words while petitioning the
directors to promote him from the Cape to an Asian factory. To
strengthen his case, he was arguing that someone with his experience
and "subtlety" of mind was wasted on the degraded natives of the
Cape, and that his abilities were more suited for dealing with "precise"
and sophisticated Asians.[19]

In fact, there is abundant evidence that Van Riebeeck's attitudes
were complex and changeable. His dislike of many Peninsular Khoikhoi
was matched by his admiration for a number of inland Khoikhoi
leaders; and he had great affection for Eva, the Khoikhoi girl he
brought up in his own home. Through his friendliness, patience, and
insight, he gained the confidence of Khoikhoi in a way no other Dutch
official was able to do in the seventeenth century. His interest in their
customs and internal affairs, though rooted in commercial considera-
tions, so far transcended that of his successors that the official journal
compiled under his direction is one of the richest sources on Khoikhoi
culture and history available anywhere.

Relations were further improved because the establishment of a
permanent settlement made the Europeans much more useful to the
Peninsular Khoikhoi than they had been heretofore. Though the
Khoikhoi were unaware that the colony was to be permanent or that
it would ever threaten their pastures and way of life, they were alive
to the fact that the fort—more than the ships—offered a regular supply
of European foods, metals, alcohol, and tobacco. The Peninsulars, who
were the experts among Khoikhoi in dealing with Europeans, indus-
triously tried to gain these goods in three ways: by trade, by robbery,

18. E.g. P. J. van der Merwe, "Die Inboorlingbeleid van die Kompanjie," in *Geskiedenis van
Suid-Afrika*, ed. A. J. H. van der Walt, J. A. Wiid, and A. L. Geyer, 2d ed. (Cape Town, Bloemfontein, and Johannesburg: Nasionale Boekhandel Beperk, 1955), 2: 350.

19. KA 3966, Van Riebeeck to XVII, April 14, 1653, p. 23.

and by offering themselves as laborers. They also revived Coree's old policy of urging the Dutch to aid them in various struggles with their enemies.

While changing circumstances were encouraging the Khoikhoi of the peninsula to tolerate and even welcome the Dutch presence, the Dutch on their side had even weightier reasons for desiring good relations with Khoikhoi. Indeed, the success of their colony and the career advancement of their commander depended upon white-Khoikhoi harmony. Van Riebeeck was in an insecure position. He had been given the Cape assignment—a humble one in the scale of Company values—as a kind of probationary post, a stepping stone to the recovery of his reputation after his dishonorable discharge from the Company's service in 1648.[20] At first, as we have seen, he strove to be promoted from the Cape to the East. At length, when it became evident that the Seventeen wanted him to serve out a full term at the Cape, Van Riebeeck rechanneled his ambitions into building up the station he had founded.

To succeed in this aim he had to ward off criticism from ship captains and official commissioners who visited the Cape. Many of these complained about the meat supply: a number said there was not enough meat, others said it was too lean and dry. Some officials wanted to close down the Cape and restore St. Helena as the Company's stopping place. In addition, many captains, tantalized by the premium which the Company paid for an early arrival at Batavia, preferred to ignore the sufferings of their crews and refused to stop at all.[21] To defend his position and to recommend himself to the directors, Van Riebeeck had to guarantee two things: that the Cape be always sufficiently supplied with good meat, and that it be peaceful and hence no financial burden to the Company. The key to attaining both these ends was successful relations with the Khoikhoi.

In a situation where both sides wanted to trade and where both dreaded conflict, it was natural that the leaders of each side should endeavor to be good neighbors. To avoid antagonizing the Dutch, the Khoikhoi normally pastured their stock at a considerable distance from the fort and controlled their veld burning so as not to threaten

20. *VRJ*, 1: xxiv. Van Riebeeck had been convicted of undermining the Company's monopoly at Tongking through private trading on his own account.

21. KA 456, XVII to Van Riebeeck, Sept. 5, 1659, p. 252; KA 456, XVII to Gerrit van Harn, Aug. 23, 1661, p. 444; KA 3967, Van Riebeeck to XVII, April 22, 1654, p. 10v; KA 3968, Van Riebeeck to XVII, March 25, 1656, pp. 3–4.

Dutch buildings. They also cooperated with Van Riebeeck in returning deserters from the ships and from the colony's military and civil establishment. From time to time they honored the Dutch with gifts of cattle or sheep, and with fine novelties like horns or the heads of wild game.[22]

Van Riebeeck devoted a great deal of time to reciprocating these courtesies. In the fort he often entertained Khoikhoi at simple feasts of bread, rice, arrack, and tobacco, and occasionally rode out to their camps with small gifts. Dutch herdsmen used their guns to dispatch wild animals that were threatening Khoikhoi herds, and Khoikhoi who had been wounded by wild animals or in war were sometimes offered the services of a Company surgeon.[23]

The most difficult part of Van Riebeeck's policy was restraining other whites from mistreating the Khoikhoi. Though, as we shall see, he was himself not adverse to violence, he felt that it must be used suddenly and massively, or not at all. Sometimes the impulse to violent action came from the ships in the bay: for example, a number of skippers warned Van Riebeeck "that if they did not get from us as many cattle as they wanted, they would go inland with hundreds of men to shoot cattle, and if the Hottentots did not want to exchange them, they would seize them."[24] At times when food was scarce, Van Riebeeck even had difficulty in stopping his own subordinates from attacking the Khoikhoi; often such men, simply by threatening Khoikhoi leaders, managed to frighten away the trade.

Much friction was engendered when Khoikhoi committed minor thefts. As early as December 1652, Van Riebeeck had noted a strange discrimination in Khoikhoi attitudes to stealing:

> whenever one of our cattle runs away, they [the "Saldanhars," which in 1652 meant all cattle-keeping Khoikhoi] immediately fetch it for us for 1 inch of tobacco; but if they can get hold of a plate of copper, they do not fail to do so.[25]

The hesitation of Khoikhoi to steal stock is explained in part by the gravity with which they regarded this crime in their own society (see p. 182). Similar inhibitions seemed not to apply to stealing metals, which they possibly did not even regard as personal property. They

22. *VRJ*, 1: 109 (Dec. 8, 1652); 2: 14 (Feb. 14–19, 1656); 2: 52 (July 22, 1656); 1: 77 (Oct. 23, 1652).

23. Ibid., 1:39 (May 11, 1652); 270 (Nov. 3, 1654).

24. Ibid., p. 203 (Jan. 10, 1654).

25. Ibid., p. 107 (Dec. 6, 1652).

occasionally took copper, but more frequently iron; for the glut in iron was a thing of the past, and the company only rarely sold it to Khoikhoi in the livestock trade. Iron was usually taken in the form of hatchets, carpenter's tools, tobacco boxes, chains, and nautical gear, and was used to make assegai heads and possibly crude knives. Khoikhoi also stole tobacco and hides. Hardly ever were any of these items recovered.

In defiance of the voices raised for revenge, Van Riebeeck shrank from punitive measures that would imperil the smooth flow of trade, and concentrated instead on preventing robberies by placing armed guards at key locations during the night. He overlooked several crimes because he hoped that the suspected culprits would come and trade at the fort. In other cases he avoided taking action himself by urging Khoikhoi chiefs to capture thieves from their own tribes and to punish them in the presence of the Dutch.[26] Though this policy did little to cut down theft in Van Riebeeck's time, it was to become a key pillar of Dutch judicial policy in subsequent decades.

The second great source of conflict between Company and Khoikhoi was the conduct of the trade in sheep and cattle. This trade was a natural extension of the small-scale intermittent barter which had been conducted in the years immediately before 1652. In those early days the ships' crews had been willing to accept cattle in almost any condition, as their intent was to slaughter them immediately. The Peninsulars had used this opportunity to rid themselves of sick and old beasts, and from the Europeans' copper they had fashioned bracelets and chains to trade inland for more and better cattle.[27] Thus to some extent their prosperity had been dependent on the European trade.

After 1652 the demand altered. Not only did the Dutch require much larger amounts (in order to feed the garrison as well as the larger number of ships calling at the Cape), but they now desired young cows for breeding purposes and oxen for work on fortifications, and later for agriculture. During the first year or two, while they were impressed by the Europeans' great stocks of copper, the Peninsular Khoikhoi were willing to satisfy a considerable part of this new demand. It was not long, however, before the Dutch were complaining that Khoikhoi herds were increasing at the same time as sales to the Dutch were declining: Khoikhoi, it was said, were willing to sell only old and thin stock.

This situation was due in part to a revival of the old inland trade

26. E.g. ibid., p. 200 (Jan. 3, 1654); 2: 40 (June 15, 1656).
27. Ibid., 1: 128 (Jan. 14, 1653).

network, and in part to the Peninsulars' new policy of brokerage. When inland Khoikhoi (then loosely called "Saldanhars") came to the fort to trade, the Peninsular Khoikhoi, who were indispensable as interpreters, insisted on supervising the entire barter and taking a percentage of the selling price. At other times they intercepted the incoming Saldanhars and told them tales which intensified their natural fear of the Europeans; the newcomers, knowing neither the language nor the going rate at the fort, often decided to sell their cattle to the Peninsulars, who then either kept them or sold them to the Dutch at a profit. So anxious were the Peninsulars to benefit from the Dutch trade, that they trailed Company expeditions into the interior in order to interfere with any barter which might take place.[28]

By these methods local Khoikhoi were able to capitalize on Van Riebeeck's desperate need for livestock and managed to triple the cost of both cattle and sheep within seven years (1652–59). They also found ways to obtain copper and tobacco without sacrificing their precious stock. Some bartered wild ducks and other birds, tortoise shells, ostrich feathers, and ostrich eggs. One group of Goringhaiqua brought in ten oxen laden with fish they had speared in a lake near False Bay. Another group, noting how the Dutch gathered salt from nearby pans, twice loaded a dozen oxen with salt and sold it at the fort for tobacco.[29]

The cleverness with which the Peninsular Khoikhoi exploited the Dutch presence was bound in the long run to recoil against them. As was normal in Khoikhoi society, their increasing wealth made them susceptible to attacks from hunters. More importantly, their role as middlemen led them into at least one war with Khoikhoi neighbors (Chainouqua?) who felt they had been cheated.[30] Their policy of frustrating contacts between the Dutch and inland groups made it almost inevitable that their many enemies would try to make common cause against them.

Van Riebeeck responded in two ways to the noose which the Peninsular Khoikhoi attempted to tighten around the colony. First, he tried to turn the blockade to his advantage by coopting Peninsular Khoikhoi to supply cattle and sheep to the fort under a monopoly arrangement. He turned both to whole tribes like the Goringhaiqua (to whom he naïvely offered Company protection in return for *all* their cattle!) and

28. E.g. ibid., p. 273 (Nov. 23, 1654); 2:36 (May 22, 1656); 370 (Nov. 7, 1658).
29. On prices see p. 162. On Khoikhoi enterprise see *VRJ*, 1:106 (Dec. 2, 1652); 2:83 (Jan. 20, 1657); 85 (Feb. 1, 1657).
30. Ibid., 1:379 (Dec. 22, 1655).

to the interpreter Harry, with whom he made several abortive contracts. At first he allowed Harry to take Dutch copper inland and bring back cattle from distant tribes; this scheme collapsed when Harry simply used the copper to purchase his own herds. Still later, when Harry had become rich, Van Riebeeck offered to pay him high prices and to make him a "paramount chief" if he would supply a fixed quota of ten cattle for every large ship (and five for every small one) that entered the harbor. This also failed. Barring a fundamental revision of traditional values, no Khoikhoi would long remain committed to an economic scheme that did not promise directly to increase his herds and flocks.[31]

Van Riebeeck's alternative strategy was to break through the cordon and make contact with inland tribes. This policy was given impetus by two factors: the Company's fervent desire to find marketable commodities in the interior, such as civet, musk, amber, and more ambitiously, gold and silver; and the expectation of the Dutch, nurtured by misinformation on the old Van Linschoten map, that they would find increasingly wealthy and powerful tribes as they pushed inland from the Cape toward the lands of Monomotapa.

Contact with the "Chariguriqua" (i.e. Guriqua) of Saldanha Bay was made as early as October 29, 1652, and was maintained thereafter by a series of coastal voyages from the Cape. In 1655, Jan Wintervogel penetrated fifty Dutch miles north of the Cape and became the first European to visit peoples whom the Khoikhoi designated as San. Strangely enough, contacts with the richest cattle-keeping tribes came somewhat later. So far as we know, the Chainouqua were not visited until June 6, 1657, and did not themselves venture to the fort until October 30–31 of that year. Though the Dutch had traded with Cochoqua and had even entertained Gonnoma, one of their chiefs, it was not until October 1658 that they negotiated with Cochoqua in the knowledge that they were distinct from the Peninsular Khoikhoi.[32] Prior to 1659, the Dutch enjoyed very little trade with non-Peninsular Khoikhoi, and it was not until just before the First Khoikhoi-Dutch War that Van Riebeeck's outward-looking policy began to bear real fruit. It may thus be said that the economic "blockade" imposed by the Peninsular Khoikhoi had held moderately firm.

31. Ibid., p. 313 (May 30, 1655); p. 337 (Aug. 17, 1655); p. 375 (Dec. 9, 1655); 2:38–39 (June 6, 1656).

32. Ibid., 1: 78 (Oct. 29, 1652); 305 (April 3, 1655); 2: 122 (June 6, 1657); 364–65 (Oct. 30, 1658).

While Van Riebeeck was pursuing the restrained policies so far described, his mind was at work on schemes to solve the problems of trade and theft in one brutal blow. In the first year of the settlement, during a frustrating phase of the trade, he had contemplated seizing the Goringhaiqua and all their cattle. The idea simmered in his mind until April 22, 1654, when he sent a full-blown proposal to the directors. The Peninsular Khoikhoi, he argued, were thwarting the inland trade, driving prices dangerously high, and threatening to harm Company servants. If the Company were to seize them—something which it could do without bloodshed—it would gain enough cattle and sheep to feed its ships and to start a permanent herd and flock in the colony. The Khoikhoi prisoners would be put in chains and set to work catching seals or digging in the (yet to be discovered) silver mines. With the Peninsular Khoikhoi removed, the way would then be open for establishing happy relations with inland tribes.[33]

The Seventeen did not reject this startling proposal out of hand, but asked Van Riebeeck to forbear a while and to report on further developments. Consequently, Van Riebeeck continued year after year to urge his proposal on the directors, while altering its supposed advantages to fit new circumstances. While he was awaiting permission from Holland, he resolved to lull the Khoikhoi into a state of false security: "and meanwhile we show them absolutely no hostility but all friendliness to retain their trust and make it grow, to the end that we will be able to handle them as we please all the better."[34]

To Van Riebeeck's disappointment, he never received approval from the Seventeen to implement his aggressive plans; he was thus obliged to seek recourse in less dramatic methods. Two main schemes were considered: Van Riebeeck himself advocated building a series of redoubts and watch-houses, while Commissioner Rijkloff van Goens favored digging a canal that would effectively cut the peninsula off from the rest of Africa. Both plans aimed, firstly, to protect the colony from potential Khoikhoi depredations, and secondly, to trap the Peninsular Khoikhoi and their stock within the colony. In an ingenious variation on the redoubt scheme, both Van Riebeeck and Van Goens suggested that some of the Peninsular Khoikhoi be lured into Hout Valley (on the peninsula) and then imprisoned there by means of five redoubts located in key kloofs. Under this scheme the

33. Ibid., 1:112 (Dec. 13, 1652); KA 3967, Van Riebeeck to XVII, April 22, 1654, pp. 13–14.
34. KA 455, XVII to Van Riebeeck, Oct. 30, 1655, p. 387. The quotation is in KA 3969, Van Riebeeck to XVII, March 5, 1657, p. 2v.

Khoikhoi would be prevented both from harming the colony and from making contact with potential allies in the interior. They would have adequate pasture for their animals, which they would be forced to barter to the Dutch on demand. Their leaders would be given copper to barter inland on behalf of the Company, while their families and stock would be retained in the valley as hostages to guarantee their speedy return.[35]

The Hout Valley scheme proved too expensive to implement, and the canal venture was abandoned when the first diggings were completely washed out by floods. Van Riebeeck thus turned to strengthening the borders of the colony with redoubts which he hoped could also serve as cattle posts.[36]

It was not, however, necessary to trap entire tribes in order to manipulate the Khoikhoi, and Van Riebeeck soon hit on another significant scheme—the taking of hostages. In June 1658, a number of Guinea slaves escaped from the colony, and Khoikhoi were suspected of harboring them. Urged by the Khoikhoi interpreter Eva and by several freemen, the council seized Gogosoa's sons, Schacher and Otegno. Then, on the insistence of the outraged Goringhaiqua, some Gorachouqua were also arrested, as was Harry, chief of the Strandlopers. Now that he had hostages from three Peninsular groups, Van Riebeeck was able to exert enough leverage to have some of the slaves returned. He was jubilant at the success of his manoeuvre, and argued that hostage-taking could be used regularly as a means of guaranteeing the flow of cattle and defending the colony against attack.[37]

The Three Interpreters: Harry, Eva, and Doman

The Dutch presence was a superb opportunity, not only for Khoikhoi tribes, but also for individual Khoikhoi who had the wit to seize it. Despite their much vaunted ability with European and even Asian tongues, the Dutch made scarcely a dent in understanding the Khoikhoi language in their first ten years at the Cape. They were consequently dependent on the first handful of Khoikhoi who learned Dutch; they relied on these interpreters, not only for translations, but also for geographic and ethnographic information and for advice on the making

---

35. Cape Archives, VC 36, Report of Rijkloff van Goens, 1657, pp. 5–19; KA 3968, Van Riebeeck to xvii, June 10, 1656, p. 300v; KA 3969, Van Riebeeck to xvii (in code), April 23, 1657, p. 359; KA 3970, Van Riebeeck to xvii, Aug. 31, 1657, pp. 4–5.

36. KA 3969, Van Riebeeck to Amsterdam Chamber, July 1, 1657, p. 410.

37. *VRJ*, 2:288–340 (June 22–Sept. 21, 1658).

of policies relating to Khoikhoi. The first ten years of the colony were enlivened by the careers of three of these interpreters, all of whom (so far as is known) had no particular wealth or rank in their own society,[38] but became, by dint of their linguistic attainments, influential with the Dutch and with their own people. Of these three personages—Harry, Eva, and Doman—the first chose to manipulate the Dutch for his own enrichment; the second, to win their affection through loyal service; and the third, to resist their colonial expansion. All three of them ultimately failed to attain their ends. All three died in poverty, having forfeited their former prestige among whites and Khoikhoi.

Harry, as we have seen, had had a great deal of experience with Europeans by the time the colony was founded. With his knowledge of English he established himself as the sole interpreter in the early years. He was well fed at the commander's table, and in return he offered his services as a guide, disclosed information about intra-Khoikhoi politics, and brought (or pretended to bring) cattle-keeping Khoikhoi to the fort to trade. It was not long before the Dutch became suspicious that he was in fact hindering rather than helping the trade. Their suspicions were confirmed on Sunday, October 19, 1653, when Harry, his wife, and children hastily deserted the fort while the Dutch were in church. Shortly afterward there was ominous news: most of the colony's fledgling herd had been stolen and the herdboy slain. Harry's responsibility for this incident was confirmed five years later by his niece Eva, a source usually eloquent on his behalf. With his newly acquired herd, Harry made his way to the nearby sand flats where he wandered about trying to evade both the Dutch and his enemies, the Goringhaiqua.[39]

It was the Goringhaiqua who finally found him and succeeded in capturing the stolen cattle. Harry was outmanoeuvred but by no means defeated. He proceeded first to make an alliance with the Cochoqua, the traditional enemies of the Goringhaiqua, and then, after almost two years' absence, he boldly returned to the fort in June 1655. Shrewdly relying on his value to the Dutch, he told Van Riebeeck that the robbery had been perpetrated by the Goringhaiqua, who, after all, were by then in possession of the missing cattle. The commander was taken in by this story, which was put forward with great

---

38. It is true that Harry was the Strandloper chief; however, all Strandlopers were despised by cattle-keeping Khoikhoi.

39. Ibid., 1:179–81 (Oct. 19–20, 1653); 184 (Oct. 27, 1653); 2:297 (July 3, 1658).

fervor and subtlety, and the interpreter was restored to his former position.

Harry then attempted to gain revenge on the Goringhaiqua by advising the very receptive Van Riebeeck to seize them and send them away by ship. He also endeavored to recoup his losses by engaging in trade as an agent of the Dutch. Here again he showed himself unreliable and managed to start his private herd with cattle he had ostensibly bought for the Dutch. Once again Van Riebeeck preferred to forgive him rather than risk a disruption of trade by taking harsh action.[40]

Harry now began to divide his time between translating at the fort and building up his own herd. By 1658 he had amassed at least 260 sheep and 227 cattle. He must now have been one of the most wealthy individuals on the peninsula, when it is remembered that the combined holdings of all the Peninsulars were put at only 3,000 cattle and 2,000 sheep. As Harry became more wealthy, the cattle-keepers began to lose their hostility toward him; and indeed, from 1657 onward, he emerged as the leading spokesman of all the Peninsulars against the rising threat of their common enemy, the Cochoqua. So remarkable was his elevation from his scrounging origins, that the Peninsular Khoikhoi began to call themselves "Harry's people" when they were speaking to the Dutch.[41]

It is unlikely that Harry ever intended to challenge or resist the Dutch in their settlement of the Cape. His power among Khoikhoi depended as much on his continuing influence with the Dutch as on his own wealth. He was very frightened of Company employees, many of whom threatened to kill him, and he risked everything on his curious friendship with Van Riebeeck. As the commander's patience with him began to wear thin, he began to fear that his doom was near. On one occasion at the fort he was "shaking and trembling with fear like a lady's lap-dog."[42]

For reasons that are obscure, the Peninsular Khoikhoi turned against Harry in the winter of 1658. During the hostage crisis, which has already been described, Doman, the Goringhaiqua's spokesman at the

---

40. Ibid., 1:319–24 (June 23–24, 1655); 351–55 (Journal of Corporal Muller, Sept. 7–Oct. 5, 1655); 376 (Dec. 12, 1655).

41. For the extent of Harry's wealth, see ibid., 2: 304 (July 7, 1658); this figure included a very few animals which he herded for others. See also KA 3970, Van Riebeeck to XVII, Feb. 22, 1658, p. 403.

42. *VRJ*, 2:78 (Dec. 9, 1656).

fort, convinced Van Riebeeck to seize Harry and impound his cattle. Harry was dragged before the council and confronted by the other interpreters, Doman and Eva, who testified that he had defrauded the Company. As punishment he and two followers were banished to Robben Island and his herds were confiscated.[43]

During the First Khoikhoi-Dutch War, Harry was twice recalled to the mainland to assist the Dutch as a guide and adviser. In December 1659, he escaped from the island in a leaky boat and crossed to the mainland over a heavy sea—an amazing achievement for an elderly Khoikhoi who had presumably never rowed or sailed on his own before. He now put aside his ambitions of pastoral wealth and settled down as a translator and spokesman, sometimes for the Goringhaiqua, sometimes for the Gorachouqua. The Dutch, who were now in a much more secure position, did nothing to deprive him of his freedom; and amongst Khoikhoi he seems to have retained some small influence, even though he had lost the leadership of the Strandlopers during his imprisonment.[44]

Harry died in 1663, the year after Van Riebeeck, his erstwhile mentor, had left the Cape.[45] Harry had been a man of many skills—a bold entrepreneur, a talented linguist, and a shrewd diplomat and manipulator of men. His life is better documented than that of any other seventeenth-century Khoikhoi; yet it is hard in this abundance of data to find evidence that his complex manoeuvres were motivated by anything other than self-interest. His relations with the Dutch were so changeable that it would be wrong to call him either a collaborator or a resistance leader. Furthermore, he was not consistently loyal to any Khoikhoi group, being at different times associated with the Strandlopers, the Goringhaiqua, the Gorachouqua, and the Cochoqua. His complex career well illustrates patterns of Khoikhoi culture that were discussed in part 1; namely, the remarkable ease with which individual Khoikhoi could move from one political unit to another, and from a cattleless economy to a pastoral economy and back again.

A contrast to Harry in almost every way was his "niece" Krotoa, or Eva (1642 or 1643 to 1674). Eva had extensive kinship ties with several Khoikhoi groups. She had one "uncle" (Harry) among the Strand-lopers and another among the Chainouqua, a "mother" with the

43. Ibid., p. 307 (July 8, 1658).
44. Ibid., 3:161 (Dec. 8–13, 1659); 183 (Feb. 17, 1660).
45. Moodie, *The Record*, p. 291.

Goringhaiqua and another with the Cochoqua. In addition her "sister," who was formerly the wife of Goeboe, the de facto Chainouqua
chief, was now (by act of seizure in war) the most important wife of
the Cochoqua chief Oedasoa.[46] It is very unlikely that Eva correctly
understood European kinship terms, because at this time there were
only one or two European nuclear families at the Cape, and no extended
families. Consequently, her revelations about her own family must be
considered in the context of the Khoikhoi classificatory kinship system.
Various interpretations are possible, but the most likely one sees Eva
as the biological daughter of a Goringhaiqua woman; her Cochoqua
"mother" and "sister" would be a maternal aunt (or father's brother's
wife) and a female cousin, respectively.

Soon after the foundation of the colony, Eva took service in the Van
Riebeecks' household, first temporarily and then permanently. It is
not known whether her family encouraged her in this or whether she
had simply been abandoned by them. Eva displayed a marked aptitude
for languages, mastering Dutch and gaining fairly fluent Portuguese.[47]
She also responded eagerly to the religious instruction of the pious
Mrs. van Riebeeck and became, so far as is known, the first Christian
native of South Africa. She wore Dutch (more correctly, "Indian")
clothes, became fond of Dutch food, and later was to admit that she
had a "Dutch heart" inside her. At the same time she kept contact
with her own people, who in those early days mingled with the Dutch
at the fort. Eva was employed by Van Riebeeck as a translator, the
most reliable he had yet found. In the hostage crisis of June 1658, she
firmly established her reputation as a friend of Dutch interests.

Shortly thereafter, on September 23, 1658, Eva left the fort on a
mysterious trip into the interior. As she was then about fifteen, it is
probable that she had reached the age of puberty and was returning
to her relatives to undergo the ceremonial prescribed for every Khoikhoi girl of her age. She went first to the Goringhaiqua; there her
mother (as we suppose, her biological mother) did not receive her—
maybe because of her association with the Dutch—and she was
attacked and robbed. Fleeing on, she found refuge with her "sister,"
who was the wife of Oedasoa, the powerful subchief of the Cochoqua.
Most probably she underwent her ritual isolation and reentry cere-

46. *VRJ*, 2:305 (July 7, 1658); 362 (Oct. 29, 1658); 3:78 (June 23, 1659); 91 (July 8, 1659);
270 (Oct. 5, 1660).

47. *VRJ*, 1:208 (Jan. 28, 1654); 3:260 (Sept. 21, 1660); 2:373 (Nov. 9, 1658); 3:308 (Dec.
26, 1660).

monies among the Cochoqua. Oedasoa was very kind to her and promised that he would marry her to a rich captain. She in turn urged Oedasoa to trade with the Dutch and informed him of Van Riebeeck's ostensibly benevolent policies. At this point she saw no conflict between her affection for her Dutch family, the Van Riebeecks, and her ties to her Khoikhoi cousins. She was particularly earnest in her childlike attempts to share her Christian beliefs with her people:

> She added that . . . she had been very ill, as also her sister, Oedasoa's wife, whom she had taught how to pray to our blessed Lord, to which (as she said and indicated by action) all the natives listened with tears in their eyes. . . . The Cochoquas had . . . told her to learn everything carefully from us so that she could teach them because, she said, she had prayed night and day, when she was not sleepy or asleep, until her sister also had recovered. . . . This was very pleasing to the natives who were desirous of further instruction.[48]

Now began a period when Eva regularly moved back and forth between the fort and the Cochoqua, exchanging her Batavian dress for Khoikhoi skins each time she went. She was of great value to both Oedasoa and Van Riebeeck, both of whom were anxious to come to an understanding. Each relied on her advice in dealing with the other, and in both societies she enjoyed a brief period of great prestige. When she was on a mission she rode on the back of an ox, a privilege which denoted high station among Khoikhoi. Eva was the only person at the Cape who was totally at ease in the very different cultures of the fort and the kraal; in coming years her dual culture was to become a curse which, along with other misfortunes, would finally destroy her. But for the moment her skills were unique and in great demand, and from them she derived a season of satisfaction and triumph.

Of Doman, [49] the third of the great interpreters, less is known than of Eva or Harry. His family background and early life are totally obscure. Yet he was probably more important than the other two, being the only Khoikhoi leader of the seventeenth century to emerge

---

48. Ibid., 2:362–64 (Oct. 29, 1658). On Khoikhoi puberty rites, see Schapera, *Khoisan Peoples*, pp. 272 ff.

49. Doman's name was probably a Khoikhoi nickname related to his translator's function (the Namaqua word for voice is *domi*), but the Dutch interpreted it as *dominee* (parson) because they initially thought that he was "such an artless person." See *VRJ*, 1:376 (Dec. 12, 1655).

as an effective advocate of resisting Dutch presence and expansion in South Africa.[50] His brief career was marked by consistent loyalty to the Peninsular Khoikhoi and by an absence of that flexibility in choosing allies which was so characteristic of Harry.

Doman's hostility to the Dutch probably dated from 1657–58, when he was taken to Batavia to prepare himself to be an interpreter at the Cape. While in Java he was apparently struck by the magnitude of the threat which the Dutch could pose to an indigenous society. At the same time he witnessed the climax of the spirited resistance which the Bantamese put up against Dutch domination of the north shore of the island. On his way back to the Cape, Doman told Commissioner Joan Cunaeus that he was attracted to Christianity, and that he was now so devoted to the Dutch that he could never live with his fellow Khoikhoi again.[51] These professions were purely tactical. Almost as soon as he landed at the Cape, he began to emerge as a fiery critic of Van Riebeeck's policies and as an advocate for the Goringhaiqua, whom Van Riebeeck intended to be the chief victims of his plots.

When Van Riebeeck seized several Khoikhoi leaders as hostages in June 1658, Doman was the first to perceive the long-term significance of such behavior for Khoikhoi independence. In the early stages of the crisis, when even the hostages themselves welcomed their imprisonment as a chance to enjoy Dutch hospitality, Doman alone protested. Before long Van Riebeeck was regretting that he had sent him to Batavia.

There now began a period of confrontation between Doman and the well-established Eva. Their animosity to each other was rooted, not only in different tribal loyalties (Doman spoke for the Peninsulars, Eva for the Cochoqua), but also in their radically different attitudes to the Dutch and their culture. When Eva passed by, Doman would tauntingly call, "See, there comes the advocate of the Dutch; she will tell her people some stories and lies and will finally betray them all."[52] He ridiculed her Christian beliefs and the Peninsular Khoikhoi followed his example. Whenever Eva divulged geographical information to the

---

50. In my opinion, Gonnema should not be regarded as a resistance leader in this sense; the bulk of the evidence in his case suggests that he acted only defensively, and only when no other choices remained to him. See pp. 127–30.

51. *VRJ*, 3:47, n. 1; *Memoriën en Instructiën, 1657–1699*, ed. A. J. Böeseken (Cape Town: Publikasie-Afdeling van die Kantoor van die Direkteur van Argiewe, 1966), pp. 16–17.

52. *VRJ*, 2:289–90 (June 22–23, 1658). The quotation is in ibid., p. 328 (Aug. 26, 1658).

Dutch, Doman tried to stop her. When the Dutch planned expeditions to the interior, he threatened their safety. Operating from a hut near the fort, he strove to intercept all inland visitors to the settlement, and pushed himself forward as the official interpreter and broker in all white-Khoikhoi transactions.[53]

In short, Doman was pursuing the traditional Goringhaiqua policies of economically blockading the fort and thwarting any conjunction between the Dutch and inland peoples. Unfortunately, by 1659 these policies had roused the ire of inland Khoikhoi. As a consequence, Doman was so bitterly hated by non-Peninsular Khoikhoi that he was terrified to venture up-country and was once beaten at the fort by the Cochoqua.[54] His widespread unpopularity was later to be decisive to his failure in the First Khoikhoi-Dutch War.

The First Khoikhoi-Dutch War and its Aftermath

In February 1657, the East India Company released a number of its "servants" (i.e. employees) from their contracts so that they could become free settlers at the Cape. These freemen were to raise livestock and hence to relieve the Company of reliance on the trade which the Peninsular Khoikhoi had rendered sluggish. They were also to grow crops that would free the colony from dependence on Batavian rice. The formation of a society of free white farmers was probably the most significant event in the history of modern South Africa, and it would one day affect the lives of millions of the region's inhabitants.

Peninsular Khoikhoi were very alive to the immediate significance of the new social order. It was now absolutely certain that the Dutch presence was permanent; moreover, it was likely to be expansive. Gogosoa and Harry objected to the settlement plan even before it was implemented: when the farms were actually surveyed and Khoikhoi pasture was put under the plough, their protests became more frequent and bitter.[55] Not only were the Khoikhoi deprived of pasture, but they were inhibited from using long-established sources of water on the peninsula. In addition, the new settlers, now released from the discipline of life at the fort, were able to vent their long-suppressed hostility to the Khoikhoi. Several acts of violence were committed, and the Khoi-

---

53. *VRJ*, 2:350 (Oct. 8, 1658); 3:17 (Feb. 8, 1659).
54. Ibid., 3:39 (May 8, 1659).
55. Ibid., 2:89 (Feb. 20, 1657); 135 (July 27, 1657).

khoi, in their own explanation of the causes of the war, ranked freeman misbehavior alongside the question of pastures.[56]

It was awkward that at the very moment when the Peninsular Khoikhoi were losing their Cape pastures, they were being pushed from the other side by the Cochoqua. As a result of Eva's patient diplomacy, the Cochoqua and the Dutch had broken the Peninsular blockade and had become friends and trading partners. Cochoqua were now coming to the Cape more often than formerly, were demanding pasture for their numerous stock, and were arrogantly asserting their hegemony over the Peninsular Khoikhoi. Suddenly, in part as a result of their own policies, the Peninsular peoples found themselves ground between two equally hostile forces.

It was not entirely coincidental that Van Riebeeck was at the same time vigorously at work devising new formulas for enslaving the Peninsular Khoikhoi. We do not know for how long the local Khoikhoi— who, until Doman's return from Java in March 1658, had no reliable spy at the fort—were fooled by Van Riebeeck's policy of hypocritical friendship. However by August 31, 1657, Van Riebeeck noted that Khoikhoi were becoming so suspicious that they would no longer come to the fort, and he expressed concern that so many of them could now understand Dutch.[57] Without doubt, the seizure of hostages in 1658 further alarmed the Peninsulars, even though only Harry was permanently banished. The Seventeen later argued that Harry's exile was a cause of the war; Van Riebeeck, who thought hostage-taking one of his brightest ideas, firmly denied this contention.[58]

It was into this very tense situation that Doman brought, not only a lucid interpretation of events, but also a concrete plan. As he had no wealth or prestige of his own, he had to win over the Peninsular leadership to his view that the colony must be scotched before it could grow further. In his arguments he probably drew on his own experiences in Batavia and on inklings of Van Riebeeck's plots which he had picked up at the fort. Gogosoa resisted his pleas and argued that

56. Ibid., 3:176 (Jan. 18, 1660); KA 3972, Van Riebeeck to Batavia, July 29, 1659, pp. 46–46v. Khoikhoi had also suffered for years from depredations committed by slaves in desperate flight from the colony. However, since the Company had eagerly cooperated with Khoikhoi in capturing and punishing the slaves, Khoikhoi did not apparently hold this as a grievance against the white colony.

57. KA 3970, Van Riebeeck to xvii, Aug. 31, 1657, pp. 4v–5.

58. KA 456, xvii to Van Riebeeck, Aug. 21, 1660, pp. 355–56; KA 3973, Van Riebeeck to xvii, May 4, 1661, pp. 578v–79.

it would be folly for the Peninsular Khoikhoi to attack the Dutch as long as the Cochoqua remained hostile. Nonetheless, Doman seems to have won the support of younger leaders; slowly he formed around himself a coalition of Goringhaiqua, Gorachouqua, and warriors of Ankaisoa. He himself assumed command of military operations.[59]

The Khoikhoi timed their attack to coincide with the onset of the rainy season, for Doman knew that in a downpour the Dutch match-cords could not burn and their powder could not ignite. In May 1659, he directed a series of quick, well-coordinated, and usually successful raids against the herds of the freemen. A cry for revenge arose through-out the small colony, and Oedasoa joined the freemen in urging Van Riebeeck to retaliate. On May 19 the Council of Policy resolved to mount a punitive expedition, and freemen were authorized to seize and shoot Khoikhoi on sight. The First Khoikhoi-Dutch War had begun.[60]

The war lasted almost a year, and though it seriously disrupted life for both sides, it resulted in few deaths. The Khoikhoi wanted to drive the Dutch out of South Africa by depriving them of their cattle and destroying their crops; they did not want to goad them into massive retaliation.[61] As a consequence, they killed Europeans only when it was necessary to achieve their limited ends. Throughout May and June the Khoikhoi attacked, often in groups of several hundreds, and usually on rainy days. They leapt about erratically in order to frustrate the Dutch marksmen. The speed of the Khoikhoi helped in large part to offset their lack of fire power: the Dutch had few usable horses, were themselves slow of foot, and had little experience with the rapid hit-and-run warfare at which the Khoikhoi were so adept.

The Dutch failed in every early attempt at offensive action, mainly because they had no reliable guides. (Harry was periodically recalled from Robben Island but was not much help.) As a result they con-centrated primarily on defense, withdrawing the freemen from their farms and taking them back into the Company's service at the fort. Slaves were released from irons and given light arms—an extraordinary expedient that showed how desperate Van Riebeeck deemed his posi-tion to be. [62] Cannons were deployed in the hope of terrifying Khoikhoi

---

59. *VRJ*, 3:46 (May 19, 1659); KA 3972, Van Riebeeck to xvii, March 19, 1660, pp. 3 ff.
60. *VRJ*, 3:36–50 (May 4–20, 1659).
61. Ibid., p. 63 (June 3, 1659).
62. Ibid., p. 51 (May 21, 1659).

intruders, and a strong central kraal was built to protect what remained of the colony's herds and flocks.

With the completion of all these defensive arrangements the struggle was virtually stalemated. The Khoikhoi had done most of the damage they could do to the outlying areas of the colony. (During the war the Dutch lost 148 of their best cattle and 113 sheep; five farms were destroyed and two others partially damaged.)[63] The Khoikhoi could do no more without making good their boast to storm the walls of the fort—an action which they were clearly reluctant to undertake. The Dutch on their side could neither harm the Khoikhoi nor recover their losses.

Van Riebeeck hoped to break the deadlock by making a treaty with the Cochoqua, who were at the time very close to the Cape. Embassies were sent back and forth between the fort and Oedasoa's kraal. For a while Van Riebeeck's hopes were high, but at length Oedasoa decided, for reasons discussed in the next chapter, to remain neutral and to withdraw to the interior. Van Riebeeck became alarmed, since from his perspective it seemed that the Cochoqua and Peninsular Khoikhoi were forming a coalition against him that would lead to a combined assault on the fort. However, this threat, like the opportunity which had preceded it, came to nothing.

In midwinter the Dutch were victorious in two minor skirmishes. In one of these Doman was seriously wounded in the shoulder and one of his arms was paralyzed. On the other occasion, Corporal Elias Giers surprised a group of Strandlopers—whose part in the war was never clearly defined—and killed several of them, including Trosoa, Harry's successor as chief.[64] The effect of these two blows was great, not directly on the military capacity of the Khoikhoi, but indirectly on their morale. The Peninsular Khoikhoi decided to trek inland, which they normally did at this time of year in any event, and to have a rest from the conflict. They took advantage of Oedasoa's permission to settle at Saldanha Bay, far from the long arm of the Dutch. In defeat the Peninsular alliance crumbled: the Goringhaiqua and Gorachouqua quarreled and parted company. Doman was increasingly abused by other leaders on account of the losses which had been suffered.[65]

Both sides were now ready for peace. The Khoikhoi made the first

63. KA 3972, Van Riebeeck to xvii, March 19, 1660, p. 3v.
64. *VRJ*, 3:100–02 (July 19, 1659); 109–10 (Aug. 4–5, 1659).
65. Ibid., p. 133 (Sept. 21, 1659).

overtures in September, and Van Riebeeck, without appearing too anxious, did everything he could to encourage them. Negotiations were conducted intermittently over a five-month period by Eva, acting on behalf of Oedasoa, and by Harman Remajenne, a freeman who had managed to keep illegal contacts with Khoikhoi throughout the war. In October 1659, the surviving Strandlopers were allowed to return to the fort; this reassured the cattle-keepers of the good intentions of the Dutch, and eventually some of them came hesitantly to the fort to parley. The Goringhaiqua concluded peace in early April 1660, followed by the Gorachouqua later in the month.

The peace terms recognized that the war had been largely inconclusive and by no means a resounding Dutch victory. The Khoikhoi were not required to return any booty acquired during the war, and one of their main grievances, the misbehavior of freemen, was to be dealt with by new procedures of complaint and redress. On the other hand, the Khoikhoi gave up their claim to the pastures occupied by the settlers and agreed to come to the fort only by certain routes laid out by Van Riebeeck.[66] Had this been a traditional war, the peace terms would have been far from disastrous for the Khoikhoi; but in a war against an alien, farming community, they had lost the crucial point: they had accepted its existence and hence the likelihood of its subsequent expansion.

In recent years historians have begun to classify African resistance movements in various categories that range from the initial "soldier-to-soldier" defense put up by traditional political units, to the sociopolitical nationalism of modern mass movements. The First Khoikhoi-Dutch War was clearly very near the traditional end of the spectrum. Doman's movement was based, it is true, on a temporary alliance of several distinct tribes, but they were all subject to one overlord and they had often been allied before against Khoikhoi enemies. It had, so far as we know, no new ideological or millennial dynamic, and it failed to develop any goals or strategies beyond those of a conventional cattle war.[67] On the other hand, Doman himself was no traditional chief but a "new man," thrust forward by events and utilizing much information which he had learned from contact with whites. Still, it should be noted that the mechanisms which allowed him to rise to

66. Ibid., pp. 195–97 (April 5–6, 1660); 204–05 (April 27, 1660).

67. It is, however, true that Doman, who had learned the use of firearms in Batavia, stole a gun for use in the war.

brief preeminence were as much a part of flexible Khoikhoi political structures as they were a result of Dutch pressure.

As for Doman himself, Eva asserted that he had kept most of the booty the Khoikhoi had captured early in the war, to become, like Harry before him, a "kinglet" on the peninsula.[68] There is no direct evidence whatever for this charge, which came from an exceedingly hostile source. In any event, the setbacks during the war shattered Doman's position, and he retained a modicum of respect among his people solely because they continued to need him as an interpreter. In December 1663 he died, unlamented by the Company, whose diarist coolly observed: "For [his] death none of us will have cause to grieve, as he has been, in many respects, a mischievous and malicious man towards the Company."[69]

The conclusion of the Khoikhoi war left the Dutch undisputed masters of the Cape Peninsula, though Khoikhoi were still allowed to pasture on land unoccupied by white farmers. During the war Van Riebeeck had placed a series of watchhouses around the colony's borders (see map 4). Newly supplied with horses from Batavia, he found that twenty riders could keep Khoikhoi in check without further fortifications. Still, as an added precaution, he began the planting of hedges of bitter almond and thorn, aimed not so much at keeping Khoikhoi out of the colony as at stopping them from driving out colonial cattle. Khoikhoi who wished to come onto the peninsula were forced to pass through the hedge at given points and to use designated routes to pastures in the Hout and Berg Valleys. By November 1660, Van Riebeeck was able to say that the settlement was now so well protected that everyone could have a "feeling of great security."[70]

The Dutch position was further strengthened by the renewal of the outward policy. In April 16, 1658, the Seventeen had empowered Van Riebeeck to encourage inland expeditions by giving a bounty to explorers. After the peace the frequency and length of exploratory ventures increased markedly. These were directed mainly at finding the empire of Monomotapa, which the Dutch wrongly believed to be in their immediate hinterland; however, the main effect of exploration was the opening up of relations with new Khoikhoi groups, chiefly

68. KA 3972, Van Riebeeck to Batavia, June 4, 1659, p. 38.

69. Moodie, *The Record*, p. 272 (DR Dec. 12, 1663). This statement is omitted from the copy of DR in the Hague archives.

70. KA 3973, Van Riebeeck to XVII, March 11, 1661, pp. 23v–24; *VRJ*, 3:279 (Nov. 6, 1660).

Guriqua and Namaqua. The Dutch were becoming increasingly less dependent on the Peninsular Khoikhoi for their meat supply.

In 1662, when Van Riebeeck left the Cape, the Dutch were in a stronger position vis-à-vis Khoikhoi than they had ever been. One would have to admit that the first commander's Khoikhoi policies had been broadly successful. But had they been just? His term of office had been marked by a strange incompatibility between his fierce proposals to the directors and his patient, subtle, and often generous actions. This ambivalence has long troubled historians. Van Riebeeck's biographer, C. Louis Leipoldt, argued that his generosity was real, while his vindictiveness was an artificial response to the anti-Khoikhoi clamor of his subordinates. On the other hand, Theal felt that Van Riebeeck's inmost inclinations were toward a violent solution, and that he pursued the policy of kindness purely out of a determination to obey orders.[71] Both of these interpretations ignored a considerable body of evidence.

The modern reader may well abandon the attempt to reconcile the two sides of Van Riebeeck's character. His response to the native Khoikhoi was, like that of many colonials in other times and places, at its deepest level dualistic. At times he was in the grip of totalitarian fantasies that derived from semirational fears of a native population whose behavior he could not predict; at others he displayed a tolerant affection born of the highest principles of his religion and nurtured in day-to-day contact with Khoikhoi. Of Van Riebeeck one may say what one can say of few men: that his actions were far nobler than his aspirations.

71. C. Louis Leipoldt, *Jan van Riebeeck: A Biographical Study* (London, New York, and Toronto: Longmans, Green and Co., 1936), p. 199; Theal, *History of South Africa*, 1:40, 45.

6

The Cochoqua and the North:
The Failure of Noncooperation

The speed at which various Khoikhoi tribes came into contact with the Dutch was naturally determined in part by their distance from Cape Town, the pied-à-terre of the Europeans in South Africa. In this regard the Cape Khoikhoi fall into three groupings: (1) the Peninsulars in the environs of Cape Town itself; (2) the so-called *omliggende Hottentotten* or Nearby Khoikhoi—the Cochoqua, Chainouqua, and Hessequa, all of whom were within fairly easy reach of the fort; and (3) the Khoikhoi of the Borderlands (Guriqua and Little Namaqua in the north and Inqua, Attaqua, etc. in the east). After the First Khoikhoi-Dutch War, the Company became increasingly less concerned with the Peninsulars, whose continuing disintegration made them less of a threat and less of an opportunity. On the other hand, the Company had more and more dealings with the Nearby Khoikhoi, the wealthiest and most tightly organized peoples in the Western Cape. The history of interaction between the Dutch and these peoples lasted until late in the seventeenth century, by which time the disintegration of these communities was, like that of the Peninsulars before them, virturally complete.

The Cochoqua and their Neighbors before 1658

The Cochoqua,[1] the Khoikhoi tribe destined to put up the strongest resistance to the Dutch, clearly excelled the Peninsulars in size, wealth, and political organization. The ensign Jan van Harwarden was the first European to visit the Cochoqua, and he reported on them enthusiastically:

---

1. Wuras ("Account of the Korana," p. 289) interprets *Cochoqua* as "sheep holders." I am more inclined to explain this name as "mountain people" (the Cape Khoikhoi word for mountain, */ku*, + *kwequa*, people). See Nienaber, *Hottentots*, pp. 217 (*berg*) and 385 (*mens*) as well as p. 82 n. 37 of this work.

in the army of the States General, where he had long served, he had never seen so many men together, distributed over a number of camps or armies, all equally strong men, living in large round huts made of mats, at least 30 or 40 feet in diameter.[2]

This was perhaps a bit of an exaggeration, for our best estimations of the Cochoqua population range only from 16,000 to 18,000. Cochoqua thus numbered two to five times the combined Peninsular population, though Van Riebeeck said once that they seemed to be ten times as large. Estimates of their stock are not consistent or particularly reliable, but they do at least make it clear that the Cochoqua far exceeded the Peninsulars in wealth.[3]

The Cochoqua roamed over the fertile pastures which stretched north from the vicinity of Table Bay to the Great Berg River and beyond. In 1664 some stray Cochoqua, possibly outpost herders, were found as far north as the Olifants River.[4] The territory of the tribe was in effect a long corridor bound by hunter-infested mountains on the east and by the sea on the west; in addition, the Cochoqua claimed a right to pasture both at Saldanha Bay and on the Cape Peninsula. Their transhumance pattern is not known, save that in the early years of the colony they seem to have moved southward in the summer months of November, December, and January.

The Cochoqua were divided into two sections under the eminent chiefs, Oedasoa and Gonnema. Doman asserted that Gonnema was the "paramount"; but the Chainouqua, a better source, said that he was only a "vice-chieftain" under Oedasoa. After some wavering, the Dutch adopted the second viewpoint.[5] In practice, however, the two chiefs treated each other as equals: on occasion they could quarrel and separate, but a sense of historical solidarity obtained between them and prevented their warring with one another.

Oedasoa was described in 1658 as a "beardless man, elderly, small

2. *VRJ*, 2:367 (Oct. 31, 1658).

3. On population, see Van Riebeeck's estimate of 17–18,000 in *VRJ*, 3:253 (Aug. 25–26, 1660) and of 16,000 in KA 3973, Van Riebeeck to Gerrit van Harn, n.d. [1660 or 1661], p. 664. This latter estimate was not repeated in the redrafting of this document for Zacharias Wagenaar (see Moodie, *The Record*, p. 247, which has only "several thousand men"). These figures are not consistent with Oedasoa's claim that Gonnema alone had 6–8,000 men-at-arms (*VRJ*, 3:360 [March 16, 1661]). Gonnema's wealth was variously put at 20,000 cattle and 15–16,000 cattle and sheep (*VRJ*, 2:370–71 [Nov. 7, 1658]). Dapper (VRS 14, p. 23) unreliably gave the combined Cochoqua wealth as 100,000 cattle and 200,000 sheep.

4. *VRJ*, 3:102 (July 19, 1659); KA 3976, DR Jan. 22, 1664, n.p.

5. *VRJ*, 2:357 (Oct. 21, 1658); 3:85 (July 1, 1659); 260 (Sept. 21, 1660).

and thin." The Dutch were impressed by his stately bearing and by the great authority he enjoyed among his people. He possessed three dwellings, which were larger than those of ordinary Khoikhoi, "and as full of assegais, arrows and bows as if they were armour rooms." He slept on an exceedingly fine mat, and was so besmeared "that the fat ran down his body, which was the highest mark of distinction." In his dealings with the Dutch he was reserved, courteous, normally temperate in his use of alcohol, and favorably inclined to Christianity.[6] When he visited the fort he was sometimes accompanied by Koukosoa, the second-in-command in his subtribe, or by his attractive daughter Namies.

Gonnema, the chief of the Cochoqua subtribe known as the Gorona,[7] was a larger man than Oedasoa but less imposing in appearance. Dapper, who is, however, not always accurate, says that he was coarse and corpulent. Gonnema visited the colony very soon after its founding. The Dutch dubbed him the "Black Captain" and held him in very low esteem. Gonnema also formed a poor opinion of the Dutch: so deep-seated was his distrust of them that for most of Van Riebeeck's period he stayed clear of the colony and left Oedasoa free to intrigue with the Dutch alone.[8]

The considerable wealth possessed by the Cochoqua in the 1650s was probably a testimony to a period of fairly successful wars with their neighbors. This wealth, however, excited the covetousness of other Khoikhoi groups and contributed to the Cochoqua's main problem —an almost complete diplomatic isolation from other Khoikhoi tribes. Though they occasionally made transitory alliances, the Cochoqua normally stood alone against enemies on three sides: the Guriqua to the north, the Peninsulars to the south, and the Chainouqua to the southeast. Furthermore, they could not outflank their enemies by allying with one of the two other great tribes of the region, for the Namaqua were normally aligned with the Guriqua and the Hessequa with the Chainouqua.

6. Ibid., 2:366–67 (Oct. 31, 1658); 405–06 (Dec. 31, 1658); 3:435 (Nov. 16–18, 1661).

7. We have only two references (*VRJ*, 2:170 [Oct. 31, 1657] and 185 [Nov. 15, 1657]) to the term *Gorona*. Harinck ("Xhosa and Khoi," p. 161) interprets this name as Korana, but both references make it clear that the Gorona were a subgroup of the Cochoqua. It was Khoikhoi custom to place the infix *ma* before the termination of a father's name in order to make an honorific name for his son. Hence Gonnema(b)'s father was probably Gono(b) or Gona(b). Since intervocalic *r* and *n* are often interchanged in Khoikhoi (Nienaber, *Hottentots*, p. 183), the Gorona are probably the people of Gono.

8. *VRJ*, 3:388 (May 16, 1661).

The hostility between Cochoqua and Chainouqua is a fairly reliable constant in the otherwise tangled history of shifting Khoikhoi alliances. Though Cochoqua and Chainouqua pastures bordered one another just a few hours away from the Dutch fort, grazing land was apparently not the main object of dispute. The real issues seem to have been the traditional Khoikhoi themes of cattle, prestige, and women. The Chainouqua chiefs claimed a higher title than the Cochoqua chiefs, whom, they said, they could rightfully remove from office. Oedasoa himself explicitly recognized the suzerainty of the Chainouqua and was occasionally forced to bow to their superior strength; yet he was anxious to assert at least a de facto independence, and it may have been partly for this reason that he pursued his constant wars. During the 1650s the contest was made personal and vindictive by quarrels over women. In a particularly bold move, Oedasoa had carried off and married the wife of Goeboe, the heir-apparent to the Chainouqua chieftainship. On another occasion the Cochoqua murdered the wife of Chaihantima, an important Chainouqua chief; a war broke out over this issue in 1659, and the Chainouqua were defeated.[9] This was only one of several Chainouqua-Cochoqua wars of which there are clear echoes in the records of the early colony.[10]

It might be expected that the Peninsulars, who lived close to the boundaries of the two antagonists, would try to play off their powerful neighbors against one another. At least in the 1650s they did not do so, but rather sided with the Chainouqua, to whom they looked for protection. This alliance, which was sealed by a marriage between Goeboe and one of Gogosoa's daughters, was necessary to the Peninsulars because of the Cochoqua's periodic attempts to assert their hegemony over them and to occupy the pastures near Table Bay.

The hatred between Cochoqua and Peninsulars went back at least one generation and was fanned by memories of past wrongs. Shortly before 1652, the Peninsulars had fallen upon the Cochoqua when the latter were licking their wounds after being defeated by another tribe. The victorious Peninsulars had then allegedly indulged in atrocities unusual for Khoikhoi, such as splitting open pregnant women. On their side, the Cochoqua had given the Peninsulars cause for bitterness;

9. Ibid., p. 162 (Dec. 14, 1659); pp. 259–60 (Sept. 21, 1660); pp. 264–66 (Sept. 27–28, 1660); p. 445 (Dec. 1, 1661).

10. See, for example, ibid., p. 70 (June 20, 1659) for a reference to Cochoqua fighting an inland tribe just before 1652, and p. 440 (Nov. 27, 1661) for news of a Cochoqua-Chainouqua war "4 years ago."

for example, Oedasoa's brother had once eloped with a Peninsular's wife and had killed another Peninsular in a hunting accident. This vendetta is prominent in our sources, but we should remember that the small Peninsular tribes were, as Oedasoa's elders once advised him, "the least of [the Cochoqua's] enemies."[11]

To the north of the Cochoqua lay the numerous Guriqua clans who, while not nearly as numerous as the Cochoqua, were fairly wealthy. Formerly the Cochoqua had entrusted the Guriqua with grazing many of their cattle, but the Guriqua, spotting a chance to enrich themselves, had dishonestly retained some of their patrons' stock. This had led to a punitive war in which the Guriqua lost even more cattle to Oedasoa than they had originally stolen, and were consequently forced to turn to the Namaqua, who became their new patrons and protectors. For this, and no doubt for other reasons, by 1661 the Cochoqua had long been hostile to both Guriqua and Namaqua. Oedasoa was especially anxious to prevent the Namaqua from moving south toward the Cape, for their numerous stock would have rapidly exhausted pastures which the Cochoqua considered their own.[12]

THE COCHOQUA AND THEIR NEIGHBORS, 1658–1672

The Dutch establishment at the Cape offered the Cochoqua a perfect chance to outflank the Peninsulars by allying with the newcomers. The Cochoqua were at first thwarted in this desire by the fact that the Peninsulars blocked the routes to the fort and monopolized all the linguistic skills necessary for communicating with the Dutch. This physical and psychological blockade was first broken by Eva's visit to Oedasoa's camp in 1658. Eva assiduously cultivated in Oedasoa and Van Riebeeck the highest regard for the other's character and intent. The Dutch sent a series of four embassies to Oedasoa's camp and presented him with gifts of copper, beads, and food; on the first trip the ensign entertained the Cochoqua chief with a fiddle concert and a soldier performed magic tricks. A healthy trade in sheep ensued from all this diplomatic activity, but the Cochoqua were disappointingly reluctant to part with cattle.

The following year, in the course of their seasonal wanderings, the Cochoqua returned to the Cape only to find the region in the turmoil of the First Khoikhoi-Dutch War. The Peninsulars begged them for

11. Ibid., p. 70 (June 20, 1659); p. 79 (June 23, 1659); pp. 444–45 (Dec. 1, 1661).
12. KA 3974, Van Riebeeck to XVII, April 9, 1662, n.p.; *VRJ*, 3:321 (Jan. 20, 1661); 329–30 (Feb. 3, 1661); 373 (April 20–23, 1661).

aid in their struggle against the Dutch, and as incentives they offered tobacco and copper, as well as cattle they had stolen from the colony. Oedasoa, however, preferred to negotiate with the Dutch. He sent a message to Van Riebeeck urging him to attack the Peninsulars, and promised that the Cochoqua would then come to live near Table Bay, where he and Van Riebeeck would be like "two brothers whose hearts beat as one." As we noted in the last chapter, Oedasoa's initiative gave courage to the desperate Netherlanders, who promptly sent a series of embassies to his camp urging him to enter the struggle, or at least to send guides to help them track down the Peninsulars.[13]

Though he was advised by his elders to accept Van Riebeeck's alliance, Oedasoa steadfastly but courteously refused all invitations to come to the fort. After fending off Dutch importunities for a while, he suddenly decided to depart inland and sent word to Van Riebeeck that he "left [the war] entirely to us to manage as best we could, since he cared as little about the matter as if it were nothing at all." Despite his words, he was not really indifferent to the outcome of the struggle, for in the coming months he urged the Peninsulars to make peace with the Europeans, and allowed Eva to act as go-between and interpreter between the warring parties.[14]

Oedasoa's decision to stay neutral was exceedingly important, for it came at a time when white settlement in South Africa was more seriously threatened than ever in its first centuries of existence. Had Oedasoa united with the Peninsulars, the combined Khoikhoi force could almost certainly have driven the intruders from the African continent; on the other hand, if he had acceded even to the Dutch request for guides, Van Riebeeck might well have realized his ambition of seizing the Peninsular's cattle and enslaving their persons.

Van Riebeeck thought that Oedasoa had been using the Peninsulars to soften up the colony as a prelude to attacking it himself. This interpretation ignored the fact that Oedasoa had more to gain in the short run from the colonists' presence than from their departure, and overlooked his efforts to encourage a Dutch attack on the Peninsulars. It is more likely—as Van Riebeeck himself also speculated—that Oedasoa had used the war to bring the defeated and dejected Peninsulars under his influence.[15] He was pleased by all that Van Riebeeck

13. *VRJ*, 3:68–74 (June 20–21, 1659).
14. Ibid., p. 79 (June 23, 1659); pp. 93–94 (July 9, 1659); p. 133 (Sept. 20, 1659); p. 162 (Dec. 14, 1659). The quotation is on p. 94.
15. KA 3972, Van Riebeeck to XVII, March 19, 1660, pp. 6v–7v.

could do to weaken his traditional enemies, but he clearly did not want them to be destroyed and their cattle forever lost to the Dutch. Therefore, by his noncommittal diplomacy, he had encouraged both sides to fight it out; and then, when the Peninsulars were obviously doing badly, he had switched to a peace policy.

If this was Oedasoa's strategy, it turned out to be brilliantly success-ful. At the end of the war the Cochoqua had the Peninsulars at their mercy. In November 1661, the combined forces of Oedasoa and Gonnema, along with numerous sheep and cattle, moved into the region immediately to the east of Table Bay. They gradually sur-rounded the Peninsulars, and without once resorting to force, pushed them back onto the Cape Peninsula. They then stationed themselves at crucial locations so as to cut their victims off from the Dutch and from the valuable pastures at Hout Bay; for a period of two weeks Cochoqua insisted on doing all the odd jobs in the colony which had formerly been done by the Peninsulars.

The Dutch felt powerless to resist their demands, much less to prevent their cattle from consuming Company pastures. The terrified Penin-sulars sent envoys to the fort (under Dutch guard) and asked Van Riebeeck for assurances of aid if they were attacked. The commander refused to help unless the Peninsulars would agree to supply a large quota of stock to every ship which entered the harbor. Even in their deep distress the Peninsulars could not accept such stringent conditions, and they chose instead to parley with the Cochoqua; after two weeks of tension, they finally induced the Cochoqua to withdraw, but only after they had signified their subjugation by sending them symbolic bundles of assegais.[16] This bloodless confrontation once again revealed Oedasoa's preference for negotiations over war, and his continuing desire to humiliate the Peninsulars and replace them as the closest associates of the Dutch. He had now clearly succeeded in attaining both these goals. By the time Van Riebeeck left the Cape in May 1662, the Dutch felt they had a "very firm alliance" with the Cochoqua and a "good, indeed a constant trade in livestock" with them. This trade far surpassed their barter with the Peninsulars.[17]

After the departure of Van Riebeeck, the history of the Western Cape Khoikhoi was marked by few dramatic incidents until the out-

16. *VRJ*, 3:436–48 (Nov. 21–Dec. 7, 1661).
17. KA 3974, Memorandum Van Riebeeck to Wagenaar, May 5, 1662, p. 8v. Translation from Moodie, *The Record*, p. 247. Statements on the cattle trade are based on figures compiled from the Dagregister of 1662 and 1663.

break of the Second Khoikhoi-Dutch War in 1673. Two main themes dominated this decade: the accelerating improverishment and breakdown of Peninsular society, and the continuation of the Cochoqua-Chainouqua feud.

The Peninsulars, having been humiliated first by the Dutch and then by Oedasoa, found their range of manoeuvre contracting. Gogosoa died sometime between 1663 and 1667,[18] and his son Schacher (Osingkhimma or Manckkagou) failed to restore even the slight intertribal authority that his father had possessed in his later years. Both the Goringhaiqua and the Gorachouqua gradually split into constituent clans, Schacher becoming only one of several clan captains: among the others were Kuiper (Dackkgy), Houtebeen (or Manckebeen), and Tomas. The Peninsulars had lost their predominant trading role as soon as the Dutch opened up contacts with cattle-rich groups like the Chainouqua; Peninsulars now traded only rarely at the fort and Dutch expeditions sent to them obtained only modest numbers of cattle.

Their position was further weakened when, on April 19, 1672, Schacher formally surrendered to the Dutch Company all Khoikhoi claims to the "Cape District" and Saldanha Bay. In a similar "treaty," dated May 3 of the same year, Kuiper ceded Hottentots Holland. In return for these concessions the two captains received amounts of tobacco, beads, brandy, and bread, which the Dutch valued at slightly more than 115 guilders. But the texts of the treaties—which were written for the benefit of European powers and were obviously not fully explained to the Khoikhoi signatories—had promised each captain a payment of 4,000 "Reals of Eight," that is, 10,000 guilders. In clauses which they may have similarly misunderstood, the Peninsular captains agreed to allow the Company to interfere in their disputes and to impose upon them a small annual tribute in cattle.[19]

The disintegration of the Peninsular tribes consisted, not only in the eroding authority of their leadership, but also in a serious decline in their population. This decline was caused by two factors. First,

18. He is last mentioned in the Dagregister of Jan. 8, 1663 (Moodie, *The Record*, p. 262), and Schacher is first mentioned as chief in KA 3980, DR May 8, 1667, pp. 72v–73. Gogosoa's death presumably took place between these two dates.

19. KA 3984, Accort ... wegens de generale Nederlantsche g'octroyeerde oostindische Comp: ... en den Hottentosen Prins Manckhagou alias Schacher ..., April 19, 1672, pp. 463–64v; KA 3986, Accordt ... wegens de vrije verenigde Nederlantsche g'Octroyeerde Oostindische Comp ... en den Hottentosen Overste Dackkgy (alias Cuijper) ... May 3, 1672, pp. 270–71v. On the fraudulent aspects of the treaties, see KA 3985, Goske to XVII, May 10, 1673, pp. 37–37v.

there was an increasing tendency for individual Peninsulars to leave their kraals and to enter the colony as propertyless laborers. This process, which in the 1660s was limited mainly to the Peninsulars, is described on pages 175–81. Secondly, the Peninsulars suffered, along with other Western Cape Khoikhoi, from the ravages of a disease that was possibly brought to South Africa by the colonists. In September 1661, the epidemic had first broken out among whites, slaves, and Khoikhoi. Soeswa and other Chainouqua leaders fell sick, Oedasoa's migrations were disrupted, and there was considerable mortality among both people and cattle. The disease, which might have been a form of dysentery, returned in 1662 and 1663. Unfortunately, we lack specific figures on the mortality rates in various tribes. It is clear, however, that most Western Cape Khoikhoi were severely stricken; and in 1666, when the disease had disappeared for some time, Commander Wagenaar wrote that the Peninsulars had declined significantly in numbers (he estimated their male population at eight hundred, or one-fifth less than Van Riebeeck's estimate of four years previously) and said that the Cochoqua "were very much diminished and melted away."[20]

Apart from the results of disease, the Cochoqua were unaffected in this period by the breakdown that was overtaking the Peninsulars, and they devoted themselves single-mindedly to their traditional feud with the Chainouqua. During this struggle, Gonnema came increasingly to the fore as the Cochoqua leader, and the ageing Oedasoa apparently lost some of his prestige and following. Nonetheless, the two chiefs were, so far as is known, always united and were able to give their people much firmer leadership then the various Chainouqua clan captains who inherited power after chief Soeswa died in 1663.

The Cochoqua had several other advantages over their enemy: they were occasionally successful in detaching some of the Peninsulars from their traditional alliance with the Chainouqua;[21] they were also in a far better position to benefit from the presence of the Dutch. For example, they were able to steal a firearm whose report terrified the Chainouqua, most of whom had had little direct contact with Europeans. Through pilferage (and barter with freemen) the Cochoqua probably obtained iron for their assegai heads, even though the Dutch refused all their requests for direct trade in iron, as well as all pleas

20. *VRJ*, 3:420–21 (Sept. 25, 1661); 437 (Nov. 21, 1661); KA 3975, DR May 26–27, 1662, pp. 173–73v; KA 3976, DR Nov. 29, 1663, n.p.; Moodie, *The Record*, p. 291.
21. KA 3981, Journael . . . den Corpal Jeronimus Croes, Jan. 6, 1669, p. 763v.

for military aid. Dutch sympathies were firmly with the Chainouqua, who were regarded as far more reliable traders than the Cochoqua.[22]

We have only incomplete information on the progress of these wars. It is likely that there were major battles in 1664 (with the Hessequa aiding the Chainouqua), 1666 (probably a Cochoqua victory), 1669 (dampened down by the Dutch), and 1671 (a major and violent Chainouqua victory). By March 1673, the balance had again swung back in favor of the Cochoqua, for the Chainouqua kraals nearest the enemy had suffered badly, and Gonnema had obtained enough booty to barter liberally with the Dutch. Sergeant Jeronimus Cruse, after surveying the situation, felt that the Chainouqua would be ruined unless the war ended soon. Eventually in fact, an "eternal" peace was concluded, but the Chainouqua were doubtless unhappy with the status quo.[23]

There can be little doubt that this interminable feud did much to weaken both tribes before their inevitable showdown with the colony. However, when the Dutch fell upon the Cochoqua in the Second Khoikhoi-Dutch War, they were in one sense intervening in the decades-old Cochoqua-Chainouqua vendetta: by eliminating the Cochoqua from the combat, they freed the Chainouqua from their most pressing danger and assured them of one more generation as a relatively independent people.

GONNEMA FALLS OUT WITH THE DUTCH

In the early 1670s a decided deterioration took place in Khoikhoi-European relations. The Cape colony was moving into a tense transition period when the Peninsular Khoikhoi were no longer a totally autonomous people nor yet a subordinate class in white society. In December 1671, Commander Pieter Hackius died after a long illness and was not replaced until ten months later. During his illness the Cape government had lacked the strong hand necessary to uphold the Seventeen's principles of benevolence toward Khoikhoi. This tendency was prolonged when, on Hackius's death, power devolved upon the Council of Policy, the small body of officials which in normal times assisted the governor in drafting and executing the laws of the colony.

22. KA 3987, DR March 15, 1673, p. 172v; KA 3978, DR Jan. 9, 1666, p. 439; KA 3981, DR Nov. 12, 1668, p. 665.

23. KA 3976, DR Jan. 29, 1664, n.p.; KA 3978, DR Jan. 9 and Jan. 30, 1666, pp. 439 and 443; KA 3981, Journael ... den Corpal Jeronimus Croes, Jan. 6, 1669, p. 763v; KA 3984, DR Sept. 16, 1671, p. 150; KA 3987, DR March 15, 1673, and March 20, 1673, pp. 172–72v, 174.

The council now veered sharply in the direction of a tough policy toward Khoikhoi, and this new posture was maintained when Isbrand Goske was installed as governor[24] in October 1672.

The new attitude was most apparent in the field of law. In January 1672, the council abruptly suspended a well-entrenched procedure whereby suspected Khoikhoi criminals were released to their tribes in return for a small ransom of cattle; henceforth Khoikhoi were to be subject to the severe penalties prescribed by Dutch law. The inauguration of this new system will be described in chapter 9, but at the moment one should note that the first Khoikhoi case tried by a Dutch court involved five of Gonnema's people accused of theft and assault. By order of the Council of Justice (i.e. High Court, consisting mainly of the same personnel as the Council of Policy), three of these were branded, and all five were thrashed and sent in chains to Robben Island for periods varying from seven to fifteen years. Unfortunately for the Dutch, the prisoners made a bold escape from the island in a rudderless rowboat and doubtless returned to Gonnema with vivid tales of the punishments they had undergone.[25]

About this time the government canceled Van Riebeeck's policy of generously entertaining chiefs who came to the fort; henceforth, the Dutch brusquely turned away chiefly visitors who did not bring cattle that were up to their expectations both in quality and quantity. Quite apart from the government's attitude, there were a number of unpleasant incidents in 1672: a white boy only eleven years old stabbed a little Khoikhoi child with whom he was playing; a freeman fatally wounded a Khoikhoi from Kuiper's kraal; and late in the year inland Khoikhoi were kept on edge by a number of roving deserters from the colony.[26]

The Dutch were gradually forming a view that the Cochoqua of Gonnema were particularly dangerous and intractable Khoikhoi. Gonnema's people had been involved in a few attacks on farmers, of which the case tried by the Council of Justice was only the latest. Much more serious was the fact that Gonnema was personally accused of

---

24. Up to this point the Company's chief official at the Cape had been designated "commander." Goske and his successor Bax were "governors," a change of terminology which reflected the importance of the Cape during the Netherlands' war with France (1672–78). In October 1678, Simon van der Stel took over the Cape as commander, but was promoted to governor in 1691; thereafter the Cape was ruled by governors or acting governors until 1792.

25. KA 3985, DR Jan. 11 and Feb. 10, 1672, pp. 258, 265v; KA 3987, DR Jan. 5, 1673, p. 142v.

26. KA 3985, DR April 7 and 29, and May 16, 1672, pp. 286, 296, 304.

directing two "massacres" of Dutch hippopotamus-hunters in 1671 and 1673. It was the second of these incidents, coming at the height of the recent tension, which induced the Dutch to begin the Second Khoikhoi-Dutch War.[27]

We may be almost certain that the white hunters were actually assailed by cattleless people whom the Khoikhoi called San (or Ubiqua). This was explicitly stated for the first incident and is extremely likely for the second, since hunters, far more than pastoralists, had reason to view the Dutch hunting parties with alarm. Attacks of this kind had often been made by hunters before the war and would continue to be made long after it. Hunters were willing to kill members of other hunter bands who trespassed on their hunting territory and doubtless had no scruples about extending this principle to whites. This was especially true because the whites with their firearms were rapidly killing off the hippopotami, which were a very valuable food source and were found only in limited numbers along river banks.[28]

The Dutch had to rely exclusively on Khoikhoi to ascertain that the attacking hunters were subjects of Gonnema. In the first case the informant was Kuiper, a Peninsular captain and a hereditary enemy of the Cochoqua. In the second, the informants were two Khoikhoi who claimed to have just come from Gonnema's kraal but were clearly not living there: in view of the nature of their information, it is unlikely that they were Cochoqua and very possible that they were Peninsulars.[29] Even if the guilty hunters were somehow related to one of Gonnema's kraals, there is no reason why Gonnema himself should be held responsible for their actions. Hunters, as I have shown, were related to Khoikhoi tribes in varying degrees of independence; and Khoikhoi chiefs, who had little authority over the day-to-day actions of other Khoikhoi, had presumably even less over hunters.[30]

27. The main statement of the Company's case is found in KA 3986, Goske to xvii, Sept. 17, 1673, pp. 7v–10v.

28. See following footnote. On San attitudes to intruders, see Schapera, *Khoisan Peoples*, pp. 156–57. For similar attacks on Dutch hunters, see KA 3975, DR Feb. 1, 1663, p. 234; KA 3997, DR March 17–18, 1684, pp. 177 ff; *Resolusies*, 3:148 (Nov. 2, 1686); KA 4008, DR Nov. 16, 1692, p. 337.

29. KA 3984, DR Nov. 28, 1671 p. 167; KA 3987, DR June 29, July 7 and 10, 1673, pp. 203v–06.

30. My treatment of the origins of the Second Khoikhoi-Dutch War may strike some readers as "revisionist." It is, however, worth noting that even Theal was willing to acquit Gonnema of involvement in the massacre of 1671 and the later massacre of 1676 (discussed below p. 131). On the other hand, Theal did accept the Company's claim that Gonnema directed the murders of 1673. See Theal, *History of South Africa*, 1:189–90, 210, 228.

Nonetheless, having determined that the whites had been attacked, the Council of Policy voted on July 11 to send Ensign Cruse and seventy-two men to rescue any of them who were still alive: if the Europeans were dead, Cruse was to take such revenge on the Cochoqua that future generations of Khoikhoi would shudder at the very thought of mistreating a Dutchman. Before the expedition had been gone three days, some whites reached the fort by sea from Saldanha Bay and informed the governor that Khoikhoi had attacked the Company's post there, killing four persons and doing damage later put at 300 guilders. Though the whites identified the attackers as Gonnema's people, three years later the Company maintained that the culprit was a certain Kees. Kees was a "San" or Guriqua who (according to his Khoikhoi enemies on whom the Dutch, as usual, relied for information) was an adherent of Gonnema and pastured much of his cattle; here again we face the problem of determining whether a Khoikhoi chieftain could give military orders to Khoikhoi or hunters outside his own tribe. For the council, however, there was no problem: it responded by sending reinforcements to Cruse's party and ordered it to "smash [Gonnema's people] into the ground, sparing no males."[31]

There were disquieting ambiguities and uncertainties in almost all the material cited by the Cape government to prove that Gonnema had been plotting against the security of the colony. Furthermore, no clear motive for his alleged actions was determined. He was not fighting to defend his pastures, which were not threatened; nor is it likely that he would risk a war with the colony, whose strength he knew well, merely to defend the hippopotami of his hunter-clients. Had he desired to destroy the colony (e.g. in pique over the court's treatment of his subjects), or had he wanted to seize cattle, his attacks would surely have been well-planned and massive, not a series of minor incidents. Undoubtedly Gonnema, along with other Khoikhoi leaders, resented the Dutch presence and was involved in some disruptive incidents;[32] it is improbable that he directed the sequence of events which led up to the war.

31. *Resolusies*, 2:115 (July 11, 1673). For the quotation, see KA 3987, DR July 14, 1673, pp. 208–09. See also KA 3989, Daghregister gehouden op de expeditie na de rebellerende Gonnemase Africanen, Nov. 11, 1676, p. 337v; Abraham van Riebeeck, "Aenteekeningen . . . ," *Briewe van Johanna Maria van Riebeeck en Ander Riebeeckiana*, ed. D. B. Bosman (Amsterdam: By the Editor, 1952), p. 42.

32. For a case where Gonnema was personally involved but where no whites lost their lives, see Moodie, *The Record*, pp. 322–23, n. 2.

It is noteworthy that, as the years passed, even the Dutch began to have doubts that Gonnema was entirely to blame for the outbreak of hostilities. In March 1677, Joan Bax van Harentals, Goske's successor as governor, wrote to the Seventeen that he had been hearing rumors that whites had often mistreated Gonnema's people under previous governors: they had "many times not only stripped [the Gonnema Cochoqua] and others of their cattle, but . . . had treacherously shot at them and cut down many of these Hottentots."[33] And when in 1679 rumors reached the fort of yet another massacre of white hippopotamus hunters, the officials expressed the cynical view that it was "very doubtful that the said Hottentots were given no reasons for such . . . thievish behavior."[34]

THE SECOND KHOIKHOI-DUTCH WAR (1673–77) AND THE DECLINE OF THE COCHOQUA

The expedition which had set out under Cruse on July 12, 1673, consisted of only seventy-two (later eighty-nine) men, and was gone only thirteen days. Nonetheless it was exceedingly successful. Guided by a Gonnema Khoikhoi whom they had impressed into their service, the Dutchmen located the enemy's kraals at dawn of July 18. The Cochoqua, warned of the party's approach, deserted their huts; but the Dutch sent their horsemen in pursuit. When the riders came into sight, the terrified Khoikhoi abandoned their livestock and fled to the mountains. Within the day the Dutch seized 800 cattle and 900 sheep and killed ten or twelve Cochoqua.[35]

The effects of this cheap but sensational victory were profound. With only the slightest prompting from the Dutch, a whole array of Khoikhoi tribes jumped into the war as the Company's allies. During the next four years of hostilities, Gonnema was virtually surrounded by enemies and devoid of friends. His foes included the Little Namaqua; the Little Guriqua; the Peninsular captains Kuiper and Schacher; the Chainouqua captains Koopman, Klaas, and Soeswa's Son; and a captain Jacob near Saldanha Bay.[36] These Khoikhoi were motivated in varying degrees by traditional grievances against Gonnema and

33. KA 3989, Bax to XVII, March 14, 1677, p. 16v.

34. KA 3992, DR Sept. 30, 1679, p. 285.

35. KA 3987, Dagelyckse aantekening . . . op d'Expeditie van d'rebellerende gonnemase affricanen . . . gehouden, July 12–25, 1673, pp. 213–16v.

36. There was, however, some suspicion that the Peninsular Kuiper was giving information of Dutch activities to Gonnema (Abraham van Riebeeck, "Aenteekeningen . . .," Bosman, *Briewe van Johanna Maria van Riebeeck*, p. 42). On Gonnema's enemies, see n. 38 below, and KA 3989, DR Oct. 27, 1676, p. 320v; KA 3990, DR Aug. 8, 1677, p. 359v.

by a desire to obtain his cattle with the aid of Dutch firearms. They greatly furthered the Dutch cause by serving as warriors, guides, and spies.

Under these circumstances Gonnema chose to pursue a defensive strategy, and he limited his offensive moves to attacks on his Khoikhoi enemies and on outlying farms of the freemen. His only serious attempt to harm the Company itself was an attack on one of its herds in 1673. In accordance with Doman's old strategy, Gonnema launched this raid in a rainstorm, which unfortunately let up too early to frustrate the effectiveness of Dutch fire power. To guard against further such raids, the Dutch began to build special palisades for the protection of their cattle. In other defensive moves, they temporarily abandoned their outpost at Saldanha Bay, strengthened their garrison at Hottentots Holland, and authorized whites to shoot all Khoikhoi whom they saw armed with assegais or traveling by night.[37]

The Company, moreover, was determined to take the offensive. In 1674 it sent out a second expeditionary force consisting of 100 Europeans and 400 Khoikhoi, of whom 250 were provided by the Chainouqua captain Klaas. It was Klaas who had located the enemy and urged the Dutch to mount the expedition, and his people were largely responsible for its success. Once again the Cochoqua put up no effective resistance, and the allies captured 800 cattle, 4,000 sheep, and a large number of weapons. The Company gave its Khoikhoi auxiliaries a large number of the sheep (some of them outright, some on loan) while it distributed many of the cattle among the burghers.[38]

Despite its one-sided nature, the Dutch did not try to end the war, which was providing them with sheep and cattle and tightening their influence over nearby Khoikhoi tribes.[39] In 1676 they mounted two more expeditions. The first of these was allegedly sent in retaliation for yet another massacre of freemen hunters by indigenous hunters said to be subjects of Gonnema; it was, however, significant that the incident took place on the Breede River, well outside the usual territory of the Cochoqua. As for the second expedition, one of its frankly stated purposes was to seize cattle to feed the homeward-bound fleet.[40] Both

37. KA 3989, DR Sept. 16, 1676, p. 306; KA 3987, Goske to Hendrick Elberts, Aug. 11, 1673, pp. 73v–74; KA 3989, DR Nov. 26, 1676, p. 343.

38. KA 3988, DR March 24 and April 7–15, 1674, pp. 103v–10.

39. KA 3988, Goske to XVII, Feb. 10, 1675, p. 23.

40. The Breede River massacre was reported by the Hottentots Holland post, which hardly ever had contact with Cochoqua: KA 3989, DR March 26, 1676, p. 207; *Resolusies*, 2:154 (Oct. 27, 1676).

ventures failed, mainly because the Cochoqua dispersed their remaining livestock and successfully hid from the advancing forces. By means of false trails and decoys of cattle, they were able to lure the Dutch around the countryside in a merry chase which exhausted the Europeans and consumed their provisions. The Dutch were badly served by their hunter spies, who brought them false information and sometimes even failed to report at all. The spies' incompetence was, however, more than matched by that of the Dutchmen, who could even mistake a herd of elephants for Khoikhoi cattle and one of their own abandoned campsites for a Khoikhoi kraal.[41]

The Dutch were so frustrated by their failure to contact the main body of Cochoqua that they turned on tribes whose association with Gonnema's alleged crimes was very tenuous. They marched into the kraals of Oedasoa, even though they had never accused him of encouraging Gonnema and had once even admitted that he had tried to dissuade his fellow chief from anti-Dutch activities. The resourceful old warrior was informed of this attack in advance and managed to escape with his followers and possessions just before the Dutch arrived. On another occasion Company forces surprised Kees, the Guriqua (or "San") captain near Saldanha Bay, killing five or six of his people and taking all his stock. In justification for this action they accepted the rather confused testimony alluded to earlier; namely, the claim that Kees had attacked the Company's Saldanha Bay post in 1673 at the behest of Gonnema.[42]

This small victory over Kees did little to alter the fact that the expeditions of 1676 had been wretched failures. As a consequence, the Dutch became more interested in ending the war, which was disrupting the cattle trade, keeping the countryside under moderate tension, and offering no further profits. The new governor, Joan Bax van Harentals (March 1676–June 1678), was rather more sympathetic to the Khoikhoi than were his predecessors, and in June 1677 he received envoys from Gonnema, who for months had been seeking peace with the Dutch and his Khoikhoi enemies. Amidst joyous shouts of "*sam, sam!*" (peace) the two sides concluded an agreement, the terms of which

41. KA 3989, Dagelyckse aanteyckening op de expeditie na de rebellerende Gonnemase Africanen . . . , March 27–April 16, 1676, pp. 217v–24; KA 3989, Daghregister gehouden op de expeditie na de rebellerende Gonnemase Africanen, Nov. 1–19, 1676, pp. 334–39v.

42. *Resolusies*, 2:115 (July 11, 1673); KA 3989, Dagelyckse aanteyckening . . . , April 11, 1676, pp. 223–23v; KA 3989, Daghregister . . . Africanen, Nov. 11, 1676, p. 337v; KA 3989, DR Nov. 23, 1676, p. 340.

were deliberately kept simple so the Khoikhoi could comprehend and remember them. Gonnema begged the Company's forgiveness for his alleged misdeeds and swore to live in amity with its Khoikhoi allies, many of whom were explicitly mentioned in the peace treaty; he promised to punish his criminals as the Dutch punished theirs and to bring a "tribute" of thirty cattle for the return fleet of each year.[43]

Despite the failure of the last two Dutch expeditions, the Second Khoikhoi-Dutch War must, unlike the First, be regarded as an unambiguous Dutch triumph. The Europeans had seized at least 1,765 cattle and 4930 sheep and had humiliated one of the strongest tribes in the western Cape; they had furthermore rid themselves of any fears that their settlement might ever be threatened by Khoikhoi using conventional military techniques.

The Cochoqua, however, were not entirely impoverished by the war, and Gonnema continued to be regarded as one of the richest chiefs in the region. For the remaining years of his life he was overtly submissive to his conquerors. He pursued escaped slaves, allowed his people to aid white hunters, and even executed "San" hunters who had escaped from a Dutch prison and sought refuge in his territory. Furthermore, he requested and was granted a *rotting*, a cane which the Company gave to chiefs who recognized its suzerainty.[44]

In late 1685 or early 1686, Gonnema died and was succeeded by a son whose name is unknown. Oedasoa died in March 1689, leaving the leadership of his subtribe to a "brother" whom the Dutch called Hanibal.[45] The passing of the great leaders hastened the decline of the Cochoqua, who were increasingly subject to attacks from hunters and Namaqua and to the disintegrative effects of the expanding colony. The new rulers failed to restore the hegemony of Gonnema and Oedasoa and rapidly became mere clan captains almost indistinguishable from the petty leaders of the Peninsulars. About this time a number of Cochoqua began to call themselves Gunjemans in honor of the dead Gonnema; the name persisted a long time and spread inland with the Cochoqua's descendants. In the 1770s, Gunjemans were found at such

43. KA 3990, DR June 4, 5, 7, 22–26, pp. 315v–22v.

44. KA 3991, DR July 8, 1678, p. 432; KA 3991, Dec. 16–17, 1678, p. 484–84v; KA 3992, DR Feb. 13, 1679, pp. 234v–35; KA 3997, March 17–18, 1684, p. 177v. The cane of office is discussed on pp. 191–92.

45. Waterhouse, *Van der Stel*, p. 155; KA 4004, DR March 29, 1689, p. 189v.

widely separated places as Stellenbosch, the Eastern (Xhosa) Frontier, and the Orange River.[46]

THE NORTHERN BORDERLANDS

The region north of the Cochoqua was inhabited by the Guriqua and the Namaqua. This area was moderately wealthy in cattle, important in precolonial trade, and significant as the meeting place of the two major branches of the Khoikhoi culture. However, it is not prominent in our narrative, since the Dutch had effectively penetrated only part of it before 1713.

The Dutch records often refer to Chariguriqua or Charigurina. The prefix *chari* is almost certainly the adjective ≠*kari* (small), and Vedder's reconstruction of the tribal name as ≠*kari-huri-qua* (Lesser Sea People) is more plausible than Wuras's "those who sprinkle water."[47] The Dutch constantly speak of Little and Great Chariguriqua, where it would probably be more correct to say simply Little and Great Guriqua.[48]

Estimates of Guriqua population are not very reliable, since no European ever saw a large number of Guriqua camped together. Van Riebeeck's early estimate of only 2,000 is compatible with his later view that their population roughly equaled that of the Goringhaiqua, whose *arms-bearing* men he put at 300. A very low population is also indicated by many travelers' impressions that Guriqua were scattered in low density over a vast region. Though Van Riebeeck once said that they had many thousands of cattle and sheep, our direct evidence suggests that the Guriqua were not extraordinarily wealthy. If one can judge from the trade figures, their wealth consisted of a higher proportion of sheep then did that of other groups—a fact which may be explained by the drier terrain in which they lived.[49] The Dutch normally met the Guriqua at Saldanha Bay or along the banks of the Berg and Olifants Rivers, which stretch north and south along the

46. Thunberg, *Voyages*, 1:225; Sparrman, *Voyage*, 2:336; Wikar, VRS 15, p. 23.

47. *The Native Tribes of South West Africa* (Cape Town: Cape Times Limited, 1928), p. 114; Wuras, "Account of the Korana," p. 289. I use the form Guriqua to distinguish these people from the later Griqua, though there may well be connections between the two groups.

48. The Little Guriqua were also known as Hosomans. The occasional references to *Co*horiqua and *Ci*cerica may point to the Great Guriqua, since *kai* is the Khoikhoi word for "great." See *VRJ*, 3:11 (Feb. 3, 1659); KA 3989, Dagelyckse Aanteyckening ..., April 6, 1676, p. 220v; KA 3992, DR Dec. 25, 1679, p. 308.

49. KA 3970, Van Riebeeck to XVII, Feb. 22, 1658, p. 402v; KA 3974, Van Riebeeck to Successor, May 5, 1662, p. 9. On trade, see e.g. *VRJ*, 2:181 (Nov. 7, 1657).

coastal plain. In the south the Guriqua often overlapped with Cochoqua at Saldanha Bay, and in the north they were often found inter-
spersed with Namaqua.

The Guriqua differed from most other Khoikhoi groups in that the
Dutch found no chief among them who exercised any authority, even
nominal, beyond his own kraal. This is perhaps the meaning behind
Harry's contemptuous but obviously mistranslated remark that Guriqua had no "elected chiefs"; Soeswa claimed that Guriqua chiefs
had only the title of *humque*, which probably meant "clan head."[50]
However, despite their disunity, it is probable that the Guriqua were
once a united tribe, which later split into Greater and Lesser segments,
and still later into the clans existing in our period. Dr. Shula Marks
has plausibly suggested that the original Guriqua may have been a
Strandloper group which acquired livestock: this theory would explain
their name (Sea People), their comparative poverty, their political
decentralization, and the fact that other Khoikhoi occasionally identified them as "San."[51]

Though they possessed small numbers of their own livestock,
Guriqua derived much of their income from herding stock for wealthy
neighbors. We have already seen that before 1660 some of the Guriqua
alienated their Cochoqua patrons and turned to the Namaqua for
protection. Thus, in most early accounts of Guriqua we find them
hostile to their southern neighbors but on good terms with those to
their north: Namaqua visiting the Cape often tarried for long periods
with Guriqua; others even arrived in company with Guriqua emissaries. However, in 1680 we get our first indication of a Guriqua-
Namaqua war, and such hostility occurred again after the turn of the
century.[52]

To modern scholars the Namaqua are the most familiar of all
Khoikhoi peoples; however, in the seventeenth century they were only
on the fringes of the Dutch consciousness, and their country and
customs were only imperfectly known. We know that by the mid-
eighteenth century Namaqua were dwelling along the banks of the
western half of the Orange River and had penetrated north into
modern Namibia, where they still remain in comparatively large

50. *VRJ*, 3:260 (Sept. 21, 1660); 303 (Dec. 16, 1660). Soeswa spoke of only one Guriqua
chief; there is, however, no direct evidence of a single chief who ruled the whole "tribe."
51. Personal communication.
52. Moodie, *The Record*, p. 262; KA 3994, DR Nov. 27, 1681, p. 219; KA 3992, Simon van
der Stel to XVII, March 27, 1680, p. 74; KZ 3193, Dagh Verhaal ... Slotsbo, Oct. 24, 1712, n.p.

numbers. However, little is known about them in the seventeenth
century, except that one segment, generally known as the Little
Namaqua, had moved south into the coastal region just to the north
of the Guriqua's pasturelands.

The Dutch became interested in the Namaqua very early. Enticed
by stories told them by Cape Khoikhoi, they had high hopes that the
Namaqua would prove profitable trading partners, and that they
would lead them to Linschoten's River of Vigiti Magna and the
Empire of Monomotapa. Between 1659 and 1664 no fewer than five
major expeditions were sent north; only two of these succeeded in
establishing effective contact with Namaqua, namely, the Cruijthoff-
Meerhoff expeditions of 1661 and 1662–63. These parties brought
back interesting information but little of apparent commercial value.

After 1664 the Company lost interest in northern overland exploration. As a consequence the Namaqua virtually disappeared from the
colony's records for seventeen years, until the energetic commander,
Simon van der Stel, took up the quest for Namaqualand in the 1680s.
By this time the Dutch were far more interested in mining copper than
in trade. In December 1681, some Namaqua emissaries had arrived
at the Cape and presented the commander with some copper they
had brought from their own country. The eager Van der Stel dispatched
expeditions in each of the following three years in an attempt to locate
the source of the metal. The first two failed, but the third succeeded
in bringing back some copper ore. In 1685 Van der Stel personally
topped off the series by leading his own expedition and successfully
reaching the copper-bearing mountains.

The accumulated evidence of the many expeditions before 1685
suggests that the population of Little Namaqualand was sparse. The
first successful probe (1661) found only one group of Namaqua led
by a chief named Akembie: its total population was estimated at 700,
and its visible stock holdings at 4,000 cattle and 3,000 sheep. This
evidence tallied well with Oedasoa's impression that "the Namaquas
had large numbers of livestock, but that their tribe was not nearly as
numerous as his and therefore he had very little to fear of them."
Subsequent expeditions encountered ever larger numbers of Namaqua,
culminating in Van der Stel's total of eight or nine kraals.[53] These
rising figures probably mean only that the Dutch were penetrating

53. *VRJ*, 3:353 (Meerhoff's Journal, Feb. 20, 1661); 360 (March 16, 1661); Waterhouse,
Van der Stel, passim. The quotation is in *VRJ*, 3:360.

farther into the region, though it is also conceivable that the Namaqua population was expanding.

The relative inhospitality of their terrain forced the Little Namaqua to migrate over a much wider area than the Cape tribes. The core of their pastures would seem to have been the area known later as Amaquasland, that is, the coastal area between the mouth of the Olifants and the Groene rivers. However, Bergh (1682) and Van der Salt rivers and on the River Zonder Eind. At times. normally in the we know that Little Namaqua penetrated as far as the Orange River for purposes of trade. They also could come quite far south for particular purposes, for instance, to attack Khoikhoi near Saldanha Bay.[54]

After Simon van der Stel's journey in 1685, the Namaqua began to appear far more frequently in the Company records. This was not because the Company had decided to exploit the copper in their region, but because Van der Stel, by the arbitrary and insensitive manner in which he had treated their chiefs, seems to have created considerable ill-will among the Namaqua. During his journey he had humiliated chiefs by haughtily asserting the Company's sovereignty over them; he had intervened in the affairs of one tribe and forced its members to recognize the chief of his own preference; and on two occasions he had compelled chiefs to judge and punish leading Namaqua who had earned his displeasure.[55]

It is hardly a coincidence that shortly after Van der Stel's return to the Cape, and for some years thereafter, the northern frontier of the colony was troubled by Namaqua attacks and threatened attacks on whites and their Khoikhoi allies.[56] Simon van der Stel was the first of several whites whose actions stirred up the northern region so that in 1701–03 it exploded in widespread violence. However, provocations from whites were not the only reasons why the Northern Borderlands suddenly ceased to be a tranquil periphery of the colony. The other reasons, along with the disturbances themselves, will be discussed in chapter 11.

54. Brink, VRS 28, p. 19; Bergh, VRS 12, p. 123; Waterhouse, *Van der Stel*, p. 129; KA 3981, DR May 17, 1668, pp. 615v–16.

55. Waterhouse, *Van der Stel*, pp. 130–33, 140–41. In one case the prisoner was finally excused from his punishment.

56. For example, KA 4000, DR July 13, 1686, p. 323; KA 7571/KZ 3179, DR March 5, 1688, n.p.; KA 4004, DR March 25, 1689, pp. 188v–89.

7

The Chainouqua and Hessequa:
The Perils of Cooperation

THE CHAINOUQUA AND HESSEQUA BEFORE 1673

To the east of the Dutch colony lay a region which, compared to the north, was densely populated in people and livestock. The two main tribes of this area, the Chainouqua and the Hessequa,[1] were extremely important in the economic history of the colony, the former from as early as 1657, and the latter chiefly after the Second Khoikhoi-Dutch War.

The Chainouqua and Hessequa wandered over a region bounded roughly by the Hottentots Holland Mountains in the west and the Keurbooms River in the east. The Chainouqua (later known as Soeswas, still later as Koopmans) pastured mainly on the Breede and Salt rivers and on the River Zonder Eind. At times, normally in the summer, they would come close to the Cape, sometimes even within sight of the Company's lodge at Hottentots Holland. In the east they apparently ventured only rarely beyond the site of modern Swellendam. They were seen as far south as the seashore, but the northern limit of their territories is unknown.[2]

The Hessequa were normally closely allied to the Chainouqua and might well have been closely related to them as well. The Hessequa lands lay to the east of those of the Chainouqua, though the two tribes occasionally overlapped at the borders. The rough boundaries of the Hessequa's pasture were Hessequas Kloof (ten miles west of Swellendam) on the west, and Attaquas Kloof (ten miles east of the

---

1. Wuras ("Account of the Korana," p. 289) interprets Chainouqua as "those who are swollen or puffy in the face." Maingard plausibly argues that Hessequa meant "men of the woods" (*hei*, tree, + *se*, an adjective ending, + *qua*): "Lost Tribes," p. 503.

2. KA 3987, DR Oct. 31, 1673, p. 249v; KA 3989, Visser's Journal, Oct. 9, 1676, p. 320; KA 3999, DR Oct. 31, 1685, p. 306; KA 4037, Dagverhaal . . . Hartogh, Nov. 1–24, 1707, passim.

Gauritz River) on the east. The Hessequa occasionally camped at Mossel Bay and on the numerous southward flowing rivers like the Kaffir Kuils and the Duivenhocks.[3]

The Chainouqua were never seen camped together in one place; thus it is impossible to make a direct estimate of their numbers. However, in 1673 it was reported that the whole tribe consisted of eleven kraals, and in 1707 Hartogh located fourteen to sixteen kraals. These observations give only roughest indication of population, since the kraal was an extremely variable unit. However, we may assume that Chainouqua were in the same population range as the Cochoqua, who were once described as consisting of sixteen kraals. In 1668 Cruse numbered the Hessequa kraals at twenty-five or twenty-six, thus perhaps confirming one's general impression that the Hessequa outnumbered the Chainouqua.[4] An idea of the wealth of the two peoples can be derived from the trade figures (see p. 160). The fact that the Chainouqua and Hessequa predominated heavily in the Dutch trade despite their distance from the fort, suggests that they were wealthier than all the other Cape tribes, particularly in beef cattle. Of these two groups, the Hessequa were probably the richer, especially during the 1670s when they were at their height.

The riches of the two tribes were clearly related to the strong leadership each enjoyed. When the Dutch arrived at the Cape, the Chainouqua were ruled by Soeswa, a very eminent chief whose influence was felt well beyond the bounds of his own tribe. Van Riebeeck credited him with preventing the outbreak of a war between Gonnema and Choro, the chief of the Gorachouqua; and Oedasoa, despite his hostility to the Chainouqua, was forced to recognize Soeswa's claims to lineage superiority. The Chainouqua themselves claimed that Soeswa was the second highest monarch of all Khoikhoi societies, being subordinate only to the Khoebaha of the Hamcumqua (Inqua), of whom he was considered to be some sort of representative.

3. Most references to the Hessequa's location put them near "Quaelberg's Casteel," "Backeley Plaats," or the Buffeljachts R.—all in the neighborhood of modern Swellendam. On other locations, see KA 3992, DR Dec. 12, 1679, p. 305; Schrijver, VRS 12, pp. 215–17, 245. Hartogh found some Hessequa well to the west of the boundaries indicated above, but this was due to the fact that they had recently been chased from their country by hunters: KA 4037, Dagverhaal ... Hartogh, Nov. 5, 1707, pp. 904v–05.

4. On the Chainouqua, see KA 3987, DR Oct. 31, 1673, p. 249v; KA 4037, Dagverhaal ... Hartogh, passim. On the Hessequa, see KA 3981, Diary of the *Voerman*, Oct. 19–Nov. 7, 1668, pp. 661–63.

They further claimed that he had the right to depose all Cochoqua and Peninsular chiefs, though they admitted that this privilege was more theoretical than practical.[5]

Soeswa made a positive impression on the Dutch. On one occasion he arrived at the fort accompanied by his daughter-in-law, whose rank was made evident by the way she dismounted her ox by stepping on the shoulders of another Khoikhoi. While being entertained by Van Riebeeck, Soeswa was regally clad in "splendid leopard skins," and his comportment was temperate and restrained. Even Commander Wagenaar, who was contemptuous of Khoikhoi in general, praised his extraordinary courtesy.[6]

Soeswa was already quite old by the time he made contact with the Dutch, and he had great difficulty in traveling. He had turned over much of his political power to his only son Goeboe and was normally found camped alone with his own kraal. It seems that Chainouqua society was already drifting toward the multipolarity of power that was characteristic of it after Soeswa's death. However, unlike Gogosoa of the Peninsulars, Soeswa continued to be highly honored: he received ceremonial precedence over his son and still had the authority to summon other kraals to his side. His physical infirmities continued to plague him: by July 1663 he was so weak that he could no longer travel, and he died shortly afterward, probably in November of that year.[7]

After Soeswa's death, power passed to Goeboe, who was, however, usually known to the Dutch simply as "Soeswa's Son." Around this time the Chainouqua began to call themselves Soeswas, probably in honor not of the son but of the father, and many of their clans continued to be ruled by members of Soeswa's lineage into the eighteenth century. Goeboe himself seems to have lived until at least 1707, though from the beginning he lacked his father's eminence.[8] In the decade after 1663 there was no discernible center of authority among the Chainouqua, despite the fact that they were engaged in a protracted, and at times desperate, feud with the Cochoqua. It was not until the mid-1670s that new leaders would arise among the Chainouqua to re-establish their self-esteem and forge a workable response to the threat of the Dutch.

5. *VRJ*, 3:258–60 (Sept. 21, 1660); 266 (Sept. 28, 1660).

6. *VRJ*, 3:267–68 (Sept. 29–30, 1660); 302 (Dec. 16, 1660); KA 3976, Wagenaar to xvii, Nov. 21, 1663, n.p.

7. *VRJ*, 3:258–59 (Sept. 21, 1660); KA 3976, Wagenaar to xvii, Nov. 21, 1663, n.p.

8. KA 4037, Dagverhaal ... Hartogh, Nov. 9, 13, 14, 1707, pp. 906–08.

Little evidence is available on the political history of the Hessequa in this early period. It seems almost certain, however, that the tribe was ruled by a strong leader, since in 1668 Jeronimus Cruse found sixteen to seventeen kraals—the bulk of the tribe—camped around the kraal of one particular chief. This chief was the "brother" of the Chainouqua chief Soeswa, and this kinship tie may explain the cordial relations which prevailed between the two tribes. It is very possible that this Hessequa chief was the Gaukou of later times, but on this point we have no definite evidence.[9]

KLAAS, KOOPMAN, AND THE COMPANY'S TRADE, 1673–1692

Dorha, better known to the Dutch as "Klaas," was the captain of one of the westernmost Chainouqua kraals. We have no way of knowing whether he was related to the eminent Soeswa family, but through his own efforts he became extremely influential not only among his own Chainouqua but among the Hessequa as well. From the early 1670s until his violent death in 1701, Klaas was the single most important figure in the history of Dutch-Khoikhoi relations.

In 1669 Klaas accompanied Corporal Jeronimus Cruse on a trading expedition to the Hessequa. When the expedition came to blows with a group of Ubiqua hunters, Klaas was surprised and delighted by the effectiveness with which Dutch firepower scattered his hereditary enemies. It was not long after this that he conceived the elements of a scheme to enrich himself by cooperating with the Europeans. His first attempts to trade with the whites were thwarted by Peninsular middlemen, but in 1672 he managed to reach the fort escorted by an armed guard of Company servants. He thereupon asked the Dutch to give him trade goods on credit so that he might barter inland on their behalf. This request was granted, but on a small scale.[10]

Two events were shortly to enhance Klaas's value to the Dutch. When the Company occupied Hottentots Holland in October 1672, Klaas suddenly had ready access to the colony with little danger from his Khoikhoi enemies. The Company now looked to him to protect their new possession and to open new trade routes from it into the

9. KA 3981, Diary of the *Voerman*, Oct. 22, 1668, p. 661v; *VRJ*, 3:333 (Feb. 17, 1661). The identification of this person with Gaukou is somewhat strengthened by the fact that in 1694 Gaukou was described as the oldest chief in the western Cape (KA 4009, S. van der Stel to XVII, April 14, 1694, p. 32).

10. KA 3981, Journael ... Croes, Jan. 16, 1669, p. 767; KA 3985, DR July 24–27, 1672, pp. 332v–34.

interior. The second new factor was the outbreak of war between the Dutch and Gonnema. Since he had recently lost a large number of cattle to the Cochoqua, Klaas was very eager to accept the Company's invitation to be its ally in the struggle. As we have already seen, he played a key role in the Dutch victory over Gonnema in 1674. The Company, which was temporarily oversupplied with livestock, was generous with its native allies. Klaas received a number of oxen and 300 sheep; in addition, he was given 300 sheep to pasture on behalf of the Company in return for all the lambs they would bear.[11]

Klaas was now confirmed in his belief that friendship with the Dutch was the key to wealth and power. For the next twenty years he pursued a pro-Dutch policy with a consistency and persistence that was remarkable and in the end, pathetic. He often came to the fort to pay his respects to the governor, or to answer questions about Khoikhoi disputes, the location of kraals, or the prospects for trade. At times he even took the trouble to inform the Company before moving his own kraal. He returned runaway slaves, supplied guides and oxen for Company expeditions, and offered refuge to shipwrecked sailors passing through his territory. The Company's enemies he regarded as his own; he would cheerfully execute Cochoqua prisoners or Ubiqua robbers in order to win the Company's favor and would attack Peninsulars who refused to barter with him as the Company's agent.[12]

The Company for its part was delighted by Klaas's exuberant loyalty. Officials regarded him as the "most unpretentious of these native barbarians" and showered him with gifts of brandy and tobacco, as well as a Dutch suit, a wig, and possibly even four guns. Klaas also managed to learn passably good Dutch, though his complex ideas were always hard to follow. So congenial did the Dutch find him that, when they were preparing for a possible foreign invasion of the colony, their contingency plans called for some of the white population of the Cape and Stellenbosch to take refuge in Klaas's territory.[13]

It was, however, preeminently as a trader that Klaas won the gratitude of the Company. Trading inland with European goods, he

11. KA 3987, DR March 14, 1673, p. 171v; KA 3988, DR April 9, 1674, 108v.

12. KA 3988, DR June 27, 1674, p. 132v; KA 3989, Dagelyckse Aanteyckening . . . , April 12–13, 1676, p. 223v; KA 3999, DR March 27, 1685, p. 249; KA 3999, DR Dec. 16, 1685, p. 314; Verhaal van Theunis Gerbrantszn van der Schelling, *RZA*, 3:170; Schrijver, VRS 12, p. 209.

13. KA 3987, DR Nov. 18, 1673, p. 253v; KA 4002, DR June 30, 1687, p. 295; Buttner, Waare Relation, n.p.

was able to benefit both himself and the Dutch and to bring to fruition a scheme that had first been tried by Van Riebeeck and Harry. Under the terms of his contract Klaas was paid only the number of *cows* which he happened to barter, the Company being at this point mainly interested in oxen. He was to repay these cows to the Company at the rate of 20 percent per year, but could keep all calves that were born to them in the meanwhile. Though Klaas was in fact very lax in his payments, the system was enormously advantageous to the Company. Van der Stel enthusiastically wrote to the Seventeen that in his first two expeditions Klaas had obtained 393 cattle of which only 57 were cows; the cost to the Company of the remaining 336 cattle was only about 238 guilders, or well under a guilder a head. This was far less expensive than fitting out an expedition for six or seven weeks and losing the labor of seventeen or eighteen Company servants who could be better employed in Cape Town.[14] Between 1684 and 1690 Klaas conducted at least six expeditions (and probably several more) and brought back at least 1,242 cattle and 823 sheep for the Company.

Through his enterprising activity, Klaas grew wealthy at the same time as other Khoikhoi chiefs were becoming impoverished through social and economic processes which I will describe in coming chapters. Klaas's new-found wealth and his influence with the Dutch probably affected in large measure his relationships with other Khoikhoi leaders. He was on the best of terms with Gaukou, the powerful chief of the Hessequa: their alliance was cemented in the mid-1680s when Klaas married Gaukou's daughter,[15] and in coming years the Dutch often found the two chiefs camped together.

Gaukou was apparently a close relative ("brother") to the Inqua chief, the overlord of the region. The Dutch called Gaukou "De Oude Heer" (the Old Lord or Gentleman), while the Khoikhoi gave him the Portuguese title *Sire*, a term by which they also addressed the Cape governors. Gaukou enjoyed great prestige among his own people, received unquestioning obedience from his son and his subchiefs, and possessed arbitrary judicial authority in excess of that of most Khoikhoi rulers. He was also highly respected among the Chainouqua and the Peninsulars. Simon van der Stel said of him, after one of his visits to the Cape, that he was "a man very rich in people and in cattle, the oldest and mightiest [chief] of all nearby nations; during his presence

14. KA 3997, S. van der Stel to XVII, April 30, 1684, pp. 416v–17v.
15. There is no direct evidence for the date of the marriage; however, in 1694 Gaukou's daughter had been married to Klaas about ten years (KA 4011, DR Jan. 23, 1694, p. 121v).

here he was able to settle and adjust all differences among the Hottentot captains through the respect he commanded."[16]

The benefits Klaas enjoyed from Gaukou's friendship were partially offset by the dangers which he encountered from two enemies: Koopman (the leader of another Soeswa kraal) and the "Ubiqua" (robberhunters). The Koopman-Klaas feud was a traditional one that was probably intensified, but not caused, by Klaas's friendship with the Dutch. We know of open conflict between the two captains in 1677, 1687, 1688, and 1690–91. In all of these cases the Company intervened, in the first two cases as an honest broker and mediator. By 1688, however, the Dutch were so impressed by the importance of Klaas's barter that they abandoned all pretence of neutrality, interposed their strength on Klaas's behalf, and forced the unlucky Koopman to recognize him as his "overlord." When, in December 1690, Koopman and some of his allies "rebelled," the Company sent a small force with authority to subdue them if they refused to submit to Klaas.[17]

The fact that Klaas was now relying on the Company's protection suggests that he had passed the peak of his own wealth and power. For some time he had been struggling to defend his holdings against "Ubiqua" attacks, and in late 1689 the robbers made away with the stock from three of his kraals while his people were suffering from an epidemic. Almost a year later the Company had been obliged to send out an armed force to protect him against further attacks by the robbers.[18] Klaas was clearly on the decline when Koopman launched the campaign which finally destroyed him.

THE DOWNFALL OF KLAAS, 1693–1701

In 1693 Governor Van der Stel abruptly abandoned the policy of shoring up Klaas's crumbling position. In July of that year two leading Khoikhoi from Koopman's kraals arrived in Cape Town and complained that Koopman's clan was about to be massacred by a combined force of six or seven thousand men made up of Klaas's Chainouqua and the Hessequa. One of the envoys testified that his own brother-in-

16. On the word *Sire*, see Nienaber, *Hottentots*, p. 349 (*kommandeur*). On the meaning of the name Gaukou, compare Namaqua *gou-ha*, "fat" and the Gauka R. (translated by the Dutch as Botter, now Bot), on which Gaukou was often camped. On Gaukou himself, see KA 4002, DR Feb. 4, 1687, p. 168; Schrijver, VRS 12, pp. 217, 247–48. The quotation is in KA 4009, S. van der Stel to XVII, April 14, 1694, p. 32.

17. KA 3990, DR July 14, 1677, pp. 337v–38; KA 4002, DR Nov. 19 and Dec. 3, 1687, pp. 375v, 384v; KA 7571/KZ 3179, DR March 3, 1688, n.p.; *Resolusies*, 3:229 (Jan. 1, 1691).

18. KA 4004, DR Dec. 27, 1689, p. 287; *Resolusies*, 3:225 (Nov. 11, 1690).

law was the main figure whom Klaas intended to kill in this attack. The brother-in-law had done nothing to deserve this fate, save that he had desired to trade with the Dutch, an ambition which Klaas was determined to thwart.

The Council of Policy chose to accept the testimonial of Koopman's envoys to their own loyalty and wounded innocence. An expedition of two hundred whites set out toward Hottentots Holland and surprised Klaas's kraal by night, the whites attacking from one side and Koopman's people cutting down survivors who tried to flee in the opposite direction. One hundred cattle and two hundred sheep were seized, and Klaas and several of his leading men were taken as prisoners to the Cape. Having examined the prisoners on charges of disloyalty to the Company, the Council of Policy decided to banish Klaas and his brother-in-law to Robben Island and to force two of Klaas's leading followers to become subjects of Koopman. By this time many of Klaas's people had already submitted to Koopman in accordance with the Khoikhoi custom whereby the newly poor hoped to recover their losses by herding for the newly rich. Klaas's hard-earned stock was apportioned between the Company and Koopman.

Van der Stel justified his sudden volte-face by charging that Klaas had for some time been plotting against the Company's interests. Not only had Klaas refused to trade with the Company, but he had also thwarted the Company's trade with other Khoikhoi; he had bartered illegally with freemen, and he had mistreated a recent Dutch expedition in his territory.[19]

These charges were at best only partly true and could in any event hardly justify such a sudden attack on an allegedly independent people. If Klaas did in fact turn against the Company after twenty years of almost servile obedience, one would expect to find evidence of his treachery piling up in the official records prior to 1693. The fact is, however, that little is to be found except a complaint that the Hessequa and Chainouqua *in general* were obstructing trade, and one court case in which some freemen were convicted of trading with one of Klaas's people but not with Klaas himself.[20]

Van der Stel's evidence did not convince many contemporaries. Kolbe stated that many people at the hearings would have spoken up

19. *Resolusies*, 3:270–75 (July 20 and Aug. 17, 1693); KA 4010, DR July 25, 1693, p. 143v; KA 4011, S. van der Stel to XVII, May 9, 1695, pp. 11–13.

20. KA 4007, S. van der Stel to XVII, April 12, 1693, pp. 35–36; KA 4008, DR Feb. 22, 1692, pp. 159–59v.

on Klaas's behalf but for fear of the governor. Certainly the episode was vividly remembered in Cape Town when Kolbe reached the Cape in 1705 and when Johan Daniel Buttner arrived in 1712: both these German visitors found informants who were extremely sympathetic to Klaas's side of the story. The Seventeen were not convinced by the charges either. Possibly influenced by Theunis Gerbrantz van der Schelling, a sea captain recently returned from the Cape, they bestirred themselves to write their first significant dispatch on Khoikhoi affairs for decades. They severely reproached Van der Stel for acting without authority and for destroying a Company ally without due process or adequate proof. Klaas was to be released immediately and compensated for his losses.[21]

If the charges were false, or only partially true, Van der Stel must obviously have had ulterior motives. He was probably influenced by the knowledge of Klaas's slipping position and by the calculation that Koopman would have made a sterner ally. Kolbe suggested that the governor may well have wanted to seize Klaas's cattle: this suspicion is perhaps borne out by the text of the resolution to attack Klaas, which begins with a long and lugubrious passage about the Company's shortage of cattle. Kolbe further charged that the ensign (Schrijver) and others involved in the cattle trade had been absconding with goods and stock belonging to the Company; because Klaas's system threatened the continuation of the official-dominated trade, they had decided to dispose of him. In view of later revelations of official involvement in the trade, we cannot dismiss this allegation out of hand, especially since Van der Stel relied mainly on Schrijver for his information on Klaas's alleged treachery. Nonetheless, Kolbe's charges, which were made decades after the event, are far from conclusive.[22]

Van der Stel himself soon came to doubt the justice, or at least the wisdom, of his act. Even before receiving the Seventeen's rebuke, he released Klaas and allowed him to pasture some cattle for the Company, provided he would never return to his own country.

21. Kolbe, *Cape of Good Hope*, 1:39–45; Buttner, Waare Relation, n.p.; KA 461, XVII to S. van der Stel, July 14, 1695, n.p. Kolbe's account and Buttner's are based on different sources. Buttner's tallies very well with contemporary evidence in the Company archives and shows intimate knowledge of some aspects of the affair, especially the inner politics of Koopman's clan. Kolbe's is more melodramatic and embellished but is reliable on the main facts: on his suggestion that Gerbrantz influenced the Seventeen, see also Verhaal van Theunis Gerbrantszn van der Schelling, *RZA*, 3:170.

22. Kolbe, *Cape of Good Hope*, 1:41–42; *Resolusies*, 3:270–71 (July 20, 1693). For an example of officials' involvement in cattle barter, see p. 229 of this study.

Gradually Klaas managed to build up at least a portion of his former wealth, restored his friendship with Gaukou, and, with or without permission, returned to his original home. He did not, however, regain his wife, Gaukou's daughter, who in the presence of the governor declared that she preferred to live with Koopman, who was now riding high with Company recognition as "chief of the Soeswas."[23] Relations between Klaas and Koopman were now even more bitter than before Klaas's arrest, having been exacerbated by intervening events and by the dispute over the woman. Throughout 1697 and early 1698, the Dutch were engaged in unending attempts to dampen down the quarrel. At the height of the struggle Gaukou's daughter decided to return to Klaas, but while fleeing she was overtaken by Koopman and murdered.[24]

By this time Klaas was a demoralized man who alternated between obsessive pursuit of his enemies and alcoholic stupor. Having now learned to distrust the Company, he used all his influence to stop his own and other Khoikhoi from trading more cattle than they could afford. On one occasion he was drinking with the leader of a Dutch bartering expedition, Ambrosius Zassé, when he suddenly got up and shouted, "I'm boss here!" and wildly attacked the Dutchman. In the ensuing struggle he vainly tried to kill Zassé with a pewter mug, a sharpened bar, and a hatchet. He then scrambled out of the tent shouting, "I'm the boss!" and struck one of his own people before being subdued and placed under armed guard.[25]

A year and a half later, in June 1701, Klaas was killed during a fight at Koopman's kraal. According to one of Buttner's informants, he had been lured there by Koopman and then murdered.[26] Koopman had finally eliminated his rival and was now unquestionably the dominant chief among the Chainouqua. Indeed, after Gaukou's death in 1707, he was the only powerful Khoikhoi chief in the south-western Cape. He apparently lived to quite an old age, and was able to establish his authority so well among the Chainouqua that most of them began to call themselves Koopmans. Approximately seventy years later, when independent Khoikhoi groups were hardly ever

---

23. KA 4011, DR Jan. 23, 1694, p. 121.
24. KA 4015, DR Feb. 4, May 6 and 27, Sept. 7, 1697, pp. 481, 515, 526–27v, 569; KA 4017, DR March 26, 1698, pp. 451–51v.
25. KA 4017, Declaration of Ambrosius Zassé and Jacob Leven, Jan. 23, 1699, pp. 354ff; KA 4017, Declaration of Pieter de Blaauw, Jan. 23, 1699, pp. 347–47v.
26. KA 4024, DR June 14–15, 1701, p. 144v; Buttner, Waare Relation, n.p.

found in the southwestern Cape, and when the name Chainouqua had long been forgotten, the Swedish traveler Thunberg discovered a small cluster of Khoikhoi who still boasted the name of Koopman.[27]

After the death of Klaas, the traditional leadership of the Western Cape Khoikhoi virtually disappeared from the records of the Dutch colony. By 1701 the Dutch no longer feared or relied on the traditional leaders, and consequently they rarely bothered even to record their names. This indifference was largely due to the fact that there were no longer any chiefs in the western Cape—apart from Koopman—whose authority extended beyond a single clan. The respected tribal chiefs of earlier generations had disappeared, and they had done so largely because they had failed to respond adequately to the threat posed by the Dutch colony. The cooperative stance taken by Klaas and Gaukou had proven as futile in the long run as the more hostile policy of Gonnema.

But why had the leadership so signally failed? No answer can be given before we examine the political, economic, and social context in which the leadership operated or before we understand the numerous ways in which virtually all facets of Khoikhoi life were eroded by contact with the alien society. Khoikhoi decline was not by and large dramatic; it was the result of several gradual processes that were barely perceptible to contemporary observers. These processes of disintegration will be the subject of the next three chapters.

---

27. KA 4037, Dagverhaal ... Hartogh, Nov. 5–10, 1707, pp. 904v–06v; Thunberg, *Voyages*, 1:227.

Part 3   Processes of Decline among the Western
Cape Khoikhoi, 1652–1701

8

The Trade in Cattle and Sheep

THE DIMENSIONS OF DEMAND

The Company's cardinal goals for its Cape station were that it should supply food and services to Company vessels, and that it should do so with as little outside help as possible. In large part these goals were readily attained: within a few years after 1652 the colony was able to provide water, fruit, and vegetables for the ships, as well as lodging, entertainment, and medical care for their crews. But never in the seventeenth century was it able to supply meat in adequate quantities without resorting to trade with the inland Khoikhoi.

This dependence on Khoikhoi sources resulted largely from the fact that the Company consumed far more stock than its ships alone required. Among the foremost of its obligations was the nurture of its own civil and military establishment at the Cape. The needs of this community were considerable but more or less subject to limitation by the Company: the growing slave population was usually fed only on fish, and the white population was not self-generating, since few Company employees kept their families with them at the Cape. The total white establishment, which had numbered only 97 in 1658, gradually rose to a peak of 520 in 1673 as a result of the war with France and England; in postwar retrenchment it was cut back to 306 in 1681 and then allowed to creep slowly upward to 714 in 1714.[1] Despite their small numbers, these people probably consumed much more meat than persons of comparable class in Europe. It was not long before the Cape was noted for a culinary culture based on mutton.[2]

The Company's hospital constituted another major drain on the meat supply. It housed not only sick sailors from vessels in the harbor but many who had been left behind to convalesce after their ships had resumed their voyages. These patients, who often numbered many

1. Statistics on Company employees are scattered. In earlier years they are often found in censuses sent over to Holland with the burgher rolls. In later years the most regular source of information is the annual "general missive" from the Cape governor to the Seventeen.

2. Mentzel, VRS 6, p. 101.

hundreds,[3] received more generous rations than sailors on board ship; consequently, the annual outlay of mutton to the hospital was often greater than that to the Company's permanent employees in Cape Town.

Nor were livestock needed solely for direct human consumption. The Company required a large herd of oxen for ploughing and for transporting materials used in the construction of fortifications. It was also obliged from time to time to turn stock over to freemen, sometimes on loan and sometimes as outright gifts. Significant numbers of cattle were disbursed in 1658, just after the founding of the settler community, and again after the initial Dutch victories in the Second Khoikhoi-Dutch War; furthermore, in 1687 the Company advertised in Europe that all immigrants to the Cape would be provided with a loan of cattle to start their herds.[4]

However, despite these various commitments, the Company used the bulk of its stock to feed its own fleets. During the first eighteen years of the colony's history, the ships received 64 percent of the cattle and 54 percent of the sheep distributed by the Company (see table, p. 153). Most of these deliveries were in the form of butchered meat, though occasionally live animals were boarded for use later in the voyage. In 1658 Jan van Riebeeck had advised the directors that they should count on delivering eight cattle and eight sheep to each visiting ship: reckoning at thirty ships a year, that made an annual total of 240 cattle and 240 sheep—a fairly modest figure.[5] In fact, however, sheep were always more plentiful than cattle, not only because they bred faster, but also because Khoikhoi supplied them more readily; hence the average consumption in this period (1655–63) was 5.4 cattle and 10.3 sheep per ship.[6] In following years the number of ships calling at Cape Town increased, but at a barely perceptible rate. In Van Riebeeck's time the annual total had only once exceeded forty; after 1695 it was usually more than sixty-five, and by the early 1720s was often above eighty-five.[7]

One would suppose that such gradual growth over a seventy-year

3. Theal, *History of South Africa*, 1:370–72.

4. *VRJ*, 2:325 (Aug. 20, 1658); KA 3988, DR April 15, 1674, p. 110; Algemeen Rijksarchief, Collectie Radermacher no. 503 (Stukken betreffende de Uitzending van Landbouwersfamilies), Ordre en Reglement ter vergaderingh van de Seventiene ... gearresteert ... 1687.

5. KA 3970, Van Riebeeck to XVII, Feb. 22, 1658, p. 400.

6. For sources of these figures, see nn. 7 and 9 below.

7. This information is derived from the port records that were forwarded annually to the Seventeen; the figures include foreign ships and coasting craft based in South Africa, though numbers in both these categories were then extremely small.

period would not put undue strain on the colony's abilities to provide. Such a strain did in fact occur, but mainly because the demand for stock *per ship* rose much more steeply than the number of ships itself. By the late 1660s the Company's ships consumed over 300 Cape cattle and about 2,000 Cape sheep per year; while not a radical departure from Van Riebeeck's estimate for cattle, this rate of consumption was almost nine times his suggested figure for sheep. By 1683 deliveries of sheep had risen to the point where many ships were given a hundred each, and few got less than thirty: the quota was now close to one sheep for every four to five sailors on board.[8]

This rising consumption was due, not so much to an increase in the size of ships, but to the fact that sailors could always eat far more meat than the trifling amounts suggested by Van Riebeeck. Demand could expand greatly to outstrip any increase in supply. The ships' crews—often numbering in the hundreds—faced voyages of many months, and the demands of their officers for more victuals were hard for a governor to resist, both from humanitarian and practical points of view: dissatisfied skippers on the return fleet could sometimes do a governor much harm by submitting unfavorable reports to the Seventeen.

The following table gives the breakdown of the Company's stock needs between 1652 and 1669, the only period for which reasonably complete figures can be obtained.[9]

THE COMPANY'S DISBURSEMENTS AND LOSSES OF STOCK, 1652–1669

	Cattle	*Sheep*
Disbursed to Freemen	390	383
Company Establishment	511	2,864
Ships	2,997	10,120
Hospital	111	3,020
Losses (robberies, deaths)	536	1,660
Other (includes sales to Company Servants and to foreign ships)	111	636
Totals	4,656	18,683

8. See n. 9 and KA 3996, Oncostboeck van verstreckte ververssingen ... in den Jaare 1683, pp. 689–708.

9. These figures were compiled from entries in the Company's ledgers under the rubrics "koebeesten" and "schaepen": the ledgers are bound in the KA series under the appropriate years. The totals are not complete, as data on 1654 and 1664 are not available. The figures for the Company's establishment were obtained by totaling expenditures assigned to "extraordinaire ontcosten" and "montcosten." In the chart, I have omitted fractions.

The Company could not sustain slaughtering on such a large scale simply by trading with the Peninsular Khoikhoi. It had either to trade farther and farther inland, or else develop herds and flocks that were large enough to satisfy the Company's needs through natural increase. The failure of the whites to follow this latter course was of momentous significance for Khoikhoi. Initially, the Company had not considered self-sufficiency a major objective, in part because it wished to avoid the expense of tending and protecting herds. However, when Simon van der Stel became commander in 1679, it had become obvious that the Dutch were spending far too much on expeditions to distant Khoikhoi tribes. Accordingly, with the Seventeen's endorsement, Van der Stel set out to make the Company independent of its Khoikhoi suppliers. By 1682 he could announce that it had 2,061 ewes and 500 ewe lambs, and was thus in striking distance of the 3,000 breeding ewes which it required to supply its annual needs of 3,000 sheep. In 1688 the Company's flocks reached 9,912 and by then could have been virtually self-sustaining.[10] Nonetheless, the trade in sheep did not cease, but continued as an adjunct to the cattle trade.

The Company's success with sheep was partially due to its policy of mating Khoikhoi ewes with Dutch rams; in this way it had produced hybrids that were deemed stronger, more prolific, more nourishing, and more productive of milk than pure Khoikhoi sheep. These hybrid sheep also survived much better on Cape pastures than did the Company's cattle (which were not hybrids), and of course bred faster, since each ewe might bear two lambs annually. The Dutch obtained sheep from Khoikhoi more readily than cattle, and such cattle as they persuaded Khoikhoi to sell were usually oxen or old sick cows; consequently, the Company had very few healthy breeding cows. These factors taken together explain why its annual losses of cattle (through disease, poor pasture, and attacks of wild animals) exceeded by many times its gains through breeding. Since its herds, unlike its flocks, never came close to self-sufficiency, the Company had to continue the increasingly difficult task of bartering cattle from its Khoikhoi neighbors.[11]

THE CONDITIONS OF SUPPLY

The Company strove to regulate the livestock trade with the same

10. KA 3994, S. van der Stel to XVII, April 23, 1682, pp. 8v–9; KA 4002, S. van der Stel to XVII, April 26, 1688, p. 19v.

11. *VRJ,* 2:326 (Aug. 20, 1658); KA 3994, S. van der Stel to XVII, April 23, 1682, p. 9.

thoroughness it applied to its spice operations in the East Indies. Its
goal was to control the price at which stock was bought and sold, and
its means were twofold: (1) to gain sole access to the sources of cheap
Khoikhoi cattle and (2) to monopolize the distribution of cattle to
consumers—in both cases by eliminating all middlemen, be they
European or Khoikhoi. To enforce its policies the Company had the
overwhelming advantage of being the sole lawmaker, prosecutor,
judge, jury, and policeman in the colony.

The freeman colony had been founded in 1657 primarily to supply
the agricultural needs of the Company. The farmers needed oxen for
ploughing and some stock for meat and milk, and the Company
willingly provided these. It was not long, however, before farmers
manifested that yearning for large herds and flocks which prefigured
the values of the *trekboer* culture of the eighteenth century. The Company was alarmed by this phenomenon, and for most of the rest of the
seventeenth century it regarded freemen more as potential competitors
in the cattle trade than as suppliers who could help relieve it of the
burdens of stock procurement.

Figure 2 illustrates the Company's problems. The dotted lines
indicate the illegitimate paths of trade which it strove to stamp out.
The solid lines represent the patterns of livestock exchange which it
considered ideal.

It was fairly easy to insulate the main buyers (Company and
foreign ships) from all suppliers but the Company. Sailors and ships'
officers were forbidden to buy from freemen, and notices were posted
on each ship forbidding trade with Khoikhoi in items other than
ostrich eggs or fish. Though Khoikhoi were often allowed to board
visiting vessels in spite of the regulations, it is unlikely that they could

Figure 2

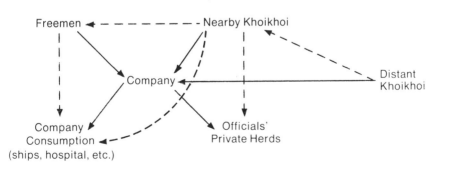

have conducted illicit trade in anything except trifles.[12] It was more difficult to guarantee that the Company would receive all the stock which freemen chose to sell, and that the price would always be the official rate of 25 guilders per head for cattle and 3 guilders for sheep. To do so the government made it illegal for freemen to sell stock even to one another without the prior consent of the commander and the Council of Policy. This prohibition was probably not well enforced, though it was occasionally reissued; the only convictions I have found under its provisions occurred just after it was renewed in 1666.[13]

The hardest task of all was to police relations between Khoikhoi and freemen. The Company appreciated that burghers were likely to "spoil" the Khoikhoi by accustoming them to more and better goods than the Company itself wanted to provide. Hence from 1658 to 1700 it imposed a total ban on all Khoikhoi-freeman trade. The enforcement of this and related prohibitions accounted for a considerable percentage of the cases tried by the Council of Justice. In the early decades the normal penalty for illegal barter was confiscation of the bartered beasts and a heavy fine (up to 25 rixdollars, roughly the equivalent of 62 1/2 guilders). Convicted Company employees were usually fined smaller amounts but were whipped and demoted. In the 1690s Simon van der Stel undertook to root out the trade by issuing even stiffer *plakkaten*: in 1696 Jan Jorgen, a burgher implicated in trading at least fifty cattle, was scourged, deprived of all his property, and banned from the colony for life.[14]

To stamp out the illegal cattle barter, the Company found it advisable to ban almost all other forms of trade between whites and Khoikhoi—even in such trivial items as ostrich feathers. One man was punished for receiving milk from Khoikhoi, another for accepting cloth which Khoikhoi had originally stolen from whites. At one time burghers were even forbidden to let Khoikhoi enter their homes, though this rule was not enforced since Khoikhoi served as domestics in white

---

12. *CGH*, 1:62 (Saar, 1660); *Kaapse Plakkaatboek*, ed. M. K. Jeffreys, 6 vols. (Cape Town: Cape Times Limited, 1944–51), 1:21, 79 (Sept. 18, 1656 and Dec. 15, 1663): this source is hereafter referred to as *KP*.

13. *VRJ*, 2:92 (Feb. 21, 1657); *KP*, 1:35 (May 4, 1658). From Jan. 17, 1660 to Sept. 18, 1666, barter among freemen in *sheep* was permitted under certain conditions (*KP*, 1:56, 94). For convictions, see KA 3979, Fiscal vs. Jacob Cornelsz et al., and Fiscal vs. Steven Jans et al., Feb. 12, 1667, pp. 683v–84.

14. For typical convictions, see KA 3973, Fiscal vs. Herman Remajenne and Hans Ras, July 10, 1660, p. 450v; KA 3975, Fiscal vs. Jacob Egbertsz, Feb. 6, 1662, p. 496; and case of Jan Jorgen in KA 4014, DR March 16, 1696, p. 874v.

households. It was also illegal for a burgher to possess Khoikhoi (i.e. nonhybrid) sheep; contrariwise, if a Khoikhoi was found with hybrid sheep, it was assumed that he had stolen them, since after 1677 whites could not legally pay their Khoikhoi laborers with such animals.[15]

These, then, were the measures the Company took to protect its monopoly: we must now examine the ways in which the monopoly itself functioned. From the founding of the colony until roughly 1670, most barter was conducted in or near the fort. This procedure was initially successful because Khoikhoi were sufficiently attracted by Dutch goods that they would voluntarily come to the colony; at first, too, they were drawn by a curiosity to see the strange building and to peer at the white intruders. The commanders took great pains to break down the fears of Khoikhoi and to quicken in them a desire for Dutch trade goods. For chiefs they laid on a simple banquet of European dishes and musical entertainment. They treated nonchiefly Khoikhoi to rice, bread, tobacco, and arrack; and they provided facilities in the fort for them to sing, dance, and sleep off the effects of their merriment.

From the Dutch point of view, the main advantages of the barter at the fort were that it was comparatively cheap and that it allowed the Company to keep its limited manpower on duty guarding the harbor. For Khoikhoi the advantages were even more significant. When they came to the fort they had the number of cattle which they were willing to sell, and no more. They could not be induced by soft words, alcohol, or the temptation of gleaming mounds of copper, to part with more animals than they considered on cool reflection to be wise. This feature was, of course, highly unfavorable to the Dutch and ultimately caused them to turn to other techniques.

Trade at the fort occurred in dribs and drabs and at irregular intervals. In the first years most sales took place in November, December, and January, since the Khoikhoi migrated to the Cape Peninsula during the dry summer season. As the trade became more institutionalized, sales tended to level out across the calendar; but as long as it remained at the fort, summer sales were slightly higher than those of the other seasons.[16] It was, however, quite impossible for the Company to predict or control the volume of trade in a given month or year. There were other problems: the presence of Khoikhoi traders in the

---

15. *KP*, 1:100 and 139–40 (June 2, 1667 and April 12, 1677); KA 3983, Fiscal vs. Jan Veth, Oct. 8, 1670, p. 332; KA 3996, Claes Pieterse vs. Jan Mostart, Sept. 28, 1682, p. 557v.

16. Statements based on trading figures scattered throughout the Dagregister.

fort led to disorders with whites, created fire hazards, and offended the Dutch sense of tidiness.[17] Furthermore, by allowing Khoikhoi into the colony the Company was giving them an opportunity to trade with freemen and to turn the trade to their own advantage.

In previous chapters we saw that it was the Peninsulars who most creatively exploited this situation. Not only did they enrich themselves by supervising Dutch transactions with inland Khoikhoi, but they also developed a secondary trade network that allowed them to buy livestock inland and sell it to the Dutch at a profit. In response to the frustrations caused by the Peninsular blockade, the Dutch periodically tried to induce individuals like Harry, or else whole tribes, to become regular suppliers at the fort. As we have seen, all these early schemes failed.[18] The crux of the problem was that both trading partners valued cattle and sheep above all other items being exchanged. Under these conditions only intermittent trade was possible; thus the Dutch, who required a steady stream of stock, were forced to venture farther inland to tap new reservoirs of cattle.

Van Riebeeck once suggested that the Company build trading posts along the migration routes of cattle-rich tribes in the interior. Although two expeditions were sent out with orders to reconnoiter ground for such a post, nothing came of the suggestion.[19] However, when Saldanha Bay and Hottentots Holland were garrisoned in the 1670s, both became minor trading forts: the former drained cattle from the Cochoqua and Guriqua, and the latter from the Western Chainouqua. These outposts accounted for only a small percentage of the total trade, as Khoikhoi generally preferred to be entertained lavishly by the governor in Cape Town than to be mistreated by a corporal at a post.[20] South Africa developed nothing comparable to the North American networks of fur-trading forts, partly because distances in South Africa were shorter than in America, but chiefly because there was no international competition spurring traders to establish themselves close to the source of supply.

The ultimate solution to the Company's problems proved to be the trading expedition. By the 1660s and 1670s several Dutch expedition

17. *Memoriën*, p. 59 (Klencke, April 6, 1663).

18. See pp. 100–01.

19. KA 3970, Van Riebeeck to XVII, March 31, 1658, p. 436; *VRJ*, 2:161 and 238 (Oct. 19, 1657, and Feb. 25, 1658).

20. There were several unpleasant incidents at the posts; see e.g. KA 7571/KZ 3179, DR Feb. 17, 1688, n.p.

leaders—notably Jeronimus Cruse, Pieter Cruijthoff, and Laurens Visser—had accumulated considerable knowledge of where and when Khoikhoi could be expected to trade and had gained some measure of rapport with their chiefs. For a while traditional barter at the fort coexisted alongside the increasingly numerous trade expeditions; however, by 1670 the former, which was dependent on the dwindling herds of the Peninsulars, had declined to 19 cattle and 271 sheep, as compared to 153 cattle and 999 sheep received from the outposts and from expeditions. The Second Khoikhoi-Dutch War further hastened the decline of the old system. By the 1680s and 1690s the expedition system was so well developed that it supplied almost all the Company's stock.[21]

The barter expeditions usually consisted of fewer than twenty men, who were drawn from the Company's garrison and commanded by a sergeant, ensign, or lieutenant. The traders, who were normally absent a month or more, carried their provisions in ox-driven wagons but supplemented these with mutton and game acquired en route. There were apparently no fixed rendezvous, except that the Hessequa were often met at Backeley Plaats (near modern Swellendam). Having located a tribe, the expedition sent out Khoikhoi runners to nearby kraals, urging them to trade. It then traveled from kraal to kraal and camped a day or so at each.

Much as they had done in the barter at the fort, the Dutch tried to lubricate the trade through judicious flattery of chiefs and captains. Normally the chief himself began the honors by offering the Dutch leader a sheep or two (according to Ten Rhyne, the Khoikhoi called this in pidgin Dutch *etom schaep*, or "eating sheep") and possibly a drink of milk in his hut. The Dutch then reciprocated with presents—in a typical case, three or four jugs of brandy, five or six pounds of rice, and two or three pounds of tobacco. (Expensive Virginia tobacco was used for this purpose, cheaper Brazilian being reserved for the trade itself.) In the eighteenth century these gifts were often called *tabetjesgoed*, from the Malay greeting *tābih*. Such gift exchanges were probably part of traditional Khoikhoi trading culture, since chiefs who had never before bartered with the Dutch insisted on them.[22] In the early years of

21. Sources as in n. 16. On March 14, 1670, Commissioner van den Brouck ordered Cape officials to halt expeditions and to encourage a revival of the fort barter (*Memoriën*, p. 92): this they found impossible to accomplish (KA 3984, Bruegel to XVII, April 19, 1672, p. 9v).

22. Ten Rhyne, VRS 14, p. 137; KA 3981, Report of Cruijthoff, Aug. 4, 1668, p. 628; KA 3981, Diary of the *Voerman*, Oct. 5, 1668, p. 659.

the trade it is unlikely that the expeditions used more than friendly persuasion to induce the Khoikhoi to part with their stock; the Dutch were constantly anxious lest harsh methods should alienate future trade.

Though expeditions were sent to the north and in circuits near Cape Town, the major thrust was into the area east of Hottentots Holland. The importance of this region is shown by the following table, the right hand column of which indicates the comparative willingness of eastern peoples to part with cattle (as opposed to sheep).[23]

SOURCES OF LIVESTOCK OBTAINED BY THE DUTCH, 1662–1713

	Cattle	Sheep	Ratio of Sheep to Cattle
Peninsulars	613	1,951	3.2 to 1
Cochoqua	2,310	9,328	4.0 to 1
Eastern Peoples (chiefly Chainouqua and Hessequa)	6,634	10,475	1.6 to 1
Northern Peoples (Guriqua and Namaqua)	99	372	3.8 to 1
Unknown or combination of two of the above	4,707	10,682	2.3 to 1
Totals	14,363	32,808	

The barter expeditions allowed the Company to draw on the largest herds and flocks in the western Cape. They also afforded excellent sources of information on inland developments and soon became instruments for interference in Khoikhoi affairs. The costs of the expeditions were high, but not intolerably so. The largest expenses were the salaries of the men who would otherwise be working at the fort, and the purchase price of trade goods; the latter expense would have been roughly the same under any system. Provisions were not a major factor: for example, in 1666 five expeditions consumed only 231 guilders in provisions while disbursing 589 guilders in copper and 948 guilders in tobacco to Khoikhoi sellers.

The triumph of the expedition system forced ambitious Khoikhoi to reevaluate their tactics. There was little hope left of effectively cutting off the Dutch from inland Khoikhoi: the last such blockade was tried by Kuiper in 1672, one of the last years in which the barter

23. Sources as in n. 16. The figures include booty as well as traded stock. The "unknown" category consists largely of stock bartered by expeditions that went to two or more regions. No figures are given for the period before 1662 because accurate tribal identifications were then rare.

at the fort was of any significance. It was still possible to conduct a secondary inland trade: in practice this usually meant that Peninsulars (mainly Kuiper and Schacher) or the westernmost Chainouqua bought cattle from the Hessequa in return for assegais and Dutch copper and beads. Some of the cattle so obtained were sold to the Company's expeditions, some were illegally turned over to freemen, but the best were probably kept as the profits of the trade. This barter attained considerable dimensions. In 1676 Visser discovered Khoikhoi at Tijgerhoek with 30 or 40 cattle and 150 sheep which they had bought from the Hessequa; the next year the postholder of Hottentots Holland saw a group of Kuiper's people with 32 cattle and 46 sheep of Hessequa origin.[24]

The Company feared that this trade would quickly raise prices and hence tried to stop it with a combination of persuasion and coercion. However, the Europeans realized that they could never suppress Khoikhoi initiative entirely, and this was doubtless one reason why they welcomed Klaas's offer to put his energies and knowledge at their service. Klaas's activities cost the Company less than the expedition system and brought in a higher proportion of cattle to sheep than was usual.

During the 1680s Klaas's barter partially supplanted the expeditions, but when he was banished in 1693 the old form perforce reemerged. By now the disintegration of Khoikhoi society was far advanced in the southwestern Cape. Both a cause and an effect of this continuing decline was the tendency of the cattle trade, once based on voluntary exchange, to evolve into an institution whereby Dutch expeditions extracted tribute in cattle from reluctant Khoikhoi. Unfortunately, we have no direct evidence from the 1680s and 1690s, when these harsher techniques evolved. However, from the reports of Zassé (1699), Starrenburgh (1705), and Slotsboo (1712) we can see the new system in full bloom.

By this time Khoikhoi were doing all in their power to avoid trade: Khoikhoi guides misled expeditions; chiefs hid their stock; and when all else failed, Khoikhoi tried to sell sheep rather than cattle. Now the barter leaders would not take no for an answer; they threatened that the governor would punish chiefs who failed to trade and demanded

24. KA 3985, DR July 24, 1672, p. 332v; KA 3989, Visser's Journal, Sept. 22, 1676, p. 318v; KA 3990, DR June 3, 1677, p. 313v.

ever-increasing numbers of stock at prices which were constant and unnegotiable. In 1699, Ambrosius Zassé told Gaukou that he could not return to the Cape with the few cattle he had been offered: "What," he asked, "will the Governor say?" To this Gaukou replied: "*Masky*, the Governor will take me to the Cape and set me in the Black Hole [a well-known dungeon]. Is that barter?"[25]

THE COMPANY AND KHOIKHOI: PROFIT AND LOSS

There can be little doubt that the cattle trade—with its artificially low prices, its lack of competition, and latterly its element of coercion —greatly helped the Dutch to limit the expenses of operating their Cape station. Figure 3 indicates the Company's average costs per head for the years 1652 to 1667, the only period for which adequate figures are available. These figures include costs of trade goods and the expeditions' provisions, but not the wages of the traders.[26]

It is apparent that sheep prices were stable in comparison with the

Figure 3: Average Prices Paid by the Company for Livestock, 1652-67
(Guilders [fl.] per head)

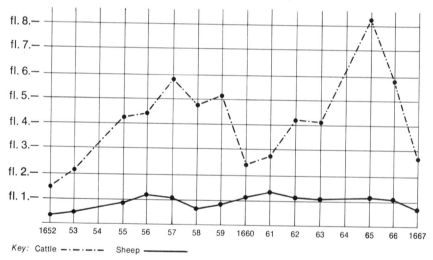

Key: Cattle —·—··—   Sheep ————

25. KA 4017, Declaration of Ambrosius Zassé and Jacob Leven, Jan. 23, 1699, pp. 350–55v; KA 4031, Dag Verhaal ... Starrenburgh, Oct. 16–Dec. 8, 1705, pp. 740–55; KZ 3193, Dagh Verhaal ... Slotsbo, Oct. 13–Nov. 22, 1712, n.p. The quotation is from the first source, p. 352.

26. The traders' wages would not be a major factor, because in this period most trading was done at the fort or very close to the fort. Average prices have been obtained by dividing total expenditures by the number of animals entered into the trade books. Note that figures for 1654 and 1664 are lacking.

fluctuating rates for cattle. This was because Khoikhoi valued cattle far more highly than sheep, and their willingness to part with the former varied with the changing size of their herds and with the degree to which Dutch trade goods were a novelty for their particular tribe. The low prices of 1652–53 and 1660–61 reflected periods of novelty for the Peninsulars in the first case, and for the Cochoqua and Chainouqua in the second. Thereafter, as Khoikhoi demand contracted, prices rose to levels that were no longer absurdly low from the Dutch point of view. (It must be remembered that the guilder was worth much more then than now: in 1662, many common sailors earned only 9 guilders per month along with their board.) Nonetheless, prices were still highly favorable to the Company, which easily obtained the requisite barter goods from its intercontinental trading system. These goods were comparatively cheap and were never needed in vast quantities. For instance, during the period 1652 to 1667 the Company bought a total of 3,819 cattle for 4,890 pounds of tobacco and 14,576 pounds of copper—a mere 1 1/4 pounds of tobacco and 3 3/4 pounds of copper per animal.[27]

Unfortunately, the Dutch archives do not provide us with comparably precise figures on prices after 1668. However, the impressionistic glimpses that we do get suggest that the going rate for cattle and sheep did not rise to a new order of magnitude in the later period. On the contrary, we can be sure that by 1700 prices had sunk to levels *below* those of the 1660s: Company expeditions in 1705 and 1712 paid only about one pound of tobacco and one bunch (*bos*) of copper beads per head of cattle.[28] By this time the trade had become so coercive that prices reflected only what the Company wanted to pay, not what Khoikhoi demanded.

Normally, of course, the Company slaughtered its stock rather than reselling it. Nonetheless, to gain a rough idea of the value of livestock to whites we can examine the prices the Company fetched in the cases where it did resell. In 1656 Van Riebeeck sold cattle to French and English ships at about 25 guilders per head, and sheep for about 5 guilders per head. Since in that year the Company paid Khoikhoi an average of 4.39 guilders for cattle and 1.16 guilders for sheep, its markup in each case was around 400 percent. Within the Dutch community, however, the selling price was lower: stock was conven-

27. Sources as in n. 9.
28. KA 4031, Dag Verhaal . . . Starrenburgh, Nov. 4, 1705, p. 749; KZ 3193, Dagh Verhaal . . . Slotsbo, Nov. 13, 1712, n.p.

tionally sold to Company servants and freemen for 12 guilders per head of cattle and 3 guilders per sheep (thus at a markup of roughly 200 percent).[29]

For the Dutch, then, the trade was advantageous in that they were exchanging goods they regarded as cheap for animals they highly valued. The Khoikhoi, by contrast, were parting with livestock—one of their main sources of nutrition, their most highly valued commodity, and the sole possessions which distinguished them from the despised hunters. In return for their livestock they received products they esteemed, but which were not foodstuffs and did not reproduce themselves. The Khoikhoi persisted in this seemingly improvident barter throughout the late decades of the seventeenth century, even as their herds and flocks were steadily diminishing. This disappearance of livestock must be counted the prime feature of the erosion of traditional Khoikhoi society. Consequently, it is reasonable to ask if Khoikhoi did not sell their independence for copper trinkets and a few pipefuls of tobacco. Is it true, as P. J. van der Merwe asserts, that "the Hottentots were stupid and ready to barter far more cattle than they could really afford"?[30] Before we settle this vexing question of whether Khoikhoi bartered irresponsibly, we must settle the seemingly more simple question of why they bartered at all.

It must be emphasized that the cattle barter was not viciously addictive; it did not make Khoikhoi pathetically dependent on whites, nor did it have malignant effects on Khoikhoi society comparable to the effects of the liquor, firearm, and slave trades on indigenous societies in other parts of the world. In fact, because of Khoikhoi conservatism and the Dutch desire to limit the range of trade goods, the social effects —both positive and negative—of the barter were slight. No cultural revolution was triggered by the trade. Western clothes, blankets, and spices—all of which might have altered traditional customs—were presented only as gifts to leading Khoikhoi and were never used as regular trade goods. Likewise, the traders did not give money to Khoikhoi; and it appears that, apart from the urban Khoikhoi who earned coins from sailors in Cape Town, seventeenth-century Khoikhoi esteemed coins only for their metallic or decorative value.[31]

29. See ledger entries in KA 3969, pp. 155, 161, 189, 190; KA 3970, pp. 281–82, 333; KA 3972, p. 189v.

30. P. J. van der Merwe, "Die Inboorlingbeleid," 2:357.

31. See pp. 207–08.

Furthermore, no revolution in military techniques was caused by the diffusion of new materials. It was a sternly executed Company policy that no guns should be sold to Khoikhoi. Apart from Klaas, who reportedly received four firearms from the Company, the few guns which got through to Khoikhoi were stolen or illegally bought from freemen. In such cases the Company usually got wind of the matter and sent out an armed party to confiscate the weapons. Khoikhoi only obtained guns in large numbers after they had been working on white farms for some time; hence firearms played no known role in the internal disintegration of traditional Khoikhoi society.[32] The Company similarly considered it unwise to give iron to Khoikhoi in large amounts, since they could use it to improve their assegai heads. Knives, small tools, and iron digging sticks were occasionally given as diplomatic gifts or as minor adjuncts to trade. However, the Company seems to have refused all Khoikhoi requests to establish a regular trade in the metal.[33]

Alcohol was not an important item of barter, and it did not corrode traditional society or undermine the determination of Khoikhoi to keep their cattle. It is true that Khoikhoi early showed a fondness for alcohol; typically, after a glass of brandy they would sing and dance exultantly and then fall into a long, deep sleep. The Khoikhoi who worked on white farms or in the town were sometimes given a *soopje* (dram) each day, along with bread and tobacco. Furthermore, at least two westernized Khoikhoi—Eva and Klaas—ended their lives as drunkards, if not alcoholics. However, there is very little evidence of alcohol producing pathological or violent behavior among individuals, and none at all for such behavior in the mass of cattle-keeping Khoikhoi in the kraals. There is absolutely no parallel here to the effects of liquor on some North American Indian societies.

This was mainly because the Company did not use alcohol as a barter item per se. Brandy and arrack (an East Indian liquor first requisitioned by Van Riebeeck because some Khoikhoi found brandy too strong) were given solely as honoraria to chiefs and to those with whom the chiefs chose to share. The amounts consumed were considerable but not enormous: for example, in 1673 Sergeant Cruse took only

---

32. *VRJ*, 3:239 (July 4, 1660); KA 3990, DR Oct. 12, 1677, p. 384v.

33. See Company's ledgers under "koebeesten" and "schaepen," especially for 1658 and 1660–63; KA 3999, DR April 29, 1685, p. 256v; KA 3973, Fiscal vs. Jan Zacharias, Oct. 9, 1660, p. 460; KA 3978, DR Jan. 9, 1666, p. 439.

one anker of brandy on a barter expedition to several tribes.[34] If the Company had intentionally or unintentionally undermined Khoikhoi society with alcohol, there would surely be record of the fact in its papers which, it must be remembered, were rarely falsified to hide moral turpitude in dealings with native peoples.[35] The freemen might have been freer in dispensing liquor than the Company, but their trade, as I shall show shortly, was too miniscule in the early years to have had much effect. A degrading dependence on alcohol was normally a result, not of the cattle trade, but of Khoikhoi absorption into white society. In general, it followed rather than preceded the disintegration of traditional Khoikhoi communities.

In short, then, the Company eschewed the more notorious forms of trade which Europeans practiced in other areas of the world, and sold Khoikhoi only copper, beads, trinkets and tobacco. Of these items by far the most important were copper and tobacco. To the Khoikhoi, copper was a pure "luxury" used solely for the manufacture of decorative bangles, beads, and rings; tobacco was even worse since it was a rapidly consumable luxury, and for this reason Van Riebeeck recommended that the Company emphasize it.[36] Yet we must remember that copper and dagga (for which Dutch tobacco later served as a substitute) had been the most important items in Khoikhoi trade long before Europeans reached South Africa. Metal ornamentation and narcotics were so deeply entrenched in Khoikhoi culture, and yet so hard to obtain in the southwestern Cape, that Khoikhoi welcomed the new European suppliers with enthusiasm. The success of the Dutch trade was due, not to any innovations caused by European products, but to the fact that they (or items like them) had long been traded against livestock in traditional Khoikhoi barter.

Different segments of Khoikhoi society had their own reasons for participating in the trade. Chiefs and wealthy men, for example, could thereby transform some of their livestock into copper, which was at once a prestigious and easily defensible form of wealth. It appears, however, that metallic values never displaced traditional pastoral ones, and few of the rich ever disposed of more than the skimmings of their herds. Indeed, by 1685 the wealthy Khoikhoi were

34. KA 3986, Memorie voor den Sergeant Jeronimus Cruse . . . , Feb. 23, 1673, p. 152. The size of the anker varied throughout Europe: according to the *Oxford English Dictionary*, the Rotterdam anker contained 8½ imperial gallons.
35. Graham Irwin, "Dutch Historical Sources," in *An Introduction to Indonesian Historiography*, ed. Soedjatmoko et al. (Ithaca, N.Y.: Cornell University Press, 1965), pp. 236–37.
36. KA 3966, Van Riebeeck to XVII, April 14, 1653, p. 16v.

begging the Dutch to halt the trading expeditions to their tribes. The perceptive commissioner, H. A. van Reede, noted that "the reputation, power, might, and wealth of these peoples consists solely in the great numbers of their stock and cattle, by which they can attract their neighbors to themselves." Consequently, it was the wealthy and ambitious leaders rather than the poor who regarded the barter as a threat:

> [The common people, however] have no difficulty in selling a beast or a sheep for a bit of tobacco from which they derive no other benefit than ephemeral pleasure; they have no difficulty squandering their necessary sustenance, bringing themselves to poverty, and finally becoming a servant of those who again supply them with other cattle.[37]

The tendency to improvidence was not limited to the poor. Khoikhoi women, it will be remembered, inherited cattle only if they had no brothers and identified only with the small number of stock which they obtained at marriage. On the other hand, they did inherit beads, rings, and ornaments, and for that reason they probably valued them more highly (and livestock less highly) than did men. Furthermore, women played such an important role in Khoikhoi society that it seems they could influence the course of the trade. In 1668 Jeronimus Cruse found the Attaqua unwilling to barter until the chief had first consulted with his wife; he thereupon came to Cruse and promised to trade sixteen pack-oxen on condition that the Dutch would give his wife a quantity of beads. The first Company employees to visit Xhosa country (1752) were struck by the contrast between female roles in Nguni and in Khoikhoi society, and implied that this explained the unwillingness of Xhosa to sell their stock for Dutch copper:

> they [the Xhosa men] treat their wives little better than slaves, keeping all their ornaments for themselves . . . without giving the slightest amount to their wives. The Hottentots by contrast will save them in order to adorn their wives with them.[38]

The traditional status of trade in copper and narcotics, as well as the role of the poor and of women in barter, help to explain why Khoikhoi were willing to part with small numbers of livestock during periods

---

37. Hulshof, "H. A. van Reede . . . Journaal," p. 202.

38. On the role of women see pp. 60–61; Schultze, *Namaland*, p. 299; Engelbrecht, *Korana*, pp. 96–97; Wikar, VRS 15, p. 195. For Cruse's observations, see KA 3981, Diary of the *Voerman*, Oct. 5, 1668, p. 659; the quotation is found in Beutler (Haupt), *RZA*, 3:309.

of prosperity. These factors fail, however, to explain the behavior of Khoikhoi if, as is often alleged, they sold animals in such numbers as to induce the decline of their herds and the collapse of their traditional economy. But were the Khoikhoi in fact so imprudent? Much evidence suggests that they were not.

First, we must remember that the so-called barter was voluntary only for the first thirty years or so of its history. The subsequent three decades were increasingly marked by the actual or threatened use of force by the Dutch. This new coercion coincided with a period when Khoikhoi livestock holdings were dangerously low and when thoughtful Khoikhoi were actively trying to stop the trade.

Secondly, even in the earlier period of noncoercive barter, the evidence suggests that Khoikhoi were tough, shrewd bargainers. The only prolonged period when they traded livestock in numbers and at prices which delighted the whites was long before the founding of the colony —from 1591 to 1609, when Khoikhoi brought hundreds of cattle and sheep to passing ships.[39] Even this exuberant selling was by no means irrational: at that point Europeans were bartering iron, a metal of crucial military significance to Khoikhoi; and the absence of this metal at the Cape and the unpredictability of European visits naturally drove up the price to extreme heights.

However, after 1652 it was clear that Khoikhoi had no intention of jeopardizing the integrity and growth of their herds for any amount of copper and tobacco. Many Khoikhoi, in fact, traded with the Dutch in order to gain merchandise with which to buy more stock. Those who traded mainly for Dutch goods did so in small quantities, and in time of plenty. They preferred to sell sheep rather than cattle; and their sales of cattle consisted largely of oxen, the loss of which would not impair their herds' growth. The cows and ewes that were sold were often lame, sick, or old: Van Riebeeck reckoned in 1659 that not one-tenth of the sheep he had obtained from Khoikhoi were healthy enough to breed from.[40] Charges of selling shoddy goods were directed not only at the Peninsulars, who were considered wily, but also at the Chainouqua, the Company's most loyal trading partners in the early years.

Even if Khoikhoi had sold only healthy and fecund animals, the volume of their sales was not large enough to endanger the maintenance of their herds and flocks. According to the daily entries in the

39. See pp. 74–76.

40. *VRJ*, 2:370 (Nov. 7, 1658); 378 (Nov. 16, 1658); 3:5 (Jan. 20, 1659); KA 3972, Van Riebeeck to XVII, March 19, 1660, p. 15.

Dagregister, the Dutch obtained 15,999 Khoikhoi cattle between 1652 and 1699, almost entirely through trade. These figures are certainly incomplete, since between 1652 and 1669, a period for which the Company's ledgers are still extant, the *Dagregister*'s figures were 11 percent too low. In addition, we know that some cattle bought by bartering expeditions never reached the fort: some were consumed en route, some died in river crossings or were killed by wild animals, and some probably found their way into private hands. If we make a massively liberal allowance for all such factors and bring the estimated total of cattle sold by Khoikhoi to 25,000 (an increase of more than 55 percent), we are still left with an average of only 532 cattle per year. Furthermore, sales over the period were fairly constant: though there were large fluctuations from year to year, there was no tendency for sales to be bunched together in one decade, or for average annual sales to rise or fall greatly over the period.

If we assume, very conservatively, that only one-fifth of all Khoikhoi cattle were cows of suitable age and health to calve, a total herd of only 2,660 head could provide the Company with its 532 cattle in one year without declining numerically. To sustain such an annual loss over many years the herd would have to be only slightly larger. Yet we know that even the lowly Peninsulars had more cattle than this in 1652.[41] The total of all Khoikhoi herds in the southwestern Cape must have been well beyond ten times this figure, and would have been able to sustain the Company's purchases without harm, had not many other factors been operative. A similar situation existed in regard to sheep: over the same period the *Dagregister* shows that the Company obtained 36,636 sheep, or somewhat more than double the same source's figure for cattle. Khoikhoi sheep, however, bred at least twice as fast as cattle; so the problems of sustaining this loss should have been no greater.[42]

41. See p. 92.

42. Dr. Shula Marks has suggested to me that this argument would be stronger if the statistical analysis were performed on individual tribes rather than on the Western Cape Khoikhoi and Namaqua as a whole. This is a good point, for it is theoretically possible that the holdings of different tribes were separately depleted as the Dutch purchased massive numbers from one tribe and then from another. Unfortunately, tribe-by-tribe analyses are almost impossible to make. This is because in a given year many livestock cannot be definitely assigned to their tribal source. However, the evidence we do have indicates little concentration of sales on a single tribe over a short span. A possible exception is the trade to the Hessequa in the early 1680s, but in this case there is no reason to believe that the tribe's herds were declining in this period. On the other hand, the concentration on the Namaqua after 1687 may well be associated with the impoverishment of that group, especially since the trade was by then becoming coercive.

In view of the foregoing evidence it is clear that the Khoikhoi did not trade their cattle and sheep to the Company in sufficient numbers to explain the poverty in which they found themselves by the early eighteenth century. The trade was partially, but not entirely, responsible for their plight; it was only part of a complex of disintegrative factors that must now be briefly discussed.

How the Khoikhoi Lost their Livestock

In chapter 2 we described an "ecological cycle" that was embedded in the economy of Khoikhoi and their hunter neighbors. The essence of this cycle was the rapidity with which stock moved in and out of individual clans and tribes as a result both of warfare between Khoikhoi and hunters and of the vendetta system. The downswing of this cycle was not so much the loss of stock by one group as the process by which the ratio of stock to human population declined throughout a large region. Several events could induce such a decline: (1) disease, drought, or a combination of the two could kill large numbers of stock; (2) political disintegration could lead to many wars and a resultant loss of stock in battle and celebrations after battle; (3) political disintegration could also leave Khoikhoi open to hunter attacks, and hunters often slaughtered captured cattle in large numbers.

The downward swing was a snowballing process which could be started or given further momentum by factors outside the fragile Khoikhoi economy. The Dutch presence created many such factors, of which the official trade was only one. Another danger was posed by the clandestine trade that sprang up between Khoikhoi and freemen in defiance of the Company's regulations. In some cases Khoikhoi brought their own cattle to white farms; in others they acted as agents trading inland on the freemen's behalf. Most of this trade derived from free farmers' desire to build up their herds, but by the 1690s innkeepers in Cape Town were also using Khoikhoi agents to obtain cheap mutton for their guests; these Khoikhoi lived at the inn and were given the skin and entrails of each sheep they procured.[43]

The extent of the illegal trade should not be exaggerated. In the years before 1690 all the cases apprehended by the authorities involved a very small number of cattle and sheep—often as few as one or two, never as many as ten. In the period before the settlement of Stellenbosch in 1679, the colony was sufficiently compact, and chan-

43. KA 3984, DR Oct. 30, 1671, p. 160; *CGH*, 2:384 (Dampier, 1691).

nels of information were sufficiently numerous, that the officials could interdict the entry of large numbers of smuggled stock into the colony. This was especially the case with Khoikhoi sheep, which were visibly distinct from the freemen's hybrid sheep.

Growing contact between farmers and Khoikhoi also created an opportunity for stock theft. Again, however, our evidence indicates that in the early years freemen stole from Khoikhoi in only very small numbers. After the First Khoikhoi-Dutch War, we hear remarkably little of disputes between Khoikhoi and freemen over cattle. The Company was in constant contact with Khoikhoi chiefs who would have informed the officials of any robberies; and officials were only too anxious to find evidence against law-breaking freemen.[44]

In the late 1680s and 1690s, however, many old restraints began to collapse. The disappearance of powerful leadership among Khoikhoi was matched by an increasingly turbulent rebelliousness among frontier farmers, and both these developments encouraged illegitimate barter and cattle stealing. In 1689 we find record of freemen robbing Khoikhoi on a large scale (in this case taking at least fifty sheep), and in 1696 we encounter burghers forming partnerships for the express purpose of trading with Khoikhoi.[45]

Long before the era of frontier looting, the Company itself had contributed to Khoikhoi impoverishment in ways unrelated, or only indirectly related, to the regular barter. Not the least of these was its eagerness to seize the cattle of groups with which it was in conflict. This affected only a few southwestern clans, but for some of these it was the coup de grace. Harry and Klaas, the two Khoikhoi who most successfully exploited the Dutch presence to create new wealth, both saw their fortunes liquidated in this manner. In addition, one very important tribe, the Cochoqua, lost at least 1,600 cattle and 4,900 sheep in the Second Khoikhoi-Dutch War: though this disaster by no means extinguished their holdings, the Cochoqua found it impossible ever to recover their former wealth.

The Company did not encourage wars among Khoikhoi societies— quite the contrary, it tried to stop them—but there is evidence that it benefited from such wars nonetheless. The Khoikhoi were more willing to barter booty freshly taken in war than they were to sell their own

44. The preceding two paragraphs are based on a survey of all the judicial records of the colony in the period 1652–1713.

45. KA 4004, Landdrost vs. Jan Rappoi and Albert Bierman, April 19, 1689, p. 697; case of Jan Jorgen in KA 4014, DR March 16, 1696, pp. 872v–74v.

stock. And in one case at least, a dispute over trade with the Dutch seems to have contributed to the outbreak of an inter-Khoikhoi war.[46] It is also quite certain that a number of human diseases of European origin played havoc with Khoikhoi societies even before 1713, and it is likely that some of these encouraged Khoikhoi to part with their cattle faster than they desired.[47]

The effect of disease was similar to the effect of inter-Khoikhoi wars. In neither case was the Dutch trade directly culpable, but in both cases the presence of the colony encouraged Khoikhoi decline, and whites reaped benefits in sheep and cattle which were thus permanently lost to the Khoikhoi economic system. It must be emphasized that it was more detrimental to Khoikhoi to lose livestock to the Dutch than to lose it to other Khoikhoi. In the latter case, those who had been deprived of their animals could hope to recover them from the conquerors in battle, or could become herdsmen for the conquerors and thus benefit on a small scale from their former stock. By contrast, whenever Khoikhoi livestock fell into Dutch hands (whether by trade, robbery, or conquest) it was virtually irretrievable.

In seeking to explain the disappearance of stock from Khoikhoi herds, it is not enough to speculate on the causes of the economic downswing: one must also appreciate the reasons why the Khoikhoi economy did not recover in traditional fashion. Even if the Dutch had not been present, such recovery would have been exceedingly difficult apart from warfare; for while cattle were lost in the system as a whole, new prosperity had to be built up in nuclear families, the tiny units of social organization that owned stock. A Khoikhoi family which had lost most of its stock would find it difficult to rebuild because it was obliged to slaughter to meet its social obligations; Schultze says in this connection that poor Namaqua often sold their last milch cow to buy a slaughter beast for a wedding.[48] Under such conditions the growth of herds could not be subject to tribe-wide planning. Further- more, considerable mathematical difficulties faced small-scale cattle breeders. A man with a herd of 450 cattle (of which 200 are cows of calf-bearing age) can hope to have well over 600 cattle the following

46. KA 3987, DR March 15, 1673, p. 172; *VRJ*, 1:379 (Dec. 22, 1655).

47. It is not possible to identify most of these diseases accurately; however, intestinal diseases were quite frequent, as were illnesses characterized by severe fevers or swelling of the throat. Venereal diseases were also contracted from whites. Smallpox was apparently not present prior to 1713.

48. Schultze, *Namaland*, p. 298.

year: a man who has only one breeding cow (and the use of a bull) might have to wait several years before a female calf is born. Under ideal conditions he could only hope to be approaching a herd of ten cattle after seven years. And conditions were rarely ideal, for the insecurities of warfare with hunters and other Khoikhoi were felt equally by the individual stock owner and by the tribe as a whole.

The Dutch military potential served to discourage Khoikhoi from one traditional means of economic recovery: coalescence around a strong military leader. While traditional wars eliminated cattle in the short run, they offered the fastest way by which a tribe could build up the stock holdings that were the essential basis of recovery in their region. The Dutch, by intervening to halt Khoikhoi vendettas, effectively blocked this means of aggrandizement for all chiefs in the immediate hinterland of the Cape. At the same time, the Europeans were only partially successful in protecting their Khoikhoi clients against the depredations of hunters which contributed greatly to their poverty.[49]

The expansion of the white farming economy was a further detrimental factor. Firstly of course, the white farmers gradually encroached on the best pastures and left the Khoikhoi with inadequate land on which to build up vast herds. More importantly, the farms offered impoverished Khoikhoi a hope of regaining their cattle in a traditional way—namely, by herding for someone else. In fact, white farmers did not usually pay high enough wages to allow Khoikhoi to return to their kraals with new stock: normally tobacco and food were the only recompense, and these were quickly consumed. Khoikhoi laborers on white farms had in effect been sucked out of Khoikhoi society at the bottom of its economic downswing and had thus been relieved of the need for patiently reaccumulating wealth through the provident husbanding of stock. The process whereby Khoikhoi became laborers on Dutch farms will be discussed in the next chapter.

Thus, the Company's trade was only one of many reasons why the Khoikhoi lost their livestock. The deleterious factors may be divided into three groups: (1) processes by which Khoikhoi livestock were directly transferred to whites (e.g. the Company's trade, the freemen's trade, robbery, military action); (2) features of traditional Khoikhoi

---

49. On Dutch policy, see the following chapter.

society which made economic decline frequent and recovery difficult (e.g. private ownership of livestock, ritual consumption of livestock, political instability, the vendetta system, the danger from hunter-robbers); (3) processes engendered by the Dutch presence which exacerbated problems in the Khoikhoi economy (e.g. spread of new diseases, interdiction of chiefly aggrandizement, expropriation of pastures, demand for Khoikhoi labor). All of these processes fed on one another in ways so complex that it is almost impossible, given the inadequacy of our sources, to assess their relative significance.

We should note, however, that almost all processes in which the Dutch were involved were ones whose destructive impact grew steadily as the decades wore on. The trade increased in impact, though not in absolute numbers, as it evolved from voluntary barter with Khoikhoi well supplied with livestock into forced tribute from impoverished tribes. Similarly, the scale and violence of robberies by whites grew markedly toward the end of the century: so too did the illegal freemen's trade. And as we shall see in coming chapters, the settlers' land holdings, their demand for Khoikhoi labor, and the ability of the Company to intervene in tribal affairs, all were slight at the beginning, increased slowly from the 1670s, and grew rapidly in subsequent decades. The combination of all these mounting pressures put severe strain on the fragile economies of Khoikhoi tribes and made it virtually certain that they would never recover from their initial losses.

9

The Khoikhoi and Colonial Society:
Structural Aspects

"Our Hottentots": Individual Khoikhoi Enter European Society

The history of the Cape Khoikhoi differs from that of most southern African peoples in one striking respect. Their eventual subordination to the European colonists was not only structural but also cultural: their descendants in the end adopted the language, religion, and many of the customs of the Europeans. However, during the period covered by this study, cultural assimilation was not nearly so prominent as the rapid incorporation of Khoikhoi into the colonial polity and economy. Before 1713, a large percentage—perhaps a majority—of Western Cape Khoikhoi had become permanent or semipermanent residents of the colony. This remarkable development had been caused primarily by the Dutch demand for labor.

The colonists needed laborers to work in the fields, on building projects, and in private households. Apart from the officials, the bulk of European settlers were artisans and soldiers who were notoriously loath to engage in manual labor[1] or freemen who could not be expected to work on the Company's behalf. The government was thus forced to decide between encouraging the emigration of labor from Europe and transporting slaves from elsewhere in its trading system. Influenced in part by East Indian precedents, it chose the latter course, and for the first 182 years of its existence, white South Africa was a slave-owning society. However, prior to 1658, when slaves were first imported to the Cape in significant numbers, the Company had tried to obtain the services of a few Khoikhoi; after 1658 this small body of Khoikhoi laborers continued to grow as an adjunct to the more important slave force.

When they were not hunting, Khoikhoi men could find free time

1. E.g. *VRJ*, 3:122–23 (Aug. 19, 1659).

fairly easily, since the routine tasks of tending livestock required few
of their number and could even be performed by women. They were
thus willing to work for the Dutch, but on a temporary basis only.
This distaste for regular labor was regarded by most Dutchmen as
"laziness." It is fairer to say that the Khoikhoi were a nomadic people
for whom fixed domicile and routine were intolerable. In return for
their labor they were offered only rice, bread, tobacco, and alcohol.
All of these items were not, at least at first, necessities, but luxuries
for which they were unlikely to endure great hardship. Since they
were of lighter build than most whites and slaves, they found heavy
jobs (e.g. carrying beams from forests to construction sites) exhausting
and hardly worth the recompense. As a consequence of these problems,
the Dutch found it exceedingly difficult to stabilize their labor supply:
often they had too few workers, occasionally too many.[2]

The colony also attracted Khoikhoi who had no stock of their own
or had been banned from their tribes for committing some crime.
Indeed, during the formative period of labor relations (1652 to the
mid 1670s) the core of the Khokhoi community in the colony consisted
of the former Strandlopers. In October 1659, members of this group
were granted permission to settle at the fort under Dutch protection,
provided that they would fish and fetch water and firewood for the
Company. This arrangement became permanent: from a mere
eighteen males in 1662 the Strandlopers grew, by absorption of other
Khoikhoi refugees, to a total population of seventy, eighty, or more,
by 1666.[3] These poor outcasts proved to be more reliable laborers
than the pastoral Khoikhoi, and increasingly the names Strandloper
and Goringhaicona disappeared from the Dutch records and were
replaced by the phrase "our Hottentots."

At this stage Khoikhoi males were engaged primarily in carrying
wood for the cooks, in doing various cleaning and washing tasks, and
in fishing. In the 1660s they were also employed in gathering shells
for lime-burning, and in 1672 a plan was implemented for Khoikhoi
to carry earth for the building of the new castle.[4] Khoikhoi women

2. The problem of training Khoikhoi to be regular laborers is one of the main themes of
Van Riebeeck's Journal. See, for example, *VRJ*, 1:157 (May 26, 27, 29, 1653); 336–37 (Aug. 17,
1655); 3:439 (Nov. 24, 1661).

3. Dapper, VRS 14, p. 69; *VRJ*, 3:144–45 (Oct. 13–14, 1659); KA 3974, Van Riebeeck to
Successor, May 5, 1662, p. 6v; Moodie, *The Record*, p. 291.

4. KA 3976, DR Oct. 24, 1663, n.p.; KA 3985, DR Oct. 8, 1672, p. 366.

were taken into Dutch homes from the very beginning and were trained as domestic servants. Van Riebeeck had several such maids, of whom Eva was the best known. Most of these were probably very young girls who subsequently left the colony when they married. As the Dutch imported more Eastern slaves with advanced culinary and domestic skills, the Khoikhoi were gradually displaced from this sector. Only in the eighteenth century did Khoikhoi domestic help reemerge on a large scale—this time on the distant frontier.

From the earliest years of the colony, Khoikhoi had brought information to the fort about happenings in the interior and had been rewarded with gifts of tobacco, arrack, and food. As an extension of this custom, the Dutch began to use Khoikhoi as letter carriers between Company posts: the letters usually contained instructions for the recipient to pay the runner a specified amount and to send him back with a reply. By 1665 this practice was so entrenched that even crucial dispatches were delayed until a Khoikhoi runner could be found. Khoikhoi, of course, were cheaper than soldiers, had detailed knowledge of the terrain, and were very fast: it normally took them only six days or a bit longer to take a message to Saldanha Bay and bring back a reply, a distance of 100 miles each way.[5]

In this early period Khoikhoi were given neither farming nor pastoral jobs despite the colony's great need in both these areas. In the case of farming, the Khoikhoi had no traditional skills to offer and could be used only in simple tasks like frightening crows away from seeded fields. It seems also that Khoikhoi had a positive aversion to cultivation, since it reminded them of despised aspects of their own culture. In 1712 some Namaqua far removed from the colony were reported to ridicule the Dutch, saying "that they were only women, who go into the fields to dig onions with a piece of iron."[6] (Thus, cultivating was equated with gathering, a woman's role.)

Khoikhoi could, of course, have been most usefully employed in pastoral tasks. At first they were not, simply because the Company would not trust them with its animals. Though the Khoikhoi did not in fact steal many cattle from whites except as an act of war, events like Harry's spectacular cattle robbery of October 1653 had given them a bad reputation. It was thus not until the 1670s that the

5. E.g. *VRJ*, 3:412, 414 (Aug. 21 and 27, 1661); KA 3978, DR Sept. 21, 24, 27, 1665, pp. 422 ff.

6. KZ 3193, Dagh Verhaal ... Slotsbo, Nov. 1, 1712, n.p.

Company (and a very few burghers) began to entrust their precious stock to Khoikhoi herders. This new attitude derived in part from a successful experiment which the Company had tried more out of necessity than conviction. In August 1670 several French ships appeared in Saldanha Bay: visits of the subjects of Louis XIV always awakened the most lively fears in Cape Town, and the Company's officials were delighted and gratified when ninety armed Khoikhoi arrived in the bay and offered to repel any possible French invasion. The Dutch supervisors at the bay decided to take advantage of Khoikhoi goodwill and sent the Company's stock to a nearby kraal for protection. This bold move was later approved by Commander Hackius. From this time onward we begin to find references to Khoikhoi working with stock in the colony. For example, in July 1673 Khoikhoi under Dutch supervision moved Company cattle from Hottentots Holland to the Cape, and in October 1674 Khoikhoi were transporting lime on oxen from Cape False to Cape Town.[7] Despite these new signs of confidence the Company probably did not entrust its stock to unsupervised Khoikhoi herders.

The Company's experiments in employing Khoikhoi were merely a prelude to the vast social transformation that would result when free burghers began to encourage Khoikhoi to live on their farms.[8] This process began in earnest in the mid-1680s and was fostered both by the intensifying poverty of Khoikhoi tribes and by the geographical expansion of the colony into Stellenbosch (1679) and Drakenstein (1687). The farmers who moved into the new outer districts had much less available labor than those who were already settled near the Cape. In 1695 there was roughly one white servant (*knecht*) for every four male white burghers in the Cape district, but only one for every seven in Stellenbosch and Drakenstein. Much more startling were the figures for slave labor: in 1695 there were 1.7 male slaves for every white freeman in the Cape, while Stellenbosch had only 0.65 and Drakenstein 0.27.

The following table presents the ratios between the slave population

---

7. KA 3983, DR Aug. 28 and Sept. 1, 1670, pp. 183–84; KA 3983, Hackius to Calmbach, Sept. 12, 1670, p. 75; KA 3987, DR July 27, 1673, p. 218; KA 3988, DR Oct. 15, 1674, p. 158.

8. For the 1670s we have only scattered indications of Khoikhoi herding for freemen: there is a possible instance from 1672 and a clear one from 1678. See KA 3986, Attestation of Ocker Cornelisz and Jacobus Zaunbrecher, July 5, 1673, pp. 323–25; KA 3991, Confession of Quisa Soucka, Sept. 5, 1678, p. 525.

in each district and the amount of work undertaken there in the years indicated. It will be seen that a radical discrepancy existed between the ratios for the Cape district and those for the outer areas; as the new farmers prospered and obtained more slaves, the gap between districts narrowed, but never in our period to the point of nearing parity.[9]

	Number of Cattle Tended per Male Adult Slave			Number of Muids of Grain (wheat, barley, rye) Sown per Male Adult Slave		
	Cape	S'bosch	D'stein	Cape	S'bosch	D'stein
1690	9.2	25.7	63.0	.94	5.5	20.0
1711	12.8	18.9	32.5	.99	2.4	3.5

Similarly striking figures could be supplied for sheep herding and for viticulture. The differing production levels can in part be explained by the assumption that both whites and slaves worked harder in the new districts, and by the fact that in the Cape district some slaves were engaged in domestic tasks. However, the main explanation for the discrepancies lies in the fact that the frontier farmers were supplementing their labor force with a massive recruitment of Khoikhoi, whose numbers are unfortunately not indicated on the rolls. We know, however, that before the epidemic of 1713 such a high percentage of Cape Khoikhoi had entered white service that most of the men of some kraals were either in Cape Town or on colonial farms.[10]

Our only information on the terms of Khoikhoi employment comes from scattered references, mainly in the judicial records. At first Khoikhoi farm laborers left their families at home in their kraals. However, by 1696 we find a reference to Khoikhoi women and children living in their own huts on a white farm. Later cases make it clear that laborers often brought their families to live with them even if these were not in the farmer's service. A striking, but probably atypical, case was that of the frontiersman Jacobus Overney, who moved around the country with an entire Khoikhoi kraal which he used to guard his large herds and help him mask his true wealth. Some Khoikhoi brought their own livestock with them when they took employment

9. Figures in this and the preceding paragraph are based on the censuses of 1690, 1695, and 1711 (KA 4005, p. 82; KA 4013, pp. 201 ff.; KA 4043, p. 689).
10. Cape Archives, C 430, Frans van der Werf to Assenburgh, Jan. 27, 1709, p. 71.

with whites: we know of one Khoikhoi who still had his herds after twenty-three years of service.[11]

The earliest references to Khoikhoi working in cultivation date from the early eighteenth century, a full generation after Khoikhoi had begun to enter burgher society in large numbers. The Adam Tas diary shows that in 1705–06 teams of Khoikhoi moved about from farm to farm cutting grain at harvest time. It was not long, however, before they were not only harvesting but harrowing, pruning vines, pressing grapes, and hauling building materials in ox-drawn wagons. In areas of fairly dense settlement Khoikhoi women tried to make a living by hawking honey and homemade brooms from farm to farm, and also fetched clay to help in the building of homes.[12]

On the frontier a cattle culture was forming in which Khoikhoi and whites jointly participated. Though there were some cases of Europeans keeping cattle for Khoikhoi,[13] the normal pattern was for Khoikhoi to tend European cattle, often at great distances from the colony. Some Khoikhoi were paid for these services in livestock and still retained the hope of establishing themselves as independent herders. While it is true that some whites were beginning to speak of Khoikhoi in the same breath with slaves, the Khoikhoi still retained much of their freedom; they still had their language, their customs, and some of their stock, even as their tribal structure was falling apart.

In Cape Town, however, the growing Khoikhoi proletariat lived in a condition in some ways more degraded than that of slaves. Their mendicant style of life contributed greatly to the widespread disdain for "Hottentots" throughout the Western world. They regularly boarded visiting ships and made for the galley: there the cooks gave them grease and animal entrails, with which they adorned themselves to the amusement and disgust of the sailors. Then, plied with alcohol and tobacco, they would dance to entertain the ship's company. They danced first on one foot, then on the other, "as if treading grapes," and repeated the chant, "Hotantot, Hotantot," which some writers take to be the origin of the name Hottentot. Other Khoikhoi for similar

---

11. KA 4014, Sentence of Anthony of Bombay, DR Dec. 29, 1696, p. 1026v–27; KA 4037, Vraagpoincten . . . Pieter Cronje, March 3, 1707, p. 780v; KZ 3193, Dag Verhaal . . . Slotsbo, Oct. 19, 1712, n.p.; Algemeen Rijksarchief, Collectie Radermacher no. 504, Contra-Deductie . . . , 1712, p. 119.

12. *The Diary of Adam Tas (1705–1706)*, ed. Leo Fouché (London: Longmans, Green and Co., 1914), p. 64. Other references to Khoikhoi skills are scattered through the judicial papers of the colony.

13. KA 4053, Landdrost vs. the Hottentot Claas Blank, Nov. 28, 1715, p. 658v.

inducements showed their genitals to prurient visitors; for the rumor that Khoikhoi males had only one testicle and females an extended labia minora, had spread widely through the ports of the world.[14]

Others made a meager living by acting as porters: they would seize a sailor's burden with an obsequious protest such as, "You Englishman, you no Hottentot." Still others were attached to Dutch houses and ran errands in return for scraps from the table. Yet, degraded as the urban Khoikhoi were, visitors were well aware that they were not slaves. As one Englishman noted: "they have a great love for liberty, and an utter Aversion to Slavery. Neither will they hire themselves in your Service longer than from Morning to Night, for they will be paid, and sleep Freemen, and no Hirelings."[15]

KHOIKHOI UNDER THE LAWS OF THE COLONY

A fundamental principle of Dutch policy was that the Khoikhoi were a free and independent people; in other words, that they were subject to their own laws and not to those of the Company, and that they could be neither coerced nor enslaved by the Company or its subjects. In the first years of contact, Khoikhoi independence was obvious enough to everyone; however, when the labor market began to alter the nature of Khoikhoi society in radical ways, many whites began to think of the Khoikhoi population as a permanent laboring class, or even as a subdivision of the slave force. In 1706 a recent immigrant, who had killed a Khoikhoi cow, was asked "if he was not aware that the Hottentots are owners of that land, and that field and grass are free and common to them for pasturing their cattle." To this question the burgher replied, perhaps honestly, that he was unaware of the fact. In response to the growing confusion about Khoikhoi status, the government responded with iterations "that these natives cannot be regarded and treated as less than free people," that beating and murder were intolerable outrages "even if perpetrated on a Hottentot," and that "the laws make no distinction [between crimes] committed against Christians and heathens."[16]

14. *CGH*, 1:219 (Vogel, 1679); 2:238 (Tappen, 1682); 2:319 (de la Loubère, 1687); G. S. Nienaber, "The Origin of the Name 'Hottentot'" *AS* 22, no. 2 (1963):89.

15. Charles Lockyer, *An Account of the Trade in India* (London: Samuel Crouch, 1711), p. 298; Dampier, VRS 5, p. 126; Beeckman, VRS 5, pp. 114–17. The quotations in this paragraph are from Beeckman, pp. 117 and 114.

16. KA 4034, Confession of Jan van Bevernasie, Nov. 29, 1706, p. 537; KA 4014, DR Dec. 29, 1696, p. 1027v; KA 4036, DR July 23, 1707, p. 236v; KA 4037, Prosecution of Pieter Cronje, March 29, 1707, p. 768v.

From the beginning, however, the Company itself had no compunctions about limiting Khoikhoi freedom if it deemed it necessary to intervene in disputes between Khoikhoi and subjects of the colony. As a rule it avoided interference in conflicts between two Khoikhoi,[17] nor did it meddle in strictly civil cases between whites and Khoikhoi (for example, disputes over labor contracts).

Of the many cases involving Khoikhoi which the Company adjudicated, the vast majority concerned robbery and the violence resulting from robbery. Stock theft was not as common as might be supposed, since both whites and Khoikhoi regarded it as a heinous crime. Under the Statutes of India, a body of law theoretically in force at the Cape, stock theft was punishable by death. Khoikhoi practice was apparently not far different. In 1676 a Khoikhoi stole and ate a sheep belonging to a white man, but in retaliation he was shot and severely wounded by the white shepherd who had been guarding the flock. The Dutch sent out an investigating committee which interviewed the guilty Khoikhoi and were shocked to hear him say "that he could not complain [about his wound] as he confessed to have done wrong." Furthermore, his captain asserted, in opposition to the view of the commissioners, that the white herdsman had been perfectly correct in shooting; indeed, he would have been satisfied if the Dutch were to hang all Khoikhoi cattle thieves whom they could catch and convict.[18]

In this stern climate of opinion cattle theft was not resorted to lightly. Most livestock robberies committed by Khoikhoi were associated with one of the two Khoikhoi-Dutch wars, or were acts involving a whole clan or tribe which could well be construed as an act of war. Few cattle and sheep were stolen by individuals so long as Khoikhoi society remained intact, and these were mostly taken by people whom Khoikhoi regarded as "San" (i.e. cattleless paupers). However, after 1685, as Khoikhoi became increasingly impoverished, the number of "San" consequently rose steeply, as did the number of robberies that had to be dealt with by judicial or military means.

More common than stock theft was the petty thievery related to begging. Whites were universally impressed by the hospitality Khoi-

17. Two exceptions to this rule were a case in 1703, where three Khoikhoi were arrested for murdering a Khoikhoi woman, and a trivial suit between two Khoikhoi in 1708. See KA 4028, DR Jan. 2, 5, 1703, pp. 45–45v; KA 4039, Jantje vs. Soufahals, Oct. 18, 1708, p. 623.

18. South African Public Library, Statuten van Indiën (manuscript originally compiled at the Cape in 1715, with later additions), vol. 1, p. 457: the regulation regarding livestock robbery was in effect only after 1688. KA 3989, DR June 21, 1676, pp. 253v–54.

khoi showed to visitors, and by the way in which they shared what little they had with their fellows.[19] As their contacts with the colonists became more intimate, Khoikhoi expected, and sometimes demanded, similar generosity from Europeans. By and large the Dutch fell in gracefully with the custom of giving a bit of food or tobacco to Khoikhoi whom they met in daily life. But occasionally a white farmer or sailor refused Khoikhoi requests either because he was irritated or simply because he had nothing to give. The insulted Khoikhoi sometimes retaliated by robbing or attacking the European. Stones could be thrown, knives drawn, and guns fired. As a result of such incidents several Khoikhoi, and several Europeans, were arraigned on charges of assault or murder.

In Van Riebeeck's time interracial cases were handled, not by the courts, but by the commander or his agent. The bulk of cases concerned petty thefts committed by Khoikhoi, and the main problem was to recover the stolen goods. In order to attain this end, Van Riebeeck began by seizing Khoikhoi cattle as security and later advanced to the point of capturing human hostages, including chiefs. He did not, however, attempt to punish Khoikhoi criminals (Harry excepted), feeling that Khoikhoi leaders should punish their own subjects.

In the five years after Van Riebeeck's departure the colony was troubled by a number of Khoikhoi attacks on burghers, soldiers, and sailors. The new commander, Zacharias Wagenaar, threatened to lock Khoikhoi in prison or banish them to Robben Island, and to this end he obtained consent from the Seventeen to punish some Khoikhoi criminals "as a deterrent to others." However, he and his successors were able to accomplish little of this sort since they rarely succeeded in apprehending the culprits: they fell, rather, into the habit of seizing Khoikhoi hostages and then ransoming them in return for a few cattle.[20]

By 1671 it was clear that the Khoikhoi totally misunderstood the hostage system: they viewed it as a means whereby the Dutch fined them for the sins of their tribesmen, rather than as a lever to bring Khoikhoi criminals to justice. Accordingly, in 1671–72 the government abruptly adopted a new tough policy. Henceforth they brusquely rejected all Khoikhoi attempts to ransom hostages and established

19. Kolbe, *Beschreibung*, p. 35. Cf. also Schapera (*Khoisan Peoples*, p. 338), who says of Khoikhoi in general that "selfishness in regard to food . . . exposes a man to scorn."

20. KA 3976, DR March 5, 1664, n.p.; KA 3977, DR Dec. 23, 1664, p. 209v; KA 456, XVII to Wagenaar, Nov. 7, 1665, pp. 832–33; KA 3984, DR Jan. 17 and Aug. 16, 1671, pp. 93v–94, 142v.

the authority of the Council of Justice to try and punish Khoikhoi. The new jurisdiction was established in two cases which involved Khoikhoi in very different circumstances.

The first case concerned Sara, a Khoikhoi girl who had hanged herself. The fiscal (prosecutor) argued that Sara's action had been an offense against the laws of the colony, since she was subject to Dutch, rather than Khoikhoi, laws and customs. She had lived in colonial society since her childhood, had worn European clothes, earned wages, spoken Dutch and Portuguese, and attended church. Since "such as live under our protection are rightly called our subjects," it was clear that her body should be dishonored just as if she had been European. The court agreed: her corpse was dragged through the streets and exposed on a forked post as food for the birds.[21]

While Sara's body was still rotting in the open air, the Council of Justice moved to establish its jurisdiction over noncolonial Khoikhoi. The defendants in the test case were five Khoikhoi charged with robbing and assaulting some whites. The fiscal defended the court's authority on philosophical grounds. Though Khoikhoi appeared at first glance to be "more beast than man," it was beyond doubt that they had the form of rational creatures, and hence that they possessed rational souls. All such beings had been endowed by their Creator with a knowledge of Natural Law (the judgment necessary to distinguish right from wrong) and the Law of Nations (law common to all peoples). It was thus appropriate for the council to try Khoikhoi under these universal codes. The court accepted the fiscal's argument, and passed sentences that included thrashing, branding, and periods of forced labor up to fifteen years.[22]

By coincidence it was also in 1672 that the court first sentenced a white, Willem Willemsz of Deventer, for murdering a Khoikhoi. Willemsz escaped from the colony but was condemned in absentia to perpetual banishment from the Cape and forfeiture of all his goods, which were to be divided between his estranged family and the court.[23]

21. KA 3984, Prosecution of Sara, Dec. 18, 1671, pp. 222v–24; KA 3984, DR Dec. 18, 1671, p. 173; KA 3985, DR Jan. 10, 1672, p. 257.

22. KA 3984, Prosecution of Five Hottentots, n.d. [1672], pp. 382–87v; KA 3984, Sentence of Five Hottentots, Feb. 10, 1672, pp. 394–95v.

23. KA 3986, Sentence of Willem Willemsz, July 20, 1672, pp. 321–22. Willemsz escaped to Europe where he obtained a pardon from the Prince of Orange; when he returned to the Cape, the authorities were reluctant to honor this pardon and, after several years of correspondence with Europe, they banished him to Batavia. This complex case is succinctly summarized in A. J. Böeseken, "Die Verhouding tussen Blank en Nie-Blank in Suid-Afrika aan die hand van die Vroegste Dokumente," *South African Historical Journal* 2 (Nov. 1970): 10.

Though this verdict established a precedent for harshly punishing white mistreatment of Khoikhoi, it also introduced a principle never deviated from in coming years; namely, that though Khoikhoi could be executed for murdering whites, the reverse would not be the case.

Even after 1672 the bulk of cases between whites and Khoikhoi were probably handled arbitrarily without recourse to the formality of courtroom procedure. Little is known about these extrajudicial cases. Some seem to have differed little from others that were in fact brought to court: for example, a case in which a Khoikhoi was thrashed for mistreating a Dutchman at an outpost and one in which a Khoikhoi was sent to Robben Island for robbing a freeman's garden. Most extrajudicial cases, however, were ones that could be satisfactorily regulated by investigating commissions without the need of imposing punishments. For example, if the government heard of the violent death of a Khoikhoi, it sent out an official party to determine if Europeans had been involved: if the findings were negative, the case was dropped. Cape officials and landdrosts also adjudicated disputes on the spot. In 1677 two officiers examined a case of a *knecht* (white laborer) who had broken the arm of a Khoikhoi; they ordered the white to recompense his victim with some rice, three pounds of tobacco, and a bit of arrack. Contrariwise, in 1693 the Cape government approved an arrangement whereby a Khoikhoi whose cattle had damaged a freeman's crop compensated the farmer with five young heifers.[24]

Most likely the vast majority of Dutch interventions were like those just described and did not result in formal legal procedure. Nonetheless, the court cases are worthy of attention because they are well documented and hence allow us to assess the quality of colonial justice with greater precision than is possible with the extrajudicial cases.

It must first be noted that the justice of the Company courts could at times be extremely unfair to white freemen. All criminal and civil cases (except very minor ones) were dealt with by the Council of Justice, which was largely identical in membership with the legislative and executive body, the Council of Policy. It is true that one (later two, still later three) representatives of the burghers sat on the Council of Justice in cases involving freemen: however, they were decisively

---

24. KA 4010, DR March 6, 1693, p. 72v; KA 3988, DR March 19, 1674, p. 101v; KA 4000, DR Feb. 6–7, 1686, pp. 212–13v; KA 3990, DR July 8, 1677, p. 336; KA 4007, S. van der Stel to Landdrost of Stellenbosch, Sept. 29, 1693, p. 188v.

outnumbered by the official members. There were no juries and normally no defense lawyers. The prosecutor, in cases where there was no plaintiff, was usually the fiscal, and occasionally the landdrost of Stellenbosch. The prosecutor was normally a close confidant of the judges, even after 1688, when the office of fiscal was made independent of control by the governor. For this reason, and because he was usually paid in fines and forfeitures, the prosecutor rarely went to the trouble of a trial unless he knew he could win: hence there were few acquittals. The system could be exceedingly iniquitous to soldiers, sailors, and freemen who were charged with robbery, smuggling, desertion, or dereliction of duty—all crimes in which the Company was both the aggrieved party and the judge in its own case.[25]

By contrast, Khoikhoi were only rarely tried in cases where the Company was the complainant. This fact, combined with the judges' political concern to preserve peace, assured the Khoikhoi a comparatively fair hearing. In some cases Khoikhoi were able to initiate actions, in others they were key witnesses establishing the guilt of whites. I have not found examples in this period of the court's discounting evidence simply because it came from Khoikhoi—though after 1713 such racialist attitudes did in fact become apparent.[26]

Eight court cases have been found that involved one or more Khoikhoi defendants in the period 1672–1713. Of these, two were disputations with plaintiffs which the court adjudicated,[27] and one was the case of the suicide Sara, already described. Of the remaining four, two were murder trials in which the Khoikhoi were convicted to be turned over to their chiefs for execution, and one was an affair of stealing and assault for which the defendants were thrashed and banished to Robben Island. The eighth case ended in a harsh sentence —execution by the colonial authorities—for some Khoikhoi who were chronic thieves but had not apparently committed murder.[28]

Probably none of these sentences were unduly severe from the viewpoint of Khoikhoi law; however, they were generally harsher than

25. These generalizations about Cape justice are based on wide reading in the Company's judicial records. My conclusions are quite similar to those of M. F. Katzen, "White Settlers and the Origin of a New Society, 1652–1778," in Wilson and Thompson, *Oxford History*, 1:219–22.

26. KA 4002, DR Dec. 5, 1687, p. 385; KA 4037, Declaration of the Hottentot Hans, Jan. 14, 1707, pp. 685–86v; KA 4090, Decision of the Council of Justice, June 2, 1729, p. 1038v.

27. KA 4026, Abraham de Villiers vs. Kleine Kapitein et al., July 27, 1702, pp. 418–18v; KA 4039, Jantje vs. Soufahals, Oct. 18, 1708, p. 623.

28. KA 3999, DR April 26–27, 1685, p. 255; KA 4004, DR April 23, 1689, pp. 231v–32v; KA 3984, Sentence of D'haurry et al., Feb. 10, 1672, pp. 394–95v; KA 3991, Prosecutor vs. Quisa et al., Sept. 14, 1678, pp. 503v–04.

sentences meted out to whites for similar crimes against Khoikhoi. During this period five cases were opened against whites accused of killing Khoikhoi. Two ended inconclusively because the accused party could not be caught,[29] and in the other three the defendants were sentenced to banishment varying from twenty-five years to life, and to confiscation of one-half to all of their goods.[30] Whites who were accused of wounding Khoikhoi received highly variable sentences: in one such case, a soldier was condemned to spend his life in forced labor after being scourged and branded, while on another occasion a freeman got off with paying a fifteen rixdollar fine to the Company and compensation of two pounds of tobacco to the wounded Khoikhoi.[31] (The lightness of this last sentence was due to the plausible claim of the freeman that the incident was an accident.) In cases in which whites killed Khoikhoi cattle, they were sentenced to a whipping and then ordered to compensate the Khoikhoi and pay a small fine to the Company.[32] In instances of cattle stealing, whites could receive very severe penalties indeed: in 1673 a woman who had stolen two Khoikhoi cows was sentenced to be thrashed, branded, deprived of all her property, and banished to Robben Island for twelve years; though she was granted exemption from the branding, the rest of her sentence was apparently carried out.[33]

In order to minimize resentment against the Company, the Dutch preferred to have Khoikhoi criminals executed by other Khoikhoi. The first such execution took place in 1673, when some local Khoikhoi brought in five of Gonnema's people and charged them with the massacre of some freemen hunters. The prisoners were tried, convicted, and turned back over to their Khoikhoi captors, because the fiscal, as he later admitted, "was heartily pleased to be relieved of the trouble of further proceedings." The Khoikhoi then beat the prisoners to death with fearful cries of "Kill the dogs! Kill them!" after which they trampled the corpses under foot.[34] In most subsequent executions the

29. KA 4013, DR Nov. 23–24 and Dec. 2, 1695, pp. 799v, 804–05v; KA 4038, DR July 7, 1708, pp. 166–67v.

30. See n. 23 above; KA 4036, DR July 23, 1707, pp. 234–37v; KA 4036, DR March 31, 1707, p. 177v.

31. KA 4014, DR March 30, 1696, pp. 887ff. (In this case the soldier had also been guilty of negligence in his duties.) See also KA 4021, Landdrost vs. Hendrick Jans, March 19, 1700, p. 737; and Jans's confession on pp. 654–54v.

32. E.g. KA 4004, Landdrost vs. Jan Rappoi and Albert Bierman, April 19, 1689, p. 697.

33. KA 3987, DR Sept. 22–23, 1673, pp. 235–35v.

34. Pieter de Neyn, Lust-hof der Huwelyken ... (Amsterdam: Willem Lamsvelt, 1697), p. 225; KA 3987, DR Aug. 20, 1673, pp. 227v–28. On the purpose of this policy, see also Hulshof, "H. A. van Reede ... Journaal," pp. 30–32.

Dutch made a point of obtaining the active participation, or at least the consent, of the condemned party's chief.

It seems that, on the whole, Khoikhoi trusted the Company's justice. Not only did individual Khoikhoi feel free to lodge complaints about the misbehavior of whites, but captains were willing to turn over their accused subjects to the Dutch courts.[35] No marked partiality against Khoikhoi is apparent from the records of interracial disputes except in the matter of unequal sentences for the same crime. The real injustice of the system may well have lain in the number of crimes against Khoikhoi that went unnoticed or unprosecuted because the necessary zeal was lacking. There was one incident in which a drunken white stabbed, and almost killed, a Khoikhoi: the government overlooked this misdeed "in hopes of improvement."[36] Whether such unpardonable laxity was common we have no way of knowing.

Neighbors, Allies, and Subjects: The Subordination of the Khoikhoi Chiefs

Like the absorption of individual Khoikhoi into Dutch society, the increasing subordination of Khoikhoi chiefs to the Company was a very gradual process, and one of which contemporary Khoikhoi and whites were probably scarcely aware. It resulted in the transformation of the relatively strong chiefs of Van Riebeeck's day into the "captains" of the well-known eighteenth-century variety—pathetic figures who had no power beyond their own families, derived their authority entirely from the Company, and lived with the knowledge that even their own children might report on their actions to Dutch officials.[37]

The subordination of chiefdoms usually took place in advance of the frontier of settlement, but it was not explicitly intended to clear the way for colonial expansion. Among the Western Cape Khoikhoi it proceeded in several phases, the first of which (1652 to the early 1670s) was marked by Dutch acceptance of the sovereignty of the Khoikhoi chiefs. It is true that the Company was willing to use its influence—and occasionally a bit of force—to induce chiefs to trade, to move their people off disputed pastures, and to return stolen property to the colony. But never in this early period did the Dutch claim sovereignty over Khoikhoi; and never, even at their most arbitrary, did they act with the supreme self-confidence they were later to display. In this

35. E.g. KA 3991, DR Aug. 24, 1678, p. 446v.
36. KA 3984, Fiscal vs. Andries Jens. Vries, July 8, 1671, p. 202v.
37. See, for example, Sparrman, *Voyage*, 1: 257–59.

period the Company also remained aloof from intertribal disputes: on several occasions when chiefs asked for Dutch aid against their enemies, they always received a firm, but polite, refusal.

Throughout Van Riebeeck's command the Dutch had had considerable respect for Khoikhoi military potential, a respect that was not diminished by the ambiguous results of the First Khoikhoi-Dutch War. Van Riebeeck's successors, however, became progressively less interested in Khoikhoi and less afraid that they could harm the colony. Admiration for Khoikhoi fighting ability dropped when a number of incidents showed that a white man with a gun could normally best any number of Khoikhoi without firearms.

Khoikhoi chiefs fell even faster than their subjects in the estimation of the Dutch. Increased contact with the wealth of the inland Khoikhoi allowed Europeans to see that their immediate Khoikhoi neighbors (the Peninsulars) were poor, weak, and despised by other Khoikhoi. On the other hand, the inland chiefs were not impressive enough to fulfill the long-standing Dutch dream of finding, just beyond the next mountain range, a Khoikhoi king whose wealth and power was like that of an Asian potentate. Each newly encountered chief deepened the disillusionment of the Europeans, and from an exaggerated respect for chiefs they fell into the opposite error of disdaining them too easily. This process was accelerated by the procession of chiefs who demeaned themselves in the eyes of the Dutch by coming to the fort and later the castle, begging to be entertained.

More important was the fact that the chiefs of Van Riebeeck's time were not being replaced by men of equal stature. Neither Gogosoa of the Peninsulars nor Soeswa of the Chainouqua was succeeded by a man who exercised noticeable control beyond his own clan. Oedasoa, who had been very prominent in Van Riebeeck's time, increasingly avoided the Dutch after 1662. In the 1660s and early 1670s contacts with the Namaqua and Hessequa were still rare, and the powerful Inqua monarch had not yet been visited. In fact, the only Khoikhoi chief who was strong in wealth and followers, and who was also in contact with the Dutch, was Gonnema.

The humiliation suffered by Gonnema in the Second Khoikhoi-Dutch War did more than any other event to reduce the status of all Khoikhoi chiefs in the eyes of both Dutch and Khoikhoi. During the war the Company referred to the Cochoqua as the "*rebelling* Gonnema Africans," an interesting slip which shows how ideas of sovereignty were shifting. At the end of the conflict the Dutch forced Gonnema to recognize a form of Company suzerainty which would be marked by the payment of an annual tribute of thirty cattle. The Company prolonged Gonnema's degradation by continuing for some years to insist on its right to the tribute; however, it showed him considerable leniency in regard to the size and frequency of his actual payments.[38]

The war had an almost equally disastrous effect on those chiefs who fought on the Dutch side: the Peninsulars Kuiper, Tomas, and Schacher; and the Chainouqua chiefs Klaas and Koopman. What these allies gained in booty they lost in dignity. In addition to keeping a considerable amount of Gonnema's stock as outright booty, Klaas, Koopman, Kuiper, and Schacher were each given 300 sheep to herd on behalf of the Company in return for the natural increase. The repayment of these sheep was staggered over a decade and was one mechanism by which the Dutch were able to tighten their control over the captains.[39] During and after the war, the captains were at the beck and call of the governor: three of them were summoned to the fort in April 1674, when the Company found that it was missing some cattle: Kuiper was dragged over the coals for alleged contact with the enemy; and several captains were sternly warned never to trade with other Khoikhoi without the Company's permission.[40]

Even more alarming from the Khoikhoi point of view was the government's newly asserted right to interfere in inter-Khoikhoi disputes. In December 1676, Schacher was summoned to the fort to answer claims that he had stolen cattle from a Khoikhoi neighbor; only when the Company ascertained that he had already returned the cattle did he obtain forgiveness. Early the next year the governor learned of an impending war between Schacher and his Peninsular neighbors Kuiper and Tomas, and he immediately dispatched a rider to bring the antagonists to the castle. It is significant that the captains united in a vigorous denial that there was any discord among them—their fear of Company intervention was evidently greater than their hostility to each other—but sharp questioning brought out the truth, and the governor imposed a solution on the disputants: the captains

38. KA 3990, DR June 25, 1677, p. 321v; KA 3991, DR Nov. 24, 1678, p. 478; KA 3996, Dagelyckse Aanteekeningh gehouden op de Voyagie ... nae de Clapmuts ..., Nov. 2, 1683, pp. 340–40v.

39. KA 3988, DR April 9, 1674, p. 108v; KA 3994, DR July 25, 1681, p. 196. For proof that better control of the captains was a major reason for lending out the sheep, see KA 3990, Bax to XVII, May 15, 1678, p. 36.

40. KA 3988, DR April 20, 1674, p. 111; KA 3989, DR Sept. 25, 1676, p. 309v; KA 3990, DR June 28, 1677, pp. 323–23v.

were induced to swear that they would never again take revenge on evil-doers but would always complain to the governor, who would then punish the guilty according to their merits.[41] The important principle thus established among Peninsular Khoikhoi was extended to the Chainouqua when, in July 1677, an expedition set out from Hottentots Holland to impose peace on warring Soeswa clans.[42]

After this date vigorous interventions in Khoikhoi affairs occurred at an accelerating pace: this was due in large part to the domineering personality of Simon van der Stel, commander (later governor) from 1679 to 1699. Van der Stel's extremely long tenure at the Cape, his decisiveness of character, and his desire for a growing agricultural colony, all contributed to the vigor and skill with which he worked against any revival of Khoikhoi independence. We have already described his attack on Klaas and his bullying of Namaqua chiefs. His view on the sovereignty of the petty captains near Cape Town can be illustrated by the case of a Captain Dikkop, whose people's herds had interfered with those of the settlers: Dikkop was seized and dragged to the castle, where the governor commanded him "to behave more decently and obediently in the future, and to follow the Company's orders exactly and without argument."[43]

Under Van der Stel the Company arrogated to itself various new powers in relation to chiefs. It did not hesitate to force one chief to acknowledge the "lordship" of another, nor even to compel rebelling subjects to submit to their rulers.[44] The governor also gained the right to install chiefs in office, though the selection of the new chief was normally made on the advice of the elders of the clan or tribe. By 1700 this was virtually a universal practice among Western Cape Khoikhoi. Van der Stel and his successors took advantage of the installation ceremony to give the chiefs classical names like Asdrubal, Scipio Africanus, Hercules, Mars, or Hanibal. It is likely that these names were intentionally ludicrous.

At his installation the chief or captain was presented with a cane (*rotting*) with a copper grip that bore a stamped imprint of the Company's coat of arms. Sometimes the captain's name and the date of his accession to office were also affixed. These canes of office may have

41. KA 3989, DR Dec. 23 and 25, 1676, pp. 367, 370v; KA 3990, Jan. 17 and 19, 1677, pp. 245, 251v–52.
42. KA 3990, DR July 14, 1677, pp. 337v–38.
43. KA 4005, DR Feb. 21, 1690, p. 108.
44. KA 7571/KZ 3179, DR March 3, 1688, n.p.; *Resolusies*, 3: 55 (Dec. 8, 1682).

dated from the Second Khoikhoi-Dutch War or even earlier, but it was Van der Stel who made them a major feature of tribal life. They soon became prized artifacts which Khoikhoi passed down from generation to generation: in 1779 an English traveler met a Khoikhoi captain whose cane had been engraved seventy-four years earlier, in 1705.[45] The implications of possessing a cane varied from region to region. In the north, where Company influence was tenuous, the captain who thus identified himself with the foreigner could bring upon himself the wrath of his neighbors. In general, however, the cane conferred a certain prestige on a chief, since it implied that the Company would aid him in times of peril. This was, in fact, the positive side of Van der Stel's policy from the Khoikhoi point of view. Not only could captains turn to the Company for redress when they were wronged by their neighbors, but they could also expect assistance in their struggle against hunters.[46]

By the turn of the eighteenth century, the Dutch control of chiefs was virtually complete in the southwestern Cape, though it extended only nominally to Namaqua country and not at all east of the Chainouqua. The chiefs who had bowed their knee to the Dutch were not yet "straw chiefs"; for, having been selected in a traditional manner, they still possessed customary legitimacy alongside the authority conferred by the governor. Yet they were heavily dependent on the Company and subject to its interference in their daily life. We have little direct evidence about the degree to which these disabilities compromised their position in the eyes of their people. However, if one may judge from the repeated experience of traditional rulers in other colonial societies, the damage to their prestige was probably severe.

45. On distribution of canes before Van der Stel, see KA 3991, DR Dec. 16, 1678, p. 484. On the long history of the canes, see William Paterson, *A Narrative of Four Journeys into the Country of the Hottentots, and Caffraria, in the Years 1777, 1778, 1779*, 2d ed. (London: J. Johnson, 1790), p. 120.

46. KZ 3193, Dagh Verhaal . . . Slotsbo, Oct. 18 and 24, 1712, n.p.; Buttner, Waare Relation . . . , n.p.

10

The Khoikhoi and Colonial Society:
Psychological and Cultural Aspects

THE WHITE MAN'S IMAGE OF THE "HOTTENTOT"

While Europeans became progressively disillusioned with Khoikhoi leadership over the years, their impression of Khoikhoi culture had always been overwhelmingly negative. This was particularly the case with the scores of transient visitors to Cape Town who subsequently published their memoirs in Europe.[1] It must be remembered that almost all visitors perceived the Cape, not as part of Africa, but as a stepping-stone to Asia; furthermore, most of them had no contact with other African indigenes during their outward voyage, and on the way home their memories were full of the splendors of the Buddhist, Hindu, and Muslim kingdoms of southern Asia. Few observers had had prior contact with nonliterate peoples or with peoples who did not adhere to a universal religion and practice a complex culture; hence they regarded Khoikhoi as more unusual than in fact they were.

Given the shortness of the visits and the rudimentary education of most visitors, it is not surprising that most attention was focused on the visual impact of Khoikhoi. Although a very few noted that Khoikhoi were "well-proportioned" or "of pleasing build," the majority of observers rarely noticed their physiques, so preoccupied were they with their body grease, which to European eyes was dirty and, to European noses, intolerable. They were not greatly shocked by the fact that Khoikhoi dressed in animal skins, but were appalled to see them wearing the guts of sheep and cattle around their necks: it was not until well after the settlement of the colony that anyone realized

---

1. My observations on travelers' impressions are based on a very large number of printed accounts. Full documentation of all these points is unnecessary in view of the analytical material found in Raven-Hart's excellent indexes to *BVR* and *CGH*. Consequently, some of the following footnotes will direct the reader to index entries in these publications.

that this custom was related to ritual sacrifice and *rites de passage*, and was not a simple manifestation of Khoikhoi aesthetic standards.[2]

Many writers found time to collect bits of information—much of it inaccurate—on Khoikhoi crafts and skills. A great deal was written on hut-making, the construction of weapons, and dancing; and somewhat less on pottery-making, metalworking, pastoralism, hunting, and fishing. It was generally, but by no means universally, agreed that Khoikhoi attainments in these fields were rather elementary. However, the simplicity of Khoikhoi material culture had much less to do with the origins of prejudice than did a number of customs that were radically foreign to Europeans' experience. Among these were the practice of finger-mutilation (the removal of a finger joint of certain persons at certain stages of life), and the practice of infanticide (burying a baby alive if the mother had died in childbirth or if the baby was one of twins).[3] Perhaps even more repulsive to Europeans were the dietary customs of Khoikhoi, who seemed, as Johan Schreyer observed, to "eat everything that we find loathsome."

> This is also to be seen in that they eat ... lice, which they neatly pull out of their hair and bite in their teeth, since they have very many of the same in their hair, in the mantles, between the rings on the arms and legs in quantities, very large and fat.[4]

Khoikhoi were also condemned for eating the entrails of animals:

> They are very piggish in their eating, since ... when the Dutch kill an ox they beg the guts, from which they do but draw the dung between their fingers and scrape it out, and so lay it on the fire; and when it is not yet half roasted they bite into it with such appetite that is a horror to see.[5]

Most Europeans, regardless of their personal level of piety, were interested in religion and tried perfunctorily to inform themselves of Khoikhoi beliefs. Since Khoikhoi had no obvious temples or elaborate ceremonies, and since the language barrier made communication on philosophical topics almost impossible, many visitors (including a man

2. *CGH*, 2: 508 ("Guts"), 510 ("Smearing"). For mildly positive impressions of Khoikhoi physical appearance, see ibid., pp. 404 (Langhansz, 1694) and 319 (de la Loubère, 1687). For an early appreciation of the ritual importance of cattle entrails see ibid., 1: 125 (Schreyer, 1668).
3. Ibid., 2: 507 ("Finger-mutilation"), 508 ("Infanticide").
4. Ibid., p. 509 ("Lice"). The quotation is from ibid., 1: 130 (Schreyer, 1668).
5. Ibid., 2: 507 ("Cookery"). The quotation is from ibid., 1: 8 (Merklein, 1653).

as eminent as Abraham van Riebeeck, the governor-general of the East India Company's empire) reached the ludicrous conclusion that Khoikhoi had no religion at all. This was the unanimous opinion before 1652 and the majority view thereafter, though some more thoughtful observers speculated that Khoikhoi dances and their interest in the sun and moon might be, in some sense, religious. In the very dogmatic climate of the seventeenth century, the alleged atheism of Khoikhoi aroused feelings of revulsion in whites and induced them to count their own blessings. It seemed deplorable, as Wouter Schouten noted in 1665, that Khoikhoi,

> although descended from our father *Adam*, yet show so little of
> humanity that truly they more resemble the unreasonable beasts
> than reasonable man . . . having no knowledge of GOD nor of what
> leads to their Salvation. Miserable folk, how lamentable is your
> pitiful condition! And Oh Christians, how blessed is ours![6]

The Khoikhoi language also contributed to the growth of prejudice; characterized as it was by click consonants in most of its nouns and verbs, it seemed far more grotesque to Europeans than any tongue they had yet encountered. They repeatedly compared it to hiccupping or gurgling, or—what was worse—to the cackling of geese or the clucking of hens.[7] When considered alongside Khoikhoi culture and seeming lack of religion, the oddity of the language stimulated speculation that Khoikhoi had "no better Predecessors than Monkeys," and that "if there's any medium between a Rational Animal and a Beast, the *Hotontot* lays the fairest Claim to that Species."[8] This oft-repeated identification of Khoikhoi with the beasts was to have a sinister influence on the armchair philosophers of the following century who, on the basis of these earlier travelers' accounts, were happy to use Khoikhoi as the link between man and the animals in the Great Chain of Being;[9] it also assured that the word *Hottentot* would long be used as a synonym for *brute* or *boor* in many Western European languages.

---

6. *BVR*, p. 199 ("Religion"); *CGH*, 2: 510–11 ("Religion"); ibid., 1: 192 (Abraham van Riebeeck, 1676). The quotation is from ibid., 1: 85 (Schouten, 1665).

7. Nienaber, *Hottentots*, pp. 79–84.

8. Ibid., p. 84; *CGH*, 2: 394 (Ovington, 1693).

9. Jordan, *White over Black*, pp. 224–25. As might be expected, philosophers who wrote enthusiastically about natural man were not as harsh on the Khoikhoi as were most of their contemporaries. Rousseau, for example, used Kolbe's description of Khoikhoi swiftness to prove the physical superiority of man in the state of nature. See Jean-Jacques Rousseau, *Discours sur l'Origine et les fondements de l'inégalité parmi les hommes* (Paris: Editions Sociales, 1971), pp. 152–53.

The unduly negative impressions of short-term visitors were not due entirely to ethnocentrism and lack of prior exposure to non-complex cultures. A contribution was also made by the conditions, alluded to in the last chapter, under which the races met in Cape Town. Even before 1652 a large percentage of travelers met, not cattle-keeping Khoikhoi, but impoverished Strandlopers; and after the founding of the colony it soon became virtually impossible for visitors to see pastoral Khoikhoi in their traditional society—though they might obtain distorted information on these matters by questioning the garrulous inhabitants of the town. The Khoikhoi whom visitors actually saw were cattleless members of an urban proletariat, many of whom begged for their living by dancing or disrobing for visitors; though Europeans were quite willing to pay Khoikhoi to degrade themselves in this way, at the same time they accused Khoikhoi of exceptional immodesty.

Then too, there was the problem of thievery, an unpleasant reality for many visitors before and after the founding the colony. Raven-Hart has noted that while many travelers prior to the mid-1670s mentioned thievishness as a cardinal sin of the Khoikhoi, many thereafter praised them for their honesty.[10] This interesting shift in perception was probably linked to the changing roles of Khoikhoi in the Cape Town of the 1670s; by this time many Khoikhoi were willing to earn food and tobacco by taking permanent jobs, and few needed iron for warlike activities any more.

In the absence of evidence to the contrary, we must assume that the well-documented attitudes of short-term visitors to the Cape roughly corresponded to those of most residents of the town, who after all came from similar backgrounds, met Khoikhoi under similar circumstances, and had themselves often been residents of the Cape only a short time. These early South African prejudices against Khoikhoi bore certain resemblances to racial attitudes forming at the same time in English-speaking communities that came in contact with negroes through the slave trade.[11] In both cases Europeans were stunned by the appearance of African peoples, dismayed by their lack of Christianity, and horrified by certain of their customs; in both cases they were inclined to draw invidious comparisons with the animal kingdom.

However, there were important differences between the two cases. Fear was not at first a predominant component in European attitudes

10. *CGH*, 2: 511 ("Shamelessness" and "Thievishness").
11. Jordan, *White over Black*, pp. 1–43.

to Khoikhoi; over the long period between the First Khoikhoi-Dutch War and the frontier disturbances of 1701–03, traditional Khoikhoi chieftains were not taken seriously as a threat to the colony, nor were colonial Khoikhoi numerous enough or embittered enough to make wide-scale revolt a likelihood. The native population was more a nuisance than a threat to most whites, apart from the hardy few who ventured into the game preserves of the "Bushman" hunters. Secondly, some of the subconscious aspects of white prejudices against blacks were absent in the case of Khoikhoi. European imaginations were not powerfully affected by Khoikhoi skin color as they were by negro "blackness," with all its identifications with evil, darkness, and the devil. It is true that Europeans loosely called the Khoikhoi "blacks" (as they did all peoples who were not "white," even the Chinese), but they usually agreed that the dark complexion of Khoikhoi was due to grease and was not innate. They described newborn Khoikhoi babies as brown, yellow, or even white.[12]

Furthermore, there were few of the sexual undertones that are often said to have characterized Protestant Europeans' responses to negroes. On the whole, white males did not find Khoikhoi women at all attractive, and, for reasons discussed later in this chapter, there was very little white-Khoikhoi miscegenation. Neither did anyone worry very much about protecting European women against Khoikhoi rapists. Khoikhoi, unlike blacks, were not imagined to have unusual sexual powers, for it was remarked that they had few children and practiced polygamy only rarely. In fact, European interest in Khoikhoi sexuality was concerned, not with fantasies about their passionate exploits, but with aspects of their genitalia which seemed odd.[13] If this obsession (for so it could fairly be called) contributed to the formation of racial prejudices, it did so directly by heightening the grotesque image of Khoikhoi, rather than indirectly, by giving rise to rivalry or envy, whether conscious or subconscious.

Khoikhoi were admired only by the very few who were curious enough to look behind the unhappy complex of superficialities which made Khoikhoi seem so un-European. One of their first admirers was H. A. van Reede tot Drakestein, a nobleman and distinguished botanist, who visited the Cape for three months in 1685 with the rank of commissioner. Van Reede perceived that "if one judges them

---

12. *CGH*, 2: 507 ("Colour").
13. Ibid., pp. 494 ("Apron"), 510 ("Polygamy"), 524 ("Testicles").

[Khoikhoi] by externals nothing good will be divined; but, having thorough instruction in their life and thought, one will find them otherwise." In the course of applying this principle, he pronounced many stereotypes about Khoikhoi to be completely false: contrary to accepted opinions the Khoikhoi were skilled warriors; they held their leaders in honor; they did have knowledge of God; and, perhaps most importantly to the patrician van Reede, they differed from the animals in that they observed the rule of law:

> they live under one another according to laws, which they hold unbreakable . . . manslaughter, adultery, lying, incest are forbidden and punishable among them; reverence for the dead and their burial places . . . are strictly maintained.[14]

A second Khoikhoi sympathizer was Johannes Wilhelm de Grevenbroek, a one-time secretary of the Council of Policy and later a settler in Stellenbosch. Grevenbroek's views, unlike those of Van Reede, were rooted in long contact with Khoikhoi and in considerable research on their customs. Though his enthusiasm for Khoikhoi was partly inspired by their submissive obedience to Europeans, Grevenbroek occasionally slipped into sentiments which the following century would elaborate into the image of the Noble Savage. The Khoikhoi, he maintained, "in whiteness of soul . . . are superior to many of our countrymen." Most of their seemingly odious qualities were not innate but derived from contact with Europeans:

> From us they have learned blasphemy, perjury, strife, quarrelling, drunkenness, trickery, brigandage, theft, ingratitude, unbridled lust for what is not one's own, misdeeds unknown to them before, and, among other crimes of deepest die, the accursed lust of gold.[15]

Because he liked to compare Western and Khoikhoi culture at the expense of the former, Grevenbroek took the trouble to write down Khoikhoi impressions of Europeans. These are virtually unique and very valuable, but it is hard to determine how far they have been embellished by Grevenbroek's own criticisms of European society. According to him, Khoikhoi initially thought that Europeans could vomit fire (from guns), and that men on horseback were centaurlike creatures, half-man, half-horse. Among European customs they most

14. Hulshof, "H. A. van Reede . . . Journaal," pp. 35–36, 203–04. Quotations are from pp. 36 and 203.

15. Grevenbroek, VRS 14, pp. 175 and 173.

disliked were the indiscriminate eating of green vegetables (food fit for cattle), belching and breaking wind, and the wearing of dainty necklaces "strung with a needle on a slender thread, bought for a greater price than the largest flocks of sheep." They also took it ill that Dutchmen "should foully insult their worship by disburdening their bowels" on the sacred "graves" of their mythical hero Heitsi Eibib.[16]

Grevenbroek was a settler and a farmer; but, as a man who had traveled widely in Europe and who wrote easily, if somewhat pompously, in Latin, he was clearly no typical frontiersman. Unfortunately, there is very little evidence available on the racial attitudes of the many whites who settled at some distance from Cape Town in the period 1679–1713. Virtually the only direct sources on up-country thinking are the letters written in the first decade of the eighteenth century by Adam Tas, in consultation with other farmers opposed to Governor Willem Adriaan van der Stel. In one of these letters the settlers displayed hostility toward free blacks which can only be described as racist; but toward Khoikhoi they had more ambiguous attitudes:

> No dependence should ever be placed on the Hottentots, who have been treated in an un-Christian manner by Christians. By nature they are more than any people in the world inclined to vengeance and would . . . , seeing their chance, attack all Christians, good as well as bad without distinction, and exterminate us.[17]

While they put the ultimate blame on the shoulders of unscrupulous whites, the farmers here attribute a ferocity to Khoikhoi which seems odd in view of the minimal violence that had accompanied the subordination of the native population. The whites' fears probably derived in part from the protracted unrest on the northern frontier in 1701–03. Perhaps even more important was the fact that Khoikhoi, now working side by side with slaves on European farms, were slowly assimilated with the latter in the white men's minds; and for the slaves, the whites had a deep-seated (and by no means irrational) fear that sometimes bordered on terror.

Increasing fear of Khoikhoi led to greater brutality in dealing with them. In 1696 a soldier in the Company's service shot and almost killed a Khoikhoi whom he accused of stealing his stirrups; at his trial

16. Ibid., pp. 181, 195, 207.
17. KA 4035, Tas et al. to XVII, n.d. [probably 1707 or 1708], p. 1035v.

the soldier testified that he cared little whether the Khoikhoi died or not, "believing . . . that by his action he had done no wrong." Ten years later a postholder in the Land of Waveren authorized a freeman to fire at will among Khoikhoi who persisted in pasturing their sheep close to his home. In the same year, three whites were convicted of beating a Khoikhoi to death over protracted periods, which they measured by the "pipeful" and spaced out with breaks for a friendly drink; they were assisted in this grim activity by two slaves, one of whom apparently dealt the Khoikhoi his coup de grace by breaking his neck with a spar.[18]

We must not assume that such incidents typified relations between whites and Khoikhoi in the rural districts. Our knowledge of them is based on judicial documents which, by their very nature, reflect the worst aspects of any society; and before 1713 the colony was so small that few settlers were sufficiently isolated from governmental supervision to possess arbitrary powers of life and death over their employees. These examples do, however, suggest that farmers and other up-country whites, now vastly outnumbered by slaves and Khoikhoi laborers, were showing new tendencies toward a callous brutality: these tendencies marked a new era when hate and fear, more than the earlier repulsion and annoyance, seemed dominant in Europeans' response to Khoikhoi.

The Failure of Comprehensive Assimilation

In the western Cape, as in many areas of Asia, the Dutch presence led to some adoption of Western culture by the indigenous inhabitants. At the Cape this process involved a much higher percentage of the native population than was normally the case in the Orient; but in another respect, assimilation at the Cape was less pervasive than elsewhere, for in the period covered by this study it was limited to Khoikhoi acquiring those aspects of Western culture which they needed to be laborers in white society. In Asia by contrast, cultural traits were transferred, not only through labor relations, but through active Christianization (in Formosa, Ceylon, and Amboina),[19] and through miscegenation. As a result, there emerged in many of the Company's

---

18. KA 4014, DR March 30, 1696, p. 890v; KA 4037, Landdrost vs. Tiele Weerts, Dec. 14, 1706, pp. 752v–53; KA 4037, Declaration of the Hottentot Hans, Jan. 14, 1707, pp. 685–86v; KA 4037, Further Confession of Jan Andriesz, March 30, 1707, pp. 688–91; KA 4036, DR July 23, 1707, pp. 234–37v.

19. Boxer, *Dutch Seaborne Empire*, pp. 133–48.

eastern settlements a large Eurasian population—which was partially received into the European community and partially relegated to its fringes—and a mixed "Indische" culture. Pauline Milone has characterized the cultural amalgamation at Batavia as "largely the pace-of-life, graces, aristocratic attitudes and arrogated privileges of Indonesian civilization mixed with some of the material uses, technology, elite fashions and Christianity of European society."[20]

The Company's accumulated experience in Asia caused Van Riebeeck and other early Cape officials to assume that a thorough assimilation of Khoikhoi to European culture was both possible and desirable. However, no official plans were made for such a campaign, and no money was allotted to carry it out. The only real efforts were made at a personal level by Van Riebeeck, his wife, and his brother-in-law, the sick-comforter Pieter van der Stael. By far the most outstanding product of their labors was the translator Eva, who, as we saw, mastered the language and customs of the Dutch and became a sincere Christian believer.

At first, Eva was an extremely successful intermediary between the Cochoqua of Oedasoa and the colonists. However, in the 1660s her position began to deteriorate. Oedasoa, who was gradually establishing direct relations with the Europeans, needed Eva's services less and less, and he became increasingly unfriendly to her after 1660. Eva also lost her European family when the Van Riebeecks sailed for Batavia in 1662. As more and more Khoikhoi mastered the Dutch language, she was no longer indispensable as an interpreter. Feeling neither at home nor fully accepted in either culture, she spent more and more time in the company of sailors from the ships, and by November 1663 she had borne two illegitimate children of European patrimony.[21]

Fortunately, in 1664 Eva, now twenty-one, was saved from her downhill life when the Danish surgeon, Pieter van Meerhoff, asked her hand in marriage. At twenty-seven Van Meerhoff was one of the most intelligent and promising men in the colony, and one of its leading experts on Khoikhoi. Commander Wagenaar—despite a personal dislike for Khoikhoi in general and for Eva in particular—encouraged this first Khoikhoi marriage by giving the couple a modest bridal feast (at Company expense) in his own home. Eva was also awarded fifty rixdollars in consideration of her former services. Soon after his marri-

---

20. Pauline Dublin Milone, "*Indische* Culture, and Its Relationship to Urban Life," *Comparative Studies in Society and History* 9, no. 4 (July 1967): 411.

21. KA 3976, DR Nov. 16, 1663, n.p.

age Van Meerhoff was appointed superintendent of the convicts on
Robben Island—a responsible enough post but a confining one for
Eva, who was used to the bustle and excitement of the fort. It may have
been at this time that she began to drink to excess, for in April 1667
it was reported that she had fallen off a bench, severely wounding her
head on the side of a staircase. The following year Van Meerhoff was
appointed to command an expedition leaving for Mauritius and
Madagascar. Eight months passed before the party returned—with
the news that Van Meerhoff had been slain in Antongil Bay in a clash
with some Madagascans.[22]

After less than four years of marriage, Eva was a widow with three
children by her late husband. The Company gave the little family a
home in an abandoned pottery, and Eva remained an acceptable
member of European society, eating occasionally at the commander's
table. Nonetheless, she began to drink heavily and—perhaps from
necessity—returned to prostitution. While dining with the colony's
elite on February 8, 1669, she shocked the assembled company by
becoming drunk and hurling abuse in the hearing of the commander;
for this outburst she was sternly lectured and threatened with banishment to an island. This so frightened Eva that she gathered up her
belongings and fled from the colony, leaving her half-white children,
destitute and naked, to throw themselves on the mercy of the Council
of Policy. In the nearby dunes she found some Khoikhoi who were
willing to buy her bedding for a bit of tobacco; she was just about to sell
her children's clothing when she was overtaken by the fiscal and
arrested.[23]

The indignant council banished Eva to Robben Island where, as it
turned out, she spent most of the remaining five years of her life;
though she was occasionally permitted to return to the mainland, she
did not, in the government's view, show sufficient moral improvement:

> with the dogs she returned to her own vomit, until finally, in
> death, she put out the fire of her lust, affording a clear illustration
> that nature, no matter how tightly muzzled by imprinted moral
> principles . . . reverts to its inborn qualities.[24]

22. KA 3977, DR April 26 and June 2, 1664, pp. 162, 168v–69; *Resolusies*, 1: 316 (April 12,
1664); H. C. V. Leibbrandt, *Precis of the Archives of the Cape of Good Hope: Journal, 1662–1670*
(Cape Town: W. A. Richards & Sons, 1901), pp. 218, 238.

23. KA 3981, DR Feb. 8–10, 1669, pp. 690v–92.

24. KA 3988, DR July 29, 1674, pp. 140–40v.

Eva died in July 1674, and in recognition of her Christian status and past services she was granted burial in the newly built castle. Her children, who had also been baptized, were supported by the church council until 1677, when Bartholomeus Borms, a friend of their late father, took two of them to Mauritius. On Mauritius, Petronella van Meerhoff married Daniel Zaijman of Vlissingen, a man of modest wealth. The couple were blessed with eight children, one of whom they christened with the name Eva. In 1709 they returned with their children to South Africa and settled in Stellenbosch.[25]

In naming her child after her own famous mother, Petronella was not echoing the general sentiment in the white community, which had thought very badly of Eva in her last years. Indeed, Eva's tragic life had helped spawn a belief that Khoikhoi could never successfully absorb the higher aspects of European culture. Prior to 1713 only a handful of Khoikhoi were exposed nearly so fully to Western civilization as Eva—and their stories were scarcely more encouraging. Sara, a girl who had spent most of her life among the Dutch as a servant and a concubine, killed herself in 1671 at the age of twenty-four. Another Khoikhoi was converted to Christianity by the Reverend Petrus Kalden, taken to Holland in 1707, and baptized as Frederick Adolf in the church at Vianen; he later returned to the Cape, where his life was deemed so immoral that he was apparently obliged to spend the rest of his life on Robben Island.[26]

Several other westernized Khoikhoi avoided such tragic ends by leaving the colony and returning to Khoikhoi society. One Pegu (or Bego) was educated in European customs by Simon van der Stel and taken to India in the service of Van Reede: when he returned to the Cape, he renounced his Christianity and became a moderately wealthy Khoikhoi captain.[27] Dobbeltje, Vogelstruys, and Cornelia—three Khoikhoi, who like Eva had worked in Van Riebeeck's household—were still living in Khoikhoi kraals in 1710 when Van Riebeeck's granddaughter Johanna Maria visited the Cape and heard them reminisce about old times. Cornelia had already been visited in 1705

25. *Resolusies*, 2: 195–96 (July 23, 1677); D. F. du T. Malherbe, *Stamregister van die Suid-Afrikaanse Volk*, 3d ed. (Stellenbosch: Tegniek, 1966), p. 1198.

26. On Sara, see chap. 10, n. 21. On Frederick Adolf, see Kolbe, *Beschreibung*, pp. 110–11; Collectie Radermacher no. 504, Contra-Deductie . . . , p. 174; Petrus Kalden, *Afgeperste Verweering . . . Tegens Twee nu onlangs uytgekomene Laster-Schriften . . .* (Utrecht: W. Broedelet, 1713), p. 52; Valentyn, *Oud en Nieuw Oost-Indiën*, 5 (2): 158–59.

27. Valentyn, *Oud en Nieuw Oost-Indiën*, 5 (2): 106; Kolbe, *Beschreibung*, p. 35; KA 4031, Dag Verhaal .. Starrenburgh, Dec. 1, 1705, p. 754; KA 4042, DR Feb. 25, 1710, p. 382v.

by François Valentyn; though it was then forty-three years since the
departure of Van Riebeeck, and though she was now in her eighties,
Cornelia still spoke very good Dutch and was, "apart from her Hottentot clothes and animal skins, so modest and well-mannered that
one [had] to be astonished."²⁸

Cornelia excepted, westernized or partially westernized Khoikhoi
did not favorably impress Europeans, and so there were no happy
precedents to spur the Company into a policy of planned assimilation.
Apart from this general pessimism, there were several other reasons
why the Cape did not experience the Batavian—let alone the Portuguese—model of cultural amalgamation. Preeminent among these
was the very small scale both of miscegenation and proselytization.

Though white males at the Cape often had sexual relations with
women of other races, these were usually slaves or ex-slaves of Asian,
Madagascan, or African origin.²⁹ Slave women were far more readily
coercible than Khoikhoi women, and many, through the degrading
conditions in which they had lived, had abandoned much of their
native codes of sexual morality. By contrast, most Khoikhoi women
in the colony retained their kinship ties to a kraal and were subject—
at least in the early decades—to traditional sanctions against pre-
marital sex and adultery. Dapper (probably relying on the research
of Georg Friedrich Wreede) says:

> When [a Khoikhoi man and woman] are caught in illicit inter-
> course, they are both whipped . . . and [sometimes] . . . permitted
> to marry each other. In case this does not take place, they wait
> to see if the girl becomes pregnant. Once she is pregnant, the
> marriage must be hastened on, no matter how bad a person the
> lover is, in order to restore the honour of the girl; for it is a great
> scandal there to have an illegitimate child; although sometimes
> it does actually occur.

As for married women, Tachard (relying on Claudius) says that
among Khoikhoi adultery was a crime punishable by death, as does
Kolbe.³⁰ While such traditional sanctions must have discouraged

---

28. Bosman, *Briewe van Johanna Maria van Riebeeck*, p. 88; Valentyn, *Oud en Nieuw Oost-Indiën*,
5 (2): 106.

29. J. L. M. Franken, *Taalhistoriese Bydraes* (Amsterdam and Cape Town: A. A. Balkema,
1953), pp. 20–25.

30. Dapper, VRS 14, pp. 65–67; Tachard, *Voyage de Siam*, p. 95; Kolbe, *Beschreibung*, p. 125.
See also Valentyn, *Oud en Nieuw Oost-Indiën*, 5 (2): 109.

Khoikhoi women from consorting with white men, an even greater deterrent to miscegenation was the distaste with which Europeans regarded Khoikhoi clothing and adornment. As one seaman, Captain Daniel Beeckman, remarked:

> By the *Dutch* laws it is *Death* for a *Dutchman* to lie with a *Hottentot-Woman*: tho' I think they need not have laid that Restriction upon them, the very Smell and Looks of such hideous Creatures being a sufficient Antidote against Lechery.[31]

Beeckman was wrong in saying that the Dutch prohibited miscegenation with Khoikhoi,[32] and we would be wrong to assume that none at all took place: apart from scandalous cases like those of Eva and Sara, there were enough Khoikhoi women loitering around the docks to give *casual* visitors an impression of Khoikhoi lewdness and for venereal disease to be transferred to the Khoikhoi population. Nonetheless, such instances were very few; and apart from Eva's, there were no intermarriages prior to 1713. Widespread miscegenation with Khoikhoi was a phenomenon, not of the early colony, but of the remote cattle frontier in the eighteenth century.[33]

During the colony's first sixty years virtually no progress was made in converting Khoikhoi to Christianity. In 1678 Eva was the only pure-blooded Khoikhoi who had been baptized, and apart from Kalden's Khoikhoi, who was baptized in Holland, we know of no others before 1713. A few others came under the influence of Christian teachings, but more often than not they abandoned their beliefs before their deaths. The first sick-visitor (i.e. lay reader) at the Cape was Willem Barentsz Wylant, who set the pessimistic tone in 1655 when he observed

---

31. Beeckman, VRS 5, p. 117.

32. There was, to my knowledge, no law directed specifically at intercourse between whites and Khoikhoi: there was certainly none that was enforced in the courts. However, on December 9, 1678, a pro forma proclamation outlawed *all* types of concubinage (*KP*, 1: 151–52). On his expedition to Namaqualand in 1685, Simon van der Stel forbade his men to sleep with Khoikhoi women on pain of flogging and dismissal from the Company's service; this, however, was not a general law. See Waterhouse, *Van der Stel*, p. 117.

33. For an impression of Khoikhoi promiscuity, see William Funnell, *A Voyage round the World* ... (London: W. Botham, 1707), p. 290. On venereal disease, see Grevenbroek, VRS 14, p. 241. One of the first hints of white concubinage with Khoikhoi in outlying districts is in C. Spoelstra, *Bouwstoffen voor de geschiedenis der Nederduitsch-Gereformeerde Kerken in Zuid-Afrika*, 2 vols. (Amsterdam: Hollandsch Afrikaansche Uitgevers Maatschappij, 1906), 1:65 (Le Boucq to Classis Amsterdam, April 20, 1708).

> it appears almost impossible to bring [Khoikhoi] to the knowledge of the truth, for the language cannot be learned. Also . . . I have twice already had one of their boys living with me, intending thereby to educate them in something good, to read and write, and also to learn their language, in order thus to bring them to the light of the truth. But it did not work out, because they are so used to running about wild, that they can't live in subjection to us.[34]

Later, when official clergy were established at the Cape, they continued to wish that Khoikhoi would become Christians so that "Ham would no longer be a servant of servants"; but they normally concluded that this would happen "only through the almightly hand of our merciful God at that time when the fullness of the Gentiles be come in." Though some clergymen proposed ways to hasten that day, none apparently took concrete steps, except Petrus Kalden, who made considerable progress in learning the Khoikhoi language.[35] Unfortunately, Kalden's good work was cut short in 1707 when, because of his association with the discredited Governor Willem Adriaan van der Stel, he was recalled to the Netherlands.

Several factors help to explain the lack of effective missionary activity at the Cape. The clergy—who never numbered more than three in this period—had their hands more than full with a large white constituency that was growing rapidly and spreading over inconveniently long distances. To evangelize Khoikhoi effectively, they would have had to learn an exceedingly difficult language, and might possibly have had to move about with a nomadic Khoikhoi tribe. No official aid was forthcoming from the Company, since at the Cape competing religions like Islam and Catholicism did not pose problems that entered into its geopolitical calculations. Such little time as could be found for moral and spiritual uplift the Company devoted to the white and slave populations: at various times small schools for slaves and whites were started, and though Khoikhoi were supposed to attend these as well, we know of only one or two who actually did.[36] Yet when all these excuses have been made for clerical inactivity, it

34. Spoelstra, *Bouwstoffen*, 1: 28 (Overney to Classis Amsterdam, n.d.). The quotation is from p. 4 (Wylant to Classis Amsterdam, April 20, 1655).

35. Ibid., p. 34 (Beck et al., to Classis Amsterdam, April 4, 1703); p. 37 (Church Council to Classis Amsterdam, April 2, 1706).

36. H. P. Cruse, *Die Opheffing van die Kleurlingbevolking*, vol. 1: *Aanvangsjare 1652–1795* (Stellenbosch: Die Christen-Studentevereniging van Suid-Afrika, 1947), p. 86.

is still hard to avoid the impression that the conversion of Khoikhoi did not rank high on the list of the Cape church's priorities.

SOME INDICATORS OF CULTURAL ACQUISITION

As a result of the hindrances we have discussed, the assimilation of Khoikhoi to Western culture was informal and haphazard rather than directed or comprehensive, and it involved only those aspects of Western ways which were appropriate to the role of Khoikhoi as members of an urban and rural proletariat. Virtually the first European cultural traits that Khoikhoi adopted were a taste for tobacco and alcohol, as well as for rice, bread, cheese, and the once-despised green vegetables. Later on they learned a variety of skills related to farming, such as harvesting, preparing wine, and driving wagons. It seems doubtful, however, that these acquired tastes and skills much altered the physical culture of their homes or their traditional style of life. Most Khoikhoi in the colony continued to wear their traditional dress well into the eighteenth century,[37] and many lived in mat huts even while on European farms. Prior to 1713 few had learned the use of firearms, and assegais were often carried inside the colony.

One slight, but potentially significant, shift of values took place in Khoikhoi attitudes toward money. In the 1680s some Siamese ambassadors were shipwrecked near Cape Agulhas; during their trek to Cape Town they came across some Khoikhoi to whom they offered large diamonds in return for cattle and sheep: the Khoikhoi showed no interest in the diamonds and would accept only tobacco and "pataques" (coins). In this same period Khoikhoi occasionally stole money, and Grevenbroek noted that they often wore a small wallet around their necks in which they kept "one or two copper coins of which they have managed to cheat our fellows."[38] Most likely, however, Khoikhoi valued money as an extension of their affection for metal decorations, and it is doubtful if at this stage they distinguished the different denominations of coins or understood in detail how Europeans evaluated money against other goods.

This was certainly the case with the Khoikhoi on the frontier: in 1682 some Khoikhoi recovered valuable pieces of eight from a shipwreck near Agulhas but were happy to trade them to the Dutch for

37. E.g. KA 4036, DR July 23, 1707, p. 235.

38. Guy Tachard, *Second voyage du père Tachard* ... (Middelburg: Gilles Horthemels, 1689), p. 321; Grevenbroek, VRS 14, p. 187. The English translation of *pataque* is "patacoon": this was a silver coin minted by the Spanish and Portuguese.

a bit of tobacco. It is even possible that Cape Town Khoikhoi, who were paid by the sailors in coin, did not have completely westernized attitudes about money. De la Loubère noted in 1687 that Khoikhoi port workers valued their wages only slightly, and in 1706 Bartholomew Ziegenbalg observed that Khoikhoi workers were "content with very little. If you will give them a *Ducat* [a sizeable amount] they will hardly take it, requiring only a *Groat* [i.e. a pittance] by reason they don't use to spend more in a Day; and they are unconcerned for the Morrow."[39] We can conclude, then, that coins had taken their place in the urban Khoikhoi value scale but that a full-fledged monetary revolution still lay in the future.

Rather more rapid change seems to have taken place in the Khoikhoi naming system. Among traditional Namaqua all sons inherited the name of their mother, and daughters took the name of their father: when sons reached maturity they were also given their father's name, to which was added the suffix -*ma*. We have relatively few recorded instances of such double names at the Cape—one example was Gamnoa-Koucha*ma*, the name of a chief who visited the castle in 1687—but names ending in *ma* were quite common; e.g. Gonnema, Eykamma, Khuma. These traditional Khoikhoi names revealed valuable genealogical information but were also confusing, because many people (including siblings) had the same name; thus, nicknames based on a person's bodily features or events in his past life became very important. Sometimes nicknames were used temporarily, sometimes permanently; and sometimes they were inherited, thus becoming new family names.[40] Some very well known personages in Cape history—like Gaukou, Gogosoa, and Doman—were probably known by nicknames of this sort.

The Dutch were oblivious to these complexities and usually only learned one of the names of any given Khoikhoi. Quite often they did not even do this, so dismayed were they by the problem of recognizing or pronouncing clicks. Long before 1652 they had begun to call Khoikhoi by European names, which Khoikhoi, wishing to be cooperative, also used in referring to one another in conversation with

---

39. KA 3995, Dagelycxe aenteekening gehouden door den adsistent Aernout Kalcoen ... , Aug. 14, 1682, p. 361v; *CGH*, 2: 321 (de la Loubère, 1687); Bartholomew Ziegenbalgh, *Propagation of the Gospel in the East* ... , 3d ed. (London: Joseph Downing, 1718), p. 12. The quotation is from this last source. For a clear (and late) example of a Khoikhoi who was in European employ but had no conception of the value of money, see KA 4053, Interrogation of Claas Blank, n.d. [1715], p. 886v.

40. Schultze, *Namaland*, pp. 303–06.

the Dutch. In Van Riebeeck's time only Peninsulars had received European names; but with the spread of white influence, more and more inland chiefs, and then their subjects, took them as well; by 1713 the majority of Khoikhoi mentioned in the documents had European names. Apart from the classical names given to chiefs by Simon van der Stel, the majority of these new appellations were Dutch. Many were originally Christian names like Cornelis, Frans, or Leendert; others were surnames like Bootman, Kruidop, or Ingerman; but most were nicknames, either favorable or pejorative, like Dikkop (Fathead), Jager (Hunter), Zwarte Kapitein (Black Captain), Schele Klaas (Squinting Klaas), Chineesje (Little Chinese), and so on.

A smaller number of Khoikhoi took complete Dutch names like Jan Pietersz or Pieter Passagie. It is probable that most such names (and indeed some of the shorter ones) were those of current or former employers. This would seem to be the origin of a name like Jan Mostaerts Dikkop, and certainly explains the case of two hunter brothers who worked at one time for the burgher Willem Schalck and subsequently were themselves called Willem Schalck and Willem Schalcks Broer (i.e. brother).[41] This latter example (from 1678) was one of the earliest in which blood relationships were shown in Khoikhoi names of European origin: by 1700, however, it was quite common for names to indicate paternity, sonship, or siblinghood; for example, Ruyters Vader, Oude Heers Zoon, Hans Broer, Jantie van Sosequa Broer. This could have easily been a transitional stage on the way to passing names down the male line as in conventional European usage; though this was commonly done among eighteenth-century Colored families like the Koks, I have found only one possible example prior to 1730.[42]

It is very difficult to determine how rapidly traditional names disappeared in Khoikhoi (as opposed to European) usage. Undoubtedly this process was slower than the documents—which naturally used European names in preference to Khoikhoi—would suggest. However, we must not be overly cautious. The process of name change was hastened by the fact that Khoikhoi had traditionally adopted nicknames, which for a time coexisted with their inherited names, but sometimes finally displaced them and themselves became heritable. It was likewise aided by the prestige which European culture

41. KA 3991, Confession of Gamako, Sept. 10, 1678, p. 525.

42. A comparison of the following two sources suggests that there was a chiefly Guriqua family with the inherited name Blaauw: KZ 3193, Dagh Verhaal ... Slotsbo, Oct. 18, 1712, n.p.; Rhenius, VRS 28, p. 144.

enjoyed among Khoikhoi at a time when their own society was disintegrating: indeed, it is likely that Khoikhoi desired European names, which identified them with the colony's masters and distanced them from the slaves (who bore either a native name or a toponym like Titus of Macassar).

In any event, the change in names was faster than the change in language, a process to which we must now turn our attention. From the beginning of their adventures in South Africa, Europeans had been frustrated in all their attempts to understand or speak even a few words of Khoikhoi. In 1601 a diarist on Sir James Lancaster's fleet noted that "in seven weeks which wee remained heere in this place, the sharpest wit among us could not learne one word of their language; and yet the people would vnderstand any signe wee made to them."[43] These difficulties persisted long after the founding of the colony, especially since the Company's policy was "that the natives there shall learn our language rather than we theirs."[44] Though several persons compiled word lists of Khoikhoi, as late as 1685 Commissioner Van Reede looked in vain for a European who could actually speak the language. (In fact, at this time there was in the colony a slave who, having sojourned a year among the Guriqua, had mastered Khoikhoi.) It is not until 1711 that we hear of a few white children picking up Khoikhoi, and not until the isolated frontier conditions of the mid-eighteenth century that such skills were common among settlers.[45]

Thus, from the beginning Khoikhoi were expected to exert themselves to learn European languages and, beginning with Coree and Harry, there were always a few leaders who showed a real genius for the task. From the time of the *Haerlem* wreck (1649) even ordinary Khoikhoi picked up words of English and Dutch and used these to greet the founders of white South Africa when they landed in 1652. In the next decade they made such progress that Van Riebeeck warned his successor never to say anything of importance within the hearing of Strandlopers. By the early eighteenth century, travelers had the impression that most Khoikhoi spoke understandable Dutch, not only in Cape Town, but in kraals one day's journey away.[46]

43. *BVR*, p. 23 (Lancaster, 1601).

44. KA 456, XVII to Wagenaar, April 29, 1664, p. 700.

45. Hulshof, "H. A. van Reede ... Journaal," p. 36; KA 3993, DR Jan. 27, 1680, p. 73; Nienaber, *Hottentots*, p. 85.

46. *VRJ*, 1: 30 (April 10, 1652); KA 3974, Van Riebeeck to Successor, May 5, 1662, p. 6v; Cnoll, VRS 5, p. 83.

Eva's achievement in speaking perfect Dutch was, however, rare; in ensuing decades even those Khoikhoi who had regular dealings with the Dutch spoke in broken dialects. We have many words and phrases of Khoikhoi Dutch scattered through Company documents and travelers' accounts, but for connected sentences we must turn chiefly to data collected by Ten Rhyne in 1673 and by Kolbe in the early eighteenth century. Two examples from these authors follow,[47] with possible literal translations.

> Dat is doet: was makom? Duytsman altyt kallom: Icke Hottentots doot makom: Mashy doot, Icke strack nae onse groote Kapiteyn toe, die man my soon witte Boeba geme.

> (That is death. What are you doing? Dutchmen always say: I will kill Hottentots. Then kill! Even if I die, I shall go straight to our great captain who will give my son [or "give me such a"] white ox.)

> Gy dit Beet fangum zoo, en nu dood makum zoo, is dat braa? waytum, ons altemaal daarvan loopum zoo.

> (You have caught this animal in this way, and now you want to kill it. Is that right? Wait; [if you do it], we will all run away.)

There is also a sentence of this type of Khoikhoi Dutch in a government document of 1672:

> Duitsman een wordt calm ons u kelem.[48]

> (Dutchman, [if you] speak a word, we [will] slit your throats.)

In this type of pidgin Dutch, which seems to have been remarkably uniform over a considerable time span, the same verb form is usually used for the past, present, and future; and to it is added -um, -om, -em, or -m. Marius Valkhoff has found examples of similar endings in pidgin and creole languages around the world (to which may be added Hollywood's American Indian "Me kill-um white man"), and in the Khoikhoi case relates the endings to the Dutch third-person masculine pronoun hem.[49] Khoikhoi Dutch was also characterized by heavy

---

47. Ten Rhyne, VRS 14, p. 141; Kolbe, *Beschreibung*, p. 100. For a fuller list of examples, see Franken, *Bydraes*, pp. 92–93.

48. Moodie, *The Record*, pp. 322–23, n. 2.

49. Valkhoff, *Portuguese and Creole*, p. 220.

semantic loads on words that would not be a Dutchman's natural choice; for example, *kallom* (from *kallen*, to chatter) to indicate speech of any sort; *braa* (from *braaf*) to mean "good," "powerful," "just," "efficacious"; *maski* or *mashi* (from Portuguese *mas que*) to mean "perhaps," "although," "no matter," or "if." Although standard Dutch articles occasionally appeared, Khoikhoi tended rather to use *die* before all nouns, even neuter ones, which would demand *het* in Dutch. They also mixed up subjective and objective cases in pronouns, often using *ik* where Dutch would require *mij*, and *ons* where Dutch used *wij*.

The simplification of the article and the heavy use of *ons* give this speech points of contact with modern Afrikaans, but also with a second sort of Khoikhoi speech which is recorded only in the judicial papers of 1706–08. It is interesting that the scribe who transcribed fragments of this language also depicted slaves as using the very same speech.

(Khoikhoi)   ons sel jou kost geeven
               ons het jouw tabak niet van doen
               ons wil dat niet doen
               Ary het my met een mes gesneden

(Slaves)   ons soek kost hier
               ons denk
               ons het vuur genoeg[50]

In these examples the verb endings in *-m* do not appear, and on the whole we are dealing here with more conventional Dutch than in the first samples. Probably these sentences are typical of the speech of Khoikhoi who had lived a generation in close contact with whites. The outstanding features of this type are that indicative verbs are always uninflected; that the verb "to have" is always *het*, a form which occurs nowhere in the conjugation of the standard Dutch verb *hebben*; and that *ons* is regularly used for *wij*. These charactertistics are so unmistakably Afrikaans that J. L. M. Franken, the Afrikaans linguist who first discovered these sentences, wrote: "The forms *ons soek*, *ons denk*, *ons sel*, *ons het* in 1706 are an indication that Afrikaans did not develop normally from the language of the fatherland";[51] in other words, that it was not the mere passage of time, but the process of

---

50. KA 4034, Declaration of the Hottentots, July 5, 1706, p. 636; KA 4037, Declaration of Hans, Jan. 14, 1707, p. 686v; KA 4037, Declaration of Hoerema and Grietje, n.d., p. 695v; KA 4038, DR Sept. 22, 1708, p. 199. For slave sentences, see Franken, *Bydraes*, p. 94.

51. Franken, *Bydraes*, p. 95.

being spoken by slaves and Khoikhoi which hastened the transformation of Dutch into Afrikaans. Another linguist, G. S. Nienaber, has argued that the Khoikhoi language may also have been a stimulus to the development of the famous double negative in Afrikaans.[52] These assertions, however, are part of a highly technical and controversial debate on the origins of Afrikaans, a subject with which we are not directly concerned in this study.

Khoikhoi learned languages other than Dutch. We have a sentence of broken (and abusive) French spoken by a Khoikhoi on a Huguenot farm in 1707: "Chin de mer, parle tu avec." And Ten Rhyne claimed to have spoken in French to the Peninsular captain Kuiper in 1673. Pegu, during his stay in the Orient with Van Reede, picked up Sinhalese, Malay, and Portuguese. Eva in her time had spoken Portuguese, as had Sara; and in 1685 a French visitor was approached in the Company gardens by a Khoikhoi who offered him two oranges with a salutation in High Portuguese.[53] Valkhoff has convincingly argued that a variant of Portuguese was the lingua franca of the slaves at the Cape, just as it was in the Company's Asian settlements.[54] The degree to which Khoikhoi mastered Portuguese would accordingly be dependent on the intimacy of their contact with slaves, and thus probably increased rapidly in the late seventeenth century. By the mid-eighteenth century the evidence is abundant that Khoikhoi on European farms regularly spoke both Dutch and Portuguese.[55]

Despite their achievements in learning foreign languages, the Khoikhoi continued to speak their own language among themselves for the whole period covered by this study. It was not until the mid-eighteenth century that the Khoikhoi tongue would begin to disappear from the western Cape.[56] The slowness with which it disappeared shows clearly that Khoikhoi learned other languages, less to assimilate to a new culture, than to acquire a skill essential to their role as laborers in white society.

Over the period 1652–1713, Western Cape Khoikhoi underwent drastic changes in their demographic patterns, their means of liveli-

---

52. G. S. Nienaber, "Iets Naders oor die Ontkenning in Afrikaans," *Hertzog-Annale* 2 (Dec. 1955): 29–45.

53. KA 4037, Vraagpoincten ... Pieter Cronje, March 3, 1707, p. 781v; Ten Rhyne, VRS 14, p. 111; Valentyn, *Oud en Nieuw Oost-Indiën*, 5 (2): 106; Tachard, *Voyage de Siam*, p. 97.

54. Valkhoff, *Portuguese and Creole*, pp. 146–91.

55. E.g. Mentzel, VRS 4, p. 49.

56. Nienaber, *Hottentots*, pp. 97–98.

hood, and the political authorities under whom they lived; these developments were rapid almost from the first, and precipitous toward the end. Cultural change, however, was in this period much slower than structural change, and less comprehensive in its effects. Khoikhoi had in effect become a subordinate caste in white society—subordinate in the sense that they did only the lowest-paid jobs in the colony, and a caste because their appearance and traditional culture set them apart both from whites and slaves, and because white prejudices denied advancement to Khoikhoi through job promotion, conversion, or intermarriage. It was significant that these patterns of subordination and social separation were established so early: for although European and Khoikhoi cultures were soon to come much closer together on the eighteenth-century frontier, it would be too late for cultural rapprochement to raise the Khoikhoi to a higher station in white-dominated South Africa.

Part 4   Denouement and Retrospect

11

Collapse of the Old Order

Khoikhoi tribes experienced at different times, and in varying measure, three major challenges from the whites: (1) penetration of their territories by Company officials, particularly traders; (2) settlement of their pastures by free farmers; and (3) displacement of their people, herds, and flocks by seminomadic cattlemen. Of these three, the Company's frontier of trade and political influence was the one Khoikhoi experienced first, and it is with this frontier that the bulk of this study has been concerned. In a sense, the Company's frontier had reached the Peninsulars fifty years before the founding of the colony; the Nearby Khoikhoi (Cochoqua, Chainouqua, Hessequa) were first affected after 1652 and the Borderland Khoikhoi after the mid-1670s. The farming frontier was established later (1657) and moved more slowly, threatening at first only the Peninsulars, and after 1679 the Nearby Khoikhoi. The cattle frontier emerged alongside the farming frontier toward the end of the century and by and large affected only the Borderlands.[1]

For most of this period, then, the Company was the major catalyst rather than the settlers, who became important only in the later stages of the process. In effect, Khoikhoi society had melted away some miles ahead of the advancing farming frontier. Why was this? Was it simply that the Khoikhoi were militarily inadequate? Can it be said of Khoikhoi, as it is sometimes said of the Australian aborigines, that their idyllic isolation had precluded the development of a military capacity which could cope with Europeans?

Such an argument ignores the fact that only a few tribes actually succumbed to the force of European arms. It also overlooks the ferocious nature of traditional warfare, particularly that between Khoikhoi and hunters. Had Khoikhoi chosen to use poisoned arrows against Euro-

---

1. The terms Nearby Khoikhoi and Borderland Khoikhoi were discussed on p. 117.

peans (as they rarely did), the early history of white South Africa could
have been far more horrifying than it was.[2] In any event, the Khoikhoi
proved themselves quite effective in guerilla campaigns against white
property. What they could not do was defend themselves or their
livestock in open battle.

Military failure was rooted ultimately in the nature of Khoikhoi
society, most particularly in the paucity of tribewide institutions that
could hold a people together through protracted challenges or help it
recover from temporary defeat. The unity of the tribe was constantly
being eroded by the ease with which both wealth and people passed
from tribe to tribe, and (thanks to the existence of the hunters) out of
Khoikhoi society altogether. The European presence seriously exacerbated these tendencies in Khoikhoi society.

Before the advent of the whites, a clan which had fallen on hard times
had four alternatives: its members could trek away to a new region;
they could revert to a hunting existence; they could offer to herd for
a wealthy chief; or they could try to recover their position through war.
When Khoikhoi society began to crumble before the Dutch advance,
a very few Khoikhoi chose the first alternative—namely, to trek inland.
Of the vast majority who remained, only a few became hunters—at
least among the Peninsular and Nearby Khoikhoi. This was because
the Dutch offered them attractive terms along the lines of the third
option: Khoikhoi could herd cattle for the conqueror, thus earning
their keep and possibly enough stock to restart their own herds and
flocks. In traditional Khoikhoi society this process of rallying around
the strong was the beginning of recovery; in this case, however, Khoikhoi society virtually lost those men who chose to work in the colony.

The only real hope of recovery lay in the fourth possibility; namely,
that strong leaders would forge wealthy communities through successful wars with other Khoikhoi. Only such consolidated tribal units
could control the cattle barter, defend pastures, and assert Khoikhoi
independence of the Dutch. But Khoikhoi society produced no great
men to save it in its hour of peril. Rather than becoming stronger as the
century progressed, Khoikhoi chiefs as a rule became weaker. This
failure of leadership, like most nonevents in history, cannot be fully
explained. However, one can discern several factors, apart from the
traditional limitations on the chiefs' power, which made the climate
unfavorable for the emergence of outstanding leaders.

---

2. See *CGH*, 2: 505 ("Bows and Arrows"), which makes clear that Western Cape Khoikhoi
had poisoned arrows but suggests that these were not a prominent part of their material culture.

While Dutch military activity against Khoikhoi tribes was guided by no overall plan, its deleterious effects on Khoikhoi leadership were profound and purchased at a very low price. When Peninsular leadership was crumbling in the 1650s, Dutch arms disposed of Doman and Harry, the only two Peninsulars who had the ability to recover the situation. While most Cape Khoikhoi chieftainships were experiencing declining leadership in the 1660s and 1670s, the Dutch attacked and defeated the Cochoqua, the only tribe (except the Hessequa) who were not. Then finally, when Klaas had revived the fortunes of some of the Chainouqua, he too was crushed.

From the Khoikhoi point of view it was unfortunate that political power in Khoikhoi society was so dependent on cattle wealth and on personal followings acquired in war. For reasons outlined in chapters 8 and 9, the Dutch presence meant that both cattle and people were fewer in independent Khoikhoi tribes than formerly. In traditional society both could be lost by a tribe or clan; but people, and even to a degree livestock, remained within the total Khoikhoi-hunter system of the "ecological cycle." By contrast, Dutch trade and labor policies drew both people and stock out of the system altogether.

The problems thus created tended to feed upon one another and become more serious with the passage of time. A Khoikhoi leader with a dwindling following would find it difficult to seize new livestock through war; this was especially the case once the Dutch began to prohibit all inter-Khoikhoi wars in the western Cape. Similarly, a chief with few cattle to lend out was in a poor position to attract cattleless Khoikhoi, who would be much more likely to go and work for a white farmer. In these ways the Dutch presence further enfeebled the traditionally weak institution of Khoikhoi chieftainship and guaranteed that no effective resistance would come from that quarter.

The Frontier of Settlement

During the first phase of Khoikhoi-European contact (the "frontier of trade and influence") the white farmers did little besides providing employment for indigent Khoikhoi. Only in a few areas were Khoikhoi displaced from their pastures by arriving settlers; more typically they were drawn away from their pasture lands into colonial territory. This pattern was due chiefly to the colony's very slow expansion in the early decades. The Company, as I have indicated, wanted to limit itself to profit-making enterprises. If it permitted expansion it did so for strategic reasons or because it desired agricultural growth to make the colony independent of imported rice.

Map 5: The Colony around 1705

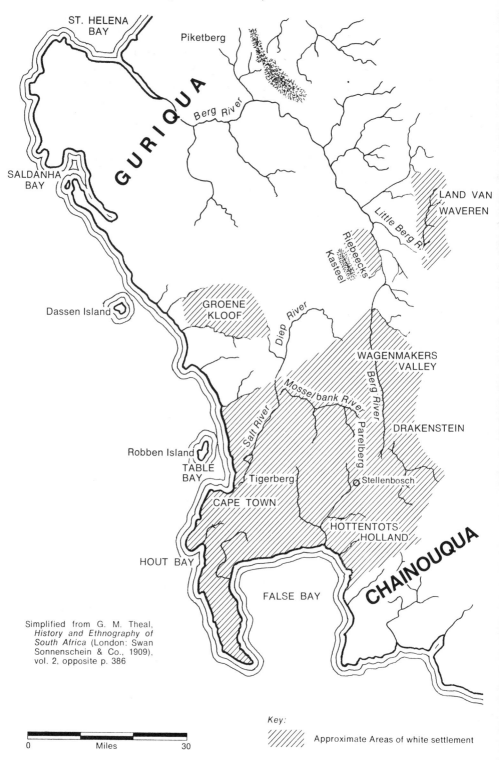

ST. HELENA BAY

Piketberg

GURIQUA

Berg River

SALDANHA BAY

LAND VAN WAVEREN

Little Berg R.

Riebeecks Kasteel

Dassen Island

GROENE KLOOF

Diep River

WAGENMAKERS VALLEY

Berg River

Mosselbank River

Parelberg

DRAKENSTEIN

Salt River

Robben Island

TABLE BAY

Tigerberg

Stellenbosch

CAPE TOWN

HOTTENTOTS HOLLAND

HOUT BAY

CHAINOUQUA

FALSE BAY

Simplified from G. M. Theal, *History and Ethnography of South Africa* (London: Swan Sonnenschein & Co., 1909), vol. 2, opposite p. 386

0   Miles   30

Key:

////// Approximate Areas of white settlement

Exploration of the interior was at first undertaken to find cattle and open contacts with wealthy peoples, not to locate land for settlement. The most intensive period of exploration was between 1655 and 1664. In 1664 the Seventeen, disillusioned by meager results, ordered a cessation of inland probes and a switch to exploration along the coasts.[3] For the rest of the century most inland discoveries were made informally by the bartering parties. The only exceptions were the Namaqualand explorations (1682–86) and two eastern expeditions (to the Attaqua in 1668 and to the Inqua in 1689).

The Company's first territorial holdings consisted merely of the fort and its immediate surroundings. As a result of the First Khoikhoi-Dutch War, this area was expanded to include the Cape Peninsula and its environs, this being the only time when pastures were formally ceded by Khoikhoi as a result of conquest. After another decade, the Company decided to expand along the west and south coasts, occupying Saldanha Bay in 1670 and Hottentots Holland in 1672. The purpose in the first case was to preempt occupation by a hostile European power, and in the second to establish an auxiliary cattle post and farming settlement. In the late 1670s the Company gradually turned Hottentots Holland over to freeman farmers, at first tentatively; then in 1683 it withdrew altogether, leaving only one official on the spot to root out any illegal barter. At this stage the Berg River was vaguely established as the limit of the farming frontier.[4]

The remaining two outward movements of the seventeenth century are better known: the foundation of Stellenbosch in 1679 and of Drakenstein in 1687. Both of these settlements were instituted by Simon van der Stel, and it was he who investigated the terrain, located the settlers, and organized the community: the autonomous frontier was still a phenomenon of the future. These new agricultural settlements were the government's response to a growing population of freemen whose sons would not be denied the right to a farm of their own. Natural increase was thus the main dynamic behind the spreading frontier of settlement; and the burgher population swelled at a fairly constant pace throughout the seventeenth century, though the totals always remained small. The only drastic population jump occurred with the influx of Huguenot refugees in 1688.[5]

3. KA 456, XVII to Wagenaar, Oct. 8, 1664, pp. 757–58.

4. KA 457, XVII to Borghorst, Sept. 5, 1670, n.p.; Theal, *History of South Africa*, 1: 178, 204; KA 3996, DR March 29, 1683, p. 206; KA 3991, DR Jan. 31. 1678, p. 364.

5. These statements are based on an analysis of the census rolls over this period. The burgher population numbered 139 in 1663, 238 in 1673, 379 in 1683, and 1,159 in 1693. By 1714 it had

The farmers moved with surprising ease into lands which formerly had supported large Khoikhoi herds and flocks. The Khoikhoi offered little resistance, mainly because their political and economic structures had been gravely damaged by the frontier of trade and influence. In addition, the tribe that would have been hardest hit by the expansion, the Cochoqua, had recently been routed in war and their herds and flocks had dwindled. Then too, the first settlers were not in a position to displace Khoikhoi entirely: though land was surveyed, it was not immediately sown. When Khoikhoi returned to these pastures after their migrations, they were apparently directed to areas where the whites had not yet established effective occupation—worse land no doubt than the Khoikhoi would have chosen themselves, but not bad enough to drive them to desperation. Consequently, it was only after the farmers had become well established that land disputes with Khoikhoi became common. Most of these incidents occurred when Khoikhoi tried to pasture their livestock on the same land that whites had planted with vineyards or grain crops. Khoikhoi cattle so frequently trampled standing crops that at one point the landdrost and heemraden of Stellenbosch petitioned the Cape government to banish Khoikhoi altogether from their districts.[6] There were also numerous cases of settlers being attacked by so-called San or Ubiqua who may well have been displaced Khoikhoi.

The experience of Khoikhoi seemed to indicate that a farming frontier can readily displace a low-density population of pastoralists, who, if deprived of one pasture, can move elsewhere. For most Khoikhoi, displacement meant merely moving to inferior pastures in or near the region of white settlement; for a very few, it meant a long trek into the interior. About these more adventurous Khoikhoi we have virtually no information prior to the time when their descendants were contacted by white explorers in the mid-eighteenth century.

THE BIRTH OF THE CATTLE FRONTIER

The slow-moving and centrally directed farming frontier began to crumble as it moved away from Cape Town. In its place there arose

reached a figure of only 1,723. The jump caused by Huguenot immigration can be seen by comparing the figures for 1686 and 1690, which were 425 and 836 respectively; these last two figures, unlike the others cited, do not include white laborers (*knechts*).

6. Cape Archives, Stellenbosch 20/1, Landdrost and Heemraden to Simon van der Stel, n.d., n.p.; KA 4034, Request of Jan van Bevernasie, n.d. [1706], p. 538; Collectie Radermacher no. 504, Contra-Deductie . . . , p. 162. For an eighteenth-century chief's description of being gradually squeezed off his land, see Sparrman, *Voyage*, 1: 259.

an expansive pastoral frontier which would one day be responsible for the dispersion of white men over much of the future Cape Province. Though it was most prominent after 1713, this new frontier originated near the Cape in the late seventeenth century and struck hard at a Khoikhoi society already reeling from a succession of challenges.

The tightly woven fabric of Cape society had always had frayed edges. Beginning in the 1650s, many individuals and groups fled from the highly regulated colony into the seemingly boundless vacuum of South Africa. These were not only resentful slaves, but also soldiers, sailors, and freemen who desired to escape duty, taxes, or what the Company called justice. Always desperate, and sometimes vicious, these fugitives often attacked Khoikhoi kraals and slaughtered livestock in order to keep alive. The Khoikhoi and the Company thus had a common interest in keeping the colony's boundaries firm, and as a rule Khoikhoi were cooperative in apprehending and returning all types of deserters.[7] By the time of Simon van der Stel the colony was so large that it could no longer be effectively managed by personal oversight of the governor and his council. The number of escaped slaves became to great, and their mood so bellicose, that in most years there were sizable bands roaming uncaptured on the fringes of the colony; expeditions were sent out constantly, with Khoikhoi enlisting in the search for vagrants in response to ever increasing inducements.

A second frontier phenomenon of long standing was the white hunting expedition. For the first thirty years after 1652, most hunting beyond the colony's borders was done by freemen who had been granted permission by the authorities, even though their activities often led to conflicts with Khoikhoi or "San" hunters. By the time of Simon van der Stel the government began to fear that the burghers were neglecting their farms for the hunt, and that they were prodigally shooting out valuable game, particularly hippopotami. By 1692–93 white hunters commonly went inland without asking permission, and the government was forced to take action to stop the growing disorder.[8]

P. J. van der Merwe has shown that the hunting experience was important in the formation of the cattle boer culture; not only did hunting allow a man to explore new lands, but it gave him the opportunity to buy or steal Khoikhoi cattle and to accumulate the small amount of capital needed to start a cattle post. Other factors which

7. E.g. KA 3987, DR June 18, 1673, p. 202.
8. KA 3999, S. van der Stel to XVII, April 12, 1686, pp. 21–21v; KA 4008, DR Dec. 1 and 5, 1692, pp. 344v, 346v; KA 4010, DR July 8, 1693, p. 131.

contributed to the genesis of the cattle frontier were the unattractiveness of cultivation under the Company's price control system and the difficulty of shipping agricultural products from the distant interior to Table Bay. Very quickly a tradition formed that each man must have his own farm, and the sons of established farmers trekked on to new land, forced by lack of water and pasture.[9] By 1730 there was scarcely a bit of watered land that was not occupied within thirty or forty Dutch miles (roughly 90–120 English miles) of Cape Town.[10]

It was Simon van der Stel who had to deal with this, as with so many new phenomena. He himself was deeply committed to the farming sector of the colony and heartily detested the new wandering population; consequently, he framed laws to bring the trekboer back under the administration of the colony. He forbade anyone to own cattle unless he was a resident of the Cape District, Stellenbosch, or Drakenstein. He further decreed that all land holdings must be register-ed, that all whites were to return within the colony's boundaries on pain of destruction of their property, and finally that all pastoralists must return to their homes each night and not follow their stock inland in search of pasture.[11] These provisions, like similar ones that were to be passed in the next century and a half, were probably ineffective.

In 1699 Simon van der Stel retired to his estate at Constantia and turned over the government to his son Willem Adriaan. Within a year two separate events radically altered for the worse the course of white-Khoikhoi relations. The first of these was the decision of the Seventeen to abolish the Company's farming and ranching enterprises and turn them over to the freemen. An order to this effect had reached the Cape in 1695 but had been resisted by Simon van der Stel who, contrary to the spirit of the Seventeen's instructions, stepped up his campaign against Khoikhoi-freeman barter. The wrath of the directors reached the Cape only after Willem Adriaan had taken office: the new governor was curtly ordered *inter alia* to abolish the Company's herds and to arrange for freemen to deliver stock to the Company. Thus, on February 17, 1700, the cattle trade was thrown open to the freemen.[12]

---

9. P. J. van der Merwe, *Die Trekboer in die Geskiedenis van die Kaapkolonie, 1657–1842* (Cape Town: Nasionale Pers Bpk., 1938), pp. 43–55; 173 ff.

10. KA 4089, De la Fontaine to XVII, Jan. 24, 1730, p. 83v. The extent of the Dutch mile varied greatly.

11. KA 4008, DR Jan. 22, 1692, pp. 124 ff.

12. KA 461, XVII to S. van der Stel, July 14, 1695, n.p.; KA 4013, S. van der Stel to XVII, Aug. 1, 1696, pp. 51–53; KA 461, XVII to W. A. van der Stel, June 27, 1699, n.p.; *Resolusies*, 3: 364–65 (Feb. 17, 1700).

Several months after this important event, W. A. van der Stel sent a group of freemen, accompanied by an armed guard, over the Roode Zand to settle in a region known as the Land of Waveren. This was a highly significant northward thrust of the frontier of settlement; for Khoikhoi it was doubly ominous, for the location of Waveren dictated an economy that would be primarily pastoral. Van der Stel assured the Seventeen that Khoikhoi posed no threat: "in this entire region, so far as we have been able to notice, there are few or no Hottentots to be found."[13]

This was a vain hope. In the following year (1701) Khoikhoi attacked farms and outposts throughout the northern borderlands; among the first areas to be hit was the Land of Waveren, and it was hit often. In this barrage of rapid assaults the Company, the freemen, and pro-Company Khoikhoi all lost much stock. The attacks lasted from March 1701 into the early months of 1702, with scattered incidents continuing into 1703. The violence was as extensive as that of the two Khoikhoi-Dutch wars, and the upheaval might well have been called a war except that the enemy was never clearly defined. Some historians have labeled the attackers "Bushmen"[14] (i.e. aborigines) and classified the struggle with the inland "Bushman" wars of the mid-eighteenth century. This misinterpretation derives from the fact that the Dutch often called the enemies Ubiquas, Sonquas, or Bosjesmans. From the beginning, however, they were fairly sure that the Guriqua were involved, and this view was confirmed by a gathering of Peninsular and Gonnema captains which declared unanimously that the attackers were "Bushmen or highwaymen, consisting mainly of the ... Grigriquas and Namaquas." Thus the enemy were not aborigines but Khoikhoi: they were "San" only in the sense that their poverty had driven them to robbery.[15]

Van der Stel and his council were convinced that these disasters were a direct result of the Seventeen's decision to open the barter. They alleged that freemen had robbed the Khoikhoi of their stock and

13. KA 4019, W. A. van der Stel to XVII, March 1, 1700, p. 61. On the pastoral nature of Waveren, see A. J. Böeseken, *Simon van der Stel en sy Kinders* (Cape Town: Nasou Beperk, 1964), p. 166. Böeseken cites as the main determinants of pastoralism the distance of Waveren from Cape Town markets and the inadequacy of road links to the capital.

14. E.g. Theal, *History of South Africa*, 1: 385–87.

15. KA 4024, DR March 13, 1701, p. 125; KA 4024, DR June 16, 1701, p. 145. It is, however, conceivable, as I suggested on p. 135, that the Guriqua were originally Strandlopers, and hence *possibly* of aboriginal descent. But by this time they were thoroughly pastoral and spoke the Khoikhoi language.

driven them to revenge. This view, which corresponded with the deeply held prejudices (and possibly the ulterior motives) of the official clique, was documented several years later by one of their members, the landdrost Johannes Starrenburgh. Starrenburgh's trading expedition of 1705 visited the region to the north of the colony and revealed a bleak panorama of desolation among Guriqua and Gonnema Cochoqua. There were few kraals to be found, and even fewer which had much stock. Many impoverished Khoikhoi had turned to hunting; others had become robbers and were themselves robbed. One kraal told Starrenburgh that some years ago a freeman named "Drunken Gerrit" had attacked them, burnt their homes, and taken their cattle. As a consequence, they had been forced to turn to theft, and the Dutch farmers had been among their victims.[16]

Starrenburgh's report gives us a vivid picture of the northern border area in a desperate downswing of the ecological cycle. Freemen had doubtless contributed greatly to this process: even the burgher enemies of Van der Stel admitted that their fellow farmers had committed acts of plunder. Nonetheless, one cannot entirely accept Starrenburgh's conclusion that freemen had caused all the misery. The landdrost had a strong bias against freemen, and his investigation took place fully five years after the fact. Furthermore, he generalized from the experience of one Khoikhoi tribe to draw conclusions about all. The actions of lawless frontiersmen were only a part—though an important part— of a confused and deteriorating situation in the region.

The northern borderlands had been, as long as we have knowledge of them, more sparsely populated and more troubled by robber-hunters than other Cape Khoikhoi areas. In the 1680s and 1690s conflicts were endemic there. As the Company's authority moved out to correspond roughly to the sphere of the Nearby Khoikhoi, the Dutch became involved in disputes between their Khoikhoi protégés and the Guriqua-Namaqua beyond the colony.[17] Against this backdrop the events of 1701–02 must be seen merely as an intensification triggered by several factors, among which may be mentioned a prolonged drought, a serious plague of locusts,[18] and the sudden intrusion of the colony into new pastures, chiefly in the Land of Waveren.

Beginning in March 1701, the Khoikhoi attacked unpredictably over

16. KA 4024, W. A. van der Stel to XVII, March 20, 1702, p. 60v; KA 4031, Dag Verhaal . . . Starrenburgh, passim especially Oct. 26, 30 and Nov. 4, 1705, pp. 743v–49v.
17. E.g. KA 4015, DR March 10, 1697, pp. 491–91v.
18. KA 4024, W. A. van der Stel to XVII, March 20, 1702, p. 55v.

the whole span of the frontier from Groene Kloof to Waveren; the raiding parties, often numbering in the hundreds, tried only to seize cattle and were usually successful. The Company responded by garrisoning its cattle posts in the region and by creating several new ones. Whenever a robbery occurred, the soldiers at the posts were alerted and ordered to ride out and chastise the thieves. At first these responses failed, but from November 1701 on the whites perfected their techniques to the point where they could recover most of the stolen cattle after each raid. Burghers and Khoikhoi also learned much about self-help: on at least one occasion a Khoikhoi captain and a burgher led a joint expedition to recover lost cattle. The success of these various strategies slowed the tempo of the attacks and finally halted them altogether.[19]

For our present purposes the most important aspect of these disorders was their effect on the Peninsular and Nearby Khoikhoi. When the Company garrisoned its posts, some Khoikhoi moved their kraals and camped under protection of the Dutch guns. The postholders were energetic in defending and recovering Khoikhoi cattle, and they were glad of Khoikhoi help on their expeditions.[20] Nonetheless, many Khoikhoi had already lost heavily in the raids, and others continued to do so. This period of chaos doubtless intensified the poverty which later travelers found in the region.

Though this series of attacks died out in 1703, the breakdown in rural areas did not end. Deserters and vagabonds wandered unchecked through the country. Burghers became openly defiant of authority, tearing down government proclamations, appearing drunk at muster, and refusing to work on the roads or pay taxes. It was during one clash with a government official that a burgher was first recorded as calling himself an "Afrikaner."[21] In an atmosphere of increasing lawlessness, Khoikhoi on farms could become victims of cruel, and sometimes fatal, punishments; those with cattle could be casually plundered.

Late in 1702 the government began to collect evidence that some freemen were despoiling Khoikhoi on a massive scale. Early in that year forty-five burghers, each with a Khoikhoi attendant, had set out toward the region later called the Eastern Frontier. Each man had

19. KA 4024, Dagregister of 1701, passim.

20. KA 4024, DR Nov. 29, 1701, p. 177; KA 4026, Feb. 2–3 and March 14, 1702, pp. 60v–61 and 67v–68.

21. KA 4033, DR Oct. 3, 1706, pp. 268–68v; KA 4037, Prosecution of Jan Cloete et al., n.d. [1707], p. 785; KA 4040, DR Sept. 25, 1709, pp. 119–19v.

provided his own ammunition and one head of cattle to consume on
the way; all other provisions and trade goods (which included iron and
dagga) had been purchased jointly from a wealthy burgher. The
adventurers eventually reached Xhosa country, where they attacked a
group of Xhosa to avoid, so they said, being attacked first. Returning
back through Khoikhoi country, the whites now turned to marauding.
They attacked first the Horisans (a "Bushman" kraal with few cattle)
and then the Heykons (the Inqua, once a very wealthy group). In this
last encounter they obtained 2,000 cattle and 2,500 sheep (of which
they subsequently returned a very few), and killed many Inqua. The
loot was divided among the white participants, the Khoikhoi assistants
getting only one cow and four to ten sheep each. The Europeans made
a covenant not to betray one another to the authorities, and wrote it
into the blank pages of a book. The book was ironically entitled *The
Christian Voyage (De Christelijke Zeevaart)*.[22]

The composition of this expedition is of interest. Of the forty-five
white participants, only eighteen were inscribed in the burgher rolls
three years later; of these, only eight had possessions significant enough
to be noted on the property rolls, and only five were married.[23] In
short, few of the plunderers were "respectable" men, but much of the
cattle they confiscated may well have found its way into respectable
hands. Appalled (so he claimed) by the accumulating evidence, and
arguing that the Company had a duty to protect the Khoikhoi, Van
der Stel suspended the free barter on October 27, 1702. The Seventeen
subsequently endorsed this action but ordered the trade reopened.[24]

The question of who should conduct the trade, the freemen or the
Company, now became entangled in one of the most famous incidents
in white South African history, the overthrow of Willem Adriaan van
der Stel by a group of prominent burghers who managed to gain the
ear of the Seventeen. The pros and cons of Van der Stel's governorship

22. KA 4027, Interrogations of Willem van Sijburg, Lambert Symonsz, Jacob Holland,
David Pennesmit, and the Khoikhoi Soetekoek et al., Oct. and Nov. 1702, pp. 442–56, 469–71.
In reconstructing the events of this expedition I have preferred white testimonies over Khoikhoi
in numerical matters; however, Khoikhoi testimonies have been preferred for tribal identi-
fications. *De Christelijke Zeevaart* was apparently a translation of *The Christian Navigation* by the
Reverend J. Flavel.

23. H. C. V. Leibbrandt, *Precis of the Archives of the Cape of Good Hope: The Defense of Willem
Adriaan van der Stel* (Cape Town: W. A. Richards & Sons, 1897), p. 138; KA 4030, Freeman
Rolls, Dec. 31, 1705, p. 454.

24. *Resolusies*, 3: 390–91 (Oct. 27, 1702); KA 462, XVII to W. A. van der Stel, July 24, 1704,
n.p.

and his dismissal were heatedly debated by contemporary observers and later by historians in the early twentieth century.[25] It has been fairly well demonstrated that Van der Stel systematically used his office to defraud the Company and deprive the burghers of their lawful place in Company markets. Furthermore, Leo Fouché argued that the governor's policy of protecting the Khoikhoi was a smokescreen for his own commercial activities: he "placed an interdict upon the cattle traffic, not to protect the Hottentots against the colonists, but to rid himself of all interference on the part of the latter, and so keep the Hottentots to himself to plunder at his ease."[26] There is indeed considerable evidence that the governor engaged in the cattle trade[27] despite his persistent denials. Though there is no evidence of Van der Stel's using violent means, it is still clear that his concern for Khoikhoi integrity was rather hypocritical. All strata of colonial society saw easy and attractive pickings in the livestock of a crumbling native society.

THE FINAL CATASTROPHE

It should now be evident that the smallpox epidemic of 1713 was only the last of many disasters to befall the Western Cape Khoikhoi. By 1713 their social structure and economy had dramatically disintegrated. The extent of this decline north of Cape Town is best described by Starrenburgh's report of 1705. For a month and a half Starrenburgh scoured that vast region in search of Khoikhoi kraals. Though he cajoled and threatened, he could obtain only 179 oxen from the very reluctant Khoikhoi. The only Guriqua and Namaqua he found were camped together in a small cluster under four captains. Of the former Cochoqua he found mixed evidence: one group of six captains under Hanibal (Oedasoa's successor) was impoverished, while the clan of Bootman (a Gonnema Khoikhoi) had a "lovely herd." As for the descendants of the Peninsulars, he found three kraals camped together near Waveren under three, four, and five captains respectively: together these twelve captains could supply only thirty-eight cattle and eight sheep; though one of their number, Scipio, was fairly wealthy, possessing more than two hundred cows. Starrenburgh also found ten

25. Leibbrandt, *Defense*; George McCall Theal, *Willem Adriaan van der Stel, and Other Historical Sketches* (Cape Town: Thomas Maskew Miller, 1913); *The Diary of Adam Tas (1705–1706)*, ed. Leo Fouché (London: Longmans, Green, and Co., 1914); Böeseken, *Van der Stel*; Algemeen Rijksarchief, Collectie Radermacher no. 504, Korte Deductie..., Neutrale Gedagten..., Contra-Deductie...; Kalden, *Afgeperste Verweering*.
26. Fouché, *Diary of Adam Tas*, p. 343.
27. Collectie Radermacher no. 504, Contra-Deductie..., pp. 138, 166–72.

tiny kraals of uncertain identity in the region immediately to the northeast of the Cape Peninsula.[28]

Starrenburgh's observations prove that the whole northern region was vastly poorer in stock than it once had been, though border Khoikhoi were probably in a worse state than those who had enjoyed Company protection. The general impression is also one of disintegrating political authority and declining population: the only apparent supraclan chief whom Starrenburgh encountered was Hanibal, and his six captains apparently ruled over a population living in only twenty-three huts.[29] The large number of captains dwelling among small clusters of followers suggests that various clans, being faced with a declining population, had coalesced into one kraal, but that each had retained its identity and traditional leader.

In 1712 Lieutenant Kaij Jesse Slotsboo led an armed party to the northern frontier in order to deal with rumored Namaqua attacks on freemen in the region. He found little evidence of burghers suffering but much of endemic fighting among Namaqua and Guriqua. As for the Nearby Khoikhoi, Slotsboo's observations give the impression of continued poverty, with here and there signs of modest recovery. The wealthy Scipio now had more than 2,000 sheep; and a group of captains (at least one of whom was a Cochoqua) lived just south of the Piketberg with 200 cows, 100 calves, a few oxen, and many sheep. Generally, however, Slotsboo met only scattered kraals whose tribal denomination he did not consider worth noting, and which could only supply trivial numbers of stock. Khoikhoi were extremely loath to trade, and did all they could to hide their cattle from the expedition. Scipio's people, when asked to barter, refused to do so, "giving as their reason that they behaved quietly and did no harm, and that they also did not come to complain [to the Company]."[30] By this time Khoikhoi clearly regarded the trade as a form of tribute extracted by the colonial government.

East of Cape Town the picture was similar but possibly less desperate. In 1699 Olof Bergh reported that the Chainouqua and Hessequa were vastly poorer than when he had visited them in earlier years. In 1707 this impression was confirmed by Jan Hartogh's expedition through the region. In twenty-four days Hartogh obtained 220 oxen and 242 sheep, a goodly number but a small one when compared to earlier

28. KA 4031, Dag Verhaal . . . Starrenburgh, passim.
29. Ibid., Oct. 26, 1705, p. 743v.
30. KZ 3193, Dagh Verhaal . . . Slotsbo, passim. The quotation is from Oct. 19, 1712, n.p.

standards. Freemen had been bartering in the region, and, as Koopman put it, "they violently took all the cattle, cows, and heifers and threw the tobacco and beads on the ground." Robber-hunters, always a threat in the region, had recently driven a section of the once wealthy Hessequa out of their land. To make matters worse, the revered Hessequa chief Gaukou had just died. On the other hand, the Chainouqua leader Koopman was still alive, and had authority over at least eight kraals.[31]

Of the region east of the Hessequa we know almost nothing. The Inqua had been severely hurt by the marauders of 1702: still, they maintained their tribal integrity for another generation in a region well beyond the colony's borders.[32] Apart from the Inqua, the 1702 expedition found no wealthy tribes between the Hessequa and the Xhosa, though it is possible that such tribes did exist.

On February 13, 1713, a fleet put into Table Bay under the command of Commissioner Joannes van Steeland. During the voyage several persons, among them the commissioner's own children, had come down with smallpox but had later recovered. Their clothes were apparently among the linen taken from the ships to the Company's slave lodge for washing. On April 9 the government learned that its slaves were beginning to die of the pox. By April 19, six to eight slaves were buried daily, and before the disease abated the Company computed its losses at about two hundred slaves. From these, the most wretched members of Cape society, the virus was transmitted to the colony's masters.

In early May the authorities buried two to five whites a day, often dispensing with coffins because wood could not be brought into town fast enough; even so, many corpses remained unburied. On May 9 two pigeons toppled from the roof of the governor's residence, rolled over, and died instantly: observers examined the bodies of the birds, and, finding nothing wrong with them, declared their deaths to be an omen of catastrophe.[33] "Now one could note melancholy along the streets; where before one saw youths amusing themselves it now became deathly, and one scarcely saw a house that was not closed by

31. Bergh, VRS 12, p. 69; KA 4037, Dagverhaal ... Hartogh, passim, especially Nov. 5–10, 1707, pp. 904v–06v. The quotation is in the entry of Nov. 9 on p. 906.

32. *Resolusies*, 5: 329 (Jan. 31, 1719).

33. KA 4048, DR April 9, May 9, 15, and 26, Aug. 26, 1713, pp. 169, 178v, 180, 183v, 210; Valentyn, *Oud en Nieuw Oost-Indiën*, 5 (2): 51–52.

death or sickness."[34] By the end of the month, the Cape region had lost 110 whites, and before the plague was over the membership of the Cape Town church had been cut by one quarter. So desperate was the situation that slaves were offered a rixdollar a day and food if they would watch over the sick and dying.[35]

In June the pestilence abated in town only to break out with renewed force in the countryside. On June 24 it was reported that there were only twenty healthy whites in all of the Drakenstein district. Many farmers could not attend to their crops, and the colony was forced to make emergency requisitions from Batavia. Not until December was the danger over for the whites: by then, bereaved persons were marrying again in large numbers and the reconstruction of colonial society began.[36]

Khoikhoi probably contracted the plague from all three groups of victims in the colony—slaves, urban whites, and farmers. Khoikhoi first began to die in late April,[37] and it was soon evident that they had far less resistance to the infection than the Europeans and slaves, and that they had no medical lore to combat it. Many died in their huts in or around the colony. As Valentyn later reported:

> the Hottentots ... died in their hundreds. They lay everywhere on the roads. ... Cursing at the Dutchmen, who they said had bewitched them, they fled inland with their kraals, huts, and cattle in hopes there to be freed from the malign disease.[38]

The Dutch buried as many of the Khoikhoi corpses as possible in order to prevent more of the "bad air" which they thought prolonged the plague. Those Khoikhoi who fled found little welcome in the interior, where their relatives refused to mingle with the pathetic refugees and often killed them. Either through death or flight the white farmers lost the majority of their Khoikhoi laborers: for the first time in many years whites appeared in the fields scything their own grain.[39]

By 1713, official interest in independent Khoikhoi tribes was so low that the documents do not give us a clear view of the extent of Khoikhoi

34. KA 4048, DR May 7, 1713, p. 177v.
35. KA 4048, DR May 31 and June 4, 1713, pp. 185–86; Spoelstra, *Bouwstoffen*, I: 133.
36. KA 4048, DR June 24 and Dec. 17, 1713, pp. 190v, 265.
37. KA 4048, DR May 1, 1713, p. 176.
38. Valentyn, *Oud en Nieuw Oost-Indiën*, 5 (2): 51–52.
39. KA 4048, DR May 6–7 and 19, Nov. 28, 1713, pp. 177–77v, 181, 256–56v.

COLLAPSE OF THE OLD ORDER

losses. In February 1714 the survivors of four kraals appeared at the castle to report that their captains were all dead and asked the governor to appoint their replacements. They announced that scarcely one in ten of their number had survived the catastrophe. These envoys came from the cluster of clans Slotsboo had found at the Piketberg in 1712, a fact which suggests that their appalling figures applied to Khoikhoi near the border region as well as to those close in. The number of "Bushman" attacks reported in subsequent years suggests that many starving survivors of the plague were regrouping into bands which subsisted by stealing cattle.[40]

The agony of the smallpox was scarcely past when the western Cape was hit by two years of intense drought, and then by seven years of recurrent stock sicknesses, including foot-and-mouth disease. During these years the colonists lost large numbers of livestock, particularly sheep: the recorded figures of colonial sheep dropped from 116,256 in 1711 to 67,104 in 1719.[41] The few Khoikhoi who had retained sheep or cattle in the western Cape must have suffered in equal measure from these disasters.

The Little Namaqua were at first not seriously touched by the disease, their community being healthy and prosperous when visited by Ensign J. C. Rhenius in 1721. In 1724, however, the same ensign found much devastation among them. In the interim the smallpox had reached the Tlhaping (a Tswana group) and was now sweeping back southward through Little Namaqualand toward the colony. Attacks by robbers were common, and the dying Namaqua were slaughtering their cattle to prevent them from falling into Dutch hands.[42]

Smallpox viruses continued to circulate among southern African peoples for a century, causing disruption whose scale and historical significance may never be fully known. However, for the Western Cape Khoikhoi it was the plague of 1713 that did the decisive damage. Not only did it kill the majority of the population, but it also eliminated those vestiges of traditional Khoikhoi social structure which Starrenburgh, Slotsboo, and Bergh had noted in the region. Our sources for the decades immediately after 1713 are poor, but we can still form a

40. KA 4050, DR Feb. 13 and 15, 1714, pp. 274v, 277v; KA 4052, DR Aug. 3, 1715, p. 377v.

41. KA 4050, DR Jan. 4, 1714, p. 253v; KA 4052, DR Aug. 6 and Sept. 11, 1715, pp. 278, 391v; KA 4054, DR Sept. 14, 1716, pp. 431v–32v; KA 4072, DR Feb. 25, 1723, pp. 1345v–46. Figures for sheep are based on the burgher census rolls, which are reliable for trends but inaccurate for absolute numbers. The same source shows a decline in cattle from 20,743 to 16,262 between 1711 and 1719.

42. Rhenius, VRS 28, passim.

vague picture of the Khoikhoi condition from scattered references in judicial papers and from the few diaries kept by travelers into the interior.

In this period few Khoikhoi, it seems, remained in Cape Town or on farms near the Cape Peninsula. Most court documents mentioning Khoikhoi deal with events in the Stellenbosch-Drakenstein jurisdiction. Here, as a memorial of 1721 tells us, most of the surviving Khoikhoi lived on white farms.[43] I have seen no direct evidence of independent Khoikhoi kraals farther south than Meerhofskasteel (north of the Olifants River mouth) or farther west than the Company's posts Rietvlei and Zoetemelksvlei near the River Zonder Eind. These latter Khoikhoi were Hessequa who apparently found intermittent work at the Company's posts but still retained independent kraals under their own leaders. The independent peoples to the north were all Guriqua or Namaqua.[44] Thus, for all the Nearby Khoikhoi except the Hessequa, the effects of the 1713 plague were catastrophic. A traditional society, already in precipitous decline, had been virtually destroyed; and the people who had lived in it had barely escaped annihilation.

43. *Resolusies*, 6: 128 (Sept. 2, 1721).

44. Bernhard Krüger, *The Pear Tree Blossoms: A History of the Moravian Mission Stations in South Africa, 1737–1869* (Genadendal: Moravian Book Depot, 1966), pp. 19 ff.; Rhenius, VRS 28, pp. 132–34; KZ 3947/8302, Dag Register gehouden op de Voyagie van . . . Jan de la Fontaine . . . , entry of July 16, 1734, n.p.; Beutler (Haupt), *RZA*, 3: 267–68.

12

Conclusion

By 1720 the transformation of the Western Cape Khoikhoi into "colonial Hottentots" was almost complete. The Khoikhoi had been reduced to a small fraction of their former population, their ancient economic and political institutions had virtually disappeared, and even their traditional culture was showing signs of erosion. All this had happened in the seventy years since Van Riebeeck had landed at Table Bay. Yet these rapid and fundamental changes excited little interest among Europeans of the time. It was not until much later, in the late eighteenth century, that a few scholarly travelers noted the pathetic Khoikhoi remnants in the colony and questioned how a people who were supposed once to have been wealthy and numerous had come to such desperate straits.

Their solution to this riddle resembled the "Black Legend" developed by Anglo-Saxons to explain the fate of Indians in Spanish America. The Dutch, said the traveler C. P. Thunberg, had simply "exterminated [the Khoikhoi] or driven them away." Count Louis Degrandpré similarly concluded that the Dutch "destroyed the Hottentot nation; they repeated at the extremity of Africa the bloody scenes for which Spain had given them an example in America."[1] In the early nineteenth century the Black Legend found support among the first persons to consult original documents on the question, namely British humanitarians bent on reforming the relations between whites and blacks in South Africa. For example, in 1836 a British parliamentary committee concluded that:

> The system of oppression thus begun [by Van Riebeeck] never slackened till the Hottentot nation were cut off, and the small remnant left were reduced to abject bondage. From all the accounts we have seen respecting the Hottentot population

1. Thunberg, *Voyages*, 1: 223; L. Degrandpré, *Voyage à la côte occidentale d'Afrique, fait dans les années 1786 et 1787* (Paris: Dentu, 1801), 2: 179.

[in Van Riebeeck's time] it could not have been less than 200,000, but at present they are said to be only 32,000 in number.[2]

The humanitarians' charges outraged many in South Africa, including the governor of the Cape Colony, Sir Benjamin D'Urban. In 1836 D'Urban commissioned Donald Moodie, a colonial civil servant, to translate and publish extensive portions of the Dutch East India Company's papers on Khoikhoi affairs. Moodie's work appeared between 1838 and 1842 under the title *The Record: Or A Series of Official Papers Relative to the Condition and Treatment of the Tribes of South Africa.* These documents seemed to prove beyond question that white-Khoikhoi relations before 1713 were remarkably unsanguinary by the standards prevailing on later colonial frontiers in America and Africa. One colonial commentator triumphantly noted that the documents indicated only two Dutch-Khoikhoi wars, in the first of which only six Khoikhoi were killed, and in the second, fewer than forty. The true cause of Khoikhoi decline, he declared, was the intro-duction of European diseases, "compared to [which] the effect of war was evidently altogether trivial."[3] This conclusion was of course exag-gerated: there were actually three wars and several armed expeditions against Khoikhoi, and the Company's documents cannot be expected to give full listings of enemy casualties. But it is true that none of these resulted in the deaths of many Khoikhoi; the greatest damage inflicted by war was on the size of Khoikhoi herds and the prestige of Khoikhoi leaders.

Though the colonists properly refuted the charges of genocide, their own explanation of disease was only slightly more satisfactory. In the seventeenth century the recurring struggle Khoikhoi had with diseases, some perhaps of European origin, was only one of many factors in their political and economic decline, both of which were far advanced and probably irremediable when the smallpox epidemic finally swept away most of their population. By that time (1713) the Khoikhoi were no longer blocking the advance of white settlement, but had already been incorporated into the colony's labor force. Thus the settlers regarded their virtual disappearance, not as a gift from God (as did New England

---

2. *Report of the Parliamentary Select Committee on Aboriginal Tribes,* p. 30.

3. "A Member of the Late Committee," "Remarks upon Some of the Results Developed by the Publication of a Portion of the Cape Records, etc.," in Donald Moodie, *Specimens of the Authentic Records of the Colony of the Cape of Good Hope* ... (Cape Town: A. S. Robertson, and London: J. Richardson, 1841), p. 3.

Puritans when their Indian neighbors were ravaged by plague), but as a *zeer groot ongemak*, a "very great inconvenience."[4]

The epidemic merely hastened and completed the collapse of the old order, a process which had been proceeding almost unnoticed for decades. How are we to explain this collapse? Obviously it was made possible by the unstable economy and weak political institutions of the Khoikhoi, both of which were rooted in the nature of pastoralism and in the continuing operation of the "ecological cycle" of hunting and herding. Also important were the periodic decisions of Company officials to strengthen the colony at Khoikhoi expense, as for example when Simon van der Stel ordered the settlement of Stellenbosch or the attack on Klaas. But Khoikhoi society did not collapse on its own, nor was it simply crushed at the behest of the colonial government. Much more crucial was the accumulated effect of actions taken by individual whites and Khoikhoi, with no thought of their ultimate significance. Thus, for example, when a Khoikhoi sold his heifer to a Dutch bartering expedition, or his labor to a colonist, he was exploiting the colonial situation for his own ends; but, though he did not know it, his immediate interests were incompatible with the continuing autonomy of his traditional society. These seemingly minor actions, and the processes to which in aggregate they gave rise, are less often witnessed by our documents than the episodes of conquest. Nonetheless, they were the fundamental determinants of Khoikhoi decline.

By "decline" I mean the erosion of Khoikhoi society as it had existed in 1652, virtually independent of European economic, political, and cultural influences. For Khoikhoi to remain "independent" (in this broad sense) five conditions were necessary: Khoikhoi must (1) enjoy secure possession of their livestock, (2) be able to maintain satisfactory living standards without losing manpower to the colony, (3) be free to make political and economic decisions without European dictation, (4) have secure and exclusive occupation of traditional pastures, and (5) retain their traditional culture. The rapid disappearance of their autonomy was due not so much to the calculated actions of Dutch governors as to the fact that the "colonial system"—by which I mean the Company and the settlers in combination—assaulted all five components of independence together: it absorbed livestock and labor from the Khoikhoi economy, subjugated Khoikhoi chiefs to Dutch overrule and their followers to Dutch law, encroached on Khoikhoi

4. Valentyn, *Oud en Nieuw Oost-Indiën*, 5 (2): 52.

pastures, and endangered the integrity of Khoikhoi culture. And it did all these things in such a way that inroads in one area undermined Khoikhoi resistance in others.

Though all five processes of decline were intimately related, they were not all of equal importance. There was one point at which the Khoikhoi were most vulnerable, and against this point the colonial system pressed first and most relentlessly, thereby triggering decline in other sectors. This crucial point was not the land, as it apparently was in many later South African frontiers, but the possession of cattle and sheep.[5] As individual Khoikhoi found themselves unable to keep their livestock, they were presented with a attractive alternative: an opportunity to work on a European farm in return for food, tobacco, lodging, and security. Since the process of losing cattle and going to work for another was deeply engrained in traditional Khoikhoi life, the situation posed by the Dutch colony demanded no novel response. Once the movement of labor into the colony had begun, other facets of Khoikhoi independence were quickly affected. Colonial Khoikhoi became increasingly disloyal to their traditional leaders, whose prestige had already been damaged by the shortage of livestock and by their failure to stop Dutch encroachment. In the colony the Khoikhoi came to realize that the Company's administration was their only protector against mistreatment from the settlers, and they submitted with surprising readiness to its laws and to those who enforced them. Finally, on the farms their culture began to change, though slowly at first, and chiefly in areas directly related to their employment.

Of course, all the processes of disintegration cannot be reduced *simply* to consequences of cattle loss. In chapter 8 I concluded that the Khoikhoi lost their cattle, not solely because of the Company's trade, but because of an array of pressures from the "colonial system," some of which led to loss of cattle only indirectly through weakening other aspects of Khoikhoi society. In other words, though the drain on cattle was the first and most dangerous aspect of the system's assault, it set in motion other processes (like loss of manpower, land, and morale) which in turn further accelerated the loss of livestock.

Thus, the leading features of Khoikhoi decline were the complex interconnections of its many causes, and the predominance of broad processes over discrete episodes of diplomacy and conquest. For these

---

5. This does not apply to the Peninsulars, who lost important pastures and suffered grave political damage as a result of the First Khoikhoi-Dutch War, well before their livestock holdings began seriously to decline.

reasons Khoikhoi decline was a mystery both to the Europeans who initiated it and to nineteenth-century investigators who vainly sought to explain it by a single cause, be it genocide or plague. For these reasons, too, the story has hardly ever been told in recent times; it has few villains, fewer heroes, and little of the drama that attracts novelists and historians to later phases of settler-native conflict in southern Africa. Yet the process of Khoikhoi decline should be understood, and not only because brown and white South Africans still live with its consequences today. For it is a fact worth pondering that the European subjugation of southern Africa began, not because statesmen or merchants willed it, nor because abstract forces of history made it necessary; but because thousands of ordinary men, white and brown, quietly pursued their goals, unaware of their fateful consequences.

Bibliography

A. BIBLIOGRAPHY FOR PART I

Articles

Acocks, John P. H. "Karoo Vegetation in Relation to the Development of Deserts." *Ecological Studies in Southern Africa.* Edited by D. H. S. Davis. The Hague: W. Junk, 1964.

Anders, H. D. "Marginal Notes to Wikar's Journal (Van Riebeeck Society XV, 1935)." *BS* 11, no. 1 (March 1937): 47–52.

———. "Observations on Certain Sound Changes in Xhosa Derivatives from Khoisa." *SAJS* 33 (March 1937): 921–25.

Bisschop, J. H. R. "Parent Stock and Derived Types of African Cattle, with Particular Reference to the Importance of Conformational Characteristics in the Study of their Origin." *SAJS* 33 (March 1937): 852–70.

Bleek, D. F. "Bushman Terms of Relationship." *BS* 2 no. 2 (Dec. 1924): 57–70.

———. "The Distribution of Bushman Languages in South Africa." *Festschrift Meinhof: Sprachwissenschaftliche und andere Studien.* Hamburg: L. Friederichsen & Co., 1927.

Böeseken, A. J. "The meaning, origin and use of the terms Khoikhoi, San and Khoisan." *Cabo* 1, no. 1 (Aug. 1972): 5–10; 2, no. 2 (Jan. 1974): 8–10; 2, no. 3 (Nov. 1975): 16–18.

Bourquin, W. "Click-Words which Xhosa, Zulu and Sotho Have in Common." *AS* 10, no. 2 (June 1951): 59–81.

Broom, R. "A Contribution to the Craniology of the Yellow-Skinned Races of South Africa." *The Journal of the Royal Anthropological Institute* 53 (Jan.–June 1923): 132–49.

———. "Bushmen, Koranas, and Hottentots." *Annals of the Transvaal Museum* 20, no. 3 (Sept. 1941): 217–51.

Cooke, C. K. "Domestic Animals, Rock Art and Dating." *SAAB* 23, pt. 1, no. 89 (April 1968): 25–26.

———. "Evidence of Human Migrations from the Rock Art of Southern Rhodesia." *Africa* 35, no. 3 (July 1965): 263–85.

Dart, Raymond A. "The Physical Characters of the /?Auni-≠Khomani Bushmen." *BS* 11, no. 3 (Sept. 1937): 175–246.

Doke, C. M. "A Preliminary Investigation into the State of the Native Languages of South Africa...." *BS* 7, no. 1 (March 1933): 1–98.

Drennan, M. R. "Archaeology of the Oakhurst Shelter, George. Part III. The Cave Dwellers." *Transactions of the Royal Society of South Africa* 25 (1937–38): 259–80.

Dreyer, T. F., and Meiring, A. J. D. "A Preliminary Report on an Expedition to Collect Old Hottentot Skulls." *Soölogiese Navorsing van die Nasionale Museum (Bloemfontein)* 1, no. 7 (Aug. 1937): 81–88.

———. "The Hottentot." *Navorsinge van die Nasionale Museum (Bloemfontein)* 1, no. 1 (Feb. 1952): 19–22.

Du Toit, Brian M. "*Cannabis sativa* in sub-Saharan Africa." *SAJS* 70 (Sept. 1974): 266–70.

Ehret, Christopher. "Cattle-Keeping and Milking in Eastern and Southern African History: The Linguistic Evidence." *JAH* 8, no. 1 (1967): 1–17.

———. "Patterns of Bantu and Central Sudanic Settlement in Central and Southern Africa." *Transafrican Journal of History* 3, nos. 1, 2 (1973): 1–71.

———. "Sheep and Central Sudanic Peoples in Southern Africa." *JAH* 9, no. 2 (1968): 213–21.

Ehret, Christopher et al. "Outlining Southern African History: A Reevaluation, A.D. 100–1500." *Ufahamu* 3, no. 1 (Spring 1972): 9–27.

Elphick, R. H. "The Meaning, Origin and Use of the Terms Khoikhoi, San, and Khoisan." *Cabo* 2, no. 2 (Jan. 1974): 3–7; and 2, no. 3 (Nov. 1975): 12–15.

Engelbrecht, J. A. "Studies oor Korannataal." *Annale van die Uniwersiteit van Stellenbosch*, Year 6, Series B, no. 2 (1928): 3–45.

Fagan, Brian. "The Greefswald Sequence: Bambandyanalo and Mapungubwe." *JAH* 5, no. 3 (1964): 337–61.

———. "The Later Iron Age in South Africa." *African Societies in Southern Africa*. Edited by Leonard Thompson. London, Ibadan, and Nairobi: Heinemann, 1969.

Goodwin, A. J. H. "Archaeology of the Oakhurst Shelter, George. Part VII. Summary and Conclusions." *Transactions of the Royal Society of South Africa* 25 (1937–38): 321–24.

———. "Metal Working among the Early Hottentots." *SAAB* 11, no. 42 (June 1956): 46–51.

Greenberg, Joseph H. "The Languages of Africa." *International Journal of American Linguistics* 29, no. 1, pt. 2 (Jan. 1963).

Grobbelaar, C. S. "Report on Eight Bushman-Hottentot Skulls from the South East Coast, Cape Province." *SAJS* 59, no. 6 (June 1963): 282–85.

———. "The Physical Characteristics of the Korana." *SAJS* 53, no. 4 (Nov. 1956), Special Publication no. 1:99–159.

Harinck, Gerrit. "Interaction between Xhosa and Khoi: Emphasis on the Period 1620–1750." *African Societies in Southern Africa*. Edited by Leonard Thompson. London, Ibadan, and Nairobi: Heinemann, 1969.

Hewitt, John. "Notes Relating to Aboriginal Tribes of the Eastern Province."

SAJS 17, nos. 3–4 (July 1921): 304–21.

Hoernlé, A. Winifred. "The Social Organization of the Namaqua Hottentots of Southwest Africa." *American Anthropologist*, n.s. 27, no. 1 (Jan.–March 1925): 1–24.

Inskeep, R. R. "The Archaeological Background." *The Oxford History of South Africa.* Edited by Monica Wilson and Leonard Thompson. Vol. 1. Oxford: Clarendon Press, 1969.

Jeffreys, M. D. W. "The Batwa: Who Are They?" *Africa* 23, no. 1 (Jan. 1953): 45–54.

———. "The Cabonas." *AS* 27, no. 1 (1968): 41–43.

Jenkins, Trefor, et al. "Red-Cell-Enzyme Polymorphisms in the Khoisan Peoples of Southern Africa." *The American Journal of Human Genetics* 23 (Sept. 1971): 513–32.

Keen, J. A. "Craniometric Survey of the South African Museum Collection of Bushman, Hottentot and Bush-Hottentot Hybrid Skulls." *Annals of the South African Museum* 37, pt. 2 (Aug. 1952): 211–26.

Köhler, Oswin. "Die Wortbeziehungen zwischen der Sprache der Kxoe-Buschmänner und dem Hottentottischen als geschichtliches Problem." *Neue Afrikanistische Studien.* Edited by Johannes Lukas. Hamburg: Deutsches Institut für Afrika-Forschung, 1966.

———. "Sprachkritische Aspekte zur Hamitentheorie über die Herkunft der Hottentotten." *Sociologus*, n.s. 10, no. 1 (1960): 69–77.

———. "Studien zum Genussystem und Verbalbau der zentralen Khoisan-Sprachen. *Anthropos* 57 (1962): 529–46.

Lanham, L. W. "The Proliferation and Extension of Bantu Phonemic Systems Influenced by Bushman and Hottentot." *Proceedings of the Ninth International Congress of Linguists: Cambridge, Mass., Aug. 27–31, 1962.* Edited by Horace G. Lunt. The Hague: Mouton & Co., 1964.

Lanham, L. W., and Hallowes, D. P. "Linguistic Relationships and Contacts Expressed in the Vocabulary of Eastern Bushman." *AS* 15, no. 1 (1956): 45–48.

Maggs, T. M. O'C. "Pastoral Settlements on the Riet River," *SAAB* 26, pts. 1 and 2, nos. 101 and 102 (Aug. 1971): 37–63.

Maingard, J. F. "Physical Characteristics of the Korana." *BS* 6, no. 2 (June 1932): 163–82.

Maingard, L. F. "A Comparative Study of Naron, Hietshware and Korana." *AS* 22, no. 3 (1963): 97–108.

———. "Hendrik Jacob Wikar: His Editors, Translators and Commentators." *BS* 10, no. 1 (March 1936): 31–40.

———. "History and Distribution of the Bow and Arrow in South Africa." *SAJS* 29 (Oct. 1932): 711–23.

———. "Studies in Korana History, Customs and Language." *BS* 6, no. 2 (June 1932): 103–62.

————. "The Brikwa and the Ethnic Origins of the Bathlaping." *SAJS* 30 (Oct. 1933): 597–602.

————. "The First Contacts of the Dutch with the Bushmen until the Time of Simon van der Stel (1686)." *SAJS* 32 (Nov. 1935): 479–87.

————. "The Korana Dialects." *AS* 23, no. 2 (1964): 57–66.

————. "The Linguistic Approach to South African Prehistory and Ethnology." *SAJS* 31 (Nov. 1934): 117–43.

————. "The Lost Tribes of the Cape." *SAJS* 28 (Nov. 1931): 487–504.

————. "Three Bushman Languages." *AS* 16, no. 1 (1957): 37–71.

Marshall, Lorna. "!Kung Bushman Bands." *Africa* 30, no. 4 (Oct. 1960): 325–55.

————. "!Kung Bushman Religious Beliefs." *Africa* 32, no. 3 (July 1962): 221–52.

————. "The Kin Terminology System of the !Kung Bushmen." *Africa* 27, no. 1 (Jan. 1957): 1–25.

Mauny, Raymond. "The Wakwak and the Indonesian Invasion in East Africa in 945 A.D." *Studia: Revista Semestral* 15 (May 1965): 7–16.

Meinhof, Carl. "Das Verhältnis der Buschmannsprachen zum Hottentottischen." *Wiener Zeitschrift für die Kunde des Morgenlandes* 37 (1930): 219–29.

————. "Der Koranadialekt des Hottentottischen." *Beihefte zur Zeitschrift für Eingeborenen-Sprachen*, vol. 12 (1930).

————. "Ergebnisse der afrikanischen Sprachforschung." *Archiv für Anthropologie*, n.s. 9, nos. 3–4 (1910): 179–201.

Nienaber, G. S. "The Origin of the Name 'Hottentot.'" *AS* 22, no. 2 (1963): 65–90.

Pettman, Charles. "Hottentot Place Names." *SAJS* 17, nos. 3–4 (July 1921): 334–52.

————. "Hottentot Place Names—II." *SAJS* 19 (Dec. 1922): 372–82.

Phillipson, D. W. "Early Iron-Using Peoples of Southern Africa." *African Societies in Southern Africa.* Edited by Leonard Thompson. London, Ibadan, and Nairobi: Heinemann, 1969.

Robinson, K. R. "Bambata Ware; Its Position in the Rhodesian Iron Age in the Light of Recent Evidence." *SAAB* 21, pt. 2, no. 82, (June 1966): 81–85.

Rudner, I. and J. "Who Were the Artists? Archaeological Notes from South West Africa." *SAAB* 14, no. 55 (Sept. 1959): 106–08.

Rudner, Jalmar. "The Brandberg and its Archaeological Remains." *Journal of the South West Africa Scientific Society* 12 (1956/57): 7–44.

Saunders, C. C. "Early Knowledge of the Sotho: Seventeenth and Eighteenth Century Accounts of the Tswana." *Quarterly Bulletin of the South African Library* 20, no. 3 (March 1966): 60–70.

Schapera, I. "A Preliminary Consideration of the Relationship between the

Hottentots and the Bushmen." *SA JS* 23 (Dec. 1926): 833–66.

Schofield, J. F. "A Hottentot Pot from the Pella District of the Orange River Valley." *SA JS* 33 (March 1937): 940–42.

———. "Archaeology of the Oakhurst Shelter, George. Part V. The Pottery." *Transactions of the Royal Society of South Africa* 25 (1937–38): 295–301.

Schweitzer, F. R., and Scott, Katharine J. "Early Occurrence of Domestic Sheep in Sub-Saharan Africa." *Nature* 241 (Feb. 1973): 547.

Seddon, J. D., and Vinnicombe, Patricia. "Domestic Animals, Rock-Art and Dating." *SAAB* 22, pt. 3, no. 87 (Nov. 1967): 112–13.

Silberbauer, G. B. "Aspects of the Kinship System of the G/wi Bushmen of the Central Kalahari." *SA JS* 57, no. 12 (Dec. 1961): 353–59.

Singer, Ronald. "The Future of Physical Anthropology in South Africa." *SAAB* 17, no. 68 (Dec. 1962): 205–11.

Singer, Ronald, and Weiner, J. S. "Biological Aspects of Some Indigenous African Populations." *Southwestern Journal of Anthropology* 19, no. 2 (Summer 1963): 168–76.

Stern, Jack T., Jr., and Singer, Ronald. "Quantitative Morphological Distinctions between Bushman and Hottentot Skulls: A Preliminary Report." *SAAB* 22, pt. 3, no. 87 (Nov. 1967): 103–11.

Tobias, Phillip V. "Bushman Hunter-Gatherers: A Study in Human Ecology." *Ecological Studies in Southern Africa.* Edited by D. H. S. Davis. The Hague: W. Junk, 1964.

———. "Les Boschimans Auen et Naron de Ghanzi: contribution à l'étude des 'anciens jaunes' sud-africains." *L'Anthropologie* 60, nos. 1–2 (1956): 22–52; nos. 3–4 (1956): 268–89.

———. "On the Increasing Stature of the Bushmen." *Anthropos* 57 (1962): 801–10.

———. "On the Survival of the Bushmen: With an Estimate of the Problem Facing Anthropologists." *Africa* 26, no. 2 (April 1956): 174–86.

———. "Physical Anthropology and Somatic Origins of the Hottentots." *AS* 14, no. 1 (1955): 1–15.

———. "Taaibosch Koranas of Ottosdal: A Contribution to the Study of the Old Yellow South Africans." *SA JS* 51, no. 9 (April 1955): 263–69.

———. "The Peoples of Africa South of the Sahara." *The Biology of Human Adaptability.* Edited by Paul T. Baker and J. S. Weiner. Oxford: Clarendon Press, 1966.

Trevor, J. C. "The Physical Characters of the Sandawe." *Journal of the Royal Anthropological Institute* 77, no. 1 (1947): 61–78.

Wandres, C. "Über das Recht der Naman und Bergdaman." *Zeitschrift für Kolonialpolitik, Kolonialrecht und Kolonialwirtschaft* 11 no. 9 (Sept. 1909): 657–86.

Wells, L. H. "Bushman and Hottentot Statures: A Review of the Evidence." *SA JS* 56, no. 11 (Nov. 1960): 277–81.

———. "Physical Measurements of Northern Bushmen." *Man* 52 (April 1952): 53–56.

———. "The Broom Collection of Nama Hottentot Skulls in the Edinburgh University Anatomical Museum." *SAJS* 48, no. 3 (Oct. 1951): 97–103.

Westphal, E. O. J. "The Click Languages of Southern and Eastern Africa." *Current Trends in Linguistics*. Edited by Thomas A. Sebeok. Vol. 7: *Linguistics in Sub-Saharan Africa*. The Hague and Paris: Mouton and Co., 1971.

———. "On Classifying Bushman and Hottentot Languages." *African Language Studies*, 3 (1962): 30–48.

———. "The Linguistic Prehistory of Southern Africa: Bush, Kwadi, Hottentot, and Bantu Linguistic Relationships." *Africa* 33, no. 3 (July 1963): 237–65.

Willcox, A. R. "Australian and South African Rock-Art Compared." *SAAB* 14, no. 55 (Sept. 1959): 97–98.

———. "Sheep and Sheep-Herders in South Africa." *Africa* 36, no. 4 (Oct. 1966): 432–38.

———. "Who Were the Artists? Another Opinion." *SAAB* 15, no. 57 (March 1960): 23–25.

Wilson, Monica. "The Hunters and Herders." *The Oxford History of South Africa*. Edited by Monica Wilson and Leonard Thompson. Volume 1. Oxford: Clarendon Press, 1969.

Wuras, C. F. "An Account of the Korana." *BS* 3, no. 3 (July 1929): 287–96.

Books and Theses

Acocks, J. P. H. *Veld Types of South Africa*. Botanical Survey of South Africa, Memoir no. 28. Pretoria: The Government Printer, 1953.

Beach, D. M. *The Phonetics of the Hottentot Language*. Cambridge: W. Heffer & Sons, 1938.

Bleek, Dorothea F. *A Bushman Dictionary*. New Haven, Conn.: American Oriental Society, 1956.

———. *The Naron, A Bushman Tribe of the Central Kalahari*. Cambridge: Cambridge University Press, 1928.

Bleek, W. H. I., and Lloyd, L. C. *Specimens of Bushman Folklore*. London: George Allen and Co., 1911.

Clark, J. Desmond. *The Prehistory of Southern Africa*. Harmondsworth, Middlesex: Penguin Books, 1959.

Cole, Monica Mary. *South Africa*. London: Methuen & Co., 1961.

Engelbrecht, J. A. *The Korana: An Account of their Customs and their History*. Cape Town: Maskew Miller, 1936.

Epstein, H. *The Origin of the Domestic Animals of Africa*, 2 vols. Revised in collaboration with I. L. Mason. New York, London, and Munich: Africana Publishing Corporation, 1971.

Galloway, Alexander. *The Skeletal Remains of Bambandyanalo*. Edited by Phillip V. Tobias. Johannesburg: Witwatersrand University Press, 1959.

Gusinde, Martin. *Von Gelben und Schwarzen Buschmännern*. Graz: Akademische Druck- u. Verlagsanstalt, 1966.

Hahn, Theophilus. *Tsuni-//Goam, The Supreme Being of the Khoi-Khoi*. London: Trübner & Co., 1881.

Jeffreys, M. D. W. *Some Semitic Influences in Hottentot Culture*. Raymond Dart Lectures, no. 4. Johannesburg: Witwatersrand University Press, 1968.

Kirby, Percival R. *The Musical Instruments of the Native Races of South Africa*. London: Oxford University Press, 1934.

Kolbe[n], Peter. *Beschreibung des Vorgebürges der Guten Hoffnung*. Frankfurt and Leipzig: Pieter Conrad Monath, 1745.

———. *The Present State of the Cape of Good Hope*. Translated by Guido Medley. London: W. Innys, 1731.

Krönlein, J. G. *Nama Wörterbuch*. Revised by F. Rust. Pietermaritzburg: University of Natal Press, 1969.

Lichtenstein, M. H. C. *Foundation of the Cape/About the Bechuanas*. Translated and edited by O. H. Spohr. Cape Town: A. A. Balkema, 1973.

Louw, J. A. *The Nomenclature of Cattle in the South Eastern Bantu Languages*. Communications of the University of South Africa, C 2. Pretoria, 1957.

Maingard, L. F. *Korana Folktales: Grammar and Texts*. Johannesburg: Witwatersrand University Press, 1962.

Mason, I. L., and Maule, J. P. *The Indigenous Livestock of Eastern and Southern Africa*. Technical Communication no. 14 of the Commonwealth Bureau of Animal Breeding and Genetics. Farnham Royal, Bucks.: Commonwealth Agricultural Bureaux, 1960.

Meinhof, Carl. *Die Sprachen der Hamiten* (Hamburg: L. Friederichsen & Co., 1912).

Mourant, A. E., and Zeuner, F. E. *Man and Cattle: Proceedings of a Symposium on Domestication at the Royal Anthropological Institute, 24–26 May 1960*. Royal Anthropological Institute Occasional Paper 18. London: Royal Anthropological Institute, 1963.

Murdock, George Peter. *Africa: Its Peoples and Their Culture History*. New York, London, and Toronto: McGraw-Hill Book Company, 1959.

———. *Ethnographic Atlas*. Pittsburgh: University of Pittsburgh Press, 1967.

The Native Tribes of South West Africa. Cape Town: Cape Times Limited, 1928.

Nienaber, G. S. *Hottentots*. Pretoria: J. L. Van Schaik, 1963.

Rudner, Jalmar, and Rudner, Ione. *The Hunter and His Art*. Cape Town: C. Struik (Pty.), 1970.

Rust, F. *Deutsch-Nama Wörterbuch*. Windhoek: Rheinische Mission in Südwestafrika, 1960.

———. *Praktische Namagrammatik*. Cape Town and Amsterdam: A. A. Balkema, 1965.

Schapera, Isaac, ed. *The Bantu-speaking Tribes of South Africa*. London: George Routledge and Sons, 1937.

————. *The Khoisan Peoples of South Africa: Bushmen and Hottentots*. London: Routledge & Kegan Paul, 1960.

Schapera, Isaac, and Farrington, B., eds. and trans. *The Early Cape Hottentots*. Publication no. 14. Cape Town: Van Riebeeck Society, 1933.

Schofield, J. F. *Primitive Pottery*. The South African Archaeological Society Handbook Series, no. 3. Cape Town: By the Society, 1948.

Schultze, Leonhard. *Aus Namaland und Kalahari*. Jena: Verlag von Gustav Fischer, 1907.

Silberbauer, G. B. *Report to the Government of Bechuanaland on the Bushman Survey*. Gaberones: Bechuanaland Government, 1965.

Stow, George W. *The Native Races of South Africa*. Edited by George McCall Theal. London: Swan Sonnenschein & Co., 1905.

Theal, George McCall. *Ethnography and Condition of South Africa before A.D. 1505*. 2d ed. London: George Allen and Unwin, 1919.

Vedder, Heinrich. *South West Africa in Early Times*. Translated and edited by Cyril G. Hall. London: Oxford University Press, 1938.

Wellington, John H. *Southern Africa: A Geographical Study*. 2 vols. Cambridge: Cambridge University Press, 1955.

Willcox, A. R. *The Rock Art of South Africa*. Johannesburg: Thomas Nelson and Sons, 1963.

B.   Bibliography for Parts 2, 3, and 4

Unpublished Documents

My description of Dutch-Khoikhoi relations is based chiefly on the records of the Dutch East India Company. At the Cape most Company documents were produced in many copies: one copy remained in Cape Town, while others were sent to Batavia and to various chambers (*kamers*) of the Company in the Netherlands. Most of the papers of the smaller chambers have been lost, but the records of the Amsterdam and Zeeland Chambers are presently housed in the Algemeen Rijksarchief at The Hague. I have relied chiefly on the Chamber Amsterdam papers, which are almost complete for the period 1652 to 1713, and have had recourse to the Chamber Zeeland only in order to fill in the rare gaps in the Amsterdam series. The Amsterdam Chamber arranged all its Cape papers into a single series, entitled "Brieven en Papieren van Cabo de Bonne Esperance overgekomen"; in the Cape Archives, by contrast, copies of the same documents were separated into several series: for example, Resolutiën, Uitgaande Brieven, Dagregister, Council of Justice, etc. In the footnotes I have normally cited only the Dutch copy of documents; the few references to the Cape Archives indicate documents from series which are not found in the Netherlands.

ALGEMEEN RIJKSARCHIEF, THE HAGUE, NETHERLANDS

Aanwinsten	1881	A VIII	J. C. Cloppenburg, Journaal van mijn Reijs in Africa. ... (1768)
Aanwinsten	1901	XLIV	Reize ... door J. Lambair ... (1671–77)
Aanwinsten	1903	XV	Journaal...Gijsbert Heeck...(1654–56)
Collectie Geleynssen de Jongh		no. 31	Briefboeck begonnen in Brotcha ... ende geeijndicht in Ammadabath ... (1631–37)
		no. 75	Daghregister gehouden op het Schip Amsterdam ... 1635
Collectie Radermacher-Schorer		no. 503	Stukken betreffende de Uitzending van Landbouwersfamilies naar de Kaap en naar Indië, 1670–1715
		no. 504	Korte Deductie van Willem Adriaan van der Stel ... met Contradeducties, 1707, 1712
Koloniaal Archief		KA 488	Register op de Brieven van de Vergadering van zeventien sedert 1692 tot 1707. (In fact, covers 1613–1706.)
		KA 455–63	Brieven Heeren XVII naar Indië en de Kaap, 1644–1717
		KA 974, 977, 984, 1033, 1046	(Miscellaneous volumes with information on the Cape before 1652)
		KA 3967–4159	Brieven en Papieren van Cabo de Bonne Esperance overgekomen, 1653–1750.
		KA 7571/ KZ 3179	Kamer Zeeland (Papers from the Cape—1688)
		KA 7588/ KZ 3193	Kamer Zeeland (Papers from the Cape—1712)

CAPE ARCHIVES, CAPE TOWN

C. 416–35	Letters Received, 1652–1715
Stellenbosch 1/1 to 1/4	Notule van Landdros en Heemrade, 1691–1715
10/1	Inkomende Briewe van Gouw. en P. Raad, 1686–1715
19/168	Extract Resolutiën van die P. Raad en Afskrifte van Briewe aan die Gouw., 1686–1715
20/1	Uitgaande Briewe van Land. en Heemrade, 1687–1718
V. C. 36	Rapporten der Commissarissen, 1657–1764

SOUTH AFRICAN PUBLIC LIBRARY, CAPE TOWN

Johan Daniel Buttner, Waare Relation und Beschrybung von Cabo de
Goede Hoop. . . .

STAFFORDSHIRE COUNTY RECORD OFFICE, STAFFORD, ENGLAND

D 593 /U/4/1/1 to 5   Four Journals of Captain R. J. Gordon

Published Documents and Travelers' Accounts

A large number of descriptions of Cape Town between 1652 and 1702 have
recently been published in Raven-Hart's compendium *Cape Good Hope*. I have
consulted many of these sources in the original, but in view of the easy
accessibility of Raven-Hart's work, I have not considered it necessary to
include them in this bibliography.

Aimé-Martin, L., ed. *Oeuvres complètes de Jacques-Henri Bernardin de St-Pierre.*
   Brussels: Auguste Wahlen et Co., 1820.
[Allamand, R. S., and Klockner, J. C.] *Nieuwste en beknopte Beschryving van
   de Kaap der Goede Hoop.* Amsterdam: J. H. Schneider, 1778.
Barnard, Lady Anne. *South Africa a Century Ago (1797–1801).* Edited by H. J.
   Anderson. Cape Town: Maskew Miller, [1924].
Böeseken, A. J., ed. *Memoriën en Instructiën, 1657–1699.* Cape Town: Publi-
   kasie-Afdeling van die Kantoor van die Direkteur van Argiewe, 1966.
Bosman, D. B., ed. *Briewe van Johanna Maria van Riebeeck en Ander Riebeeckiana.*
   Amsterdam: By the Editor, 1952.
Collectanea. Publication no. 5. Cape Town: Van Riebeeck Society, 1924.
Degrandpré, L. *Voyage à la côte occidentale d'Afrique, fait dans les années 1786 et
   1787.* Paris: Dentu, 1801.
Fouché, Leo, ed. *The Diary of Adam Tas (1705–1706).* London: Longmans,
   Green, and Co., 1914.
Funnell, William. *A Voyage round the World.* . . . London: W. Botham, 1707.
Godée Molsbergen, E. C., ed. *Reizen in Zuid-Afrika in de Hollandse Tijd.* 4 vols.
   Linschoten Vereeniging Series, nos. 11, 12, 20, 36. The Hague: Martinus
   Nijhoff, 1916, 1922, 1932.
Great Britain. Historical Manuscripts Commission. *Report on Manuscripts in
   the Welsh Language.* Vol. 1, pt. 3. London: Eyre and Spottiswoode, 1905.
Haafner, Jacob. *Lotgevallen en Vroegere Zeereizen van Jacob Haafner.* . . . Amster-
   dam: Johannes van der Hey, 1820.
Hulshof, A. "H. A. van Reede tot Drakestein, Journaal van zijn verblijf aan
   de Kaap." *Bijdragen en mededeelingen van het Historisch Genootschap (gevestigd
   te Utrecht),* vol. 62 (1941).
Jeffreys, M. K., ed. *Kaapse Plakkaatboek.* 6 vols. Cape Town: Cape Times
   Limited, 1944–51.
Kalden, Petrus. *Afgeperste Verweering . . . Tegens Twee nu onlangs uytgekomene*

Laster-Schriften.... Utrecht: W. Broedelet, 1713.

La Caille, Abbé de. *Journal historique du Voyage fait au Cap de Bonne-Espérance .... * Paris: Guillyn, 1763.

Leibbrandt, H. C. V. *Precis of the Archives of the Cape of Good Hope. Journal, 1662–70; 1671–4 and 1676; 1699–1732.* 3 vols. Cape Town: W. A. Richards & Sons, 1901, 1902, 1896.

———. *Precis of the Archives of the Cape of Good Hope. The Defense of Willem Adriaan van der Stel.* Cape Town: W. A. Richards & Sons, 1897.

Le Vaillant, François. *Voyage de Monsieur le Vaillant dans l'intérieur de l'Afrique.* 2 vols. Paris: Chez Leroy, 1790.

Lichtenstein, Henry. *Travels in Southern Africa, in the Years 1803, 1804, 1805, and 1806.* Translated by Anne Plumptre. 2 vols. Publication nos. 10, 11. Cape Town: Van Riebeeck Society, 1928, 1930.

Lockyer, Charles. *An Account of the Trade in India.* London: Samuel Crouch, 1711.

Mentzel, O. F. *A Geographical and Topographical Description of the Cape of Good Hope.* Translated by H. J. Mandelbrote. 3 vols. Publication nos. 4, 6, 25. Cape Town: Van Riebeeck Society, 1921, 1925, 1944.

Moodie, Donald. *Specimens of the Authentic Records of the Colony of the Cape of Good Hope....* Cape Town: A. S. Robertson, and London: J. Richardson, 1841.

———. *The Record....* Cape Town: A. S. Robertson, 1838–42.

Mossop, E. E., ed. and trans. *Journals of the Expeditions of the Honourable Ensign Olof Bergh (1682 and 1683) and the Ensign Isaq Schrijver (1689).* Publication no. 12. Cape Town: Van Riebeeck Society, 1931.

———, ed. and trans. *The Journals of Brink and Rhenius.* Publication no. 28. Cape Town: Van Riebeeck Society, 1947.

Mossop, E. E., and Horst, A. W. van der, eds. and trans. *The Journal of Hendrik Jacob Wikar (1779) and the Journals of Jacobus Coetsé Jansz (1760) and Willem van Reenen (1791).* Publication no. 15. Cape Town: Van Riebeeck Society, 1935.

Neyn, Pieter de. *Lust-hof der Huwelyken....* Amsterdam: Willem Lamsvelt, 1697.

Paravicini di Cappelli, W. B. E. *Reize in de Binnen-Landen van Zuid-Afrika.* Edited and translated by W. J. de Kock. Publication no. 46. Cape Town: Van Riebeeck Society, 1965.

Paterson, William. *A Narrative of Four Journeys into the Country of the Hottentots, and Caffraria, in the Years 1777, 1778, 1779.* 2d ed. London: J. Johnson, 1790.

Raven-Hart, R. *Before Van Riebeeck: Callers at South Africa from 1488 to 1652.* Cape Town: C. Struik (Pty.), 1967.

———. *Cape Good Hope, 1652–1702.* 2 vols. Cape Town: A. A. Balkema, 1971.

The Reports of Chavonnes and his Council, and of Van Imhoff, on the Cape. Publication no. 1. Cape Town: Van Riebeeck Society, 1918.

Silleman, Daniel, and Thysz, Lourens. *Ongeluckig, of Droevigh Verhaal van't Schip de Gouden Buys*. . . . Enkhuizen: Hendrik van Straalen, n.d.

Sparrman, André. *Voyage au Cap de Bonne-Espérance et autour du monde*. . . . 2 vols. Paris: Buisson, 1787.

Spoelstra, C., ed. *Bouwstoffen voor de geschiedenis der Nederduitsch-Gereformeerde Kerken in Zuid-Afrika*. 2 vols. Amsterdam: Hollandsch Afrikaansche Uitgevers Maatschappij, 1906.

Stavorinus, John Splinter. *Voyages to the East Indies*. . . . Translated by Samuel Hull Wilcocke. 3 vols. London: G. G. and J. Robinson, 1798.

Suid-Afrikaanse Argiefstukke. *Resolusies van die Politieke Raad*. 6 vols. Cape Town and Johannesburg: Publikasie-Afdeling van die Kantoor van die Direkteur van Argiewe, 1957–68.

Tachard, Guy. *Voyage de Siam*. . . . Paris: Arnold Seneuze et Daniel Horthemels, 1686.

————. *Second Voyage du Père Tachard*. . . . Middelburg: Gilles Horthemels, 1687.

Terry, Edward. *A Voyage to East-India*. . . . (Original edition 1655.) London: J. Wilkie, 1777.

Thom, H. B., ed. *Journal of Jan van Riebeeck*. 3 vols. Cape Town and Amsterdam: A. A. Balkema, 1952, 1954, 1958.

Thunberg, C. P. *Voyages de C. P. Thunberg au Japon par le Cap de Bonne-Espérance* . . . . 2 vols. Paris: Benoît Dandré, Garnery, Obré, 1796.

Valentyn, François. *Oud en Nieuw Oost-Indiën*. Vol. 5(2). *Beschryving van . . . Malabar . . . Japan . . . Kaap der Goede Hope*. . . . Dordrecht and Amsterdam: Joannes van Braam & Gerard Onder de Linden, 1726.

Waterhouse, Gilbert. *Simon van der Stel's Journal of his Expedition to Namaqualand, 1685–6*. London: Longmans, Green, and Co., 1932.

[Ziegenbalgh, Bartholomew.] *Propagation of the Gospel in the East*. . . . 3d ed. London: Joseph Downing, 1718.

Secondary Works

Böeseken, A. J. "Die Nederlandse Kommissarisse en die 18de Eeuse Samelewing aan die Kaap." *Archives Year Book for South African History* 7 (1944): 1–253.

————. "Die Verhouding tussen Blank en Nie-Blank in Suid-Afrika aan die hand van die Vroegste Dokumente." *South African Historical Journal* 2 (Nov. 1970): 3–18.

————. *Nederlandsche Commissarissen aan de Kaap, 1657–1700*. The Hague: Martinus Nijhoff, 1938.

————. *Simon van der Stel en sy Kinders*. Cape Town: Nasou, 1964.

Bosman, D. B. "Uit die Biografie van 'n Hottentottin. 'n Eksperiment in Beskawing." *Die Huisgenoot*, July 3 and July 10, 1942.

Botha, C. Graham. *Collected Works.* 3 vols. Cape Town: C. Struik, 1962.

Boxer, C. R. *The Dutch Seaborne Empire, 1600–1800.* London: Hutchinson & Co., 1965.

———, ed. *The Tragic History of the Sea, 1589–1622.* The Hakluyt Society, 2d series, 112. Cambridge: Cambridge University Press, 1959.

Cope, John. *King of the Hottentots.* Cape Town: Howard Timmins, 1967.

Cruse, H. P. *Die Opheffing van die Kleurlingbevolking.* Vol. 1: *Aanvangsjare 1652–1795.* Stellenbosch: Die Christen-Studentevereniging van Suid-Afrika, 1947.

Engels, Louise J. "Personal accounts of the Cape of Good Hope written between 1652 and 1715." *Africana Notes and News* 8, no. 3 (June 1951):71–100.

Forbes, V. S. *Pioneer Travellers of South Africa.* Cape Town and Amsterdam: A. A. Balkema, 1965.

Franken, J. L. M. *Taalhistoriese Bydraes.* Amsterdam and Cape Town: A. A. Balkema, 1953.

Froidevaux, Henri. *Reconnaissances et projets d'établissements français sur la côte occidentale de l'Afrique australe sous le règne de Louis XIV (1666–1670).* Extract from the *Revue Coloniale.* Paris: Paul Dupont, 1899.

Godée-Molsbergen, E. C. "Hottentotten, Slaven en Blanken in Compagnies-tijd in Zuid-Afrika." *Handelingen en Mededeelingen van de Maatschappij der Nederlandsche Letterkunde* (1912–13): 102–18.

Goodwin, A. J. H. "Commentary on 'Jan van Riebeeck and the Hottentots.'" *SAAB* 7, no. 26 (June 1952): 86–91.

———. "Jan van Riebeeck and the Hottentots, 1652–1662." *SAAB* 6, no. 25 (March 1952): 2–53.

Irwin, Graham. "Dutch Historical Sources." *An Introduction to Indonesian Historiography.* Edited by Soedjatmoko et al. Ithaca, N.Y.: Cornell University Press, 1965.

Joubert, S. P. F. "Die Veehandel tussen die Hollanders en Hottentote aan die Kaap, 6 April 1652–8 Mei 1662." M.A. thesis, University of Stellenbosch, 1923.

Katzen, M. F. "White Settlers and the Origin of a New Society, 1652–1778." *Oxford History of South Africa.* Edited by Monica Wilson and Leonard Thompson. Vol. 1. Oxford: Clarendon Press, 1969.

Kock, W. J. de. *Suid-Afrikaanse Biografiese Woordeboek.* Vol. 1. Cape Town: Nasionale Raad vir Sosiale Navorsing, 1968.

Krüger, Bernhard. *The Pear Tree Blossoms; A History of the Moravian Missions in South Africa, 1739–1869.* Genadendal: Moravian Book Depot, 1966.

Leipoldt, C. Louis. *Jan van Riebeeck: A Biographical Study.* London, New York, and Toronto: Longmans, Green & Co., 1936.

Le Roux, H. J. "Die Toestand, Verspreiding en Verbrokkeling van die Hottentotstamme in Suid-Afrika 1652–1713." M.A. thesis, Stellenbosch

University, 1945.

MacCrone, I. D. *Race Attitudes in South Africa: Historical, Experimental and Psychological Studies.* Johannesburg: Witwatersrand University Press, 1965.

Malherbe, D. F. du T. *Stamregister van die Suid-Afrikaanse Volk.* 3d ed. Stellenbosch: Tegniek, 1966.

Marais, J. S. *The Cape Coloured People, 1652–1937.* Johannesburg: Witwatersrand University Press, 1962.

Marks, Shula. "Khoisan Resistance to the Dutch in the Seventeenth and Eighteenth Centuries." *JAH* 13, no. 1 (1972): 55–80.

Merwe, P. J. van der. "Die Inboorlingbeleid van die Kompanjie." *Geskiedenis van Suid-Afrika.* Edited by A. J. H. van der Walt, J. A. Wiid, and A. L. Geyer. Vol. 2. 2d ed. Cape Town, Bloemfontein, and Johannesburg: Nasionale Boekhandel Beperk, 1955.

————. *Die Noordwaartse Beweging van die Boere voor die Groot Trek (1770–1842).* The Hague: W. P. Van Stockum & Zoon, 1937.

————. *Die Trekboer in die Geskiedenis van die Kaapkolonie, 1657–1842.* Cape Town: Nasionale Pers, 1938.

Milone, Pauline Dublin. "*Indische* Culture, and Its Relationship to Urban Life." *Comparative Studies in Society and History* 9, no. 4 (July 1967): 407–26.

Mossop, E. E. *Old Cape Highways.* Cape Town: Maskew Miller, [1927].

Nienaber, G. S. "Die Vroegste Verslae Aangaande Hottentots." *AS* 15, no. 1 (1956): 29–35.

————. "Iets Naders oor die Ontkenning in Afrikaans." *Hertzog-Annale* 2 (Dec. 1955): 29–45.

Report of the Parliamentary Select Committee on Aboriginal Tribes, published for the Aborigines Protection Society. London: William Ball, Aldine Chambers, 1837.

Robertson, H. M. "The Economic Development of the Cape under Van Riebeeck." *South African Journal of Economics* 13, nos. 1–4 (March–Dec. 1945): 1–17, 75–90, 170–84, 245–62.

Schmidt, K. L. M. *A Bibliography of Personal Accounts of the Cape of Good Hope in Printed Books, 1715–1850.* Cape Town: University of Cape Town, School of Librarianship, 1955.

Scholtz, J. du P. *Taalhistoriese Opstelle; Voorstudies tot 'n Geskiedenis van Afrikaans.* Pretoria: J. L. van Schaik, 1963.

Smith, J. J. *Theories about the Origin of Afrikaans.* Hofmeyr Foundation Lectures, 1. Johannesburg: Witwatersrand University Press, 1952.

Spilhaus, Margaret Whiting. *South Africa in the Making, 1652–1804.* Cape Town, Wynberg, and Johannesburg: Juta & Company, 1966.

Theal, George McCall. *Ethnography and Condition of South Africa before A.D. 1505.* 2d ed. London: George Allen and Unwin, 1919.

————. *History of South Africa under the Administration of the Dutch East India Company, 1652–1795.* 2 vols. London: Swan Sonnenschein & Co., 1897.

————. *Willem Adriaan van der Stel, and Other Historical Sketches.* Cape Town: Thomas Maskew Miller, 1913.

Thom, H. B. *Die Geskiedenis van die Skaapboerdery in Suid-Afrika.* Amsterdam: Swets & Zeitlinger, 1936.

Valkhoff, Marius F. *Studies in Portuguese and Creole, with Special Reference to South Africa.* Johannesburg: Witwatersrand University Press, 1966.

V[arley], D. H. "A Note on Coree the Saldanian." *Quarterly Bulletin of the South African Library* 1, no. 3 (March 1947): 78–81.

Index

Livestock (*cont.*)
  goats, 57–58; care of, 58–59; and wild
    animals, 59, 98; blood of, 60; fat of,
    60–61; as fines, 61; in Khoikhoi
    dress and adornment, 61, 193; theft
    of, 98, 182; Company's use of, 99,
    151–54; Company distributes to
    allies, 131, 142, 190; hybridization of
    by Company, 154, 157; Khoikhoi loss
    of, 170–74, 233, 238; Company
    seizes, 171; Khoikhoi-freemen dis-
    putes over, 171, 185, 191; Khoikhoi
    guard for Company, 178. *See also*
    Pastoralism; Trade
Lords Seventeen, 143; found Cape
    Colony, 87–88, 90; on van Reibeeck's
    term at Cape, 97; on enslaving
    Khoikhoi, 102; on First Khoikhoi-
    Dutch War, 111; on inland explora-
    tion, 115, 221; order Klaas freed,
    146; on livestock breeding, 154;
    consent to banishment of Khoikhoi,
    183; on freemen's barter, 224–25,
    228. *See also* Dutch East India
    Company
Louis XIV, 178

Madagascar, 202, 204
Maingard, L. F., 6, 7, 37
Malay (language), 159, 213
Manckebeen, 124
Mapungubwe, 18
Marks, Shula, 135, 169 n
Marriage. *See* Khoikhoi; Miscegenation
Matabeleland, 17
Matelief, Cornelis, 74, 75, 77
Mauritius, 71, 202
Meerhofskasteel, 234
Meinhof, Carl, 6
Metals. *See* Brass; Copper; Iron
Middleton, Sir Henry, 74
Milone, Pauline Dublin, 201
Milward, John, 81
Minors, William, 81
Miscegenation: between whites and
    Khoikhoi, 197, 204–05; in Asia,
    200–01; prohibited, 205
Money, 164, 207–08
Monomotapa, 101, 115, 136
Moodie, Donald, 236
Mossel Bay, 12, 77, 92; Da Gama at,

64, 72; Dias at, 72; Hessequa at, 139
"Mountain Climbers," 27
Mozambique, 73
Murdock, George Peter, 14

Namaqua, xv, 44, 66, 117, 133, 134,
    172, 189; early history of, 19–20; and
    Cape Khoikhoi, 21, 45; use term
    "San," 28; and hunters, 34, 40;
    social structure of, 43–45, 61; tribal
    divisions of, 45, 49; use of name, 46 n;
    cattle culture of, 56, 57, 58, 61; in
    Khoikhoi trade, 65; first encounters
    with Dutch, 116; and Guriqua, 119,
    121, 135; hostility to Gonnema, 130;
    numbers and location of, 135–37;
    Dutch expeditions to, 136, 221;
    humiliation of, by Van der Stel, 137,
    191; attack colony, 137, 225–26;
    trade with Dutch, 160, 169 n; not
    subjugated by Dutch, 192; decline of,
    229, 230; alleged attacks of, 230; and
    smallpox, 233; after *1721*, 234
Namibia, 10, 36, 135; Namaqua occupy,
    19; hunters in, 27; metals from, 65
Namies, 119
Namnykoa: dagga among, 63
Nanningai, 27
Naron, 6, 8, 14
"Nation": use of term by Europeans, 43;
    not equivalent of Hoernlé's "tribe," 45
Nearby Khoikhoi: defined, 117; and
    Company frontier, 217; losses in
    northern disturbances, 227; nearly
    destroyed, 234. *See also* Chainouqua;
    Cochoqua; Hessequa; Western
    Cape Khoikhoi
Newgate men: left at Cape, 79
Nienaber, G. S., 213
Nieuwveld, 20
Noble Savage, 198
North American Indians, 12, 158, 165
Northern Borderlands: infested by
    robbers, 39–40, 226; Namaqua attacks
    on, 137; disturbances in, 225–27
Northern Bush: term originated by
    Bleek, 6
Northern disturbances (*1701–03*), 137,
    197, 225–27; effects of, 199

Oedasoa, 113, 119, 121,